carlos monsiváis

linda egan

carlos monsiváis culture and chronicle

in contemporary mexico

the university of arizona press

tucson, arizona

The University of Arizona Press
© 2001 The Arizona Board of Regents
All rights reserved

∞ This book is printed on acid-free, archival-quality paper.
Manufactured in the United States of America
First Printing

06   05   04   03   02   01   6   5   4   3   2   1

library of congress cataloging-in-publication data

Egan, Linda.
  Carlos Monsiváis: culture and chronicle
  in contemporary Mexico/Linda D. Egan.
    p. cm.
  Includes bibliographical references and index.
  ISBN 0-8165-2137-9 (cloth: alk. paper)
    1. Monsiváis, Carlos, 1938—Knowledge—Mexico.
    2. Mexico—Civilization—20th century.
    3. Mexican essays—20th century—History and criticism.
    I. Title.
  PQ7298.23.O686 z64   2001
  808'.0092–dc21   2001001660

british library cataloguing-in-publication data

A catalogue record for this book is available
from the British Library.

to my son kevin, who gave me life.

Introduction   ix

contents

Introduction

Carlos Monsiváis is a major writer of twentieth-century Mexico and its most celebrated cultural critic. Not only in his country but throughout Latin America and in important sectors of the United States, he is influential for his transcendent analyses of contemporary Mexico's sociopolitical realities. He is author of five collections of literary journalism pieces on Mexico called *crónicas* (chronicles): *Días de guardar* (1970), *Amor perdido* (1977), *Escenas de pudor y liviandad* (1981, 1988), *Entrada libre: crónicas de la sociedad que se organiza* (1987) and *Los rituales del caos* (1995). With the seven essays of a more recent collection, *Aires de familia: cultura y sociedad en la América Latina* (2000), he extends his concerns about Mexico to the entire Latin American region and won the Premio Anagrama for essay, in Barcelona. He has edited a groundbreaking anthology of Mexican chronicles, *A ustedes les consta* (1980), and anthologies also of Mexican short stories and poetry, as well as a selection from his longest-running newspaper column.[1] Widely cited by cultural and literary analysts, Monsiváis is also one of the most prominent critics in Mexico of literature and of other cultural discourses such as photography and painting. In this arena, the prologue is a particular specialty of his.

Among other book-length works, he has recently augmented his single volume of fiction, a collection of satirical parables called *Nuevo catecismo para indios remisos* (1982, 1992), coauthored a retrospective examination of the 1968 Student Movement,[2] published a biographical homage, *Salvador Novo: lo marginal en el centro* (2000), and produced two beautifully illustrated tributes, one a charming essay on letter-writing in Mexico, *El género epistolar: un homenaje a manera de carta abierta* (1991), the other a commentary on political cartoons, *Aire de familia: colección de Carlos Monsiváis* (1995).[3] His publications are, in fact, virtually innumerable, housed over the last four and a half decades in newspapers and magazines and in a growing number of academic journals edited on both sides of the U.S.–Mexican border.

He is most heralded for his analytic and often satirical descriptions of the popular cultures of Mexico City, and, as leader of the heavily politicized Generation of 1968,[4] his work bears a leftist ideological edge. Emmanuel Carballo remembers that, as a young reporter-critic, Monsiváis and his intellectual companions had from the start confused literary enterprise and political activism (Carballo, "Sabio" 43). Monsiváis devotes his creative project, then, to a trinity of nation-building concerns: the artistic, social and political phenomena of Mexico's immediate and recent history, as these bear upon the progressive democratization of his society.

His first book of chronicles slipped into the mainstream of the Latin American *boom*'s literary ferment with stylistically exuberant pieces akin to the U.S.–style New Journalism of which Monsiváis was and remains a devoted reader. In many of *Días de guardar*'s texts he dialogues openly with U.S. literary journalists such as Tom Wolfe and Norman Mailer, as well as with other North American culture intellectuals. The core of this collection is a series of crónicas now frequently mentioned in the bibliography of so-called Tlatelolco literature: prose, poetry and drama inspired by the spontaneous bid for democracy embodied in the Student Movement, which government soldiers shut down on the night of October 2, 1968, when they ambushed students, parents, workers and children gathered for a political rally in the Plaza de las Tres Culturas, or Tlatelolco Square.

If with *Días de guardar* (1970) Monsiváis eternalizes deeply symbolic "days of observance" such as those of 1968's portentous summer and fall, the exemplary chronicles of *Amor perdido* (1977) memorialize protagonists of Mexico's recent history; among them, the writer of *boleros*, or romantic ballads, Agustín Lara; the singer of *rancheras*, or "country songs" (Monsiváis, *Aires* 62), José Alfredo Jiménez; communist activist Benita Galeana and labor boss Fidel Velázquez. In this series of metonymic biographies, Monsiváis shows us the life of a nation just entering mass-mediated modernity.

By the time he invites us to watch *Escenas de pudor y liviandad* (1981) with him, much of capital life has become a soap opera; these chronicles probe beneath the kitsch melodrama of popular urban culture to figure scarcely perceptible but real changes in the Mexican society's temperament. Monsiváis loiters in funky dance dives and eavesdrops on poor working-class girls to take the pulse of a massively mediated and marginalized urban body that is almost wholly unconsciously learning to decolonize itself.

The impulse to freedom rises to consciousness in *Entrada libre* (1987), when a series of crises in the center (Mexico City) and periphery (rural towns) calls forth extraordinary civilian resistance. Since publication of *Días de guardar*, Monsiváis had been patiently documenting his optimistic expectations for democratization in a column he began writing for the literary supplement *La Cultura en México*, an important organ for the Generation of 1968 that Monsiváis directed for years. The title of his column, "Para documentar nuestro optimismo" [To Document Our Optimism[5]], eventually acquired a cotitle, "Por mi madre, bohemios," which offers a parodic toast to Mom in a notably masculine political arena. The column still runs under that title today, in the Mexico City daily *La Jornada*.

The optimism illustrated in his column is the sort a reader has to dig for, in the way that Monsiváis's analytical-synthetic mind tirelessly grubs for seeds of democracy amid deep structures that cultivate meanings larger than the crises of Mexico's past and immediate history. That spirit of self-liberation sprawls outward in splendid disarray through the texts gathered for *Los rituales del caos* (1995). In this collection, Monsiváis continues to document his eternal optimism. We go on visits to cultural sites with the *cronista* (chronicler, journalist), perhaps to a patio where the credulous wait in a long line for a cure from the local miracle worker, or to a Gloria Trevi rock concert to hear the scandalous Mexican Madonna's "himnos anticonformistas" [hymns to nonconformity] (*Rituales* 170), or maybe only to Monsiváis's apocalyptic imagination, where he delights in listing some of the ways in which beleaguered inhabitants of super-crowded Mexico City turn the negative into sources of a compensatory pride (*Rituales* 19). While we are in these places, the narrative ritual he performs allows us to observe Mexico's culture of poverty with 3-D glasses that coax into focus the redemptive signs of emergent change.

an informed and reliable spokesman for mexico

In view of the cumulative weight and quality of his writings, Monsiváis is held to be Mexico's most informed and reliable spokesperson on cultural and sociopolitical issues, one of Latin America's most prestigious intellectuals, according to the Barcelona publishing house that brought out Monsiváis's prize-winning *Aires de familia* in 2000 (back cover). I will return to the way colleagues and other readers of Monsiváis regard the man and his works. For now, in light of what is the principal object of his ongoing production, two *popular culture* "proofs" might best speak to his ever-rising status on the Mexican intellectual scene, what one tongue-in-cheek Mexican journalist has referred to as "la *monsivaítis,* raro fenómeno de mitificación de un intelectual" [Monsivaitis, a rare instance of the mythification of an intellectual].[6]

the man as myth

Proof #1. In the January 1993 issue of *Caminos del aire,* Mexicana Airlines's in-flight magazine, a color closeup of Carlos Monsiváis straddles both pages. He is cuddling one of his numerous cats in front of a wall of books. The accompanying four-paragraph, bilingual blurb reads like an advertisement; to a transnational market, Mexico is selling what has lately become one of its most user-friendly products for domestic and foreign consumption, a cultural phenomenon identified as Carlos Monsiváis, the critic and chronicler of Mexico City, born there "in 1936" (Quintana 15; my sources say 1938). A sound bite of biography follows: Monsiváis studied economics and then literature at the national university and he's been a journalist and cultural analyst for thirty-five years.[7] Next, a list (incomplete and inaccurate) of his books. At the last, the indulgent confidence revealed in tones perfected by *National Inquirer.* His personal plans for the near future are as original as his literary projects. The quote that ends the piece is patented Monsiváis, whose opinion of the mass media—of which, of course, *Caminos del aire* is a part—is not nearly as endearing as his appearance: From now on I propose to believe everything I read in the newspaper, he says (15).

Proof #2. In an August 1995 issue of perhaps the most prestigious cultural supplement currently published by a newspaper in Mexico City, the essay, "Historia personal del caos" [A Personal History of Chaos], is narrated through a review of Monsiváis's then most recent book, *Los rituales del caos* (Ochoa Sandy 7). The supplement special includes a montage of testimonials by leading intellectuals, critics and artists who agree here to participate in what *La Jornada*'s editors headline as "Monsimanía" (Cayuela Gally 4–6). The editors playfully present Monsiváis as a Star—something like one of the pop culture idols he is fond of psychoanalyzing. The medium is the message.

A series of illustrations for these testimonials dramatizes the paradox. Now made the subject of a metacultural cartoon, Monsiváis is ridiculed as a Man of Action who spends his life with a book in his lap (the street vendor cries, "¡Llévese su póster de Monsiváis LEYENDOOOO!" [Get your poster of Monsiváis READING!!!]). Perhaps most significantly, he is caricaturized as a publicly owned cultural artifact to be (mis)handled and (ab)used: A man sobs that Monsiváis is protesting because "estamos cayendo en el chiste barato" [We're stooping to the level of cheap jokes] and a clown applying makeup retorts: "Ha llegado el momento de ignorar a Monsiváis" [The time has come to ignore Monsiváis].

the outsider in the middle

To *La Jornada*'s educated readership, the evident subtext unmasks an opposite truth: Monsiváis is to be taken very seriously, albeit with a light heart. The object of all this tongue-in-cheek adulation surely invited the cheap joke on himself; he might well have also delighted in the one published earlier in which he is depicted as a typewriter on a deserted isle receiving its wisdom directly from the Hand of God (A. Ruiz, "De la vida" 10). Through such self-deprecating representations, the cronista models for his fellow citizens in the knowledge-and-power class the cleansing value of antisolemnity. The full-color cover of *Los rituales del caos* caricaturizes a crowded subway car in Mexico City, full of punkers, hookers, other members of the vast urban underclass and, squeezed in the center, the recognizable figure of Mr. Middle Class Monsiváis. Inveterate *flâneur* of the largest and fastest growing city in the world, indefatigable student of the out-of-luck, born-to-lose survivors of the apocalyptic postmodern megalopolis, the intellect behind the most brilliant journalist in Mexican history stares with bespectacled eyes at the jostling masses. He holds a reporter's notebook, a sign of his dual citizenship in The Two Mexicos—one Oral and one Literate[8]—and a sign also that the insider is outside in the "real world" to serve as the self-sequestered bourgeoisie's eyes, ears . . . and conscience.

Monsiváis is depicted "in the middle" of the two Mexicos as a cultural conduit, a translator who interprets the nation's impoverished Other Within to the miniscule monied class that "others" the emerging megacity's copper-toned rural migrants, the mass that fuels Mexico's demographic explosion while inciting, in behalf of the bourgeoisie, the wry observation that everyone who should be born has done so already (Monsiváis, "Espacios" 275).

a speaker of artful truths

Among other objects of this study, I will explore Monsiváis's ideas, together with his moral and social purpose in writing. If the crónica is literature and, when practiced by a writer of Monsiváis's caliber, literature of canonical status, it is first journalism, a truth genre. The theoretical and literary merits of Monsiváis's writings, then, are predicated on an understanding of the credibility of his reportorial voice. Such a view of Carlos Monsiváis, the reporter as professional writer, is the focus of chapter 1—and comprises the limit of most critical interest to date in him. Of equal importance, however, is the way he uses his journalistic voice to create literary texts of enduring appeal. This study thus progresses from Carlos Monsiváis the journalist to a consideration of his works as aesthetic objects.

Carlos Monsiváis's narrative talent, technique and artistic intent align him with boom and postboom fictionalists; he began publishing contemporaneously with Carlos Fuentes in 1954, Monsiváis at 16 inaugurating his career with a crónica on a political rally attended by painters Frida Kahlo and Diego Rivera, the twenty-six-year-old Fuentes with an exclamation point of a book containing six short stories *(Los días enmascarados).* With his 1958 novel *La región más transparente,* Fuentes is widely held to have launched the Latin American narrative boom of the 1960s and 1970s, the years when Monsiváis was publishing in journals like *Medio Siglo* the first literary claims to his eventual fame. When one takes into account the generic implications of his truth genre—whether the literature he writes is fact or fiction—the purely aesthetic features of his writing stand out more remarkably still.

Remarkably, because he creates enduring literature with the prosaic, often scarcely newsworthy, facts of daily public life. Worthy of remark as well, because if he did not do so, he could not be called Mexico's foremost chronicler. He might instead be known simply as a journalist, an essayist, a historian or even, on rare occasion, a writer of short stories. As his longtime friend and colleague, José Emilio Pacheco, says, not as a writer of fiction but as a chronicler was Monsiváis destined to become the great narrator of a Mexico City that was becoming what is now called "el DF"—the Federal District (39).

mexico's "new chronicle" as literature

To assess the literariness of Monsiváis's writings, I consider it necessary to weigh the literary potential of the genre Monsiváis calls the *nueva crónica* [new chronicle] and I have called "la crónica actual de México" [the contemporary chronicle of Mexico].[9] As with any other writer, one can read Monsiváis most successfully with as precise an idea as possible of the parameters of the literary form he most often relies on. If Fuentes's *La muerte de Artemio Cruz* is at its literary best when read as a novel, rather than, say, as a history of the Mexican Revolution and its aftermath, then Monsiváis's "Yo y mis amigos" (*Días* 65–77), for example, makes the most of its literary potential when read as a crónica, rather than, say, as a short story, a confession or an editorial attacking the nationalist Mexican government's massacre of student demonstrators in 1968. Accordingly, in Part I's analysis of Carlos Monsiváis as theorist, I will postulate a poetics of the contemporary crónica, identifying a rhetoric which, as I see it, structurally distinguishes the chronicle from related genres such as the news article, the essay and the short story, the forms most often confused with the chronicle.

What cultural theorist Néstor García Canclini has observed in the masses as a tendency to substitute biographical anecdote for textual criticism (*Culturas híbridas* 103) holds true for almost all those of a small but growing number of critics who have written substantively on Monsiváis's works. While he is frequently cited by academic essayists in and out of Mexico, principally in sociopolitical or cultural treatises but also in literary analyses, critics who allude to aesthetic aspects of Monsiváis's writings have to date not given them the kind of close narratological reading routinely accorded novelists and short story writers.

emphasis on textual analysis

Monsiváis's many "parts" necessarily function together and simultaneously; thus, shifts in my focus to the referent, or to the form or to the ideological intent of Monsiváis's work will somewhat artificially isolate a given aspect of the whole. In every instance, however, I will rely on textual analysis. *What* Monsiváis says is inextricably interwoven with *how* he says it. Whether emphasizing his role as a journalist (chapter 1), as a theorist of culture and the chronicle (chapters 2 through 5) or as author (chapters 6 through 10), this study will characterize Monsiváis's particular way of representing the factual through what he has called "el juego literario" [literary play] (*A ustedes* 13). In structure, handling of narrative voice, lexicon and trope, the earlier Monsiváis of *Días de guardar* and *Amor perdido* is virtually indistinguishable from other exhibitionists of the boom. His persona in *Escenas de pudor y liviandad* is only slightly less experimental. By the time *Entrada libre* and *Los rituales del caos* appear, we note that his discursive personality has distilled itself into a more synthetic blend of editorialism and artistry. At the same time, however, his lifelong addiction to the verbal bomb known as the aphorism has intensified the cronista's characteristic hermeticism—and his equally characteristic humor, without which Monsiváis would not be Monsiváis, nor the crónica very much itself.

Among the goals of this study, then, is a consideration of Carlos Monsiváis as an author of literature, to identify in his writing what Hayden White calls "the content of the form"—the semantic excess to be assessed in any narratively structured discourse, whether history intended to be objective, patently invented fiction, or crónica, a form built upon the contents of both history and fiction.

For many years, Monsiváis has been challenging the literary community to take the crónica with canonical seriousness. In a text that has become an oft-cited classic of literary criticism, his 1976 "Notas sobre la cultura mexicana en el siglo XX," he observes that in Mexico "la poesía lo es todo" [poetry is all] (356), remaining more powerful even than the novel. With his characteristic acumen, Monsiváis finds causal links among Mexico's still-predominantly oral culture, its enduring religiosity and the privilege accorded the poetic genre, which insistently invades Mexican prose forms. Easily memorized, poetry passes into popular culture where this presumably most impractical of genres is obliged to be of use to convey advice, emotional inspiration or life-affirming wisdom (357). Monsiváis could here be suggesting a process by which Mexican journalism absorbs the emotiveness of poetry while infusing this formal element in turn with practical utility, a process that constructs the very genre he is using to write his criticism.

What I have come to think of as "Monsi's Complaint" is formalized a decade later in a text solicited by one of the most prestigious academic fora of the Mexican literary establishment, the *Nueva Revista de Filología Hispánica*, published by El Colegio de México. As a self-avowed Outsider who works on the perimeter of the Academy, Monsiváis uses the podium offered him to reproach his audience's unbalanced critical focus. He demands to know,

¿Por qué el sitio tan marginal de la crónica en nuestra historia literaria? Ni el enorme prestigio de la poesía, ni la seducción omnipresente de la novela son explicaciones suficientes del desdén casi absoluto por un género tan importante en las relaciones entre literatura y sociedad, entre historia y vida cotidiana, entre lector y formación del gusto literario, entre información y amenidad, entre testimonio y materia prima de la ficción, entre periodismo y proyecto de nación. ("De la Santa Doctrina" 753)

[What accounts for the chronicle's quite marginal place in our literary history? Neither poetry's enormous prestige, nor the ever-present seduction of the novel, are sufficient explanations of the almost absolute disdain for a genre so important to relations between literature and society, history and daily life, information and entertainment, testimony and the raw material of fiction, journalism and the task of building a nation.]

Five years later, in his prologue to an anthology of chronicles, Monsiváis's appreciation of U.S. New Journalism's narrative reportage summons the lingering critical question: Why, he asks, is nonfiction thought to be the opposite of fiction when it is or can be imaginative, creative and full of artistry? (Monsiváis, prologue to Valverde and Argüelles 18–19). Because the chronicle's marginalization in the academic community stems largely from anachronistic application of a lingering nineteenth-century standard that considers "literature" to be synonymous with "fiction," I will take up this generic and semantic question in detail. The form that Monsiváis has perfected in Mexico will be shown to be a *mestizo* [crossbred] genre in which both the "high" culture of Eurocentric canonical literature and the "low" culture of American mass media are seamlessly fused. This hybrid form may be as unworthy of literary analysis as any novel ignored by a language department, but in talented hands it can be as deserving of canonical status as Juan Rulfo's *Pedro Páramo* or Elena Poniatowska's *La noche de Tlatelolco*.

Carlos Monsiváis's concern for the status of the chronicle's imaginatively narrated reportage is shared by many who question the traditional literary canon's bias against nonfiction. We can recall Tom Wolfe's classic 1975 defense of the New Journalist's narrative style, and even before that, Norman Podhoretz in 1974 recommending "The Article as Art." The attitude that identifies the aesthetic or literary with fiction is an unwarranted prejudice that has distanced literary discourse from the world of factual reality and weakened it, making it seem a supplementary and inessential activity, says the author of a recent study on the Latin American modernist chronicle (Rotker 111). Gérard Genette, from his solidly mainstream position, lodges a "protest . . . against the overly unilateral practice of what might be called *restricted narratology*," even as he declines "to redress the balance here by undertaking a study of the characteristic features of the discourse of factual narrative" ("Fictional/Factual" 756).[10] Still, being willing to question "the pieties surrounding the canonical monuments," as Edward Said has characterized the "religious consciousness," or "priestifying," of university canon makers ("Opponents" 150), is a healthy step toward rationalizing our literary belief system.

The challenge of addressing the fact-fiction dualism is memorably issued by Barbara Foley in a 1979 essay on the reportage literature of the New Journalists. After citing leading theorists in the then-budding critical field and their (on the whole, unsatisfactory) studies, Foley concludes that "a theory of the nonfiction novel, and of the generic identity of other such mixed narrative modes is . . . badly needed ("Fact, Fiction" 398). By the time I had arrived at the same conclusion, fifteen years had passed without notable progress in the Academy toward the goal of articulating a workable theory of the relationship between history and fiction that could be useful for textual exegesis. If we expand the dualism to include not only history but the immediacy of journalism and the daily, lived reality of popular cultural practices, we can see that a theory of the chronicle genre can challenge the definition of literature as it has been defined in Eurocentric terms since at least the end of the eighteenth century. I do not propose to merely append a popular cultural dimension to the concept of the literary, but instead to join other critics in propping the door open to ever-changing possibilities of what merits serious academic study, as Wlad Godzich and Nicholas Spadaccini do, for example, in *Literature Among Discourses*.

During my search for an archaeology of the crónica, I hope to elaborate existing theoretical approaches such as John Beverley's on the *testimonio* [testimonial] genre, a form perhaps most readily exemplified by Rigoberta Menchú's autobiographical report on the oppression and resistance of Guatemala's indigenous people (Menchú, 1983). Whereas Beverley argues for inclusion of such texts (typically spoken to a scribe) on exclusively ethical-ideological grounds ("Second Thoughts" 129), I argue for inclusion of the crónica on formal (aesthetic) grounds.

The countercanonical changes being fomented by current postmodernist, poststructuralist and postcolonialist sensibilities have begun to bring the metropolitan critical community closer to Monsiváis's always more inclusive understanding of what constitutes literature. With respect to Latin American literary studies, works such as Martin Lienhard's *La voz y su huella* (1991), Carlos Pacheco's *La comarca oral* (1992), or Walter Mignolo's recent work on colonization of language figure among a growing body of knowledge on the ways popular-oral expression absorbed by and into literature are helping turn critics in refreshing new directions (Pacheco, *Comarca* 17–18). Beverley's *Against Literature* is another prime example of both the spirit and the letter of this canon-stretching intent. Still, while books and doctoral dissertations have been written, for example, on Elena Poniatowska's non- or parafictional works, the current surge of critical interest in truth genres has not yet refunctioned Monsiváis as a literary author. Rationalizing such a change of perception and reception is a principal goal of this study.

a review of the criticism

Monsiváis has of course never been ignored in the intellectual community of Mexico. In the capital's small, tightly configured intellectual group, it would be impossible not to notice a talent as big as Carlos Monsiváis's. Already in the 1950s and early to mid-1960s, Monsiváis was consolidating a distinctive voice and sought-after critical stance. Still, Monsiváis remains more cited in essays on other writers than he is the subject himself of autonomous literary analysis. On the general topic of Mexican literary criticism, Emmanuel Carballo could be paraphrasing how I see most comments to date on Monsiváis: "No agarran la obra por los cuernos, en el mejor de los casos palmean sus cuartos traseros" [Nobody grabs the work by the horns; at best they pat it on the behind] (*Francotirador* 9). Practicing what he has denounced, Carballo's 1966 critique of Monsiváis goes not much deeper than observations about the writer's self-critical attitude and his sense of humor; he predicts Monsiváis will replace Salvador Novo as the Cronista of Mexico City (*Monsiváis* 7).[11]

Gustavo García, reviewing *Amor perdido* in 1978, briefly mentions the book's literary qualities as a compendium of cultural manias and phobias, stylistic tics and erudition in service to a nostalgic look back ("Rostros" 29). In another review of the same collection, García sketches his definition of the genre of *Amor perdido*'s texts—"la crónica es la articulación coherente de una realidad consignable . . . y una postura política" [the chronicle is a coherent link between a verifiable reality and a political posture] ("México bien vale" 42). Twenty years later, Juan G. Gelpí also cites *Amor perdido* to explore the symbiotic relationship he sees between massification of Mexico City and a new chronicle genre that supplements inadequacies of the "culturalist" essay (such as Octavio Paz's *El laberinto de la soledad*) to reflect an essentially carnivalesque Mexican reality (83–84).

Also writing in the summary review mode, Antonio Alatorre waxes ecstatic on the surprise he found in Monsiváis's 1980 anthology of modern-era crónicas. Alatorre credits Monsiváis with having introduced him to the marvelously *literary* world of the footnoteless chronicle, and praises him for doing so in a critical study full of "monsivaisismos" and presented in "un libro perfecto, una de esas obras que permanecen, que hacen época" [a perfect book, one of those epochal works that endures] (37).

What these and other reviewers of books published by Monsiváis say is true enough, as far as their comments go. The regret is that they go so short a distance toward criticism. Adolfo Castañón's assessment of Monsiváis offers characterizations—many of them metaphors of brilliant precision—without attempting textual analysis. The title of Castañón's essay—"Un hombre llamado ciudad" [A Man Named City]—indicates where his and virtually all of the as yet scant commentary on Monsiváis focuses: on the man himself, the cultural Star of the airline magazine, the target of the Intelligentsia's Monsimania, the self-mocking butt of cartoon jokes, "uno de los últimos escritores públicos del país y quizá uno de los últimos nombres que las multitudes mexicanas sean capaces de reconocer" [one of the last public writers of the country and perhaps one of the last names that the Mexican masses are able to recognize] (Castañón, "Hombre" 19).

Exceptions stand out. Until a more recent and sophisticated essay published in 1999, María Eugenia Cossío's 1984 analysis of "El diálogo sin fin de Monsiváis" in the *Hispanic Journal* stood as an isolated example of literary criticism of texts by Monsiváis, with titles, exact quotes, page numbers—and emphasis on how the author selects and orders words to achieve effects, to represent realities, to deconstruct previous texts, to (re)construct an illusion of orality. The more recent article, Sebastiaan Faber's "La metonimia en una crónica de Carlos Monsiváis: hacia un periodismo democrático," published in *Literatura Mexicana* (Mexico City, UNAM), is a provocative reading of one of the author's paradigmatic chronicles that ably combines narratological theories of metaphor and metonymy to situate Monsiváis's brand of personal journalism in relation to the neobaroque, U.S. New Journalism and a unique kind of utopian nonfiction reportage. I will elaborate these and other technical concepts. Similarly, a 1991 analysis published by Claudia Ferman in *Nuevo Texto Crítico* describes elements of postmodern textuality in a (strangely configured) trio of texts treating contemporary urban culture: the novel *Cristóbal Nonato* (Carlos Fuentes, 1987), the republished chronicles of *Fuerte es el silencio* (Elena Poniatowska, 1980) and a single text of Monsiváis appearing in a 1987 issue of *Nexos*. In the section on Monsiváis's attack on Mexican nationalism ("Muerte y resurrección"), Ferman cites the text to illustrate the postmodern character of his writing. Again, I will be building on these points.[12]

eclectic theoretical foundations

The eclecticism of Mexico's new crónica and, in particular, of Monsiváis's boundless reportorial interests has guided construction of my theoretical affiliations. For example, he once told a roomful of university students that study of religion is basic to understanding Mexico (*Confrontaciones* 30). It is equally true that anyone wishing to fully grasp Monsiváis, who knows more about the Bible than the archbishop (Benítez 4), ought to begin with a study of religions: the popular Christianity of medieval Europe and that of colonial New Spain, as well as prehispanic Aztec thought, and at least passing knowledge of the fundamentalist Protestant sects sinking roots throughout contemporary Mesoamerica.

In a similar way, other critical-theoretical groundings have claimed my attention. For example, because Mexico belongs to the two-thirds of the world that has experienced colonialism, and because Monsiváis consistently points to Mexico's three centuries of Spanish colonial rule as the starting point of many of his society's problems, colonial and postcolonial theories (of which identity theory is a noteworthy part) thus serve me, if only to perceive how Monsiváis adapts the typical postcolonialist stance.[13]

Other examples: Mexico's belated and still incomplete entry into modernity coincides with consolidation of a postmodernist ideology and aesthetics; both theories help situate Monsiváis in Mexican letters. Western-style postmodernism had begun to destabilize traditional Mexican notions of the postmodern just when the Latin American narrative boom was internationalizing Mexican literature and inaugurating a theoretical interest in magical realism and the Latin American neobaroque; Monsiváis must be viewed with respect to both the baroque and the neobaroque.[14] At the same time, Mikhail Bakhtin's works were coming out in multilingual translations and seizing powerful hold on the critical imaginations of both the United States and Mexico. Contemporaneous with Bakhtin's rise to privileged status in the theoretical arena, Walter Ong, Walter Mignolo and other students of orality and literacy were facilitating the burgeoning interest in noncanonical (para)literatures—such as the crónica of the conquest and that of contemporary Latin America. Monsiváis is up to date on orality theory, into which I also delve, to appreciate how he (re)constructs popular speech in his chronicles, and to assess the literary traits of the new chronicle's ancestry, which stretches from Herodotus and Nezahualcóyotl to Bernal Díaz del Castillo, Guillermo Prieto and Salvador Novo, all of whom Monsiváis has absorbed. He has consulted Barthes, Foucault, and Derrida on language and power; thus, structuralism, poststructuralism, deconstruction and New Historicism join my background studies.

Within this partial list of affiliations I must of course emphasize the vast theoretical field which is indispensable to reading Carlos Monsiváis: Cultural Studies and, of particular emphasis within that interdisciplinarian maze, theories of Popular Culture. Even if Monsiváis did not occasionally drop into his discourse names such as Walter Benjamin, Raymond Williams, Michel de Certeau or Pierre Bourdieu, one would note in his texts the implicit presence of Cultural Studies' throngs of theorists and know, as well, that to extract Monsiváis's metatextual theory of popular culture (a task I will undertake in Part I), one would need grounding in cultural analysis, especially that of Mexico, the United States and Europe.

The immense weight of (popular) culture in virtually every existing approach to Carlos Monsiváis demands autonomous analysis. Movies, popular music, cartoons and comic books function both as privileged objects of his writing and as elements of a metatheory of popular culture seamlessly interwoven into reportage and wordplay. When I examine his ideology in relation to theoretical postures in Latin America, the United States and Europe (chapters 2 and 3), it becomes evident that Monsiváis is at once a heterodox pioneer and a mainstream spokesman in the field. Insights into the professional authority of Monsiváis's journalistic voice and of its critical and moral force in the lived reality of Mexican culture will ground elaboration, in chapters 4 and 5, of a poetics of the contemporary chronicle of Mexico. This process will involve a review of the genre's historical ancestry and analysis of its relation to neighboring narrative forms as well as textual structures such as voice and point of view. Close readings are intended to indicate boundaries between essay, crónica and short story and, as well, to illuminate the literary weight of Mexico's new chronicle.

The culmination of this study (chapters 6–10) will then focus specifically on the canonical status of the contemporary chronicle as written by Carlos Monsiváis. I devote one chapter each to the principal collections of chronicles that Monsiváis had published on Mexico at this writing.[15] Throughout these analyses, I seek to reveal the poetic subtlety of his discourse's "resistant" nature and to weigh its semantic density. Amid current sensibilities variously denominated as postmodern, neobaroque and carnivalesque, Carlos Monsiváis occupies a space that I will define without exhausting other possibilities for characterization. While I hope to continuously make evident the inter- and intratextual relations of these works with others, my concluding remarks will aim at a unifying vision of "the whole of Monsiváis."

In this multifaceted reading of a work and a prominent writer, I wish to evade certain traps which today's hyperconscious theoretical and critical community has set and frequently sprung. In exploring the ways that Monsiváis employs the privileged object of his reportage—popular culture—to construct both a theory and a literary style, I hope not to spawn what John

Docker describes as a kind of "pop sublime." While I agree with Monsiváis and other theorists that high or elite culture owes more of its substance to the influence of "low" or popular culture than is generally recognized, neither Monsiváis nor I want to unduly idealize the popular by practicing "aesthetic utopianism" (Beverley, "Cultural Studies" 19). Popular culture is not elite culture in disguise and does not want to be.

I want also to avoid miring myself in self-deprecating qualifiers. As the contestatory thrust of postcolonial and postmodern theory continues to press Eurocentric, Western views outward from the center of critical privilege, academics housed precisely within that now-problematized position produce a critical discourse that increasingly threatens to throttle itself with apologies not only for being written by someone (perhaps) white and (certainly) middle-class in the hyperprosperous North, but also for being written at all. John Docker sees this anguished criticism as "a kind of postmarxist epistemological vertigo, a poetics of witty self-reflexivity and self-disturbance" (xxi). Such metacriticism can produce undesirable effects.[16]

For one, by implying a fear of being thought perhaps insensitive or inadequately informed, the overly self-reflexive critic may inadvertently "orientalize" the object, emphasizing, rather than closing, the gap between the writer's embarrassed centrality and the object's assumed marginality. In the instance of this book, Carlos Monsiváis is so central to Mexican cultural studies and is to such a degree respected in Latin America, the United States and Europe, that I will certainly not be tempted to think of him as in any way "subaltern," despite the fact that the object of *his* discourse very frequently is represented as subaltern, or at least economically, socially and politically marginalized in a society not only postcolonial (having spent three hundred years as a possession of Spain) but, arguably, neocolonial (being now more than ever under "dominion" of, especially, North American cultural and economic influences). That is one reason why Monsiváis still, after forty years, focuses his efforts on the vast underclass of Mexican society. Another is that his way of viewing—and writing about—what he observes consistently transforms the image of the subaltern into self-empowered agency. By respecting the "conceptual opposition between consumption and criticism" (Radway 515), I hope always to distinguish adequately between the object of my discourse and the object of Monsiváis's.

The breadth and depth of Monsiváis's knowledge, as well as his evident cosmopolitanism, earn him the stature of an international writer and theorist. Still, because all culture is grounded in local realities, I hope to provide a critical account of Monsiváis's art and thought as they are rooted in the history and contemporary life of Mexico.

I note, finally, that the Mexican nationalism Monsiváis persistently scrutinizes recommends a particular sensitivity in prospect of a reader such as Christopher Domínguez Michael, who in a 1995 essay appears to wish U.S. academics would refrain from publishing books such as this one:

> La proliferación de los mexicanistas en los departamentos de lengua española de Estados Unidos ha provocado la producción en masa de monografías anodinas, asombrosas por su aldeanismo y notables por su desconocimiento de la cultura universal, hispánica y mexicana, ortodoxamente enclavadas en algún modelo teórico—antes marxismo, hoy desconstruccionismo—que aplicadas como receta de cocina a cualquier escritor mexicano, nos hacen pensar que la desaparición del intelectual humanista en Estados Unidos tiene consecuencias nefastas para los estudios de la literatura mexicana en ese país. ("Treinta años" 269)

> [Mexicanists proliferating in Spanish departments in the United States have inspired a massive output of uninteresting monographs, astonishingly provincial and remarkably ignorant of universal, Hispanic and Mexican cultures, chained by orthodox thinking to one theoretical model or another—Marxism in the past, today deconstruction—which, applied like kitchen recipes to any and all Mexican writers, persuade us that the disappearance of the intellectual humanist in the United States implies fateful consequences for Mexican literary studies in that country.]

I am not persuaded that North American Mexicanists are yet proliferating, nor that their emergence has somehow edged out intellectual humanism in the United States. However, I have as little use as Domínguez for the kitchen-recipe use of theory or for critical provincialism, too much of which can indeed be detected, and not only on the U.S. side of our border. With this monograph I intend anything but an "ill-fated" assault on the quality of Mexican literary criticism and, last but not least (to plagiarize Monsiváis), an anodyne rite.[17]

In short, throughout the course of this study I will speak as a strategic intellectual: This is *a* reading of Carlos Monsiváis, which includes *a* theory of the contemporary Mexican chronicle, produced by *an* Anglo American woman of a certain age born in the United States, a native English speaker bilingual in Spanish and a card-carrying member of the Western Academy of the twenty-first century.

It might be useful to add that in a previous incarnation I spent ten years as a reporter and then editorial page editor of a midsize California daily and also taught college newswriting. At the time I was writing editorials I possessed two degrees in Hispanic languages and literatures, which specifically informed my journalistic vision. It was then that I began to appreciate the extent of U.S. media ignorance (and bias) about Mexico and its historically tempestuous relationship with the United States. Subsequently, as a newswriting teacher, I acquired an enduring admiration for American New Journalists such as Joan Didion, John McPhee and Tom Wolfe. By the time I embarked on the doctoral road to a university career, I knew I wanted to discover the Mexican equivalent of Norman Mailer or Annie Dillard and had the good fortune to be directed by a Mexican Mexicanist working in a U.S. Spanish Department (the intellectual humanist Sara Poot Herrera). She urged me to begin my exploration of Mexican literary journalism by sampling Carlos Monsiváis, Elena Poniatowska and José Joaquín Blanco. I was immediately hooked on their seductive blend of fact, ingenuity, humor, impudence, outrage, compassion and lyricism.

The challenge of cracking the baroquely bakhtinian code of Monsiváis's texts makes for enduring entertainment. It also inspires a critical will to spotlight the severe beauty of this philosopher's poetically hard-headed view of the world, Mexico's place in it and the privileged citizen's role in both.

carlos monsiváis

I

carlos monsiváis journalist and theorist

1

carlos monsiváis

authority to speak

Carlos Monsiváis is Mexico's most recognized cronista, not only because of his evident erudition and artistry, but also because he has cultivated over four decades a public presence that is overwhelmingly accepted as trustworthy. Held to be singularly well-informed, responsible and moral, Monsiváis is authorized by his own professionalism to speak to Mexico about Mexico like no other in Mexico. Monsiváis is "el mejor conocedor de la sociedad mexicana. . . . Quien no lo ha leído no conoce el país ni a su gente" [the one who best understands Mexican society . . . If you haven't read him you know neither the country nor its people] (Benítez 4). For his colleague and close friend, fellow cronista Elena Poniatowska, his analyses of social movements steer the Mexican people toward a more desirable future: "su lealtad a la cultura popular, su crítica al gobierno, su insistencia en la eficacia de la sociedad civil le ha dado a México una quilla" [his devotion to popular culture, his criticism of the government, his insistence on an efficient civil society, have given Mexico a keel] ("Monsiváis: cronista" 6).

If Carlos Monsiváis is uniquely "owned" by his readers (Castañón 19), it is in part because they identify the man with the journalist who speaks in his texts. Narratologists have mapped and named the layers of fictional discourse that a (real) reader must traverse from the narrator to the implicit author to the virtual or real author. Writers of empirical discourses, however, are given a conventional advantage; their readers are encouraged to assume that the narrator of a history or journalism article is also the flesh-and-blood individual who selected and ordered the words (e.g. Cohn, "Signposts" 792; Genette, *Narrative Discourse* 213–4).

If the implicit author of, in this case, a crónica is thought to be a credible spokesperson, then it is likely that his or her figurative representation as narrator will also be taken as uniquely "authorized" to speak. This technical aspect of reception is paramount in deciding whether a narrator speaks truth or fiction, and I will return to it when I take up the question of the specificity of the chronicle genre. Of prior constitutive importance is the perceived authority of the cronista as an ethical being and expert witness.[1]

By his own admission and the testimony of his friends, Carlos Monsiváis is not easy to get to know.[2] "La persona más pública y notoria coincide en Monsiváis con la persona más reservada y aun recóndita que conozco" [The most public and notorious of persons coincides in Monsiváis with the most reserved and, even, secretive individual I know], says José Emilio Pacheco, Monsiváis's friend and colleague since their youth. Monsiváis "se nos escapa siempre, se pone a salvo, no se deja cercar" [ever escapes us, placing himself out of reach, refusing to let himself be hemmed in] (39). For those he lets inside the perimeters of his intimacy, however, there is warmth to spare. Elena Poniatowska considers Monsiváis the most generous of friends who will share his knowledge and who radiates enormous compassion. From the seventies on, "Monsiváis se convirtió en el consejero auricular universal. . . . Todos somos deudores de su número telefónico" [Monsiváis became everybody's telephone counselor . . . We have all benefited from having his telephone number] ("Décadas" 9–10). Such testimonials from within Monsiváis's circle reinforce the humanitarianism perceived by those who know him only through his writings and what others say.

Carlos Monsiváis Aceves was born May 4, 1938, toward the end of Lázaro Cárdenas's six-year presidency (1934–1940). On the eve of the vertiginous changes that would come with rapid industrialization in the middle decades of the century, the most revered leader of Mexico's postrevolutionary era steered his nation leftward and onto the threshold of secular modernity with vigorous efforts to implement the land, labor and religious reforms promised by the 1910 Revolution, the constitution that resulted (1917), and the subsequent Cristero Rebellion (1926–1929). These challenges to the traditional Church order included inauguration of a socialist teaching program in the schools. Baby Carlos Monsiváis rolled over, learned to sit up and began defining his first self within a deeply religious Quaker family of a Mexico not yet urbanized. Still, the weight of Mexico's burgeoning population was beginning to shift away from rural areas. Technology, especially in communications, became a major magnet drawing the indigenous population into the vortex of a fast-growing capital city.

film colonizes the consciousness

Mexico's radio culture was already strong in the decade of Monsiváis's birth; when the silent film era that had captivated Mexican viewers since the first years of the century acquired sound, movies would quickly come to dominate the collective cultural consciousness, from top to bottom of the social hierarchy. In its Golden Era (1930–1950), the cinema would be many things to the developing Mexican nation; among others, it would compensate for a general lack of literacy and civic participation, melodramatically script the government's nationalist rhetoric and reshape the Mexican's view of himself and herself (Monsiváis, A través 67, 165, 74–78).

going to school at the movies

Monsiváis observes that the excessively sentimental character of Mexican film in the 1940s, especially, mirrored a collective worldview that was deeply imprinted with the sacrificial melodrama of a Catholic populism centered in its cult of the Virgin of Guadalupe. The transition was made smoothly from veneration of the self-abnegating indigenous Mother to veneration of the film industry's sacralized and sacrificial woman. Monsiváis observes that film reworks oral culture and, together with radio, helps fashion a great undertaking in those years: the assimilation of technology, industrial economies and domestic conveniences, which somewhat compensate for fluctuations in a Mexico caught in transition. In the capital, specifically, "el cine es la escuela de las psicologías individuales, es la visión de lo deseable" [the movies teach psychology to spectators; they are a vision of what people desire] (*A través* 60).

The movie screen is, in sum, the archetypal consciousness with which Mexican society dialogued about itself from 1932 on (91). Meanwhile, outside the theaters, the motor vehicle was accelerating transformation in commercial and social arenas. Taking advantage of some incipient cracks in the patriarchy's immutable wall, women had begun to claim a place in public life and were organizing a suffrage campaign that would give them the vote just when Carlos Monsiváis was learning how to report on public events.[3]

a critical detachment

He had begun to cultivate his talent for critically distanced involvement in society from the moment his mother Esther taught him to read (Menocal 17). Recalling a childhood that was passed acquiring books and assimilating their contents (Monsiváis, *Monsiváis* 18), Carlos Monsiváis indicates that he always felt most comfortable among "los voyeuristas sociales" [those who spy on society] (Monsiváis, *Escenas* 346); he became an observer who witnessed national life at a remove that would be as moral as it was intellectual. Early on, he was inculcated to a lifelong habit of daily Bible reading in a household characterized as Protestant fundamentalist (Monsiváis, *Monsiváis* 15). "El pecado fue el tema central de mi niñez y la idea de algún modo . . . ha seguido rigiéndome hasta ahora" [Sin was the central theme of my childhood and that idea somehow still rules me even now], he says, when already at 28 he is asked for an autobiography (15). From his observer's perch, built up deeply on sacred and secular knowledges, Monsiváis would feed his consciousness while gathering data on his society.

With self-deprecating irony he confesses having never been inclined toward athletic glory but instead to have indulged in a kind of "pornografía: el alumno Monsiváis, del Sexto A, propone la creación de una biblioteca" [pornography: Sixth Form A student Monsiváis proposes creation of a library] (Monsiváis, "Viaje al corazón" 6). Casually, as though his education were like everyone else's, he reveals that he polished off Homer and Virgil and the Protestant classics in grade school, immediately switching to Gómez Nerea, Jane Austen, Dickens and other teachers of satire, Martín Luis Guzmán,

Rómulo Gallegos, Eugenio Sué and Euclides Da Cunha, not to mention
Batman and Robin, the Billikins classics, Zane Grey and Agatha Christie:
"Mi descubrimiento del mundo literario y mi renuencia a sumarme a las
acciones mayoritarias me redujeron a condición de simple testigo" [My discovery of the literary world and my refusal to join with the majority reduced
me to a mere witness] (Monsiváis, *Monsiváis* 41).

Born into the petit bourgeoisie, Carlos Monsiváis acknowledges that
he grew to manhood without experiencing firsthand the economic misery
that—lived by others—sustains his will to chronicle the untold Mexico
(Menocal 22). But, a Protestant child of divorce in a predominantly Catholic society, he did know the sting of being an unappreciated minority. His
"suspect" family circumstances and religion, as well as Monsiváis's openly
bookish inclination, subjected him at a young age to malice and resentment
(Monsiváis, *Monsiváis* 15). Today he lives where he grew up, in a comfortable house in Colonia Portales, then an area on the quiet outskirts of the
capital, today a working-class neighborhood swallowed up in the largest and
fastest growing city in the world. His passion for literature was surely not
exclusively the defense mechanism of a lonely child; he did want, after all,
to be a fireman when he grew up (61). Still, on looking back he sees that
perhaps he did not have a childhood ("Viaje al corazón" 6).

a reporter who participates in the news

As one of Mexico's most credible public witnesses, Mon-
siváis is of course not "simply" an observer. Reading well between the scant
autobiographical lines he concedes, and scavenging for the odd personal
detail dropped into other texts, one learns that Monsiváis practices a brand
of personal journalism that does not preclude his taking sides and, even,
courageous action to back his convictions. In 1961, he, José Emilio Pacheco,
Benita Galeana and José Revueltas participated in a 62-hour hunger strike
to protest violence against striking railway workers and the imprisonment of
political dissidents. With her humanizing eye for detail, Elena Poniatowska
tells of seeing the small group of civil protesters on the sidewalk, "arrebuja-
dos en las cobijas, desmelenados y ojerosos como niños a quienes el sueño
se les enreda en las pestañas" [huddled in blankets, dishevelled and with
circles under their eyes, like children with sleep tangled up in their eye-
lashes] (*Fuerte* 82). (Monsiváis, of course, deflects potential admiration with

the parodic confession: "Acepté un chocolate de manos de las Hermanitas Galindo" [I accepted a chocolate offered by the Galindo sisters] (*Monsiváis* 47).

In a crónica of 1970, the conscientiously impersonal narrator called the *Observador* suddenly and for a brief moment flashes into biographical focus. At the urging of two women who, like Monsiváis, had traveled to the Oaxaca coast to observe an eclipse of the sun, the narrator rushes to inquire and, "al presentar su escuálida identificación de prensa, obtiene un trato . . . deferencial" [on presenting his squalid press credentials, obtains deferential treatment], by which he persuades police to release two pot smokers apprehended on the beach (Monsiváis, *Días* 101). A year later, he cosigns a letter to the editor protesting the government's deployment of paramilitary goons to attack student marchers (Sánchez Susarrey 29).

To cite a last instance here of Monsiváis's active brand of reporting, while in the rural town of Tuxtla to gather information for a 1987 chronicle on government violence against rural teachers, he witnesses an act of brutal payback: Townspeople seize a bureaucrat and roughly shave him bald. Now the reporter steps in to share his didactic point of view: that shaving enemy heads is an act of desperation and unacceptable "en quienes encarnan la decisión democrática. Nada justifica este atropello, insisto" [in those who would embody a democratic choice. Nothing justifies this attack, I insist] (*Entrada* 194). The townspeople argue back, citing uncountable years of injustice suffered silently. Monsiváis does not force a resolution of the issue. The text and relations between Mexican officials and rural citizens remain subject to revision.

carnival's fool

More typically, Carlos Monsiváis comments on the news without acting to create it. He does so conscious of the value of maintaining an Outsider's posture, a stance he considers naturally his as a consequence of having always been "precoz, protestante y presuntuoso" [precocious, Protestant and presumptuous] (Monsiváis, *Monsiváis* 12). This is the stance of Bakhtin's fool. John Docker characterizes carnivalesque fools and rogues as figures of a theatrical cast of mind who "possess the time-honoured privilege to be other in this world, the right not to make common cause with any of life's available categories; the right not to participate, to be in life but not of it, to be life's perpetual spy and reflector; to make public what is usually regarded and guarded . . . as private. . . . They have the right to blunt language and to anger, to rip off masks. . . . They don't exempt themselves from parody, mockery, abuse, for not only are such figures laughed at by others, but they also laugh at themselves" (199).

As a carnivalesque witness, Monsiváis patiently cleared a singular trail through Mexican cultures, using his scene-shaping eye to track the random, still-living, details of national life and give them a deep focus. The senseless and the trivial would yield their meanings in the seamless flow of history-in-the-making: their pathos, absurdity and sublimity. In dramatizing "la enorme significación de los actos mayúsculos y minúsculos de la sociedad" [the huge meaning of major and minor acts in society] (Monsiváis, "Guillermo Prieto" 35), Monsiváis would explain the Mexican Mask's presence, just before wrenching it away.

This he would do with the training and discipline he assumed in the fifties and sixties. Novelist Sergio Pitol remembers a day in 1957 when Monsiváis, already overcommitted at nineteen and falling into the pattern of a lifetime, kept him waiting at a restaurant. Pitol, five years older than the Poet, as Monsiváis was known on the university campus, wanted the younger writer to cast a last critical eye over a manuscript Pitol hoped to publish. In a few impressionistic strokes, Pitol sets the scene of their meeting: a Mexican capital and countryside that hadn't yet seen into their own souls through *La región más transparente,* a Mexico still primed to launch itself from the burgeoning "new narrative" of *Al filo del agua* (Agustín Yáñez 1947) and *Pedro Páramo* (Juan Rulfo 1955) into the explosively renovated narrative of the sixties and seventies. In this transitional epoch, a teenaged Monsiváis was casting about for the vehicle that would carry him through life—trying out poetry and radio drama and short fiction and newswriting and chronicle.[4] At the same time, twenty-nine-year-old Carlos Fuentes was leaning on a writing scholarship to pile up the pages of his first novel. He, Sergio Pitol, José Emilio Pacheco, Salvador Elizondo and the youngster Carlos Monsiváis worked together to publish the literary journal *Medio Siglo.* Monsiváis's scrupulously critical eye had already made him the mentor of older writers (J.E. Pacheco 39).

Hostile to praise for his own work, he would withdraw "como una ostra que tratara de esquivar las gotas de un limón" [like an oyster squirming away from drops of lemon juice] (39). High praise came anyway, through Carlos

Fuentes, who wanted Monsiváis and Pacheco to join the staff of the prestigious weekly, *La Cultura en México*, then directed by Fernando Benítez. Catching sight of Fuentes and Benítez together one day, both young men fled, "muertos de timidez" [stricken with shyness], to hide themselves in a bookstore (39). A few years down the line, Carlos Monsiváis would take over direction of the cultural supplement, which through the sixties and into the seventies would be one of the chief organs of the intellectuals who came of age during and after the 1968 Student Movement.[5]

mexico at mid-century

The state of the nation as Monsiváis and other developing luminaries were launching their careers is the reality that the heir to Salvador Novo would x-ray: Politically, Mexico had swung hard to the right after Cárdenas, with a violently anticommunist government willing to torture and assassinate rural activists, union organizers and protesting teachers. The day-to-day business of meeting a vastly changing people's needs was hampered by endemic corruption in a paternalistic system as terrified of being swallowed up by the United States as it was of remaining underdeveloped (Agustín, *Tragicomedia 1940–1970* 83). Economically, despite a small middle class just gaining a sense of itself and a lust for instant gratification of pent-up desires, abysmal gaps stretched between the rich and the poor, with factories operating at forty percent of capacity in spite of a brutally rapid industrialization. Increasingly, emigration north to the U.S. job market was a necessary "safety valve" and a concomitant impetus to the "agringamiento" [gringo-izing] of Mexico (71–2).

Only a third of Mexico's children regularly attended school while population growth was so rapid that its economic dangers were alarming officials (Meyer and Sherman 645). The triply oppressed woman (held down by Arab, Spanish and Aztec ancestries) struggled for autonomy against an "atroz machismo mexicano" [atrocious Mexican machismo] (Fuentes, *Tiempo* 82) while overall, the mass of Mexicans remained content to follow wherever its nationalistic, demagogic government suggested it go. An unprofessional and graft-riddled press was, Fuentes says, one of the chief causes of civic death in Mexico (75).[6]

Despite these and other disadvantages, reform nonetheless pressed into evidence: Women gained the vote at last in 1953, muralism faded before innovations in painting, a newly universal music provided alternatives to the traditional mariachi, ranchera and bolero; a generation raised on Freud began to take a deliberative, scientific look at the presumed essential character of the Mexican. Octavio Paz asserted his primordial power in that direction, with 1950's *El laberinto de la soledad,* and in poetry and criticism. Alfonso Reyes was the uncrowned king who presided over the court in which Paz and Fuentes were beginning to dazzle the world. Reyes welcomed bright young culture junkies into his library-house. He and Paz are of course among the heroes Monsiváis names in his literary ancestry (*Monsiváis* 49–50). Pacheco recalls tutorials he and his new friend Monsiváis enjoyed with Paz and Fuentes late in the fifties: "No puedo contarlo sin estremecerme, les leíamos nuestros textos en los cafés hoy arrasados de la avenida Juárez. Cómo agradecer esa generosidad ya irrepetible" [It still moves me to speak of this. We read them what we had written in cafes, now demolished, on Juarez Avenue. How can we express our gratitude for such a unique generosity, never to be duplicated] (39).

Monsiváis and his contemporaries were coming of age intellectually in a Mexico that, on the whole, was adjusting with understandable fitfulness to far-reaching structural changes that stimulated developments in cultural production between 1950 and 1970. Industrialization brought with it a new salaried class and an insecure bourgeoisie that quickly exposed itself to the correction of relentless satire, but whose children would kick open the prudish society's doors to let in irreverence and scandalous new ways of perceiving and articulating reality. They would be Mexico's rebels with a cause at the vanguard of the Student Movement of 1968, when Carlos Monsiváis, seasoned at 30 and seated to the left of power, would be one of its most able observers.

With industrialization would also emerge a technological assault on Mexico's traditional way of doing business. Most significantly for the long-term character of the so-called "essential Mexican," the new technologies would accelerate urbanization, increase massification of cultural tastes and foment acceptance of an internationalized notion of the modern. These changes would also facilitate political innovation of a kind Mexico's grandfatherly government could not, and did not want to, envision: radical movements of anonymous citizens seeking fundamental change in the relations traditionally maintained between power and people in Mexico (García Canclini, *Culturas híbridas* 81–83). The trend toward secularization would con-

tinue strengthening the Mexican people's "will to disbelieve" (Shotwell 6),
criticize, take responsibility, or, as Monsiváis puts it, to press for "la (silen-

ciosa) democratización desde abajo" [(silent) democratization from below]
(*A través* 211). The long, gradual sea change that throughout the sixties was
beginning to take place in the Mexican masses would soon seduce Carlos
Monsiváis into giving up poetry and fiction to concentrate on a career in
journalism (except, of course, for the odd detour into writing rock 'n' roll
lyrics or reading a part in a play[7]).

launching his career

As a visiting lecturer at the University of Essex in England,
when Raymond Williams was leading debate over the place of British Cultural Studies in academe, Monsiváis wrote to Poniatowska. The part of that
September 14, 1971, letter she shares lets us participate vicariously in Monsiváis's career decision: "Yo me sigo preparando para un acaso imposible
trabajo periodístico. Todo lo que leo, veo, escucho lo refiero de inmediato
a una especie de archivo de experiencias utilizables. Me gustaría enormemente dedicarme a la crónica, al reportaje. . . . Leo un libro diario y veo
de dos a tres películas y me inundo de revistas [I continue to prepare for a
career in journalism that may turn out to be impossible. Everything I read,
see and hear I file immediately in a kind of archive of usable experiences.
I would very much like to dedicate myself to writing crónica, to reporting.
. . . I read a book a day and I see two to three movies and I bury myself in
magazines] (Poniatowska, "Décadas" 8).

Twenty years later, heaped with awards by a news-reading public's ever-
greater appreciation, the cronista directs what has become an international
career from his home, a two-story library and museum where the patron
sleeps. A great many of his thousands of books are in English—he divides
his reading about half and half between Spanish and English—a lot by U.S.
literary journalists he admires and some by U.S. thriller writers like Thomas
Harris, creator of the unforgettable Hannibal "The Cannibal" Lector.[8]

Monsiváis had spent some months of 1965 at Harvard University as
the first Mexican representative to an international seminar. He remembers
that period away from home as fundamental in his professional prepara-
tion. Those roiling times of sex, drugs and rock 'n' roll brought him into
contact with members of radical student organizations, such as the Student

Nonviolent Coordinating Committee (SNCC, antisegregationist, Civil Rights organizers) and Students for a Democratic Society (SDS, "radical" New Left activists),[9] and with equally radical new literary influences such as Tom Wolfe and Norman Mailer. As do many Mexican intellectuals, Monsiváis regards the U.S. government and the North American people and their culture separately. In the autobiography he wrote the year after his return from Harvard, he is critical of official U.S. attitudes and actions in the international political and socioeconomic sphere (Vietnam and Civil Rights), but he cheerfully embraces the culture and its self-critical capacities while astutely employing his praise of the United States to sharply contrast the Mexican system (*Monsiváis* 60). The United States, as itself and as Mexico's intimate neighbor, naturally figures prominently in most Mexican cultural and historical analysis. Monsiváis will cite the North American instance continuously throughout his career, and his essentially dual attitude—critical and captivated—will acquire theoretical sophistication over time.

His decision to turn down further job offers abroad and to refuse salaried employment in Mexico acquires symbolic weight, as well. When Monsiváis tells Elena Poniatowska, early in the 1970s, that he will work as an information gatherer on Mexico from within Mexico, because "no es éste el momento para irse de México" [this is not the time to leave Mexico], he is announcing a kind of mission, a moral commitment not to be seduced by a foreign university recruiter but to accept the risks of self-employment in a country that even a few years ago might pay no more than $25 for a serious piece of freelance reporting. He could have been speaking of himself instead of an early role model when he wrote of the nineteenth-century nationalist Guillermo Prieto: "*Salvar a México* es la única tarea que justifica histórica y humanamente a quienes la intentan. *Vivir en México* es la condena por el pago amoroso del compromiso sacificial" [*Saving Mexico* is the only task that historically and humanly justifies the work of those who attempt it. *Living in Mexico* is the punishment received in exchange for the sacrificial obligation lovingly fulfilled] (prologue, "Prieto" 15).

Poniatowska, as adept as Monsiváis at the transcendent detail, reports that he told her of his decision to stay in Mexico while "parpadeando dos veces para que no se le vea en los ojos el agua de su devoción" [blinking twice to hide his tears of devotion] ("Décadas" 8).

Monsiváis and the "mafia"

While I realize this paints an emotional portrait of a kind of romantic hero, it is not inaccurate. Neither is it complete without the flintier image of the Monsiváis who is a don in the Mexican cultural "mafia" that has been characterized as a group that was in the beginning "dinámico, inquietante y enriquecedor" [dynamic, disturbing and enriching] but which in time came to be perceived as "la semilla del autoritarismo aristocrático intelectual" [the seed of an aristocratic authoritarianism in intellectual circles] (Agustín, *Tragicomedia 1940–1970* 219). By the mid-sixties, members of this self-named mafia directed the most influential cultural publications in Mexico, including *Revista Mexicana de Literatura, Revista de la Universidad, La Cultura en México* (cultural supplement of the magazine *Siempre!*, headed during a strategic era by Monsiváis), *Revista de Bellas Artes, Cuadernos del Viento* and *Diálogos*. I know of no official roster of the Mexican intellectual mafia, but it is easy enough to see that its members include such figures as Carlos Fuentes, Sergio Pitol, Juan García Ponce, José Emilio Pacheco, Jorge Ibargüengoitia, Fernando Benítez and Elena Poniatowska (if any woman is named it is often Poniatowska).[10] They in turn cite as their godfathers the writers of the Contemporáneos group, Octavio Paz, the painter Rufino Tamayo and Alfonso Reyes.[11]

The elite group of cultured Mexicans in which Monsiváis is a leader has of course drawn criticism, some of it bearing the cruel edge of personal resentment on the part of artists who attribute their lack of success or other difficulties to unfair treatment by the mafia rather than to the tastes of a consuming public. The state of literary criticism in Mexico, and Latin America in general, is the subject of an enormously complex and important public dialogue that in itself exceeds the intent of this book. I am inclined to situate the topic in the context of evident correlations between a critically objective cast of mind and a highly literate, economically developed society on the one hand, and, on the other, a more anecdotal, impressionistic approach in a still largely oralized, developing society. If "el subdesarrollo es no poder mirarse en el espejo por miedo a no reflejar" [underdevelopment is not being able to look in the mirror for fear of not seeing one's reflection] (Monsiváis, *Monsiváis* 57), the merciless—and exemplary—critical aptitude of extraordinary intellects such as those of Octavio Paz, Carlos Fuentes, José Emilio Pacheco and Carlos Monsiváis might well appear to hold an unreasonably harsh mirror to the face of their country's intelligentsia. I suspect, in fact, that the

Pacheco who can flash an ironic smile at the "política del desaliento" [politics of discouragement] that Monsiváis as critic exercised, already at 19, would be in the minority of any nation's cultural community.

Rather more commonly, one would likely find a conflicted state of mind such as the one Ignacio Trejo Fuentes, probably inadvertently, reveals in his *Faros y sirenas*. This book offers a revealing case study of the (a)critical attitudes I mention here to elaborate the nature of Carlos Monsiváis's narrative authority as a journalist specializing in the nonfiction crónica. Trejo Fuentes is best known in Mexico for his newspaper writing, but he is also a university-trained literary critic. With *Faros y sirenas* he produces a book of metacriticism whose first half describes the objective kind of literary criticism produced in Europe and the United States; the second half condemns the state of Mexican literary criticism, finding it lacking in audacious judgment (102), too often an evident bid for personal publicity (101) and, in general in the year 1988, immature, superficial or vindictive. Trejo Fuentes seems opposed to the kind of personalized, ideological "criticism" that either cravenly lauds a buddy or equally cravenly bashes an enemy.[12] This studiously objective discourse falls apart, however, when he engages the subject of the so-called mafia, which he says is guilty of sectarianism and a brutal *caciquismo* that commits what he calls literary crimes; these amount to assassination of both character and career (139–41).

Until shortly before this moment in the book, Trejo Fuentes had employed footnotes and other elements of the academic writing apparatus. From this point on, however, the text transmogrifies into a (rather tiresome) crónica which openly relies on the emotional first-person narrator whose vocabulary takes a sharply colloquial turn toward accusations of "mezquindades" [meanness] practiced by mercenaries and assigns blame to mafiosi critics who behave like the cliché of a heart-taking Aztec priest, practicing a kind of "terrorismo intelectual perverso" and "devastador" [perverse and devastating intellectual terrorism] (133, 141).[13] The resultant text is a strange hybrid that cites completely orthodox critical theory and at the same time espouses an inimitably personal ideology. It unwittingly constitutes a kind of meta-metacriticism that illustrates what it decries.

This is most tellingly the case when one notes the curious absence of any mention whatsoever of Carlos Monsiváis. Every other intellectual writer-critic of Mexico is mentioned prominently, as either a saint or a sinner on the review circuit. As a widely acknowledged critic whose honesty and irreverent humor make him, like the late Jorge Ibargüengoitia, "insoportable, insobornable" [intolerable, incorruptible] (Paz, *Puertas* 273), and prominent on one short list of five all-time Mexican literary critics,[14] Monsiváis happens also to be a leading member of the so-called mafia that Trejo Fuentes is attacking. Not long into what has become a diatribe against a certain group of cultural "criminals," the name of Carlos Monsiváis begins to pound loudly through the silence of its absence. Trejo Fuentes had to have consciously, deliberately, avoided using the name.[15]

In a 1998 interview with what is arguably Mexico City's most solidly nonsectarian news magazine, *Proceso*, Monsiváis spoke of his and other prominent cultural leaders' participation in Mexican literary tradition, a topic that provoked a question on the various mafias of the mid-century. Monsiváis's response put these influential groups in the perspective of a small, developing intellectual community, where they would naturally be more noticeable than in, say, the more widely dispersed cultural elite of the United States: "En lo básico, la idea de la mafia fue una invención del rencor y de la sensación de verse excluidos" [Basically, the mafia was an idea generated by the resentment of those who felt left out] (Cited in Ponce 17).

the disinterested
intellectual sharpshooter

While it is true that his "espíritu militante" [militant spirit] (Martínez 264) causes Monsiváis's admirers to see him as a kind of intellectual sharpshooter, it is essential to point out that he aims at the text, not its author—the latter being a terroristic tactic he likens to mob justice. In dramatic (and no doubt intimidating) contrast to those who practice character assassination (including attempts on our chronicler's literary life), Monsiváis aligns himself with Western modernity's universal notion of the intellectual. This is a member of the knowledge class that transcends social divisions (Frow 14) and boundaries of reified local chauvinism. Such a trans-class individual is a "mental technician," an image-maker and manipulator of symbols (Marsal 6–7) for society at large. At an impersonal remove, Monsiváis inserts his observations on individual public acts and events into an historical perspective. With equal parts fact and imagination he grafts what Roderic Camp calls transcendental values onto contemporary problems, with the intent of suggesting to a broad public what might be the most humane and rational solutions (cited in Skirius, "Intelectuales" 3). This he does independently of power structures, the better to awaken the collective conscience to its responsibilities for self-governance (29). The key to the intellectual's catalytic role in this democratizing process is his (or her) capacity to "increase a society's self-knowledge by making manifest its latent sources of discomfort and discontent" (Coser x). In the process, the intellectual must fight against a natural tendency to doubt the critical judgment that sets them rigorously apart from the madding crowd. Monsiváis struggled against this irrepressible yet discomfiting syndrome when he wrote to Poniatowska from England in 1971, when he was establishing his bonafides as a public intellectual. He wrote: "Creo que el problema de mantener . . . una actitud crítica, disidente, es un problema de lucha contra la locura. No es posible que uno tenga razón contra todos, contra la prensa, la televisión, el modo de vivir de los amigos y las apetencias secretas de poder o de fama o de lo que sea. . . . Es una de mis angustias permanentes, la búsqueda de la razón de mi razón" [I think the problem of maintaining a critical and dissident attitude is a problem of fighting against insanity. It surely cannot be possible to be right against everyone else—the press, television, your friends' way of life and secret lusts for power and fame or whatever. This is a constant source of anguish for me: my search for the rightness of my attitude, for the logic and ethics of my reason] (cited in Poniatowska, "Monsiváis: cronista" 5).

A pair of chronicles, published the summer after the outbreak of armed rebellion in Chiapas, will help illustrate some of the elements of intellectual independence that characterize Monsiváis's journalistic work. The first, titled "Respuesta de Carlos Monsiváis a *Marcos*," takes the form of a public letter to the Chiapas rebellion's (in)famous Subcomandante Marcos, who has sent Monsiváis an email invitation to participate in an event of political reconciliation planned by the Chiapas rebels (the National Liberation Army of Zapata).[16] They call the event a National Democratic Convention; it was scheduled for later that summer of 1994 and, in form and well as substance, it resounds with echoes of the 1968 Student Movement's democratic call for dialogue with citizens, government and history.

Monsiváis's public response to Marcos demonstrates the generic elements that make it a crónica as opposed to a straight news article or editorial; although it provides reportage of new information and background facts, it combines these with editorial analysis and packages the whole in a recognizably personal style that draws, among other things, on parody, metalanguage, metaphor and symbol, lyricism and baroque rhetorical strategy.

My present concern, however, is for the critical content of the page-one piece, insofar as it illustrates the authority Monsiváis assumes as an intellectual who observes the Big Picture from outside the Clubhouse. While he is clearly on the side of liberty and justice, he is not so clearly a fan of the Ejército Zapatista de Liberación Nacional (EZLN) nor, especially, of the rebel army's charismatic spokesman. Seldom inclined to wave a flag of any color, Monsiváis constructs a critically independent response to the Chiapas movement's Masked Man.[17]

The response (Monsiváis, "Respuesta") opens with metalanguage that introduces subtle but significant contradictions. While it *is* a letter answering a letter, Marcos's email becomes public because Monsiváis chooses to make it so, while the cronista's letter is public from the outset. The implication is that Monsiváis values communication with the rebel leader most for its potential to inform and instruct the general public.

Monsiváis further complicates this text's reception by deferring mention of its substance in order to openly reveal how he decided whether to use the familiar *tú* or the formal *usted* form of "you" in addressing Marcos. He wants it understood that he will use the familiar form, not because the distinction between formal or familiar tone has lost all possible distinction in today's posttraditional society (1), but precisely because he wants to send and receive signals of trust (16). At the same time, Monsiváis implicitly cites one of the Spanish *tú*'s other possible uses: to imply the false intimacy that a fan assumes with a popular culture idol. Subtly, Monsiváis queries the rebel's self-dramatization as a media star. In fashioning a mini-disquisition on the distinctions between psychic and social intimacy and formality, Monsiváis lets it be known that he thinks it prudent to leave a skeptical space in which to wonder if, behind his mask, Marcos might be hiding something less than useful for an aspiring democracy.

Immediately thereafter, the journalist in Monsiváis reports the news (he is writing because Marcos wrote him to invite him to the Convención Nacional Democrática sponsored by the EZLN) and, in the same sentence, comments on that news. Marcos has increased his own internal debate, he says, making it clear he's been in conflict over the Chiapas rebellion since its outbreak six months earlier. Throughout the remainder of the text, Mon-

siváis will explain that these doubts emerge not from the ends of the rebellion but from the violent means it employs.

He announces his willingness to remain optimistic by first siding with
the EZLN's stated objective: change. Pointedly, he personalizes his point
of view, thus distinguishing Carlos Monsiváis's beliefs from those of the
EZLN or anyone else. His view on the subject of change is that Mexico's political system is outmoded and ineffective, crippled by "ineptitudes e impuni-
dades, y . . . la barbarie ejercida en nombre de la estabilidad" [ineptitude,
impunity and barbarism exercised in the name of stability] (16); that its
so-called electoral system is anything but plural or truly elective; that "los
agravios monstruosos del neoliberalismo" [the monstrous injustices of neo-
liberalism] of recent conservative regimes have exacerbated what has always
been the Chiapas Indians' lot under colonial and postcolonial rule. His
next argument reinforces his provisional tolerance of the EZLN. He theo-
rizes a cause for the historic injustice—racism—and thereby intensifies his
expressed admiration for political gains he credits to the EZLN.

While straight news reports may concentrate on the latest rebel pro-
nouncement or demand, the most recent government response, the numbers of killed or wounded, for example, Monsiváis's discourse seeks the
transcendent meaning behind the headlines: The EZLN's attacks had, at
a minimum, deprived the Salinas regime of its triumphalist air and irre-
vocably revealed the shabbiness of the spin it put on all its paper accom-
plishments; it had further reminded the collective Mexican conscience once
again of its deep-seated hatred of its weakest citizens, of the unconscionable
poverty and misery suffered always in still-feudal Chiapas. Most particularly,
with respect to Mexico's continuing quest for true democratization, by symbolically masking itself, the rebel group had exposed the country's system
of strongman politics (*el presidencialismo*) as the true masked barbarian and
stimulated calls for widespread support of a genuine civil society.

Having aligned his ultimate political goals with those stated by the
EZLN, the journalist-critic now gets to the heart of the message he wishes
to send his countrymen, via this "letter to Marcos." He will cite and explain
a series of paradoxes that he, Carlos Monsiváis, has seen in the Zapatista
movement from its inception. It is ironic, for example, that an armed movement has inspired completely nonmilitary sectors of the community. And,
he adds, where there exist paradoxes, questions abide: "Las victorias políti-

cas del zapatismo, tan importantes como son, no alcanzan a disminuir lo otro: los muertos y los heridos, los desplazados, los inconformes con el EZLN que viven en territorio zapatista, los inmensos problemas del abastecimiento, el deterioro de las ya de por sí deterioradas condiciones de vida en la región" [Zapatism's political victories, important as they are, do not compensate for the other reality: the dead and wounded, the displaced persons and those in Zapatista territory who dissent from the EZLN's point of view, the immense problems of supplies, the deterioration of the region's already impoverished condition] (16).

This part of the text assumes the strongly personal "I" typical of the journalist who writes crónica. In the same way that U.S. New Journalists used their personal involvement in reporting the news to strengthen the credibility of their views, Monsiváis here uses an open letter format to eschew a journalistic objectivity that might be perceived as contrived; he instead puts on stage his own thought processes as a model of critical thinking for La Jornada readers to observe and emulate: "Y, explicándomela como incentivo moral en meses de tal dureza, continúo reacio a la 'mística de la muerte digna', el aspecto que menos me interesa del zapatismo, su continuación del cristianismo sacrificial por otros medios, la retórica ancestral y revolucionaria que tú [Marcos] formulas con tanta vehemencia y en ocasiones con tanta brillantez, y que, sin remedio, me deja fuera" [And, even as I chalk these months of hardship up to a moral incentive, I am opposed to the "mysticism of honorable death," the aspect of Zapatism that least appeals to me: its perpetuation of sacrificial Christianity by other means, the ancestral revolutionary rhetoric that you formulate with such vehemence and, on occasion, with so much brilliance and which, nonetheless, leaves me cold] (16).

By speaking in the autobiographical first person here, Monsiváis enjoins his fellow citizens not to agree with him automatically, perhaps because of the well-established authority of his public voice, but rather to respect the process he dramatizes of a citizen who gathers his own facts and thinks about them independently. His kind of critical thinking acknowledges both sides of a question. He admits, for example, that he is of course "al tanto de que ustedes a nadie tienen que pedirle perdón" [aware that you and your followers need ask no one's pardon] (16), and at the same time he realizes that the long-suffering Indians of Chiapas have a personal stake in a multigenerational conflict that he, Monsiváis, cannot presume to share, except in a theoretical sense. On the other hand, that theoretical sense—that universalized, intellectual and "impersonal" view—is precisely what the majority of the nation needs to adopt in this case: "Desde mi pespectiva, y sólo a ella puedo atenerme, me resulta excesivo el arrebato de muerte de muchos de sus pronunciamientos" [From my perspective, and I can speak only from that viewpoint, the ecstasy of death strikes me as excessive in many of your pronouncements] (16).

. The "arrebato de muerte" he refers to is the "mysticism of dignified death" he had mentioned earlier. This mental orientation reveals an anachronistic taste for martyrdom that is rooted equally in Mexico's prehispanic warrior cults and in the indigenous and mestizo peoples' fervid adoption of a post-Conquest Catholicism that stressed (and continues to stress) a rhetoric of sacrifice. The heart of Monsiváis's critical assessment of the Chiapas movement is enclosed in his plain-language critique of the EZLN's Second Manifesto as extremely bellicose and unfortunately imbued with "vientos del martirologio" [whiffs of martyrology]. With blunt frankness, Monsiváis attacks what he perceives as the EZLN's irrational proposal to achieve radical democracy through radical violence. The cronista believes in the former, but not in an armed band as guarantor of the transition to democracy (16).

Now he openly hammers home his point: Does it make sense to convoke a convention while remaining armed? Can anyone trust an electoral system backed with guns and a discourse of revolutionary redemption? What a shame it would be, Monsiváis judges, if this proposed convention turned out to be just another in a long line of leftist pretensions to being a Constitutional Congress. Deliver us all, he said, from exhumed stalinist sermons, from marxist puritanism in the style of Lenin or Che Guevara, from what is finally so much militant machismo (16). Let us instead involve this nation's youth in discussion of rational public policy.

ombudsman and devil's advocate

It is this permanent and transcendent goal that has kept Monsiváis in Mexico and writing about Mexico all his life. In closing his response to Marcos, he makes a rare autobiographical allusion to his long, patient career as self-appointed ombudsman of his society. Thanking Marcos for his letter, he acknowledges with a self-deprecating touch of parody that "me hizo pensar, durante largos y cálidos sesenta segundos, que mi trabajo no ha sido en vano. (Detente oh momento, eres tan reconfortante.)" [it made me think, for sixty long, cozy seconds, that my work has not been in vain. (Stay, oh moment: You are so comforting.)] (16).

As Mexico's self-appointed Devil's Advocate, Monsiváis insists on thinking against the grain precisely in order to rock the mainstream's boat: "Monsiváis es el primer escritor libre del México moderno, el primero que empieza a tomarse las grandes libertades y a decir las grandes barbaridades" [Monsiváis is the first unmuzzled journalist of modern Mexico, the first to begin taking big liberties and to pronounce outrageous truths] (Blanco, *Crónica* 85).

Monsiváis also shares with the *genus* Intellectual a tendency to temper his unfettered criticism with a playful, humorous presentation. Given Monsiváis's Bible-reading background and its influence on his style, his pitiless deconstruction of Mexican reality (including an autopsy of its cultural production), and his irrepressible attraction to parody, Lewis Coser could have been thinking of this Mexican critic as a model for the Intellectual he defines. This is an exemplar who acts at once as priestly upholder of sacred tradition, as a descendant of "those inspired madmen who preached in the wilderness," and as a medieval court jester (viii); in Bakhtinian terms, a Wise Fool whose mocking of authority holds out "the irrepressible hope for humanity that life is not necessarily preordained towards loss, failure, and tragedy, that fate is not inconquerable" (Docker 217). Or, as Poniatowska puts it: "Detrás del humor, de la ironía, de la burla, surge un alegato profundo a favor de la tolerancia, la libertad, los derechos humanos, la crítica como actividad intelectual por excelencia, la sociedad abierta" [Behind his humor, irony and mockery can be heard a profound statement in favor of tolerance, liberty, human rights, criticism as a quintessentially intellectual activity and an open society] ("Monsiváis: cronista" 6).

Mexican cartoonist El Fisgón admiringly describes Monsiváis as just such an irrepressible optimist, an evil genius (*malvado*) whose principal critical weapon is humor in all its forms: rabid irony, violent caricature, cruel mockery, poisonous nicknames: "es un canallesco parodista. . . . un hombre brillante, genial . . . [a quien] ya sólo le falta un país que lo entienda" [He's a roguish parodist . . . , a brilliant man of genius who's only missing one thing: a country to understand him] (in Cayuela Gally 5).[18] Ultimately, Monsiváis authorizes his criticism of others by first taking aim at himself; he is always ferociously self-critical (Poniatowska, "Décadas" 8).

In his 1993 study of changes in Mexico's intellectual life from 1968 to 1992, Jaime Sánchez Susarrey insistently returns to Carlos Monsiváis as the most meaningful representative of the organic intellectual engaged with the collective morality. He notes that Monsiváis and other prominent thinkers and writers such as Carlos Fuentes and José Emilio Pacheco have agreed since early in the 1970s on Mexico's need for a committed intellectual, one who rejects the purist notion of remaining not only independent of the ruling group but also at the margin of all political parties and their platforms. While Monsiváis is one of the marxist and socialist parties' most consistent critics, he has remained unswervingly loyal to leftist liberal values and quixotic postures that he calls lost causes. By the time the Neocardenist Movement of the 1980s was struggling to achieve meaningful status as an opposition party under the banner of Cuauhtémoc Cárdenas (son of the 1930s president Lázaro Cárdenas), Monsiváis was among leftist intellectuals who helped guide formation of a new coalition of oppositional splinter groups, which became the PRD, or the Partido de la Revolución Democrática (Party of Democratic Revolution).[19]

Similarly, in the economic arena, Monsiváis has mostly avoided the moral and professional compromises that would come with dependence on a paycheck. Although he has directed journals, occasionally served on editorial boards, and contributed regularly to newspapers, academic journals and literary magazines, the cronista has made a point of guarding his financial and political autonomy. He is making a statement both ethical and autobiographical when he asserts categorically that he has never worked outside his home, that he has no bosses, that he neither supervises nor is supervised by anyone (Egan, "Entrevista" 19). He also recognizes his extreme good fortune in being able to live and work as a free agent while, historically, Mexico's intellectuals have commonly been co-opted or, at least, constrained, by the government's employment powers.

Thus, in the crónica studied above, Monsiváis lets Marcos and his vigilant readers know that now, as always, he will avoid as much as possible even the appearance of complicitous sectarianism. He will not agree to the status of special invitee to the convention. In case anyone doubts the reasons for his gracious refusal of Marcos's offer, he explains that to accept would seem to identify his judgments with the achievements of the convention's governing board; it would compromise not only his independence but the *perception* of his autonomy.

Instead, he counters, "me propongo asistir como periodista, con todo y anotaciones de la Redacción (la R.)" [I propose to attend as a journalist, complete with my Editor's comments] (16). His *La Jornada* readers and, he assumes, Marcos himself, are sufficiently familiar with his long-running newspaper column, "Por mi madre, bohemios," to recognize "la R" as his trademark alter-ego in the column, the sarcastic voice of The Editor who every week gives democrats in Mexico a hilariously serious lesson on how to deconstruct the doublespeak that passes for news and turn it into genuine information for a responsive civil society. A Monday in Mexico without the satirical column would feel like walking without the "imprescindible piedra en el zapato de la vida" [indispensable pebble in the shoe of life] that the political analyst's acerbic commentary has become over the last thirty-two years (Poniatowska, "Monsiváis: cronista" 6).

As a good-faith proof of his intention to remain objectively "outside" the event upcoming in Chiapas, Monsiváis in the crónica assumes The Editor's snide voice to suggest that he couldn't possibly pass up an opportunity to "cronicar otro Condominio de Babel" [report on another Condo Tower of Babel] (16). This is vintage seriocomic Monsiváis. Having sat for forty years in the midst of auditoriums resounding with the "Babel" of Mexican citizens experimenting messily with the interminable dialogue of democracy,[20] Monsiváis finally "places" the neo-Zapatistas where he suggested they belong at the start of his crónica: in the country's portfolio of popular culture, doing what Unofficial Culture does at its best: resist, refunction, recycle, reform. The EZLN, says Monsiváis, ought to start with existing reality—a frighteningly inadequate political system and government—and work from within, without violence, to de- and reconstruct it.

This is what Monsiváis himself does with his writing; he gets within observer distance of power and its consorts (here, the EZLN and various government factions opposing it) to spy out the hidden truths of their rhetoric and then, from within the same sociopolitical circles but outside the range of those who would co-opt him, he tells it the way he sees it. An indispensable narrative strategy in what I think of as "good crónica" is the election of details with the power to excavate transcendent universality from beneath the banal surface of the fleeting event. This literary tactic is the raison d'être of the new chronicle of Mexico and serves as evidence of a reportorial competence and writing talent that contribute to the "authorization" of a chronicler's voice; the artfulness of speech may, in the end, be the strongest justification for believing that the journalist is a truthteller.

hunting democracy in the jungle

As an illustration of this aspect of Monsiváis's narrative authority, I will now comment on the second of the pair of crónicas that I mentioned earlier. This one can be seen as the companion of the one we examined above on the Chiapas crisis.[21] In his July 27, 1994, open letter to Subcomandante Marcos, Monsiváis had acknowledged being invited to the planned National Democratic Convention in Chiapas and informed that he would be attending as an observer only; he also enumerated his doubts about the democratic legitimacy of the armed rebellion and left his ultimate stance on the EZLN up in the air, with notable journalistic skepticism. He particularly regrets the EZLN's reliance on the florid rhetoric of the martyr. In the text we'll now look at, coverage of the convention itself, Monsiváis is, as promised, quite visibly present as an eyewitness to the historical event; he allows us to contrast his outsider stance to that of Poniatowska, who attended in a dual capacity as chronicler-reporter and participant (319); he ends this text as he had the earlier one: with notable journalistic skepticism. The trek back from the wilds of Chiapas to the streets of Mexico City was as exhausting as the journey out, he notes, but "en los camiones y al paso por los pueblos la esperanza de paz se afirma y disemina. Si esto es así el viaje valió la pena" [on the buses and passing through villages, hope for peace is affirmed and disseminated. The trip will have been worth making if this is the case] (323).

As a photo opportunity, a camping expedition and a chance to get a good news story, the convention itself is of but passing interest to Monsiváis. Its truest value would be the reverberating after-effect and follow-through represented by genuine progress toward social justice throughout Mexico. Monsiváis is no more convinced of the EZLN's ability to deliver those promises than he had been when planning to attend the unique event, but the experience presented Monsiváis the symbol hunter with a good kill.

Tucked away in his sharpshooter's perch, the Intellectual in search of the transcendent image zeroed in on a number of sights and sounds signifying something more than the sum of their hours of duration. An observant reader will respond to inter- and intratextual appeals to the memory of past readings and will coauthor the "real" meaning of this report on Chiapas. At a minimum, it will be clear that the most fruitful way to view this historic meeting of civilian activists is, precisely, as a part of the fluid, unfinished whole called History.

The convention, for example, takes place in a town called Aguascalientes. When Monsiváis once refers to it as the New Tenochtitlán and later as the New Aguascalientes, he invites us to step far back from the chaos of the event under observation in order to see it in the perspective of Mexico's turbulent history, which first (as Tenochtitlán, pre-Conquest Aztec capital) represents the storied continuity of the Mexican indigenous past and, at the same time, the persistence right up to the present of its defeat and enslavement by the European master. As a New Aguascalientes (the original being the central Mexican state and city where in 1914 representatives of the many armed factions of the Revolution met to elect a constitutional president), the EZLN convention is either where new hope for democratic peace will be conceived, or where such hopes will be drowned in torrents of rhetoric and menaced by the visible threat of armed violence.

In 1914, "alguna otra fecha legendaria" [another legendary date] (320), the Aguascalientes convention failed to achieve its goals, mainly because revolutionary Mexico's myriad power factions were reluctant to compromise in pursuit of their individual goals. In 1994, Monsiváis suggests, yet another National Democratic Convention filled with Zapatistas results ambiguously in grandiose rhetorical moments, dramatic photo opportunities for armed revolutionaries and civilian constitutionalists, and an adjournment that leaves ultimate gains of the meeting in doubt.

Beside such overt allusions to prehispanic times, the Conquest and the Mexican Revolution, Monsiváis plants more subliminal suggestions to historicize today's land revolt in Chiapas. From the first subtitle to the last lines of this chronicle, Monsiváis develops a photographic image of the event, emphasizing by negative contrast the way Time unstoppably unrolls a national history as moments which, although pregnant with unrevealed meaning, dissolve into blurred impressions amid the all-too-human concerns about maddening bureaucracy, food shortages and other missing creature comforts, unobserved timetables, and the pursuit of notable sound bites. If a writer such as Monsiváis does not "freeze the frame" with his words, the durable import of an event such as Chiapas will be borne away on the wind—or, in this case, a downpour of biblical dimension and possibly of biblical revelation (322–23).

If we examine up close the texture of Monsiváis's "Foto panorámica: la generación de Aguascalientes" [Panoramic shot: the Generation of Aguascalientes] (313, first subtitle), we can perceive multiple views stacked like double and triple exposures. Answering the dramatic Masked Man's call to a political colloquium in the middle of an all-but-inaccessible guerrilla hideout in the jungle is at first sight a lamentable cliché: the media-manipulating Photo Op. It is much more than that, as this time-exposed text will slowly reveal, but it is also a cliché Photo Op. He will go out of his way to show Marcos's studied use of the strategically deployed symbol, such as his mystique-maintaining mask and an exemplary national flag (320, 323), and will thereby suggest that the convention might turn out to be no more than a metaphoric co-optation of the legitimate government's prerogatives.

The implicit criticism of the photographic trope intensifies when we realize that this "generational photo"—a first of its kind—includes all the guests of the guerrillas: "personas altamente representativas y los que con dificultades se representan solos" [highly representative individuals, as well as those who would have a hard time representing even themselves] (313). Lest we dismiss this "generation" of photo subjects as mere victims of a journalist's cynicism, Monsiváis insists on the metaphor so steadily that, through the sheer weight of his List of attendees, he assembles a word picture of the ideal he has nourished in four decades of crónicas: democracy from below oozing up out of anonymity, democracy in the glorious messiness of its mismatched special interests, democracy at last (or, at least, as a real hope) in a postmodern Revolution conducted in part by email.

The last time a many-splendored throng of would-be democrats gathered to dialogue with the Mexican government, hundreds of them ended up shot down in cold blood (Tlatelolco 1968). Monsiváis froze that frame in a by-now classic series of crónicas published in his first collection, *Días de guardar* (1970). His following anthology, *Amor perdido* (1977), begins with a textual masterpiece that this narrative still-life, the one he prints in 1994, is meant to recall to mind. That crónica, titled "Alto contraste (A manera de foto fija)" (*Amor* 15–57), begins by inviting us to stand with the writer-critic before a black and white portrait while he invites his audience to project a negative critique onto his apparently innocent description of the pre-Revolution photographs of Porfirio Díaz and members of his society. The discourse on these photographs is framed as a symbolic Self-Portrait of the Mexico that lived through a revolution ostensibly fought for social, economic and political justice, only to end up, sixty years later, dragging the bodies of unarmed citizens from Tlatelolco Square.

In beginning his 1994 crónica with a similar rhetorical strategy, Monsiváis incites us to compare mental images and see that real change has taken place and continues to develop. His nation's history has made painfully slow and uneven progress toward a genuine democracy of modernity, but it has made progress. The cronista's eternally optimistic zeal to snap such shots of his society's coming of age is what makes Monsiváis include himself in the cliché photo, down at the bottom of the frame, among "los veteranos de las causas perdidas" [veterans of lost causes] (313).

As he so often does, Monsiváis insists that we read him with unresolved contradiction: Yes, the neo-Zapatista rebellion is quite possibly another in a long line of lost causes in Mexico, but at the same time it won't be a dead loss if it can entice some city slickers with "habilidades campiranas . . . perfectibles" [perfectible camping skills] (317) to depart from a public square at five o'clock in the morning on a tortuous journey into the jungle reaches of what in his sixteenth-century chronicle Bernal Díaz del Castillo calls the province of Chiapa.

And Monsiváis does want us to think about that most famous of the chronicles of the Indies, Bernal's imperishably fascinating account of the Conquest of Tenochtitlán-México by Hernán Cortés (1519–1521), which triumph was followed anticlimactically by the non-Conquest of what was known as Las Hibueras. This account of Cortés's disastrous journey with Gonzalo de Sandoval through the jungles of Chiapas, Guatemala, Honduras and Nicaragua (Bernal Díaz, chapters 163–190) contrasts vividly with triumphalist reports of the campaign to take the highly urbanized center of the Mexican empire. Las Hibueras was at the margins of the vast land offering Spain the gold-bearing grandeur of Tenochtitlán's floating palaces; lost in its crocodile-infested rainforests, Cortés achieved none of his objectives and lost all but his life before landing in a small Spanish outpost at the very edge of the newly "conquered" territory. Bernal says the fearsome captain spent the night weeping.

The soldier's account of the same jungle campaign is more ambiguous than Cortés's; a kind of reverse triumphalism shows the Conquerer and other Spanish captains steadily declining in heroic stature and narrative centrality while Bernal gains because he is more adept at sneaking into Indian villages at night to steal chickens (2: 270–4), more experienced at responding to native resistance (2: 198), more heroically willing to defend the Indian against unjustified Spanish brutality (2: 200–11).

This is the historical con*text* we should have in mind as we read of the Conquest of Democracy in Chiapas's Lacandon Jungle, whose army of civilians includes the cronista Carlos Monsiváis, a soldier for peace, freedom and justice. If in Bernal, Cortés the Conquerer could find neither Indians to vanquish (they all hid from him) nor gold to seize, the irony for Monsiváis is to find himself reporting on "una organización al margen de la ley [que] le propone un encuentro a la sociedad civil" [an organization on the fringes of the law that sets up a meeting with civil society]: The EZLN is suddenly a band of guerrillas bearing "armas que aspiran a ser inútiles" [weapons that aspire to become useless] (320, citing Marcos).

If Bernal's heroic reportage includes a litany of the wounds he received in the epic conquest of Mexico—more than three in the Hibueras campaign alone (2: 193, 203, 236)—Monsiváis's neo–*Historia verdadera* of the Chiapas expedition incorporates elements of a discourse of failure that makes note of the wound our hero-chronicler receives in the line of duty. The Lacandonian resistance has organized a campaign that involves a forced march at three in the morning, during which Monsiváis trips and injures his foot (Bernal is wounded in the leg on a dangerous scouting expedition (2: 236)).

Except for analysis of two speeches given by Subcomandante Marcos, virtually all of this crónica consists of banal details of human interest that clash ironically with the epic bid for democracy advertised by the EZLN, in just the same way Bernal's fixation with the banalities of soldier life—having dog for dinner, for example—clash with the official project of The Conquest. With deadpan irony, Monsiváis details a litany of snafus and other organizational crises, assuring us with dry understatement that the Zapatistas have yet to become terrific hosts, *"To say the least"* (317).

After days of delays and discomforts, the cronista has no conquest to report. The "natives" are in hiding. It's hard to find "chickens." There is certainly no "gold" to claim. He can offer only details of his painful personal ordeal, reminiscent of Bernal's complaints about the cold and the hunger, the pain and the fear of the common foot soldier. Monsiváis's backpack is as heavy as the weapons Bernal had to lug all over New Spain. All around him the shared misery is so great that he can take refuge only in self-pity. By

5:30 in the morning, after being up and on the march in the rain for more than twenty-four hours, he collapses wherever he can find a place to be still. A paramedic field-dresses his foot. He snatches two hours of sleep.

The morning reveals a feat of extemporized empire building. If Cortés and Sandoval had once built fifty bridges to get their bedraggled army across a switch-backing web of rivers and streams, some six hundred men and women of the EZLN have managed to construct a huge convention center in just twenty-eight days, in the all-but-inaccessible midsection of the jungle. The actual work of the convention, however, is delayed time and again. Nearly forty-eight hours after marching into camp, the schedule is still on hold. Delegates tell jokes, sing, recite poems. Finally, they break into fights over whether Cuauhtémoc Cárdenas and Subcomandante Marcos should be on the same banner (318).

The convention gets under way at last. Shortly after, a cloudburst forces everyone under a tent, which soon collapses. The conquistadors of civil self-governance break into a messy retreat from order. Both national flags rip apart in the storm and the shreds blow into the empty spaces now occupied by thousands. What Monsiváis dubs the "sociedad neohidrocálida" [neohydrotropical society] breaks camp the very next day, to avoid being defeated again by Nature. Marcos sends them off with a last *arenga* (323), much like the fervid pep talks Cortés reportedly delivered to his long-suffering troops.

The journalistic essence of "Crónica de una Convención" lies in reportage of Marcos's first address to the assembled civilians. The full import is appreciated if one has read and remembered the previous crónica, Monsiváis's open letter to Marcos. In that text, we recall, Monsiváis had consciously distanced himself from the sacrificial consciousness of the martyred fatalist that he finds characteristic of still premodern Mexico ("Respuesta" 16). Weeks later, physically returned to the feudal world of the Lacandon Jungle, Monsiváis hears Marcos declare:

> Nosotros, los muertos de siempre, los que tenemos que morir de nuevo para vivir, esperamos de esta CND [National Democratic Convention] la oportunidad que nos negaron los que malgobiernan este país, la oportunidad de regresar después del deber cumplido a nuestro estar bajo tierra . . . al silencio que callamos, a la noche de que salimos, a la muerte que habitamos . . . la oportunidad de desaparecer de la misma forma en que aparecimos, de madrugada, sin rostro, sin futuro, la oportunidad de volver al fondo de la historia, del sueño, de la montaña. (322)

[We, the eternally dead, we who have to keep on dying in order to live, expect from this convention the opportunity denied us by those who misgovern this country, the opportunity to return to life after having done our duty below ground, after the silence we kept, the night out of which we emerged, the death we inhabited . . . , an opportunity to disappear the same way we appeared, at dawn, without a face, without a future, an opportunity to go back to history's basement, back to sleep, back to the mountains.]

Coming after pages of reportage detailing the banal workings of democracy in the anonymous confusion of a great throng, this speech is placed like a museum artifact, in a large transparent space where a rhetorical vision of collectivist self-sacrifice is displayed as an archaic anomaly. Monsiváis does not judge the speech as good or bad, right or wrong—although he does analyze it as a verbal construction (321). He quotes Marcos verbatim, reports the ensuing cloudburst, transcribes shouts from the audience ("Zapata lives!" and "If only Zapata were alive!"), permits a quick flash of his black humor: "Murmuro con resignación: 'Si Zapata no hablara, con nosotros se empapara'" [I murmur with resignation: "If Zapata were not talking, with us he would be sopping"] (322).

Watching Marcos's audience run for cover from the rain, Monsiváis observes that Nature has undone the elaborate visual symbolism of Marcos's stage set. Later, Marcos says he'll take his mask off if the people want. And they beg him not to, because "Marcos sin pasamontañas no es admisible, no es fotografiable, no es la leyenda viva" [Without his mask Marcos is inconceivable; he cannot be photographed, he's not the living legend] (323).

Thus Monsiváis ends his chronicle as he began it, focused on the theatricality of Marcos and the meeting, on Mexico's ritualized public life, on his society's deeply ceremonial mindset. Such careful symmetry of structure is typical of a Monsiváis text, whose purpose is always at least both literary and informational. In this instance, intertwining the technical and the factual in an entertaining parody of a long-ago conquest narrative expands the potential signified well beyond the sum of the signifier's parts. The shots taken of the event symbolize its historical import only at a first remove from the literal. Beyond that, as happens with Bernal's torrentially detailed account of the Conquest, this crónica becomes a freeze-frame view of the informal workings of democracy, of a society whose Inner Adult very slowly comes into focus. Reporting how democracy "happens" is like watching grass grow. The challenge Monsiváis took up nearly half a century ago was to use words to design a visible landscape of civil society. To carry out that ongoing task, he developed a rigorously self-critical consciousness before he was out of his teens, and remained faithful to that Outsider's stance. He identified anonymous, lived, daily culture as the surest source of the authentic democratic mindset and adopted that journalistic object as his lifelong newsbeat. Aided by the power of the short nonfiction narrative to carry the authority of his voice, Monsiváis has elaborated over decades an understanding that the nation's psychic energy feeds simultaneously from the bottom and top of its society.

2

modernity, democracy, and popular culture in mexico

The cultural forms and practices emerging spontaneously from everyday life occupy the center of Carlos Monsiváis's narrative as both object and mode of representation. The resulting discourse is a kind of metalinguistic metaculture, an artifact simultaneously popular and elitist that satisfies on many levels: journalistic, historical, sociological, dramatic, artistic, metaphysical and theoretical. Within the broad scope of Mexican daily life and the cultural history behind it, the texts Monsiváis selects for his book collections acquire the status of high art; these, for the most part, celebrate the anti-art of calendar painting, punk rock, hippiespeak, pinup queens, provincial miracle workers, beat-up old boxers, soccer matches, meetings about water supplies in dusty town halls, aged camp followers, beauty pageants in the slums, sweatshop seamstresses, boys in the 'hood and songs about prostitutes.

To situate Monsiváis in relation to mainstream thinking in Cultural Studies requires a brief historical overview that takes in the development of popular culture as an academic discipline in the Anglo world. In the 1960s and 1970s, while Monsiváis was building his reputation as the guru of such "low" culture in Mexico, U.S. and British universities were reluctantly surrendering a few square feet of space to academic heretics who were preaching in the wilderness about the importance of a "new humanities" that they were calling Popular Culture.[1] Monsiváis found kindred spirits among trailblazing Europeans who, to mention only a few notable names, include Walter Benjamin, Elias Canetti and Raymond Williams.

Strong resemblances can be found between Monsiváis and the Walter Benjamin who strolled Germany's pre–World War II streets in obsessive pursuit of the minutiae of lived life, which he saw as a metaphor in direct correspondence with the historical substructure of Western modernity (Arendt 11).[2] Monsiváis's trademark parodies of biblical discourse, as well as his consistent pursuit of the intimate Mexican mind among the masses gathered at soccer matches and rock concerts, echo the similarly utopian concerns of Elias Canetti, Bulgarian theorist of relations between power and the masses.[3] In England, an older contemporary was to be found in Raymond Williams, who figures among groundbreaking theorists of the influential school of British Cultural Studies and who would quickly gain respected space in Monsiváis's library.[4] Among U.S. students of popular culture, Monsiváis has admired since the beginning of his career the way New Journalists such as Tom Wolfe and Norman Mailer confer the autonomous permanence of literature upon reportage of the fleeting drama of an antiwar march or a New York cocktail party.[5]

Monsiváis engages and adapts the brilliant work of his international colleagues as he constructs an evolving image of (post)modernity and democracy in Mexico. He historicizes his local space, documenting a Mexico "en el trayecto de una sociedad semifeudal a una de masas" [moving from a semifeudal state to a mass society] (Monsiváis, "Estética" 7), at the same time making durable art out of what Homi Bhabha has called the "scraps, patches and rags of daily life" ("DisseminNation" 287).

Training a philosophical eye on the "scraps" of contemporary life releases into that reality a powerful redemptive force. In this sense, one could view Monsiváis's overall work as a kind of crime reportage about victims, problem-solvers and account-balancing epiphanies in Mexico. A

favored focus of this journalism exposes the way Mexico's Establishment
exploits traditional culture as an ornament used to fake an image of itself as
a government of, for and by the people (Monsiváis, "Duración" 38). Thus,
popular culture and its study are a dual democratizing tactic.

37

modernity,

democracy,

and

popular

culture

in mexico

criticism as construction

As important as it is to Monsiváis to expose impunity, authoritarianism, and hypocrisy as fault lines in the dominant culture, he holds
it equally essential to move beyond criticism to construction. Accordingly,
Monsiváis focuses his deconstructive project on the attitudes and cultural
practices of the (overwhelmingly marginalized) people themselves, whom
he sees as ultimately responsible for their own liberation into the mainstream of a civil society enjoying autonomous, democratic self-rule. If in
Monsiváis's nation-building view, the Establishment's False National Culture has kidnapped Everycitizen of Mexico, his decades of reportage have
pursued a plan to rescue the individual consciousness. Monsiváis aims his
cultural enterprise at empowerment.

His unstinting exposés of seemingly endless Mexican maladies might
seem to evidence an incurable pessimism; in fact, his black vision (typically
shaded with cruel hilarity) denotes an inextinguishable optimism. Criticism,
after all, makes sense only if fed by hope for change. Monsiváis's coverage
and critique of local social struggles and mini-worlds of culture express
a foucauldian-gramscian desire to propagate from below diffuse, informal
contestations to the hegemonic impulse. The vast part of his study of the
"science of the ordinary" (de Certeau 13) reflects what happens for lack of
alternatives at the macropolitical level, and points out what can happen
when, in myriad micropolitical arenas, anonymous citizens create their own
responses to limitation and want.

A distinguished frontrunner in many fields of analysis, Monsiváis is
also, among scholars of the contingent, refreshingly immune to "politically
correct" attitudes. The state of mind he brings to his work is complex
and seldom explicit. His narrator appears as a pragmatic and self-critical
observer-philosopher, a thinker of (r)evolutionary stance who nonetheless
cannot be budged from certain fundamental premises. Antivictimist where
many of his colleagues seem to enjoy counting the ways they suffer for the
sins of Others, nonsectarian where it is common to cast blame and calumny

abroad, well read to a legendary degree, Monsiváis is antichauvinist, anti-nationalist and ideologically unfixed.

While perennially aligned with the left-liberal agenda in Mexico, Monsiváis is an equal-opportunity oppositionist: He will lambast the rhetoric of orthodox Marxists as quickly as that of forked-tongue fascists in the ruling party. And while he is openly critical of U.S. government policies that demean Mexican autonomy, he will just as openly cite U.S. culture and its self-critical mentality as models for the plural society he would like to see constructed at home (for example: Monsiváis, *Días* 28–44, 65–77; "Civili-zación" and "Duración"). In short, he is a thinker of independent, trailblaz-ing and frequently resented iconoclasm who lifts his lance against myth and doublespeak without regard to whose cause they falsely represent. Mon-siváis would gore God's ox if he thought it blocked the road to a more truly just society.

His extraordinary capacity for synthesizing infinite detail often leads to surprising notions about democracy and its chances in Mexico. Conclusions he reaches can appear startlingly out of context provided, in their aphoristic compression, they are perceived in the first place. Often contained in the pithy philosophy of the *sentencia,* his sense of humor makes him a popular hero among Mexican newspaper readers.

Whatever the narrative technique or tone of voice he deploys, its thrust is always directed toward transformation. Monsiváis admires the elegant and articulate writings of his literary predecessors, nineteenth-century *cos-tumbrista* analysts of traditions and social mores, writers like Guillermo Prieto and José Tomás de Cuéllar. But Monsiváis's extraordinary knack for verbally mirroring Mexican customs, unlike theirs, is not meant to fix a defi-nition of Mexicanness. Quite the contrary: Monsiváis delves with great detail into the national character of Mexican film, into the national context for Mexican cartoons and comics, into the national modes of rock music, the national way to steer a dance partner with the left hand or the national way to live by the macho code of honor precisely so that he might dislodge those local characteristics from any essentializing definition of *mexicanidad.* When he synthesizes great dollops of Mexican history to contextualize a phenomenon of immediate and ostensibly ephemeral reality, it is to fore-ground—and perhaps foretell—a rupture, a subliminal change in the collec-tive worldview.

This is not to say that Monsiváis denies that his compatriots conduct their daily affairs with a peculiarly Mexican flair; he does not wish to de-Mexicanize his society in the interest of helping it learn from the United States a pluralist capacity for self-criticism. In his view, democracy and secular self-consciousness are a universal state of mind that will find no space to grow in Mexico so long as it remains xenophobically obsessed with a national cultural identity.[6]

39

modernity,

democracy,

and

popular

culture

in mexico

a founder of popular culture theory

To see Carlos Monsiváis as a walking museum of culture is to take in only the frontal view. To see him whole is to observe how he works simultaneously behind the scenes, so to speak, to bring things to the exhibits and place them in relationships of contiguity that tell an unofficial but compelling story about Mexico and its people. More than any other in his nation's community of intellectuals, Monsiváis has contributed to the founding, not only of popular culture as a discipline, but also of a methodology and theory that to the allure of culture as spectacle add the substance of durable symbolic and philosophical meanings. In the last three decades or so, Cultural Studies and, within this amoebic field, the subset of Popular Culture, have gained a solid sense of being and definition.

At the same time, a degree of this "contested terrain of study [that is] inherently resistant to disciplinary purity" (McRobbie 48) must, by definition, elude definition. The notion of "popularity" involves a spontaneity, autonomy and refusal that can easily disappear when too closely aligned with academic concepts of discipline. From the outset, then, Carlos Monsiváis devoted himself to a seductive field that would always and yet could never be fully available for mastery. That places him in a tradition in which popular culture has remained for years a perennially "new" object of research that keeps getting discovered because it keeps getting lost or hidden from consciousness.

At least since humans began chronicling their perceptions of differences between lifestyles, popular culture has been recognized. Classical historians of religion might have been the first (Western) analysts to contrast an orthodox culture (Christianity) with a heterodox orientation (magic, superstition)(D. Hall 8).[7] The Greco-Roman discovery of the "popular" led to subsequent rediscoveries: the enthusiasm of elite poets of the Renaissance Spanish court for collecting popular ballads (Menéndez-Pidal), for example; for another, the European and, by then, Spanish American intellectual class's eighteenth-century discovery of popular culture (Burke 216). Still later the popular tradition would be cultivated by artists of the Romantic era in the mid-nineteenth century and the decadent turn into the twentieth (Paglia; Praz).

By the time the industrial revolution had radically reshaped relations between urban and rural spaces, its ever-more-rapid advances in technology would tool the Modernist sensibility of the first half of this century. The "great divide" (Huyssen) deepened between a self-defined elite culture attached to museums, opera houses and universities, while the masses and their "vulgar" tastes were held at bay "below."[8] By the middle of this century, scholars seeking popular culture's definitive parameters were rejecting dichotomies and instead taking an eclectic view of the mass mind.

In the latter half of this century and with Bakhtin's far-reaching influence, definitions of the popular multiplied; theorists weighed relations among the traditional (folkloric or the indigenous), the ultracontemporary (mass, or "pop") and the consumer cultures. A survey of critical and theoretical literatures in the United States, Europe and Latin America reveals a difference in approach to these theorizations that has decreased over time. Until the last decade, one could perceive a clear division of labor, so to speak: The Anglo world appeared to work toward universalist theories that deliberately placed traditional folklore in a separate camp while striving for nonideological ("objective") analyses of widely held beliefs and customs of contemporary society[9]; Latin America tended toward more inclusive definitions that embraced indigenous traditions, as well as displays of notably sectarian and nationalist concerns about socioeconomic injustice, vindication of repressed populations and cultural imperialism.[10]

More recently, Latin American analyses tend to assimilate critical and theoretical languages of Anglo-European schools, in keeping with pressures that generalize urban and transglobal cultural values while fostering practices that reflect or grow out of a deepening postmodern sensibility.[11] "Authoritarian populist discourse," historically out of place in the United States, is now decreasingly evident in Latin America. The shift accompanies new definitions and concepts of state and nation (Franco, "Marcar" 36); "the cultural studies that has emerged from Latin America during the last decade is theoretically sophisticated and subtle" and "seems to lack the explicit Marxism and feminism of the researchers and activists who emerged in the 1970s" (O'Connor 60).

This can be explained in part by the emergence of an electronically transmitted, global, language of cultural analysis which serves "to flatten and narrow the dominating concerns of cultural studies, predisposing communication to the abstract rather than the concrete, historicized and localized" (B. Schwarz 386). As Walter Mignolo observes, the "locus of enunciation" of Latin American culture theory has shifted from a recognizable locale south of the U.S.–Mexican border to a place less geographical than psychic or intellectual ("Introduction"). In the context of cultural criticism, the postmodern mind reacts against the self-enclosure of Modernist elitism and attacks the concept of hierarchy by refusing to discriminate (morally, ideologically and, sometimes, even aesthetically) between high and low art.

41

modernity,
democracy,
and
popular
culture
in mexico

the new chronicle as new historicism

Monsiváis's thick descriptions yield a rich, open-ended definition of culture and its subgenres. His is a metatextual and evolving view of a living historical process that resists easy definition, as does popular culture itself. Culture is shaped by its unavoidable relation to history and to politics, all three of which emerge intertwined from realities that can be observed and reported but not fully apprehended. I would align Monsiváis with New Historicists who "combat empty formalism by pulling historical considerations to the center stage of literary analysis." Like them, he describes culture in action, seizing upon an event or anecdote and rereading it in such a way as "to reveal through the analysis of tiny particulars the behavioral codes, logics, and motive forces controlling a whole society" (Veeser xi).

With such an historicist approach in mind, we can build an image of Carlos Monsiváis's understanding of popular culture as one would a pyramid. The base is the all-inclusive concept of culture, that behavior which, in separating humans from other animals, involves "a social and political process of meaning-making" (Fiske, *Reading* 1), a chaos in which the perfection of order begins (Monsiváis, *Rituales* 15). On this generic foundation, Monsiváis positions a pair of building blocks in dialectic proximity: one is the national, or official, culture, purloined or invented and then promoted by power brokers; the other is the multifaceted universe of anonymous, spontaneous, self-interested and self-directed "popular" cultures:

> De acuerdo a definiciones implícitas, . . . el Estado, a lo largo de las últimas décadas, emplea los términos *Cultura nacional* e *Identidad,* a modo de bloques irrefutables, autohomenajes que nunca es preciso detallar. . . . *Cultura popular* es, según quien la emplee, el equivalente de lo indígena o lo campesino, el sinónimo de formas de resistencia autocapitalista o el equivalente mecánico de industria cultural. El término acaba unificando caprichosamente, variedades étnicas, regionales, de clase, para inscribirse en un lenguaje político. ("Notas sobre el Estado" 33)

> [According to implicit definitions, in the last few decades the State has used the terms National Culture and Identity like irrefutable and self-evident proofs of the State's cause for self-adulation. . . . Popular Culture is, according to whomever uses the term, the equivalent of the indigenous or rural, a synonym for forms of self-styled capitalist resistance or mechanical equivalents of the culture industry. The term ends up unifying, capriciously, ethnic, regional and class differences, finally inscribing itself in a political idiom.]

While he recognizes the sociopolitical and economic hegemony's desire to represent a single legitimate culture to embody "national identity," Monsiváis discovers stress fractures in the monolithic weal, picks at the cracks in its façade, drives wedges between latent inconsistencies, solders paradoxes, shatters a supposed oneness given apparent unity by the church, the media, the intellectual elite, an obsolete one-party political system and an industrialization project that would deny regional or other divisions (Monsiváis, "De algunos problemas" 37):

> La trampa es el adjetivo canonizador: *nacional,* que históricamente ha querido decir la necesidad de unificación a cualquier costo. Un axioma: lo nacional es forzosamente positivo y la diversidad es un estorbo. . . . Creer efectivamente en la pluralidad, desde las posiciones del Estado, equivaldría a dispersar el mando, a cederle al clero el voto de las mujeres, a permitir al indígena la difusión de la barbarie, a convertir en amenaza social al paria urbano. Mejor clausurar todo acercamiento "heterodoxo" a la pluralidad y crear una hegemonía de tolerancia represiva: *la cultura nacional,* descrita oficialmente. (40)

> [The deception is in the canonizing adjective "national," which historically has meant the need for unity at any cost. An axiom: that which is national

is undoubtedly positive and diversity is an impediment. . . . To believe effectively in plurality, so far as the State is concerned, would be the same as breaking up its rule, giving clergy the women's vote, letting the Indian spread his barbarity, promoting the urban pariah to a threatening degree. It's better to close off all "heterodox" movement toward pluralism and to create a hegemony of repressive tolerance: *national culture,* as officially described.]

43

modernity,

democracy,

and

popular

culture

in mexico

a dynamic duo: the national and the popular

The "national culture" Monsiváis goes on to describe in dismaying detail is, in fact, a *leitmotiv* that binds his work together from his first collection of chronicles to the present. Carlos Monsiváis has come to represent a virtually uniform devotion to the topic of popular culture, but his work reveals that, without its concomitant focus on the national culture, Monsiváis would have little reason to describe and interpret counterhegemonic paradigms: "Cultura nacional, cultura popular. Es tan enorme en México la fortuna de ambos términos en nuestros ámbitos políticos y académicos, que previsiblemente, a ese auge no lo acompañan definiciones, difíciles de alcanzar y de riesgosa aplicación" [National culture, popular culture. In Mexico, the fortunes of both terms are so huge in our political and academic fields that, predictably, their rise in importance is not accompanied by definitions, which in themselves are difficult to arrive at and risky to apply] (Monsiváis, "Notas sobre el Estado" 33).

defining popular culture

Thus, Monsiváis stacks innumerable subgenres of culture upon the two foundational blocks of official and popular cultures. In defining the latter, he most often points to "urban popular culture" and the "culture of the masses." Ultimately, however, he inverts the pinnacle of his culture pyramid: "todo lo que hemos vivido es tan sólo cultura popular" [Everything we have lived is but popular culture] ("Civilización" 29). All culture is popular.[12] Specific aspects of the mass urban culture he privileges can be organized into broad thematic categories.

Modernization. A broad field, modernization includes secularization, urbanization, technology and industrialization, as well as related

subthemes such as language(s), education, orality, tradition and leisure time. Free time is a key liberty to emerge from modernization, which

> alcanzó y liquidó al terruño, modificó los usos de los tiempos muertos, sembró de antenas la patria chica, inició la tolerancia al conjuro de la explosión demográfica (desde la sacristía ya no se observan con claridad los enredos en los multifamiliares), y—algo muy importante—diversificó el tedio. Aún late con monotonía el corazón (persiste la ausencia de alternativas), pero un inmenso popurrí de sensaciones ha reemplazado a la vida isóctona. (Monsiváis, *Escenas* 278).

> [reached and liquidated each individual patch of earth, modified the use of free time, planted antennae in all localities, gave rise to tolerance for the spell cast by the population explosion (sexual liaisons in huge apartment complexes can no longer be clearly observed from the sacristy) and—something very important—diversified boredom. The nation's heart still beats to a monotonous rhythm (there are still too few choices), but an immense potpourri of sensations has replaced the historical sameness.]

The economy. This topic merits autonomous recognition because of Mexico's historically emotional attitude toward the changes that contact with transnational modernization has implied. The theme of capitalism is implicated in massive migrations from the countryside to Mexico's huge cities and north to U.S. job markets.

Politics and society. These posit historical problems such as "personalism" (rule by a strongman rather than the law); government authoritarianism (dictatorship disguised as democracy); "Mexicanism" and "National Unity" (vestiges of totemism and collectivism); poverty and the national culture associated with it (often a "managed anxiety" imposed by power); illiteracy (another "national characteristic" fomented by those in power); third-worldism and racism (a colonial construct imposed on migrants in the United States *and* in Mexico, especially rural Indians and urban "nacos" (Monsiváis, "Los de atrás II" 14, "De las ciudades" 588–99, "Notas sobre el Estado" 38).

History. History is organically tied to events before and after the conquest. In keeping with his journalistic project, Monsiváis most commonly situates his crónicas in relation to the more recent past, from the mid-nineteenth century through the Mexican Revolution and the rapid period of industrialization it brought, up to the traumatic historical mile-

stone known as "1968," or Tlatelolco (the government massacre of citizens demanding greater pluralism).

Mass culture. The heart of what Monsiváis calls posttraditional or post-Guadalupana culture in Mexico ("Muerte" 19), mass culture is a sensibility and praxis orchestrated by the media: the consorts of modernization, urbanization and multinational capitalism. In addition to all-important film, radio, television and pop music, cultural massification also implies the diffusion of subliteratures such as comic strips, *fotonovelas* and a proliferation of other consumer products and effects.[13] One of the most dramatic of these includes an important theme: the counterculture known as the Onda (in the Anglo world: hippies and beatniks). This includes the drug culture, rock music, politics of the New Left and other languages associated with cultural rupture.

45

modernity,
democracy,
and
popular
culture
in mexico

Sexuality. Femininity and feminism, sexism and machismo, homosexuality and gender-bending androgyny are implicated in a view, at least early on, of mass culture as a diffuse, devouring feminine entity that resuscitates the image of a Mother Goddess ruling over a newly tribalized society. Monsiváis adapts both McLuhan's and Ong's concepts of a secondary orality brought by the Electronic Age and presses hard on the wounds of patriarchy. His views coincide with those who see feminism as "perhaps the ultimate overthrow of authority" (Zimmerman 175) and thus an indispensable condition of democratic reform.

Language. As a theoretical construct, language implies the heteroglossia that Monsiváis reports in order to depict a society just learning to speak against the official discourse, as well as metalinguistic tactics to foreground (re)articulations of power relations. For Monsiváis, language is always a site of both cultural control and the transfer of power into the hands of individual citizens. His battleground is not the geopolitical field of irreversible historical developments but the semiotic space of the consciousness, where a society's psychosocial impulses are encapsulated in an array of discourses. These can be manipulated to transmit to the mass mentality a series of untruths that can assume the permanence and power of myth (Maccoby 183).

Like other critics of culture, who in general are notably self-conscious about the way culture theory fuses with its object (Connor 61–62), Monsiváis sometimes assumes the metalinguistic stance of the cronista-at-work,

processing observed data and extracting theoretical generalizations from the immediacy of their lived reality. One of his favored textual personae is the *Teórico Súbito* [Instant Analyst], the witness feeling compelled to interpret and synthesize what occurs in the midst of the moment.

subgenres of popular culture

The vast jumble of urban popular culture that Monsiváis juxtaposes to the hegemony's notion of sociopolitical functionality includes, without entirely subsuming it, the culture characterized as "mass mediated." These forms are in various ways fitted to subcultures such as melodrama, kitsch, camp, "pop," rural tradition and, overall, what he calls the aesthetics of poverty. Allusions to these subgenres recur throughout his works.

Melodrama. Mexico's historically most recognizable aesthetic mode, melodrama perpetuates classism and a feudal morality, largely through film. It promotes a cinematic nationalism offering to Mexico's naive public a series of archetypes and stereotypes in an entertaining compendium of lifestyles. These are presented by the government-controlled media industry in a humorless and absolutely acritical context that encourages cathartic rages and sorrows (Monsiváis, "Landscape" 238, 242, 244[14]) through a kind of emotional blackmail (Monsiváis, "Civilización" 25). As a central ingredient of the aesthetics of poverty, melodrama shapes Mexican art production: "el habitante de la cultura popular va a las sensaciones como el snob a los museos" [Popular culture's denizen seeks sensations the way the snob goes to museums] (Monsiváis, "Notas sobre cultura popular" 111).

Kitsch. This *cursi* [pretentiously vulgar] aesthetics, whose failure of elegance, or "la elegancia históricamente posible en el subdesarrollo" [the degree of elegance historically possible in an underdeveloped state] (Monsiváis, *Amor* 64), embodies Mexico's most natural notion of beautiful. Parodying the elitist kitsch of the late Romantic poet Bécquer, Monsiváis makes us imagine:

> ¿Qué es el *kitsch*? ¿Y tú me lo preguntas, tú que has visto la monumental cabeza de Juárez y la serie de conjuntos escultóricos en la República donde, gracias a la costumbre, el desastre artístico se vuelve señal hogareña? ¿Y tú me lo preguntas, fanático de las películas mexicanas de antes, público cautivo de los tenores que asesinan a mansalva "Granada" y "Júrame"?

¿Y todavía finges inocencia, tú, testigo de concursos de belleza, fiestas de quinceaños, bodas de plata y de diamante, homenajes a los héroes vivos, muertos y aún por nacer? ¿Qué es el *kitsch*? ¿Y tú me lo preguntas? ("Espacios" 276)

[What is *kitsch*? And you ask me, you who have seen the monumental bust of Juárez and sets of such sculptures throughout the Republic where, thanks to tradition, artistic aberration reflects home life? And still you ask me, you fanatic of classic Mexican movies, you captive audience of tenors who massacre with impunity "Granada" and "Júrame"? Do you still pretend innocence, you witness of beauty pageants, *quinceañera* parties,[15] silver and diamond wedding anniversaries, homages to heroes living, dead and yet-to-be-born? What is *kitsch*? And you dare to ask me?]

47

modernity,
democracy,
and
popular
culture
in mexico

Kitsch serves as a source of cultural identity for Mexico's masses, not least because it stimulates emotions: Everyone has feelings and therefore everyone can feel at home with a cursi aesthetic experience (Monsiváis, "Estética" 6–8).

"Camp" culture. Camp is an elitist form of kitsch that Monsiváis holds to be "la extensión final, en materia de sensibilidad, de la metáfora de la vida como teatro. . . . El amor de lo no-natural, del artificio y la exageración. . . . Camp . . . es . . . aquello tan malo que resulta bueno" [the ultimate meaning, with respect to aesthetics, of the metaphor of life as theater. . . . Adoration of the unnatural, of artifice and exaggeration . . . Camp is that which is so bad that it's good] (*Días* 172). His definition departs from Susan Sontag's "Notes on Camp," a now-classical meditation that holds such knowing parodies of kitsch to be based on innocence and an ironic vision of the world. Using a deliberately "campy" style to nationalize this theory, Monsiváis shows that Mexican Camp can be conscious (the self-mockery of, say, a James Bond movie) or unconscious (the unintentional humor of provincial poets and antipornography campaigns, for example).[16]

"Pop" culture. An all but obsolete mode closely allied to the false values promoted by fashion fads and publicity (Monsiváis, *Rituales* 24), pop culture is almost camp in its over-the-top devotion to made-up styles and media-generated loyalties to such artifice.

Rural culture. This is characterized by anachrony, a high birth rate, institutionalized violence, an implacable machismo linked to protection of the family, and vague, sacralized notions of State, Modernity and Mass Media (Monsiváis, "Lo popular en el espacio urbano" 44). When des-

peration forces families from the province to the city, rural culture clings to rooftops and tiny rooms "en donde caben familias que se reproducen sin dejar de caber" [where there's room for families who reproduce without ever failing to find room] (Monsiváis, *Rituales* 18); urban vestiges of the farming life reproach failed agrarian reform policies.

The aesthetic of poverty. This is a sensibility that manifests in any of Mexico's cultural subgenres, in tragic measure because the country's culture industry has dedicated itself since the 1930s and with enormous efficiency to the goal of generating media products designed to "festejar las limitaciones, ensalzar el bienestar final de la falta de recursos" [celebrate limitations and extol a lack of resources as the ultimate state of well-being] (Monsiváis, "Lo popular" 43). Because endemic poverty and the sociopolitical dynamics which sustain it have precluded development of a clearly defined "high" culture, Art and Beauty in Mexico usually come down to a vague awareness of "las sensaciones placenteras de *Lo Bonito*" [the pleasing sensations of *Pretty Things*] (*Rituales* 68), which we might take as the equivalent of English's inarticulate "gosh, that's pretty, isn't it? I sure like that."

teaching a language of modernity

As with any ritual, these and other tangible forms of popular culture are based upon collective psychic needs. In Monsiváis, description of the immediate real in his entertaining style is always a lure. His writing is designed to bring up from Mexico's Unconscious the larger meanings rooted in history or theory or some other phenomenon at near or far remove. And when we examine this catch, we find we have netted Monsiváis's deep-water concern: a perennial desire to teach Mexico a "language of modernity" ("No con un sollozo" 718–19). When Monsiváis makes a list of elements associated with contemporary mass urban culture, for example, his concern is less with objects and actions than with the consequences they imply. He describes urban culture from the inside out, as a process of culture *formation,* or *transformation* of consciousness.

A typical list of this kind is the litany of mass urban cultural traits (seen from a subaltern point of view), which I assemble, in loose translation, from two Monsiváis texts (*Cultura urbana* 2, "Lo popular" 42–43): (1) Material and psychological repression of the popular classes; (2) Feelings of impotence or insignificance that lead to historical fatalism; (3) An uncertain relationship

with the State (i.e., "the police"); (4) Conditioned obedience to Authority; (5) Diminished Church influence in daily life; (6) Persistent aspects of provincial culture, including local traditions, spatial time and a sense of Fiesta (suspension of rules and obligations), most notably affecting the city's poor; (7) Preservation of popular transmission of knowledge: oral narratives, home remedies, etc.; (8) Dogmatic and/or naive views of knowledge/schooling; (9) Updated machismo and sexism; (10) The feminization of poverty (a dramatic increase in female heads of household); (11) Technology as the ultimate and most irrefutable educator of the masses; (12) Political exploitation of religion and technology (subliminal imagery, etc.); (13) Mass-mediated transformation of capitalist growth itself into a marketable commodity; (14) Nationality as a conditioned reflex of commercialism; (15) A linear vision of order and progress; (16) Leisure time that is more manipulated than "free"; (17) A belief that underdevelopment is a permanent end rather than a stage.

All this the hegemony sustains in order to foster a belief in the "obvious inferiority" of the poor and marginalized and at the same time naturalize—and in fact necessitate—their oppression (Monsiváis, *Cultura urbana* 2). This is a breeding ground for the tragically paradoxical, says Monsiváis. Programmed marginalization can produce emotional reactions that affirm rather than refute oppression: "Por ejemplo, el resentimiento ante el racismo, por estar a la defensiva, concluye aceptando las reglas de juego" [For example, resentment of racism, because it is a defensive posture, ends up by accepting the rules of the game] (2).[17]

For Monsiváis, popular culture is defined by its plurality. Mexico's holder of all cultures, the "popular" is anything and everything that any sector of the people find of interest. Popular culture, in short, is the life of the country, the possibility of democracy and the postmodern's promise of justice: "Es el momento de aparición de lo marginado, lo reprimido, lo invisibilizado de las formas o exigencias culturales del proletariado, los grupos indígenas, las mujeres y las minorías sexuales" [This is when the marginalized make their appearance: the repressed, those who had been rendered invisible by forms and cultural dictates of the proletariat, indigenous groups, women and sexual minorities] ("Los de atrás" II 22). As Poniatowska has observed, "mejor que nadie, Monsiváis sabe que la historia de un país no se hace en el Congreso sino en la plaza pública, en la calle, en las misceláneas, en las vecindades, en las cocinas, y que si en las Lomas y en el Pedregal los ricos se petrifican, la cultura popular es parte de la con-

stante transformación de nuestro país" [better than anyone else, Monsiváis knows that the history of a country is not made in Congress but in the public square, in the street, in neighborhoods, in the shops on the corner and in the kitchen, and that, if in the residential enclaves of Las Lomas and Pedregal the culture of the rich slowly petrifies, popular culture remains a lively part of our country's ongoing transformation] ("Monsiváis: cronista" 6). With such transcendent values attached to popular culture, a lifelong dedication to its study can, theoretically, show Mexico how to liberate its self-colonizing consciousness.

Through tactics associated with the methodology of U.S. New Journalism of the sixties (what we might simply call literary journalism), the gathering and analysis of popular cultural data has developed into a new theoretical and critical field. This is the hands-on investigative technique of a scholar who dares to leave the Ivory Tower. It is the decidedly metacultural stance of the Instant Theorist, for example, who observes the masses venerating the rock star Raphael (Monsiváis, *Días* 45–60), or the hectoring narrator who chastises both himself and his readers for judging the way poor girls wear their hair and pile on eye makeup; with blatant disregard for the conventions of "objective" journalism, the narrator enters the consciousness of a young girl to snarl: "¿Y a usted qué le importa, pinche racista?" [What the hell do *you* care, you damned racist?] (Monsiváis, *Escenas* 149).

the ephemeral anchored in theory

Even when one takes what Monsiváis says at face value, his texts provide excessive journalistic meaning and allure. As simultaneous markers for less evident signification and as sources of an enduring artistic value, Monsiváis's multiaccented crónicas demonstrate how the elusive stuff of informal culture can be captured for study and fixed to theoretical positions. To observe with him the "happening" of minutiae in their spontaneous historical contexts is to travel with him below the visual-verbal surface toward the conclusions that can be apprehended only through anticentripetal readings; these rely on irony, metaphor and other devices that open the text to diverse interpretation. From discourses "activated" in this way (Fiske, *Television* 84–107), we can extract Carlos Monsiváis's immanent theories of culture.

the dialectic of culture formation

These theories intersect with widely recognized approaches to analysis of discourse and of sociopolitical phenomena that can be subsumed under headings of "theories of dominance" and "theories of resistance," a pair that implies dynamic interaction. For purposes of metaphoric illustration, we can visualize Monsiváis's ideology as a dialectic of culture formation analogous to the Aztec creation myth known as the Quinto Sol, or Fifth Sun, a cultural artifact frequently reconverted in monsivaisian texts. In the original ideology, the first four suns (epochs) failed, much like the antediluvian Hebrew era, because their constitutive elements lacked diversity and flexibility. The fifth sun, however, also known as "Four Movement," embodies a recycling spiral of space and time that destabilizes dichotomies and promotes shape-shifting transformations of time, space, gender and class (Labbé 35).[18]

51

modernity,
democracy,
and
popular
culture
in mexico

Students of the postmodern's decentering and destabilizing spirit may wonder at its apparent kinship with archaic thought, one of whose preeminent features is an androgynous vision of the universe that, in seeking a permanent synthesis of opposites, tends to equalize masculine and feminine powers and to reach from the center to draw peripheral elements inward (Séjourné 82). Students of Carlos Monsiváis will recognize the fertile union of both modalities in his treatment of fundamental topics such as machismo and feminism, as well as his tendency to fuse other divisions, some of which will be examined in the further course of this study.

theories of dominance and resistance

With this exegetic clue in mind, then, we return to the dialectic of dominance and resistance. With the former we can group four subcategories: (a) what is widely known as dependency theory, which posits an uneven relationship between center and periphery, or Metropolis and Third World; (b) so-called cultural imperialism, or colonization of underdeveloped societies by postindustrial cultures and multinational capitalism; (c) perceived media manipulation (a marxist-influenced belief in the subjection of passive consumers to thoughts determined by the power class) and (d) mass culture itself, often described as a flood of "dangerous" feminine influences that now dominate society. This theory contains its own resistant theory ("backlash," or masculine counterattack).

With the latter half of the dialectic we can also group four theories: (a) migration and "border" culture; (b) movements to promote indigenous cultures; (c) popular cultural theories such as clawback, excorporation, refunctioning and reconversion; and (d) a progressively less essentialized feminism that recognizes differences of class, culture, race and, even, gender among women.

Dependency Theory. This view embodies concepts "which attempt to explain the disastrous nature of . . . Latin American economies as vassals of First World financial lords" (Foster, "Popular" 11–12); it is a victimist stance based on confrontation with an Other and a refusal to scrutinize the Self (Chanady 20–22). Without perhaps wanting to, then, dependency theory tends to mire thinking in circles of frustration: Developing nations cannot succeed because others did. Vargas Llosa has termed this victimology "una de nuestras más tenaces ficciones" [one of our most tenacious fictions] (Vargas Llosa 376).

Even as he acknowledges its historical bases, Monsiváis patiently deconstructs this "visión de los vencidos" [viewpoint of the vanquished] ("Duración" 42).[19] For example, in an important text that details how official negligence led to a disastrous explosion in an overcrowded urban slum, the cronista demonstrates that the problem lies not with capitalism itself but with power's misuse of and failure to regulate it. Tensions felt with shocking power during the 1930s–1960s, an era of extremely rapid change in Mexico, were incorrectly attributed to foreign influences when, in fact, they arose out of internal structural changes (García Canclini, "Híbridas" 84). Coinciding with this view, Monsiváis suggests that Mexico's mission as it completes its modernization project is to humanize capitalism so that its liberating potential can be fully developed: "Dependency theory" as a way to describe the ways that democracy depends upon a healthy give-and-take between power and people.

Theories of Cultural Conquest. Accompanied by notions of economic domination, the terms "imperialism" and "colonization" here imply a deliberate assault on an alien society's way of life. But such a view, says Monsiváis, gives the United States too much credit for control of the Mexican domestic cultural process ("Penetración" 85). It may be popular to speak of the "McDonaldizing of other countries" and the "Yankeefication of Mexico" (Rollin 1, 7). For our cronista, it is better to parody outrage over

Americanization: "Nomás eso nos faltaba: un MacDonald's en lo alto de la pirámide" [That's all we needed: a McDonald's on top of the pyramid] ("Duración" 42). In fact, says Monsiváis, the exchange of cultural influences north and south of the U.S.–Mexico border is free, unsurprising, virtually uncontrollable and potentially liberating.

The supposed Americanization of Mexico has been going on for as long as Mexicans have crossed into the United States to work and gone back home bearing American blue jeans and radically upgraded expectations of comfort, so how can defenders of Mexico-for-Mexicans condemn, for example, "a los jóvenes de las clases populares, que al americanizarse en diversos niveles creen así exorcizar su estruendosa falta de porvenir?" [the youths of popular classes who, on Americanizing themselves in various ways, believe that they are thus ridding themselves of their thunderous lack of future?] (Monsiváis, "Duración" 42) How can you deny the human desire for comfort? (Monsiváis, "Para un cuadro" 94) Instead of being alarmed about the supposed de-Mexicanization of Mexico, says Monsiváis, consider whether U.S. models can teach Mexicans how to live more comfortably with—and as—themselves (42): "Ante el impulso de la americanización los mexicanos, cada uno a su manera, harán caso del consejo de Sedar Senghor: asimilar sin asimilarse" [In the face of the drive to Americanize themselves, Mexicans, each in her or his way, will heed the advice of Sedar Senghor: assimilate without being assimilated] (45).[20]

Manipulation. Theories of the media's power to colonize the thinking, tastes and behavior of the masses betray a paranoid view of foreign culture used as a weapon to subjugate the third world (Hinds, "Latin" 406).[21] Monsiváis, however, coincides with thinkers like Laura Kipnis, who scoffs at the programmatic pessimism of Frankfurt School theorists (34–35). The cronista labels "muy clasista el determinismo que promueve la *teoría de la manipulación* y supone a todo un pueblo juguete de titiriteros" [as very classist the determinism that promotes *theories of manipulation* and presupposes an entire nation acting like toy puppets] ("De algunos problemas" 45).

When Monsiváis looks at mass communications from the perspective of their production by corrupt newspaper publishers or state-managed television stations, he observes how they contribute to the survival of debilitating theories of dependency and inferiority (*Cultura urbana* 7–8). On the other hand, when he views the media from the perspective of the anonymous individuals who make up the masses, they become assets contributing to the decolonization of the Mexican mind and, thus, antihegemonic tools of resistance. For this Mexican analyst, the *actual* victims of a mass-mediated system of beliefs may be his society's historical lack of alternatives, the tenacity of its religious traditionalism and its apparently irremediable poverty (Monsiváis et al., "México ante la adversidad" 35; Monsiváis, "Variedades" 14–15, *Rituales* 120–24).

Feminism. As a theory of domination, feminism is equated with a complex of contemporary discourses involving renewed interest in the Feminine Divine and the resurgence of Nature's power over that of (presumably masculine and elitist) Culture-with-a-capital-C. From its inception in the era of industrialization, the feminized culture of the masses, seen as a "scandalous, grotesque body believed capable of engulfing everything from below" (Radway 523), has been a subtext of the Modernist project: the masses as "women, knocking at the gate of a male-dominated culture" (Huyssen 47). As with other theories of domination, to see modern urban culture as dangerously in thrall to antimasculine forces reflects patriarchy's historic fear of civilization—and its manhood—being swallowed up by the indifference of "female" nature (Ong, *Fighting* 77). Monsiváis is clearly conversant with the theory, but throughout his work he prefers to represent women as midwives of justice and bearers of democracy (Monsiváis, *Días* 54–56). In this opinion he aligns himself with the principal theorists of postmodernism and, more recently, with those who recognize, even in feminism, a deconstructible Master Narrative.

When he positions himself on the side of the prochoice debate in Mexico, for instance, Monsiváis observes with satisfaction "la transformación de razones del feminismo en argumentos de la sociedad civil" [the transformation of feminist reasoning into arguments for a civil society] in which individuals make reasoned choices within the law. He notes that the abortion issue transcends personal drama to represent, as well, a collective tragedy about the difficult morality of a secular, plural, society ("De cómo un día" 85).

Recuperation and Reterritorialization. Against theories of dominance, those of resistance roughly correspond. For example, against the concept of dependence on an Other for one's national well-being, one can posit notions of recovery. An important one involves a kind of utopian out-selection (Monsiváis, "Milenarismos" 172) embodied in the economics of demography. As high birth rates and low job formation in Mexico press waves of immigration outward from centers of unemployment in Mexico and into North American job markets, one way of fighting the country's historical dependency is to engage in a "reconquest" of the perceived dominant culture. This concept can be clearly detected in comments of immigrants made to a Mexican journalist sent north to conduct interviews in California cities colonized by the voluntary relocation of entire Mexican communities. A Redwood City man literally embodies new theoretical terms such as transnational and deterritorialized[22]: "Voy a Michoacán y lo veo muy lindo, pero muy pobre y polvoso. Esto la verdá es Michoacán y todo California ya es México. Ellos nos la quitaron y ahora nosotros la estamos recuperando" [I go to Michoacán and it's all very pretty, but very poor and dusty. This (Redwood City) is in fact Michoacán and all of California is Mexico. They took it away from us and now we are getting it back] (cited in Gurza 1). Reporting that, in her observation, U.S. Anglos appear to have abandoned the city of Los Angeles to Latinos and Asians, the Mexican news correspondent cites another transplanted compatriot, who, unencumbered by the baggage of legalities and national immigration policies, has crossed from one concept of "cultural imperialism" to another: "Nosotros tenemos siempre nuestro corazón en México, pero pa que es más que la verdá, Los Angeles ya es México. A los gringos ya los corrimos pa las colinas, y la ciudad es nuestra" [Our hearts always belong to Mexico, but to tell the truth, Los Angeles is by now part of Mexico. We've run the gringos off to the hills, and the city is ours] (14).

Now, even as U.S. anti-Hispanic ballot initiatives express Anglo fears that their traditional culture is being taken over through the Latinization of North America, theories of cultural colonization must be redefined along a bicultural, binational border. In northern Mexico and southern Texas, notions of state authority have lost legitimacy: "The reunification of the Lone Star State and northeastern Mexico is history quietly and boringly in the making" (Kaplan 24). One hysterical prediction in 1988 asserted that the "reconquest" of territory that Mexico claimed prior to the 1848 Treaty of Guadalupe would be a certainty by the year 2000 (Langley 166).

The borderland around Tijuana and Ciudad Juárez is where a Chicano's future identity is conceived, says Monsiváis (prologue, "De México" 19).

And, just as surely as a portion of Mexico's popular class voluntarily re-defines its national identity, all of "México se va a convertir en una nación de chicanos," he says [Mexico is going to become a nation of chicanos] (in Egan, "Entrevista" 22). Seamlessly uniting cultural borders, Monsiváis situates his project in the postmodern territory of borders, hybridity, globalization and shifting signifieds wherein concepts of both "dependency" and "resistance" to it are rendered archaic (Egan, "Mechicanos" 79).[23]

Indigenous Cultural Resistance. Within Mexico, fears of both Americanization and internal colonialism nourish a strong if anachro-nistic movement to restore Indian languages, art and philosophy to prom-inence in Mexican public life. Resistance "fighters" reject nonindigenous culture as a monolithic Other. One of the most widely cited of those who seek a return to Mexico's pre-Western roots speaks, in the last decade of the twentieth century, of his country's past as something that ended in 1521: "la civilización mesoamericana . . . es el punto de partida y su raíz más pro-funda" [Mesoamerican civilization is its point of departure and its deepest reality] (Bonfil Batalla, *México* 23). For Bonfil Batalla, Mexico's only real past is Indian and is, although deeply buried, still viable. He claims it is possible to restart the history that was temporarily suspended by colonial domination and to promote, at the dawn of the twenty-first century, reconstruction of viable indigenous communities (243).

When visiting Mexico as a tourist, Richard Rodríguez, an American of Mexican descent, has observed evidence that Bonfil Batalla's radical perspec-tive is not without basis in the culture: "Mexico has taken its national iden-tity only from the Indian, the mother. Mexico measures all cultural bastardy against the Indian. . . . Mexico equates barbarism with Europe" (52).

As Rodríguez develops the trope, we see indigenous America as a ves-tige of the Columbian fantasy of having arrived in fabulous India, a pro-cess of inside-out racism (Edward Said's "orientalism") that is a linchpin of Carlos Monsiváis's cultural theory. Of three principal strands of thought on the problem of Mexico's considerable indigenous population—(1) to segre-gate surviving Indian communities in order to save them; (2) to integrate them into the hegemonic culture, and (3) to help them fend for themselves in a plural society—Monsiváis chooses the third. For him, organized pro-tests of communities such as Juchitán are not so much instances of *cultural* resistance as they are *political* defenses of the right to make autonomous choices in lifestyle (*Entrada* 160–63). If Mexico's Indians are at risk of "losing" their traditional culture, it is because they first have been deprived of opportunities to acquire education, economic well-being and equal treatment under the law.

57

modernity,
democracy,
and
popular
culture
in mexico

His theory of resistance to cultural imperialism would ally rural Indian with blue-collar mestizo in an unsupervised guerrilla war with no generals. Each would ward off mind-controlling interpellations of the official culture with whatever activity, ruse or procedure he or she could find at hand. One that Monsiváis himself uses, for example, is his unsparing campaign against a tenacious popular culture tradition: the racism that still, half a millennium after the conquest, feeds genocidal hatreds against social "pariahs" with telltale "facciones cobrizas" [coppertoned features] (Monsiváis, "Notas sobre el Estado" 38, "Los de atrás II" 14).

If Monsiváis recounts cruel naco jokes that rose from the ashes of a spectacular fire in which many urban Indians died, it is to deconstruct them (*Entrada* 143–50). Similarly, he attacks racism by highlighting a provincial rock group's message that *"Naco is beautiful"* (*Escenas* 243); explaining the origin of the term "naco" ("Léperos" 170); revealing that distaste for the masses in Mexico hides the middle class's contempt for "el mar de semblantes cobrizos que . . . invade . . . [el] panorama visual" [the sea of copper-skinned faces invading the viewscape] (Monsiváis, "Espacios" 274–75); exposing the racist paternalism behind a beauty pageant for "las jovencitas cobrizas" [young copper-toned beauties] (*Escenas* 59–60); satirizing the way photographic art can objectify the native Mexican by turning him into an icon of traditional (dead) culture—"¡Qué plástico es el indígena!" [The Indian is so plastic!] ("Testimonios" 2)—or lambasting the hypocrisy of indigenist rhetoric, which consists of "un saludo reverente al pasado indígena y el desprecio hacia los indios que no terminan nunca de extinguirse" [a reverent acknowledgment of the indigenous past and disdain for those Indians who seem unwilling to become extinct] ("De algunos problemas" 41). Implicit in all these statements is the reminder to Monsiváis's privileged readers that they are who define and direct the persistence of racism (Monsiváis, "Léperos" 169):

> El racismo mexicano desdeña a la mayoría de los habitantes de un país, les echa literalmente en cara la ausencia de atributos valederos, pondera la excelsitud inalcanzable del físico de las minorías, extirpa con brutalidad

cualquier sueño de los jóvenes nacos ante el espejo. ¿Quién los defiende, si en los mass-media incluso, para representar a sirvientas indígenas o princesas lacandonas [de Chiapas] se utilizan a rubias platinadas?

[Mexican racism disdains the majority of a country's inhabitants, literally throwing in their faces their lack of valid attributes; it praises the unattainable excellence of a racial minority's physical features; it brutally eradicates the dream of every young naco standing before a mirror. Who will defend them, if even in the mass media, platinum blondes are used to represent indigenous servants or Lacandon princesses?] (*Escenas* 243).[24]

Feminist-Humanist Resistance. The largest subjugated social sector in Mexico is the half of the nation that is female. If Indians were denied citizenship—"En esta esquina, la Nación, fuera del ring, los parias" [In this corner, the Nation; outside the ring, the pariahs] (Monsiváis, "Notas sobre el Estado" 38)—women historically were ignored: "las mujeres: la nación fuera de México" [Women: the nation outside of Mexico] (38). Mexico's ideology of masculinity is not only legendary; it is a felt reality in virtually every aspect of life. Discourses of resistance to this historical oppression have lately acquired a complexity and, even, ambiguity that goes beyond a simple rejection of patriarchy.

Monsiváis's noted loyalty to the cause of liberating women's democratizing energies has dated at least from 1954, when he acquired a closer view than most men had of the emotional, philosophical and practical consequences of women getting the vote in Mexico. Since then his natural sympathies for the woman as one more of many oppressed peoples have acquired the theoretical certainty that none of Mexico's major economic, sociopolitical, spiritual and moral needs can be properly formulated, much less successfully realized, without the full and free participation of women. An ideology of femininity emerges, text by text, keeping pace with the time(s) his works mark.[25] He is clearly happy to report, after the July 2000 elections that at last ratified Mexican claims to being a pluralist political system, that in each party organization, the talent, discipline, efficiency and hard work of women was a definitive factor in the campaigns (Monsiváis, "Viaje de un largo día" 2).

Carlos Monsiváis is, in fact, at the forefront of what is now a measurable cadre of male writers who are at least sympathetic to women's issues, if not overtly feminist. Matthew C. Gutmann's book on the redefinition of machismo, for example, is as much a report on women as it is on men in contemporary Mexico City. Jesús Martín-Barbero's study (which relies extensively on Carlos Monsiváis) of mass society applauds the enormous role of women in construction of a barrio's distinctive identity. Jorge Castañeda includes a decent discussion of women's movements in Latin America in his study of left politics (225–30). And in a recent issue of *Debate Feminista* on links between feminism and democracy in Mexico, more than a third of the 44 contributors are men. Half a century after Mexican women got the vote, these facts may represent slow progress, but, as Monsiváis would point out, they can at least document cause for optimism.

59

modernity,

democracy,

and

popular

culture

in mexico

Popular Culture. Each of the three types of resistance theory mentioned above has been included by now in a global left-liberal view of popular culture as resistant to the official, dominant or hegemonic culture. This is a more flexible, dialectic and potentially hopeful stance that gives individual citizens credit for being not only able but willing to use in independent ways the cultural capital made available to them by government or the elite classes. With a tongue-in-cheek nod to Ortega y Gasset, I think of this oppositional theory as the true "rebellion of the masses." As the constitutive heart of Carlos Monsiváis's ideological project, this underground resistance of the Mexican masses will be the object of separate analysis in the following chapter.

3

lessons of pleasure in culture and chronicle

To situate Carlos Monsiváis in relation to mainstream thinking in Cultural Studies, I have relied predominantly on his more explicit—or
essayistic—enunciations. I now want to focus on how Monsiváis's most
implicit—or literary—texts serve as repositories of his theories on culture. A
pair of slow readings in this chapter will isolate details from which theoretical statements can be extrapolated, without ignoring that these are permanently implicated, through poetic language, in the chronicle's simultaneous
uses as pleasure, art and opinion.

First, a word about theoretical language. The vocabulary in current use
to describe ruses that the "rebellious" masses employ to secure an autonomous sociocultural space is a bellicose and inventive discourse reminiscent
of the aggression that narratology attributes to "the logic of narrative pos-

sibilities" (Brémond 389). The powerless and the poor are said to engage in clawback, struggle, cannibalization, tactics, strategies, weapons deployment, poaching, backlash, excorporation,[1] negotiation, bricolage, pastiche, parody, contestation, refusal, rearticulation, recombination, recycling, refunctioning, redefinition and reconversion. The ruling class's standard bearers, meanwhile, are said to do what they can to control, manage, contain, incorporate, exclude, define, produce, correct and naturalize. (Interestingly, this lexicon presents official culture as creator and popular culture as (re)user. Official culture manufactures the car. Popular culture modifies the engine and disrupts the neighborhood.)

The (undesired and perhaps unwitting) binarism produced by the "official" theorizing of Cultural Studies academics is probably one reason Carlos Monsiváis usually avoids trendy terminology. Instead of naming popular culture's artifacts, he prefers to show them being made or used, in progress, live and on location. That is why, if he invokes set phrases like "resistance theory" or "theories of manipulation," it is to foreground their inability to adequately depict the unfixed relationships of people and power. His theories emanate from discourses running below the narrative surface.

With chapter 2's rehearsal of the principal strands of thinking on popular culture as prior authority, I will now identify implicit theories in a selection of Carlos Monsiváis's crónicas. Without wishing to overdramatize the density of his discourse, I emphasize the multifarious uses of culture in his narrative: Monsiváis talks *about* culture *with* culture in order to theorize *on* culture by way of teaching *through* culture and, not incidentally, explaining *how* culture produces culture. While virtually all his writings are dedicated to cultural analysis, the texts in his book collections embody the most complex interweaving of functions which this referent can simultaneously serve in a single discourse. I have selected two of these for in-depth analysis—one centered on a rural subject, the other on an urban space.

multiple layers of meaning

As a prereading guide, a third analysis is offered as an example of the way Monsiváis's multiple-purpose discourses include an invitation to engage in theoretical dialogue with the author. Among the several possible readings of the chronicle I refer to, on the death of famed ranchera singer José Alfredo Jiménez (*Amor* 87–97), readers may elect to

(1) Reminisce about a national cultural icon; these readers will be well-informed by what this text explicitly says about the singer's life and times and entertained by the generous citation of lyrics from his most remembered songs. In his roles as historian, biographer and news reporter, Monsiváis does not let his creative agenda overwhelm documentary fact;

(2) Consider the possible transcendence of the artist's life, consciously or unconsciously absorbing additional meanings implicitly conveyed in structure, language and manipulation of voice and point of view: José Alfredo as metonym for an entire historico-cultural era in Mexico, an emblem of tension between stasis and change, a mirror of the Mexican's mode of being and his essential psychology (*Amor* 87);

(3) Discern a philosophical framework linking the previous readings—one that informs and entertains, and another that interprets and immortalizes—to an ongoing theoretical debate among Mexico's intellectual elite on the country's historical reliance on dependency theory to explain why much-vaunted advances into modernity have not diminished intractable poverty.

At this level of reception, the text that apparently wants nothing more than to pay particularly eloquent homage to a revered artist exceeds its potential as memoir to become a razor-sharp swipe at official culture and the neocolonial State that subjugates its own people while casting blame elsewhere; it is, ultimately, a tutorial for all of Mexican society, whose average citizens the writer depicts as susceptible to the "discourse of melancholy" that encourages them to wear the wounds of history on their skin as "an eyesore to the colonizer" (Bhabha, "Postcolonial" 65).

(4) Delve deeper still, because the author, known as a defender of the people, appears to here be blaming *them*, members of his Mexican audience, for the suffering that everyone knows is not their fault. In fact, the funerary piece Monsiváis is offering on their dearly beloved José Alfredo appears to imply that the man and his fans have been duped into believing a myth that the national culture industry had fabricated about Enemies of the Nation who forced poor Mexicans into an economic and culturally dependent position in the world. In sum, the author seems to be telling his Mexican readers to begin to see José Alfredo's maudlin Mexicanness as a kind of conditioned reflex (88–89),

a form of "desahogo inducido" [induced catharsis] imposed on them by
those who manipulate the culture of poverty (94). He has dramatized a
dependent state of mind that it is time to give up.

the culture of poverty

The first sustained textual analysis I have promised offers
the four levels of reading just discussed and, in particular, it shows the
dynamics of the dependent mindset from another angle. In "Protagonista:
el Niño Fidencio: todos los caminos llevan al éxtasis" [Protagonist: The Boy
Fidencio: All Roads Lead to Ecstasy] (*Rituales* 97–108), Monsiváis takes us
inside the world of a provincial miracle-worker of the early decades of the
twentieth century.[2] Mexico's persistent culture of poverty is shown to be
deeply rooted in its traditional religiosity, especially in the form of popular
Catholicism.[3] While documenting mass religion's evolution from healers of
the 1930s to self-styled prophets of the 1980s, Monsiváis burrows beneath
folkloric exoticism to locate a thread running against the ideological pattern.
Then he pulls on it to see what unravels.

As investigative journalist, he first reveals the pattern: a universe assembled from

— Myths, rituals, sacred centers, ecstatic trances, pilgrimages, witnesses
   and testimonies to miracles, a litany of non-Biblical saints and other
   charismatic figures—the world of Boy Fidencio is, in short, an independent nation of millenarianism and spiritual practice easily subsumed
   under the term "superstitions" (97);
— A personality who incarnates this marginalized world's myriad elements; here, The Boy Fidencio who, from childhood, was marked by
   circumstances that permitted the credulous masses to accept him as
   holy and to worship his authority over them;
— A familiarity with misery as a requirement of his divine authority (102);
   poverty as generator of moral perfection;
— A following of disciples, priests and worshipers who comprise an autonomous god-and-church system; and
— A series of acts, miracles and ceremonies featuring (1) intertwined
   religious and secular belief systems and (2) condemnation by official
   authorities of church and city.

This description of the religion of poverty (assembled from statements dispersed throughout the crónica[4]) is the raw material which, when Monsiváis dramatizes and illustrates it, will create a theory of culture that also yields, as by-products, information and entertainment. I want to focus now on the way Monsiváis helps culture explain itself in this text.

A brief introduction historicizes the account. The first sentence—"¿Cuáles son los límites de la sacralidad en medios de intensa privación?" [What are the limits of sacredness in environments of extreme poverty?] (97) —asks a question of limitless reach: Fidencio's story belongs to Mexico, but also to Latin America and, ultimately, wherever in the world that masses of society's forgotten poor find comfort in a religion of their own devising.

Beckoning us closer to this exotic world, Monsiváis invites us to see detailed meanings of "superstition" in his word-portrait of José Fidencio de Jesús Constantino Síntora, one of twenty-five children of Socorro Constantino and Mari del Tránsito Síntora. In his refunctioning of the legend, Monsiváis smudges accepted understandings of the concept of the faith healer who practices a "mesianismo enlodado" [mud-splattered Messianism] (97). Boy Fidencio is a strange young man born in 1898 in Iránuco, a village in the state of Guanajuato. Foregrounded details are pregnant with hidden meanings that the discourse will, in due time, deliver. Among the potential symbols: the young boy enjoying himself in the kitchen, but getting his greatest pleasure from assisting at childbirth and washing the soiled bedclothes afterward (98); young Fidencio, orphaned at an early age and subject to great physical abuse and economic privation; "el mocito de voz afeminada" [the young man of effeminate voice] (98) who, already a healer at twenty-nine years of age, claims, "soy virgen como Cristo" [I am a virgin like Christ] (100).

Being one of an unmanageably large brood of children, a boy of girlish voice in a ferociously machista environment who liked to cook, perform as a midwife and do laundry, an orphan relegated by misery and violence to the sidelines of society—these are the elements of transgression, abandonment and helplessness indivisibly joined to the popular mysticism of Mexicans who lament, "nací para sufrir" [I was born to suffer] (100). When the president himself travels to the state of Nuevo León to seek a healing session with Fidencio in 1928, the national anthem is sung on his arrival; in answer, the local faithful shout out Boy Fidencio's own personal hymn, "La hija del penal," a corrido of the Revolution adopted by the cult.[5] Monsiváis guides our reception of this fact by citing only those song verses that appeal to the Virgin of Guadalupe; the tune's hero, like the rest of disadvantaged Mexico, is steadfastly and "compensadamente guadalupano" [devoted to the Virgin of Guadalupe, like a compensation prize] (Monsiváis, "Vísperas" 3).

"Calles, el anticlerical furibundo, y Fidencio, el monaguillo, se encuentran" [Calles, furiously anticlerical, and Fidencio, the altar boy, meet face to face] (*Rituales* 103) is a duality that hints at the meeting's supreme irony. Western and northwestern provinces of Mexico were gripped in the especially savage cruelty of a religious civil war in 1928,[6] and President Plutarco Elías Calles, ex–Revolutionary general, was leading the battle against traditional links between Church and State, which tie was specifically attached to the people's historic devotion to the Virgin of Guadalupe. This national icon had been the heart of Mexico's concept of self as an independent nation since Creole dissidents of the late colonial era redefined her as a purely Mexican goddess. The irony exceeds the fact that official culture's highest authority was seeking union with popular culture's most venerated figure, however; of two "national" hymns sung that day, the official one had tacitly paid homage to the outlawed ideology: religion as tolerable dissidence and rebellion (Monsiváis, "Milenarismos" 165).

By now, Monsiváis's selection and placement of details has empowered the facts to redefine themselves, almost without his overt assistance, into something that transcends their basic referentiality. The list he provides of eight of Fidencio's many curative strategies is, therefore, already double-functioned as fact and symbol (*Rituales* 100–101). Looking for significant linkages among the details he includes in his parodic dictionary of medical terms, we are rewarded with a textbook enumeration of how ordinary citizens, in creating cultural meanings for themselves, make do with what's at hand. Fidencio and his assistants dunk people with skin disorders in sulphurous waters while bathing the demented at dawn, after beating them (a logical "punishment" of those who would not respond to healing techniques in broad daylight before the believing masses). The mute, the paralyzed and the insane are also given "kineterapia"—the Boy swings them back and forth.

When we arrive at the items called "meloterapia" and "impactoterapia" we are certain Monsiváis has deliberately doubled his voice in a technique I think of as discursive découpage. Meloterapia's top layer informs that Fidencio sometimes sang at his patients to cure them. Underneath is the irony that his favorite medicinal melodies were fighting songs of the Revolution. Similarly, the polysemous impact therapy's literal layer refers to the fact that Fidencio stood on a roof and threw food at the crowd down below: "el tomatazo, guayabazo o manzanazo lanzado por el Niño equivale a una bendición" [the smack of a tomato, guava or apple thrown by the Boy is like a blessing] (101). Below that historical solemnity lies hilarious slapstick: We envision witnesses handing up crates of tomatoes to Fidencio, whose strenuous physical workout unavoidably "symbolizes" the concrete, external, aggressive nature of oral culture. This perception is ratified by a risible detail nonchalantly appended: "También Fidencio provoca choques psicológicos en el paciente dejándolo en la jaula de un puma (sin dientes y garras). Según los testimonios, esta terapia resulta infalible con los sordomudos" [Fidencio also visits psychological shocks on the patient by leaving him in a cage with a puma (toothless and clawless). Witnesses say this therapy works infallibly with deaf-mutes] (101).

With the same nonserious solemnity, which deconstructs the legend's serious affirmations of truth, the cronista rounds off the list, mentioning surgery, tooth extraction, herbology and other remedies from popular tradition (101). The inference is that, in search of a mystical experience or an end to suffering, those without access to the dominant culture's solutions will accept humiliation and, even, physical martyrdom when ordinary popular medicine fails them.

The author does not have to explicitly ask us to feel outrage in behalf of this flock of the hopeless and hopeful, for by this time, he has subtly reengineered the traditional construct of Fidencio to let us see an explicit historical reality behind the mystical façade, and the quite human showmanship propelling Fidencio to fame. When Monsiváis ridicules these faith-healing tactics, he is not demeaning the credulity of the poor nor their attempts to solve their problems; he *is* asking us to see Fidencio, however, as a much more complex signifier of the culture of poverty than his legend intends.

Nowhere, for example, does the legend draw attention to the faith healer's unmystical eagerness to be photographed, always in poses reminiscent of museum paintings of Jesus (99). Also worth noting: This "caudillo de peregrinaciones" [pilgrim boss] keeps a harem of his own personal nuns nearby (99). Monsiváis need not explain the incongruity of the Spanish word for a secular strongman-dictator *(caudillo)* being paired with the mystico-ethical connotation of pilgrimages. We are warned early on that we should beware of judging a legend by its facts. And, in the back of our minds, there grows a suspicion that those who manipulate the dominant ideology have themselves written, or at least helped disseminate, this myth about the wonderful spiritual compensations available to Mexicans without money.

The two strands of culture theory we can extract from this reading, then, function in dialectic tension. One describes the culture of poverty in which "las creencias nos compensan de las carencias" [faith makes up for our deficiencies] ("Vísperas" 3) and suggests that, beneath the posturing of the elite ruling class, this popular sensibility remains the hegemonic thought system. Implicated with this strand of thought is an alternative view of popular religion as a psychic resistance to official culture's attempts to contain by incorporating its destabilizing potential. When Fidencio dies, the Church accords him recognition, not as the founder of a new religion but as an especially miraculous Catholic saint (*Rituales* 99). In this view, the outward trappings of conformity are rejected in the only way available to the poor and powerless: in ecstatic mental and emotional flight from reality.

mysticism's nonconformist appeal

To suggest that the pseudo-mystical maneuvers of religious charismatics are evidence of potentially democratic free-thinking is in itself an act of resistance to the dominant ideology. Given a sharp critical edge in this monsivaisian text, pathetic and/or inspirational images of faith healing do not inspire awe, as the legend wishes, but instead bare the dysfunctional soul of an abused child who grows up to perpetuate an historical cycle of abuse.

These and other points comprise a theoretical understanding of religious mysticism as (1) inextricably linked to poverty, (2) counterhegemonic and (3) creative: an ongoing process of (popular) culture displacement, transformation and production.

Notwithstanding probable changes in the appearance that popular religion will continue to assume, it will remain a space of autonomous choice and meaning-making for multitudes of individuals who will be following, not the dictates of the dominant culture, but their own self-interest. Monsiváis observes this with good-humored tolerance and no small theology: "Quizás tenga razón el aforista: la gente no creería en Dios en lo absoluto si no se le permitiera creer en Él erróneamente" [Perhaps the aphorist is right:

people would not believe in God at all if they were not allowed to believe in Him mistakenly] (106).

The crónica ends with two summaries. The first makes it clear to his economically and educationally privileged readers that Fidencio's mysticism is a fundamental part of an historical culture of marginalization that includes an irrepressible impulse in the masses to pay lip service to orthodox Church culture while worshiping with the old gods in their hearts.[7] More significantly still, this popular religion clings to archaic visions of the cosmos as entirely sacred "porque lo secular no existe y el Siglo (la Historia) transcurre en lontananza" [because the secular does not exist and Time (History) takes place extremely far away] (107). If for 500 years there is no change in the sociopolitical and economic circumstances of the masses, especially those left to fend for themselves in the solitude of the countryside, time will also stand still. In that static space, individuals poised on the eve of the past (Monsiváis, "Las vísperas del pasado") cannot grasp a sense of individual agency and will instead embrace "la voluntad de sacrificio" [the will to sacrifice] to collective norms and obligations (Rituales 107). In short, Carlos Monsiváis indicts Mexican leadership for giving the poor nothing more substantial than a sense of belonging that is rooted in what León-Portilla calls "un sentido náhuatl de la vida" [a Nahuatl sense of life] (Antiguos 171), the melancholy hopelessness of "un pueblo perennemente afligido por la idea de una destrucción inescapable" [a people perennially afflicted with the notion of their inescapable destruction] (172).

Monsiváis seeks a final meaning of Fidencio's life inside the collective consciousness: "La mística de la marginalidad es un enclave de la resistencia psíquica: quienes siguen a los iluminados no entienden conceptos clave en la cultura dominante: fanatismo, superstición, herejía, irracionalidad. . . . No habitan el lenguaje que los expulsa" [the mysticism of marginality is an enclave of psychic resistance: Those who follow the enlightened ones do not understand key concepts of the dominant culture: fanaticism, superstition, heresy, irrationalism . . . They do not inhabit the language which expels them] (Monsiváis, Rituales 108).

Now we understand that, for Monsiváis, Fidencio's religion is a dialect of Spanish, a language sufficient for the needs of the community of its speakers, a semiotic mechanism that unites consciousnesses (recall that both "religion" and "to bind" share a common Latin root[8]). Like language, religion is an effective means of the most serious communication and might even antedate linguistic language as we know it (Burkert 19). What most interests Monsiváis in popular religion, however, is its basically optimistic function as a tool for human survival, with the potential to be used either to dominate or to liberate.

Fidencio's world is a microcosm of society, which is culture that is ritual that is the making and speaking of "religious" meanings. Monsiváis's finely tuned ear captures the dominant culture—not Fidencio's heterodox commune—speaking heretical prejudice while committing an act of human sacrifice upon its society's most defenseless members. Within this discursive register, "el término guadalupano no tiene un significado religioso sino socio-cultural" [the meaning of the term Guadalupan is not religious but sociocultural] (Monsiváis, "Vísperas" 3), and a low-income pilgrim to the Virgin's shrine, which sits next to the National Palace in the heart of the capital, can be forgiven for thinking, "Lo peor de los ricos, es que teniéndolo todo le quitan el tiempo a Dios pidiéndole cosas" [The worst thing about the rich is that, having everything already, they take time away from God by asking him for things] ("Espacios" 273).

Carlos Monsiváis knows that the people he presumes to speak for are not hearing this and, perhaps, that those he speaks to are not listening. Still, with utopian persistence, he stretches his consciousness between psychosocial fissures such as the abyss that separates Boy Fidencio and the Pope. He practices this literary ritual in the hope of achieving, long before Judgment Day, a coincidence of opposites among the Mexican peoples.

classism and elitism in the capital

Now we will follow Monsiváis to the megalopolis, where the poor of millenarian rural spaces become the poor of an urban landscape in which "nadie se preocupa—no es asunto pensable—por las condiciones de vida de indígenas y parias urbanos. Inconcebible que habiten *casas;* a ellos les corresponden chozas, tugurios, meros hacinamientos" [nobody is concerned—it would be unthinkable to care—about the standard of living of Indians and other urban outcasts. It's inconceivable, even, that they should live in *houses;* huts, shacks, just a bit of space amid a pile of bodies—that's good enough for those people] (Monsiváis, "Ciudad de México" 11).

The abyss we now contemplate is not only between religious and secular worldviews, or between archaic and modern perceptions of reality; the division explored in "Dancing: el Salón Los Angeles" (*Escenas* 97–102) also defines three of Monsiváis's most persistent concerns, themes that also preoccupy postmodernist and postcolonialist thinkers: centralism, classism and elitism.

In "Dancing," our cronista reports on an encounter between a group of university academics and the clientele of a blue-collar nightclub. The scene's true incongruity is not immediately apparent. A problematical entry to the discourse obscures our perception of the who, what, where and why of the situation. Even when we think we have figured these out, other divisive tactics call attention to the poorly matched partners of "Dancing." Semantic mésalliances such as "proletariado intelectual" [intellectual proletariat] "folclor urbano" [urban folklore] and "Autocrítica de los Demás" [Self-Criticism of Everyone Else] jolt the sensibility. Irony, sarcasm and parody dislocate understanding. Promiscuous coupling of journalistic and fictional registers keeps us off balance. Unsanctioned shifts in point of view disconcert. Unauthorized insertion of extraliterary genres provokes. Throughout, we are tricked into laughing at subjects who move us to pity and outrage. Altogether: a reading experience that deliberately frustrates.

The first line of the text drops us into the middle of a conversation made of multiple dialogues whose strands of speech criss-cross a space we eventually identify (after two pages) as a table on the edge of a dance floor in a *barrio* nightclub. Without further external markers to identify them, we guess that the speakers are members of the "high class" who are gossiping with a malicious sense of superiority about the "low-class" people they have come to analyze. Quite a bit later in this report, the narrator reassures us that our preliminary detective work has correctly discerned outlines of the chronotope. Now he specifies that he is there in the company of "hordas de investigadores, de ayudantes de profesor, de becarios, de estudiantes de posgrados . . . , periodistas, jóvenes funcionarios, historiadores franceses y gringos eruditos, actrices, socialistas aliviandos, críticos y directores de cine, pintores sin clientela pero con proposición estética básica, todos pisteando y rumbeando, . . . seguidos por las cámaras del Canal 13 *(Programa especial)* . . . " [hordes of investigators, teaching assistants, research fellows, post-docs, journalists, young civil servants, French historians and learned gringos, actresses, accidental socialists, film critics and directors, painters without patrons but with a sound sense of aesthetics—all of these dancing or heading for the floor, . . . [with] Channel 13's Special Program camera in hot pursuit] (98–99).

The last detail—discovery that Angel Rama's Lettered City was on a televised expedition into the Wild Urban Kingdom—metaphorically miniaturizes a vast discourse on art and life, another presumably incompatible pair that in postmodern discourses are nonetheless shown to be incestuously joined: contemporary social life "scened" like video in a sound-studio reality.

So far, our view of the popular culture being practiced in the club Los Angeles is funneled through the ears, a somewhat disconcerting experience for readers. Monsiváis has forced both his book-oriented witnesses and his readers to make meaning with the tools of the objects under scrutiny, the under- or uneducated masses who inhabit a still mostly oral culture. The technique confers a degree of ephemeral immediacy on the information we receive and puts us at a disadvantage. How are we supposed to make lasting sense out of data that fly past our ears and out of perception? Within the limits of the obvious—we are, after all, reading a text that Monsiváis wrote, published and later transferred to the permanency of a book—Monsiváis has inserted the symbolic whole of the lettered elite's secondhand culture into the firsthand dance of "low" culture. He wants us to see how fish out of water swim.

artful demotion of the elite

Suddenly, as though the narrator had turned down the volume on the background music, one voice stands out: "Lo pinche del mexicano al bailar rumba es el trabajo que le cuesta mover los hombros" [The worst thing about the Mexican dancing rumba is how hard he finds it to move his shoulders] (98). Playing dirty with high culture, Monsiváis has duped a self-important academic into announcing error as fact. Listeners who have read another chronicle in this same collection, "Dancing: el secreto está en la mano izquierda" (137–40), can measure the ignorance of this academic "expert" on popular culture. In the previous text, the most credible expert on the rumba, the barrio Mexican who loses himself night after night in a cultural form he is creating—generously enlightens the clueless narrator. The dancer tells him that "el mexicano se menea de la cintura para abajo. . . . Los cubanos y los puertorriqueños alzan los hombros. Nosotros casi no" [We Mexicans shake from the waist down . . . Cubans and Puerto Ricans move their shoulders up and down. We almost never do that] (139).

As though chastened by this intratextual rebuke, the elite knowledge brokers of "Los Angeles" fall silent. Taking over the discourse, the narrator now gives us reliable journalistic facts about this "velada inolvidable" [unforgettable evening] in the Guerrero neighborhood (98), which information makes it clear that we must read this chronicle on at least two levels. On the first, we learn documentable facts about an artifact of Mexican popular culture. On the more transcendent level, however, we reflect on an elite that fancies itself separate from and superior to the class of compatriots it momentarily colonizes with ethnographic intent, the unemployed workers turned here into guinea pigs: "Les cayó una nube de historiadores orales: '¡Vengan, vengan, aquí hay un obrero, contémplenlo! ¿Cómo desplaza usted la cadera? ¡Explíquese y descodifique!'" [A plague of oral historians descended on them: "Come on guys, look! Here's a blue-collar worker. Say, how do you move your hips? Explain and decode yourself!"] (100)

A foundational point of the narrator's analysis of the analysts is that, when official culture invades the blue-collar sanctuary, its habitués slip away the minute they see they've been discovered (100). Popular culture has no intention of sticking around to justify the elite class's job description. Still, the would-be ethnographers remain, encouraged to step out on the dance floor with self-deluding remarks: "Ahora estoy contento porque estoy no entre universitarios sino entre trabajadores" [I'm happy now because I'm not with university people, but with working folk] (99). This begs the question: How is it that the nation's avant-garde suddenly acquired such a "pasión popular" [passion for the popular]? (100)

The answer is as complex as culture itself. We must not forget, for example, that the truth(s) we seek are revealed through the eyes of a narrator who, although he shames his companions at every opportunity, remains a member of their culture. He presents the jargon-laden discourse of the academic as a particularly noxious form of paraliterature, about as illuminating as an adult comic book (100). The TV camera, matched to high culture as its natural dance partner, records the professorial soul's hypocrisy: What for the popular classes is authentic creation of culture is a sterile simulacrum of the pleasure of the dance for the bourgeois who come slumming in Colonia Guerrero. The Ph.D.s who shove their bodies through a semblance of the rumba project an image not of who they think they are but of who they want to be.

Ostensibly, they are there as disinterested observers of a culture they need to know intimately in order to conduct research on the production of ideology (101). In fact, they are seen to resemble their predecessor Fray Bernardino de Sahagún, who interviewed defeated Aztecs for decades in order to learn the culture's secrets, the better to destroy that culture from within (1: 36). A like intent is not far buried in the consciousness of invaders of the Salon Los Angeles who affect a knowledge of the language of popular dance as they interview surviving natives. Seemingly in disgust for his social class's perfidy, one of the visitors, whose voice we assume is the author's, snorts: If there were any corresponding logic in life, all the music stores would right this minute be overflowing with unemployed workers buying Mozart, Wagner, Vivaldi, Lukas Foss and Philip Glass (Monsiváis, *Escenas* 101). In the Salon Los Angeles, the gross lie of this truth exposes arrogance and aggression as the "devastación muy propia de . . . élites" [kind of depredation we expect of the elite] (101).

This is a complex revelation because we know that the voice announcing it has made a career of invading foreign habitats to study the native fauna. However, because this critic does not exempt himself from his negative views of the presumptuous strangers, in whose world he is simultaneously an insider and an outsider, we are willing to see the ethnologist Monsiváis at work in dance halls, soccer stadiums and guerrilla-held jungles in the guise of an activist dedicated to curtailing elitist depredations and protecting endangered species in the cultural ecosystem. Accordingly, when Monsiváis uses his mastery of elitist Spanish to destroy from within his intended convert, we applaud his subversive "imperialism." He has made a point of becoming fluent in professorese precisely in order to reveal the emptiness of signifiers such as "metodología audaz y nueva" [audacious and innovative methodology], "sesudo análisis" [sensible analysis] and "explicación racional a las secuencias ontológicas" [rational explanation of the ontological consequences] (100–101).

classism as a constructed lie

This text's self-satisfied holders of doctorates in fact suffer both ignorance and illiteracy, says Monsiváis. When a television interviewer asks a "transmigrado rural o como se diga" [rural migrant, or whatever] about his dance style, and the man answers with simple clarity: "No tengo ritmo predilecto, todos me pasan, el caso es no quedarse hecho un palo" [I have no favorite rhythm: I can manage them all; the thing is to avoid looking stiff as a board] (102), an anthropologist disconcerted by the lucidity of the answer mutters: "se está desclasando." [He's speaking outside his assigned class]. In reality, Monsiváis implies the opposite. When the anthropologist and others of his social rank criticize the disadvantaged Mexican citizen they expose their own weaknesses without recognizing that no one in the Salon Los Angeles, rich or poor, in fact belongs to his presumed class. "¿Has conocido un investigador de tiempo completo que no esté al tanto de la trama de la telenovela de moda?" [Have you ever known a full-time academic who wasn't up on the latest plot development in the soap opera everyone's watching?] (98) Monsiváis has put his finger on the least defensible point in the intelligentsia's strategy of containment: the discovery that their complex discourse, darkened with forests of footnotes, is a mask that rationalizes a "nostalgic deep desire not to be intellectual" (Frith 179), a yearning to have escaped "del cubículo al cubil" [from the carrel to the cave] in order to now find themselves having a great time among the underclass (Monsiváis, *Escenas* 100). And, should they manage to incorporate the productive capacity of the pure cultural habitat they have invaded and drive away the natives, they will soon follow (101) in hopes of closing the "cultural distance" that separates them from the materiality of popular culture.

Of course, they require a pretext such as "doing research" for this inexcusable attraction to "la monotonía sublime del faje y el coito" [sublime monotony of sexual congress] (Monsiváis, *Escenas* 99). Fixing his x-ray eyes on high culture's vulnerable chest, Monsiváis extracts its secret desire to participate in "la obsesión de la semana" [mania of the moment] (99), holding up to view the intellectual's compulsion to join the rest of humanity in seeking his cultural and psychic roots. This subject was drawn to the dance floor, not by his ego, but by his id. The siren song of carnival's grotesque realism has inverted the mind-body hierarchy and (re)awakened in the university set "la emoción de los olores raros" [the feelings stirred up by exotic smells] (100). Historians, journalists and sociologists may now in truth create a genuine cultural product.

an implicit theory
of culture formation

The crónica ends as it began, amid a flux of voice and movement, signs of culture in progress. Despite (or perhaps as a function of) this explicit lack of closure, the following implicit theoretical points can be isolated for discussion:

(1) Authentic culture is self-validating and extemporaneous creation by a "free" agent operating autonomously, outside his or her foucauldian

work station. It is what people do when they are entertaining them-selves, feeling obligated neither to adopt defined attitudes in service to the image of them designated by the System nor to adjust their behavior to fit what an Other expects of them. It is spontaneous action inspired simply by the desire to not stand around like a stick.

(2) To be "popular," culture must emerge naturally from vital circum-stances, in keeping with the medium inspiring its creation and use. Once taken over and re-presented by official culture, it ceases to be pop-ular. At the same time, every social class is inherently capable of gener-ating popular culture. "Popular" is not necessarily a synonym of "low."

(3) The dense texturing of true popular culture is seductive. So powerful is its attraction that official culture feels obligated to control what is perceived, consciously or unconsciously, to be a potentially dangerous base of social autonomy. Unsupervised human action in a mass culture invites hostile takeover of its assets.

(4) The mass media, a related but distinct phenomenon, assist in the fab-rication of imagined destinies of irresistible allure. These are opportu-nities to escape a cultural space experienced as painful or stultifying. The media concretize the impulse to emigrate to anywhere-but-here as, instantly and everywhere, they distribute images both real and artificial, which in turn multiply openings in society for new cultural production. The media project a model to which the masses may adhere or from which they may depart.

For example, it is doubtful that the dynamic art being created in Salon Los Angeles was permanently suffocated when elite observers entered the original creative space, but if in fact that source of cultural craftsmanship had been eliminated, there would be no real harm done: the social being's need to make culture (to make meanings of and with his life) will always open new sites of creation that Others will always be tempted to visit.

(5) Takeover of popular culture by the middle and upper classes is a natural and historic process that persistently levels out unreal aspects of elite culture's creations, reintegrating them with spaces of ordinary human activity. In renewed touch with its "roots," high culture can (theoret-ically) share its civilizing, transcendent and self-critical values more equitably with all of society; at the same time, contact with the "gro-tesque realism" of the popular can help it clarify its human(ist) values.

Elsewhere, Monsiváis acknowledges the rich uses to which popular agents put elitist cultural artifacts; he revels, for example, in the "cursilería impecable" [impeccable vulgarity] of the bolero, which poaches on modernist poetry's exquisite elegance in order to idolize the prostitute heroines of torch songs (*Amor* 61). Far from embodying the barbaric half of Latin America's prototypical cultural construct, the unlettered populace of Mexico is capable of filling its prodigious memory with lines from Díaz Mirón, Plaza, Acuña and Amado Nervo (Monsiváis, "Mano" 74). Monsiváis has observed that among the benefits withheld from Mexico's deprived masses are those sequestered by full or functional illiteracy, low book sales, high book prices, and a dearth of public libraries (Monsiváis, "De cultura y política" 72; Monsiváis et al. *Derecho* 5).

promotion of the popular

In effect, "Salón Los Angeles" reiterates entertainingly the way Monsiváis has insisted throughout his career on the democratizing and humanizing power of "low" culture to deflate high culture's delusions of grandeur. In an academic venue around the same time as publication of *Escenas de pudor y liviandad,* Monsiváis was enunciating one of his fundamental hypotheses: that popular culture itself is an artificial category invented by high culture as proof of its unique authority ("De las relaciones literarias" 46). The cultural dance in contemporary society in fact involves perpetual repartnerings of low-brow, middle-brow and high-brow modes of meaning-making. As their name implies, the mass media function as a matchmaker to help join popular and high cultures (a movie by Buñuel about the forgotten poor, a novel by Puig about Rita Hayworth, a museum exhibit of José Guadalupe Posada's cartoons, an exhibit in Washington, D.C., of Agustín Víctor Casasola's photographs of the Mexican Revolution, a crónica by Monsiváis on lurid newspaper crime reportage).[9]

Monsiváis reminds Mexico's elite cultures that, to propagate, they must make themselves more accessible to popular users. Monsiváis wants his society's cultural custodians to become voluntary shareholders in a publicly owned enterprise that depends for its vitality as much on the individual, anonymous contributions that trickle up from the masses as upon investment strategies managed by the board of directors: The manufacture and distribution of cultural capital, then, conceived not as a top-down enterprise, but as passage through stages of information on a continuum. "Hoy todo participa de todo" [Today, everything is part of everything else] (Monsiváis, "De las relaciones literarias" 60).

To these descriptive components, Monsiváis adds the prescriptive reminder: Radically unequal distribution of economic wealth impedes realization of the high-low dialectic's potential to decenter exclusive authority, validate pluralism and equalize respect for difference. So also does an elite class that devotes its power and influence to the goal of naturalizing the effects of its ineptitude and corruption. From within that elite class, then, Monsiváis uses the power of his language to denaturalize—to make ridiculous the seemingly impregnable authority of the haves, and to make preposterous the acceptance of misery as the lot in life of Mexico's born-to-lose have-nots. That is why he dedicates the great mass of his literary production—and the overwhelming weight of his public authority—to the revelations he finds amid the bad smells of a barrio nightclub's bathroom, or in any of numberless such humble places where, unbeknownst even to themselves, Mexico's masses perform the work of self-emancipation.

From beneath his society's often-negative appearances and upon its broad popular base, new political and social structures are emerging. On the strength of these, as the voiceless and nameless learn to become a profoundly disruptive presence in middle-class and elite enclaves, there is hope of a new economic structure also arising. Into this irresistibly powerful energy source Carlos Monsiváis plugs his literary project, to broadcast the news of change that his consciousness picks up like a microphone.

His preferred medium of transmission is the crónica, a literary genre whose abundant vitality and mixed bloodlines reflect perfectly the nature of its referent. Elite and plebian forms coincide in a seriocomic discourse that places itself provocatively between the assertiveness of journalism and the inventiveness of fiction. This congenital crossbreeding has historically inspired a kind of literary racism that relegated the crónica to the margins of the Academy. Yet, as I will show in the next two chapters, this genre deserves honor as the constitutive soul of Mexican and, indeed, of all Latin American literature.

carlos monsiváis, cronista
the art of telling the truth

Like the cultural themes that are its favored subject matter, the contemporary crónica of Mexico is a mestizo form whose generic identity is to be found in the way its function and its form work inseparably. On the one hand, the crónica claims to be a truth-genre pertaining to the field of journalism. At the same time, its ostentatious use of narrative technique aligns it with the field of creative writing. This mix of the nonfiction and fiction modes is the source of a durable allure that has preserved its essence since classical antiquity and made it the progenitor of all American literature. From the early nineteenth century, however, the Western Academy erected an arbitrary barricade between functionality and form, a move that cast the modern-day chronicle into an ontological and critical limbo.[1]

In this chapter, I will address problems arising from that arbitrary relo-cation of nonfiction narrative. One is the difficulty of identifying the crónica: distinguishing it from such neighboring genres as essay, straight news, *tes-timonio* and short story. Another concerns its reception, problematized by doubts about the nature of the form and, thus, how to read it.[2] As a result of the first two difficulties, there are problems with the chronicle's evaluation, primarily displayed in its evident marginalization in the academic commu-nity. In response to these and other conditions that have historically stigma-tized the crónica, I want to propose a theory of this genre, to establish that its exemplary texts may be judged durable art and that the chronicles of Carlos Monsiváis are paradigmatic and canonical examples.

what's in a name?

One aspect of the first problem mentioned lies on the very surface of the controversy: Critics have yet to agree on what to call it. An inventive variety of names is given to literary journalism in Latin America and the United States, reflecting a vacillation over generic specificity that still prevails. It is worth listing some of the terms I have come across, many of which Monsiváis himself has used. In Spanish, these include *periodismo de autor, ficción documental, sociología auxiliar, crononovela, socioliteratura, metaperiodismo, periosía, periodismo cultural, relato de no-ficción, periodismo interpretativo, neocostumbrismo*, and (the very awkward) *"no(crónica)vela."* In English, the list includes *transfiction, faction, transformation journalism, cre-ative nonfiction, documentary narrative as art, apocalyptic documentary, para-literary journalism, midfiction, metareportage, liminal literature, radical news analysis, higher journalism, journalit, postmodern journalism, parajournalism, participatory journalism, the New Nonfiction*, and *poetic chronicle*.

Taken together, the names strain inventively to model how the genre itself bridges empirical and poetic worlds. Many of them also gesture toward the importance of the narrator-author and his or her perceived "authority" to speak truth, a point of key importance developed in chapter 1 and to which I will return in discussion of elements that constitute the genre. Although some of the terms suggest that the form belongs on the fictional side of the divide, most identify it with journalism.

A more serious problem of reception is reflected in confusion over the name of this literary nonfiction genre (which I have said will be called crónica or chronicle in this study). With respect to the *modernista* chronicle's generic heir a century later, revitalized by Monsiváis, Elena Poniatowska and others in the wake of 1968's sociopolitical upheavals, Christopher Domínguez Michael notes that use and abuse of the form have made it all but indistinguishable from any other neighboring genre (*Antología* 2: 68). It's a popular opinion. Speaking explicitly of the essay, but implicitly also of the chronicle, José Miguel Oviedo refers to a "género camaleónico" [chameleonic genre] that tends to adopt whatever shape it pleases (*Breve historia* 11). Whether in regard to the essay or the chronicle, virtually all critics agree that the genre is "escurridizo" [slippery] (Escarpeta-Sánchez 158); it eludes definition, whether because it has been considered an incomplete or deficient genre that only imperfectly generates its meanings (García Monsiváis 18), or because some of its formal aspects resemble those of the short story (Gómez-Martínez 119). In general, critics do not distinguish Monsiváis's chronicles from his essays (or from the occasional text that crosses over into fiction) (Argüelles 13; Blanco, Crónica 86; Castañón, "Ensayo" 73; Skirius, *Ensayo* 19–20; Zavala 161).

Another aspect of the critical dilemma I am describing is explained by the hybridity of form that is an identifiable trait of the whole of Latin American literature (Fuentes, *Valiente* 181–86; González Echevarría, *Historia* 10–12, *Myth and Archive;* Carpentier 46–48; González, *Journalism* 14–16; Navarro 146; Pupo-Walker 24; Retamar 56–57; Rowe and Schelling 200–201). Monsiváis characterizes the resultant intertwining of fact and fiction, especially in the crónica, as a coupling of (female) literature and (male) journalism: "Como hermana y hermano / vamos los dos cogidos de la mano" [like sister and brother / we go along holding hands] ("Notas sobre la cultura" 356).[3]

denying that a problem exists

A not uncommon response to the mix of reportage and invention in the crónica is to dismiss the formal conundrum as irrelevant. When noted Mexican philologist Antonio Alatorre reviewed Monsiváis's groundbreaking anthology of modern Mexican crónicas in 1981, he expressed delight at "discovering" an entertaining and (for him) new literary form; any effort to determine whether it should be considered fact or fiction he considered "bizantino" [byzantine] (38). A decade later, editors of an anthology of the "nueva crónica de la ciudad de México" restate the view (Valverde and Argüelles 12). Attempts to assign generic identity to any text may be contemptuously characterized as "un invento del academicismo, de la pereza clasificatoria" [an invention of academicism, of the indolent classificatory mind] (Huerta 6).

Another way to dismiss the relevance of generic specificity, not-so-readily apparent as such, is to go along with metaphysical theorists like Jacques Derrida, Roland Barthes and Jean Baudrillard, whose radically decontextualized readings undermine the common-sense reader's efforts to determine a text's truth value. The principal thrust of their poststructuralist thought has been to destabilize or deny a possible dividing line between fact and fiction and indeed to so obfuscate the ontological status of discourses that empiricism itself has been made provisional. In the face of historical evidence of the permanent human desire for the authority—and the allure—of fact, and notwithstanding that to satisfy that desire is to believe it possible to recognize a nonfiction discourse, deconstructionists assert no difference between living life and reading about it, or recognizing a real or imagined referent (Barthes 145–48; Baudrillard, *Selected* 88–90, 122–26; Derrida 232–33; White, "Fictions").

To thus trivialize the content of a form seems naive, at best. It is at least glaringly inconsistent with the ease with which the vast consensus of critics is able to identify a novel, for example, despite a general agreement, also, that "the novel willfully defies definition" (Waugh 5) and that its instability is one of its identifying characteristics (Bakhtin, *Problems* 204, 270–72, *Dialogic* 324–31).[4] Far from eliminating their claims to generic specificity, the formal impurity of documentary fiction, the essay, the chronicle and, even, the short story and the novel may affirm their individuality (Prince, "Narrative Studies" 276).

reading a text as it wishes

That theorists commonly hold the chronicle and the essay to be synonymous forms of equally imprecise contours falsely posits an insuperable ontological collapse. Essay and chronicle can—and ought to—be read according to their unique textual intentions: what each work "wishes" to say. In this respect, E.D. Hirsch, Jr., speaks of an "intrinsic genre" (89) and Walter Mignolo of the "metatext," an implied discourse paralleling the openly declared narration and serving as a metaexegetic guide to the act of reading ("Metatexto" 360–61, 379–80). Detecting in the text its own generic parameters functions "to contain the possibilities of reading" (Fiske, *Television* 114).

The mutual expectations of writer and reader complement each other and constitute the genre, which process produces implications for interpretation according to a set of conventions (Hirsch 80–81, 91–99; Ryan 720). "Through genre, a text is and makes sense" (Prince, "Narrative Studies" 281). A fictionalist may choose to present her story as real, and a journalist may employ narrative fiction techniques, but in either case, "to transgress intelligently, . . . one must know the rule" (Brooke-Rose 290). I proceed, then, on the understanding that a search for the rule delimiting the contemporary Mexican crónica's formal parameters is a prerequisite of its being properly read and receiving just attention from literary scholars.[5]

Despite trends beginning in the 1960s to open the literary canon to nontraditional genres, scholars are still reluctant to bestow their analytical gifts on the dual-faced discourse of Mexican and U.S. New Journalists. Tom Wolfe's 1973 complaint has lost little of its force: He was disgusted that university critics in "the grip of the damnable Novel" ("New Journalism" 20) were frankly hostile to the North American chronicler's appropriation of the language of fiction. Monsiváis echoes Wolfe's frustration over the new-style literary reportage's marginalization by the *Establishment* ("Alabemos" 201). He wonders why the crónica merits so little attention in Mexican literary history, compared to poetry's enormous prestige and "la seducción omnipresente de la novela" [the ubiquitous seduction of the novel] ("De la Santa Doctrina" 753). This original and inventive form, which manages to reveal as false the canonical difference between literature and journalism, still inspires, in 1992, a stubborn will within Academe to defend those demonstrably arbitrary borders (Monsiváis, "Prólogo" in *Fin de Nostalgia* 19).

To be sure, writers of antiquity had little practical concern for the difference between factual and made-up truths. As a matter of historical record, fictionality is a construct of a modern world made anxious by the loss of theological certitude (Kermode 67). It is perhaps not surprising that, yet possessed of many premodern features, a text's generic specificity and truth value may have inspired little practical interest. What surprises is the tenacity of the Academy's grip on a line of literary demarcation that unjustifiably banished nonfiction discourses from the privileged ground of high culture. This posture, less elite than effete, reversed values that had pertained for millennia (Schorske 110; Shotwell 1–7) and was never truly tenable.

I do not mean to suggest that standards for literature worthy of study, dissemination and emulation should be eliminated, much less relaxed. On the contrary. I believe, with Monsiváis, that official and popular cultures are codependent. Elite culture could not benefit from the popular arts if it stopped distinguishing itself from those informal orders of creativity, nor could the community as a whole be nudged "upward" toward a higher humanism, unless some standard of canonical judgment existed to sort classes of art. My point is that *fictionality* is not a sufficient marker of literariness and that *nonfictionality* is not in itself a reason to declare a work not literary.[6]

an indigenous theory of the chronicle

While I am elaborating a theory that to my knowledge has not been stated elsewhere, I keep in mind that the "concept of genre looks forward and backward" to new, uncharted territory and to existing traditions (Guillén 109). I want to expose an "indigenous theory" (Genette, *Narrative Discourse* 264) that arises out of the works themselves. This process ought to confirm that the crónica:

— Includes history and, "al verter literariamente vivencias locales y nacionales, es inmejorable aliada y cómplice de la Historia" [because it translates local and national experiences into literature, is the incomparable ally and accomplice of History] (Monsiváis, "De la Santa Doctrina" 755), but itself is not history;

— Belongs to the field of journalism but exceeds the brief both of straight news reportage and of opinion-page essay[7];

— Enjoys close kinship with the essay, but stretches and ultimately overwrites that form's staid bounds[8];

— May contain the testimony of witnesses or others—some of the genre's most memorable texts are made entirely or substantially of (apparently unmediated) speech[9]—without being or becoming what is understood today in Latin America as *testimonio*[10]; and

— Ostentatiously helps itself to the same narrative tools used by the short story and the novel, and thus may, at least in part and some of the time, resemble fictional discourse. A self-declared referential genre, however, it seeks to justify its truth-claim. As reportage literature, it assigns equal value to its *function* and to its *form*.

the chronicle's function

I will take up the question of function first, in primary instance because that is as far as most scholarship to date goes in pursuit of an understanding of the crónica. Martin Stabb, who has written frequently on this "notoriously ill-defined" nonfiction genre, could speak for most in his decision not "to become involved in . . . technical discussion" of the formal specificity of "certain unclassifiable texts wherein expository, 'essay-istic' elements blend . . . with narrative material" (*Dissenting* 95). His anti-methodological reliance on ideological considerations (e.g. in "The Essay") casts the genre into a hermeneutical limbo.

José Joaquín Blanco also concentrates on function in his study of the contemporary Mexican crónica because, "como todo gran arte . . . no se limita a la cárcel de su género específico . . . sino que busca conjugarse con todo tipo de disciplinas y de conocimientos" [like all great art, it does not confine itself to the jail of its specific genre, but seeks accommodation with every kind of discipline and knowledge] (*Crónica* 109). The chronicle is indeed interdisciplinarian and complex, but to "confine" the crónica to its generic specificity is potentially to set it free from the widespread disregard that it suffers in the critical community.[11]

Along these same lines, it is reasonable to assume that, in a nonfiction text like the crónica, "the synchronous interplay of story and discourse is undergirded—no matter how shakily—by the logical and chronological pri-ority of documented or observed events" (Cohn, "Signposts" 782), but this assertion alone, without concrete reading guides, may well leave a person wondering how to determine if the undergirding of documented events in, say, E.L. Doctorow's *Ragtime* or the five texts of Carlos Fuentes's *El naranjo* indicates that these discourses are nonfiction (they are not). Susan Rotker's otherwise admirable study of the modernista chronicle as progenitor of the contemporary crónica nowhere answers the persisting question: If an extra-textual referentiality that resists being "disappeared" by word play is the key to a chronicle's claim to status as a truth genre, how is the finally factual nature of the discourse to be verified?

The question is essential to a theory seeking to understand the process of meaning-making that houses interchanges between the fictive and the real in a presumed truth-text (Iser 20). The answer, so persistently evaded, is also of unavoidable import. Practicing a scrupulously slow reading, I will attempt to isolate moments when we can observe the discourse choosing to align itself with the real, which accounts in first, fundamental, measure for the chronicle's very being. Within the discourse to which it gives life, the real binds a seemingly paradoxical form to its ideological and ethical objectives.

a short history of the genre

These objectives are shaped by the historical context situating the discourse. Antedating the classical romance that evolved into the modern novel, the chronicle is an ancient genre defined by a gift for always seeming to be newly invented, the better to mirror the freshly evolved parameters of a culture in transition. Monsiváis's version of this assertive discourse can claim a literary lineage that unwinds in an unbroken line from Hellenistic, Roman, Semitic and early Christian histories to a rebirth in medieval Spain and another, spectacular, rebirth in the New World, where it assimilated to its written European heritage the historic memory of the Mesoamerican civilization. A significant portion of this political and spiritual legacy was preserved in first instance by Spanish missionaries and conquerors in their chronicles. This primordial American literary form then molded itself to a series of revivals and revisions in the seventeenth, eighteenth and nineteenth centuries that brought it to another resurgence in the middle of the twentieth century, still the recognizable offspring of Herodotus's *Histories*.

The historical chronicle in question evolved from epic poetry, about the fifth century B.C. in Hellenistic Europe, as an artistic form of expression that recorded and recreated changes in human consciousness and social structures, a project of dual historiographical and aesthetic functions. In medieval Europe, the personal nonfiction account was renovated during a period of reawakening popular realism in the form of autobiographical religious accounts using a mixed style that combined the sublime of allegorical figuration and the everyday concreteness of lived reality (Auerbach 159–62). On the eve of the Renaissance, the old chronicles of Spain emerged as a new way of mirroring both elite and popular cultural aspects of contemporary society in a time of radical change (Ticknor 182). The discovery of America, which added an earthshaking new fact to Europe's known reality, gave birth to a dramatically new truth-account narrated by participants in the recorded events.

Monsiváis, together with virtually all Latin American literary giants, fed his moral consciousness and his aesthetic imagination on the Chronicle of the Indies, a genre that sprang into being on the cusp of antiquity and modernity. He recognizes that "historiofabulists" (Sale 61) like Bernal Díaz del Castillo intended to write history and, thus, that the colonial chronicle pursues ends that do not correspond with Belles Lettres. Out of the textual plenitude of the colonial American chronicle, however, were born all the prose genres that have developed in Spanish America, including the new journalistic accounts of the eighteenth century; the nineteenth century's new *costumbrismo* (literary sketches of contemporary culture and politics); the new crónica that emerged at century's end from newspaper pages offering a paradigm-shifting emphasis on style; the new way of recording immediate history in the crónica written during and just after the Mexican Revolution, and the new way of capturing sociopolitical sea changes that attended rapid industrialization and urban growth as Mexico approached the mid-century.[12] Yet another "new" crónica, practiced since the late sixties by Carlos Monsiváis and his contemporaries, has produced an entertaining and sophisticated literary forum where the postindustrial age's many cultural revolutions are acted out.

the conscience of the sixties

Profound psychic stresses that accompanied the onset of a new social paradigm in the mid-twentieth century were not as knowingly countered as it has become fashionable (and possible) to do, thanks to the New Age's self-help and recovery industries and an otherwise general surfeit of information thrust on society by a ubiquitous technoculture. Since the 1960s, the Information Age and its satellites—cultural and economic globalization, the Pill and other medical empowerments, feminism and other mass-mediated shifts in collective expectations—produced almost inconceivable facts: civil unrest and violence; imperialism and chaos abroad; assassination of heroes; radical negation of the familiar and reliable, a process aided by institutionalized nonconformism and mind-altering drugs; the computer-capable imagination's will to send human beings to walk about in a fantastically distant space and, even, to obliterate Time itself, or conventional notions of it. These and many other "unthinkable" and "impossible" scenarios in a violent, chaotic, and fragmented modern era cast expectations into doubt while inspiring apocalyptic judgments about the "perplexing fictivity of the 'real'" (Zavarzadeh 24), nonfiction's elimination of facts (Boorstin 144), and "the end of difference" (Baudrillard, *America* 47–48).

Those who comment on the contemporary chronicle of either Mexico or the United States attribute its particular truth-claim to the angst inherent not only in its postcolonial condition but also in its immediate connection to those traumatic social dislocations of the 1960s: "The New Journalism— that genre-blurred mélange of ethnography, investigative reportage, and fiction—is widely and rightly considered to be *the* characteristic genre of the sixties" (Staub 54). Bakhtin would recognize in both the U.S. and Mexican new chronicle the seriocomic genre's journalistic interest in the topics of the day (*Problems* 199), as well as its tendency to concentrate on crises, turning points and catastrophes and on "threshold" spaces where the impetus and effects of crises and structural transformations occur (149). The crónica's imaginative recreation of such public milestones appeals to its society's collective yearning for concrete, real-izable certainties at a juncture in its life when received truths and ways of relating are wavering or shrinking to a white dot on the screen. Elsewhere I have observed that the genre Carlos Monsiváis assumed as his has always been the hero of literary tradition, always available as a touchstone of reality when society suddenly falls head first into an epistemological vacuum ("Crónica" 310).

In Mexico, cronistas have been registering the shocks of critical historical thresholds since Columbus fought to reconcile his expectations of urban oriental splendor with the jungle full of naked people that reality forced upon him in 1492. The chronicle continued to adjust itself to Mexican struggles with wrenching change, in years like exclamation points: 1521, 1810, 1910 and 1968. Those who write crónica in Mexico today speak specifically of the 1968 student massacre in Tlatelolco Square as a crucial year, an "año parteaguas" [watershed year] (Avilés Fabila 104). That year, said Monsiváis, made Mexico's historic reliance on self-deception obsolete (*Días* 74). Tlatelolco was the incommensurable event which, in a sense, ended Time and then restarted it in Mexico—just as, in its 1521 moment of massacre, the original Tlatelolco square of Aztec Tenochtitlán witnessed the triumphant European calendar stop indigenous Time.[13] Tlatelolco in 1968 then recast itself as the utopian year (Franco, "Marcar" 34) that sustained a generation's literary consciousness. That generation felt, and feels, morally obligated to tell the truth about lies that the Mexican government would defend to the point of torturing and "disappearing" Mexican citizens (Johnston Hernández 28; Poniatowska, *Fuerte* 78–180).

The true realities conveyed in their inventive reportage were perceived as too big to fit into either the inadequate realism of the novel or the government-controlled pages of newspapers: too pressingly present to be distanced in the epic or tragic mode of fictional narrative. They sought a textual vehicle with enough horsepower to carry their heavy ideological agenda and spacious enough to accommodate their ambitious artistic aspirations: thus, the "neocolonial" chronicle of 1968.

Braided strands of imagination and reality in this (most recently) new chronicle comprise a dual purpose of inseparable parts, one philosophical and critical, the other artistic and emotional. Its moral, political and cultural goals cannot be effectively pursued without the flexibility of figural discourse and, in the context of a declared truth-genre, that combinatory strength is wasted on anything less than the power of the real. The crónica deliberately relies on poetic language to turn the entry-level truth of raw information into deeper and more complex understandings. When its aesthetic function has added to the authority of its reported facts a measure of moral perception, critical will and suggestive symbolism, the chronicle discourse closes its circuits and transmits its power.

a critical mirror of society

This power is directed at change presented simultaneously as utopian ideal and pragmatic action: long-term and short-term goals. In the short term, the crónica positions itself in a public space to hold a critical mirror up to society caught in the act of (re)inventing itself. These public spaces are as varied as all of culture itself, but the cronista, practicing what has aptly been called transformational journalism, will choose to report on thematic sites where struggles over power implicitly contain the greatest potential for change. To help us glimpse the long-term goal, the crónica levitates to gain a more panoramic view, whence it becomes clear that the short-term objectives dramatized in the text are aimed cumulatively at the broader goal of renovating society overall. In the crónica's long view, greater equity and many more alternatives can be seen to appear over the horizon.

A memorable chronicle of the 1985 earthquakes and their aftermath can show how the cronista interweaves both these semantic goals in a single discourse (Monsiváis, *Entrada* 17–122). One of the short-term objectives emerges from snippets of testimony that unwind on the page to the rhythm of insistent references to time. The voices of representative individuals—a rescue worker, an archbishop, a grieving mother, a political activist—become a chorus of demands for inept and obstructionist government authorities to step out of the way and let citizens act on their own to rescue loved ones, retrieve possessions, excavate solutions: "Queremos enterrar a nuestros muertos, nomás eso" [We want to bury our dead, that's all] (49). The principal long-term strategy emerges piecemeal from among the material, emotional and spiritual chaos until we are ready for one citizen's summation: "Si quieres entender el tamaño de esta confrontación, no la examines de anécdota en anécdota; revisa el conjunto y verás una enorme rebeldía civil en nombre de los derechos humanos y del respeto a la vida . . . Y en esta rebeldía civil, que es defensa de la ciudad, debe fundamentarse también la reconstrucción urbana" [If you want to understand the scope of this confrontation, don't look at it anecdote by anecdote; review the whole thing and you'll perceive a huge civil rebellion in the name of human rights and respect for life. . . . Upon this civil disobedience—a defense of the city— urban reconstruction ought also to be based] (50).

The comment sums up the "utopian" goal of democratization in both the Mexican society and the crónica whose discourse models and mirrors progress toward a plural society. It declares the genre's desire to criticize constructively: seek reform; foment and register change; transform minds and media; empower the disenfranchised; modernize the individual and collective consciousness of the local and the global community—to become, in short, a participatory democracy, building from within each person and the anonymous collectivity, upward toward the privileges and profits of power. The uninvented realities of a community galvanized into civil responsibility by an earthquake gave Monsiváis not only the investigative topic of "Los días del terremoto," but also many "found" tropes of further-reaching import: images of destruction and construction, of inside and outside, of descent and ascent (and of dissent and assent). These coalesce through the narrative's expansive powers to multiply meanings. A journalistic report of a natural catastrophe remains useful as historical archive while simultaneously offering a timeless criticism of centralist authoritarianism; a sophisticated meditation, legible from within any society, on the fragility of democracy and who is responsible for its rescue and long-term care; and a moving evocation of the human spirit at its personal best.

reconstruction of the consciousness

Sharp eyes will detect between the crónica's short-term objectives and long-term goals the mediating tactic of renovating the individual consciousness. The contemporary chronicle's politically, socially and morally "compromised" art concentrates the diffuse forces and influences of daily life into dramatic summaries that can be felt, grasped and adopted as tools for self-empowerment. To assert with outrage that the filth and hopelessness of a Tijuana slum is proof that "no tiene fondo la inmoralidad de los gobiernos" [the immorality of government knows no bounds] (Garibay, *Lujo* 36) is to deploy journalism's power of denunciation; to zoom in on a Tijuana outhouse and force us to see into the abyss where human excrement lies covered with government fliers exhorting citizens to hang onto their freedom—that is to send art in to demonstrate with indelible power the unspeakable "filth" of a government that drops its defenseless poor through a figurative black hole (39).

postmodern revisionism

This revisionist spirit situates the contemporary crónica within the postmodern narrative (r)evolution that had been gathering expressive force in Mexico at least since Revueltas's *El luto humano* (1943), Yáñez's *Al filo del agua* (1947), Rulfo's *Pedro Páramo* (1955) and Fuentes's *La región más transparente* (1958). In its varied fiction and nonfiction manifestations, the literary postmodern reflects at large the same fusion of life and art within the same shifting paradigm that I have been describing in relation to the crónica genre's refashioning. Indeed, those paradigmatic shifts are identified with the postmodern episteme and, further, are commonly attached to the year 1968 (Best and Kellner 23).

In the domain of literary power, the politics of interpretation began to demand crossing of borders and obstacles. Among these trespasses, one of the first is "from literature, which is supposed to be subjective and powerless, into those exactly parallel realms, now covered by journalism and the production of information, that employ representation but are supposed to be objective and powerful" (Jameson 113). As key players in the "crisis of representation," which Lyotard configures as a worldwide battle for the control of knowledge, those targeted structures include, especially, presumably objective genres such as journalism and history. While on the one hand the breakup of "grand narratives" such as Marxism and free-market capitalism can prompt the kind of hysterical sense of erasure that Baudrillard's apocalyptic discourse models, it also authorizes assertive genres to cast about for ways to enhance their credibility and, thus, their continued usefulness in society.

Postmodern theory sets aside a space for that experimentation, which includes the necessary deflating of historical discourse's "rhetoric of anti-rhetoric" (White and Manuel, *Theories* 10) and exposure of the deceptive transparency of traditional journalism's mythical objectivity (Lanser 45; Weber, "Artistic" 18–19). The most controversial technique of narrative fiction incorporated by postmodern journalism is, precisely, the autobiographical and metahistoriographical "I" that constructs a blatantly subjective reportage Weber calls "involvedese" (*Literature of Fact* 135). Even more destabilizing in an assertive discourse is the undocumented representation of the thoughts of others. This is the crónica's most adventuresome departure from tradition and the one that demands the greatest reading—and narrating—competence.

Without wanting to rehearse here exhaustive theoretical and critical works on this and other areas where the postmodern's revisionist zeal extends into discourse, it is relevant to note the contemporary Mexican crónica's close association with and implication in the literary postmodern's principal manifestations: the Latin American *boom* and linguistic modes linked to it (most notably, the neobaroque and the carnivalesque), postcolonial writings (especially documentary fictions and testimonio) and discourses of the "new humanities" (particularly cultural studies and popular culture).

the chronicle's form

The ideological uses of art in the crónica are clear and important. However, these are less immediately evident than the values of entertainment and self-expression that lie in plain view on the surface of the chronicle's self-consciously literary discourse. The crónica makes quite clear that it enjoys dressing up its reportage in the fashionable language of narrative. By invoking what has come to be thought of as the fictionalist's privilege,[14] this literary nonfiction genre:

— Informs and comments by means of scene rather than summary;
— Includes dialogue: As a masterful user of "literate orality" (Ong, *Orality*

160) and represented diglossia (Goody 279–80), the chronicle delights in reproducing informal speech-effects;

— Lingers over characterization of witnesses and other figures central to the "story" it is telling;

— Trespasses in autobiographic or self-parodic first person upon the impersonal, third-person terrain where traditional readers feel most comfortable; indeed, it

— Violates at will the quintessential rule of nonfiction by invading what Monsiváis calls the "interioridad ajena" [consciousness of the other] (A ustedes 13), a point of view most scholars still hold as an unmistakable marker of fictional discourse;

— Thrusts its opinions, emotions, criticisms and other personal stances upon the public, engaging the reader in a dialogue that may co-opt, conspire or challenge;

— Impedes closure, propping the text open with intertexts, epigraphs, subtitles and extraneous genres such as popular songs;

— Freely (and sometimes with deliberate hostility) uses other languages, usually without warning, explanation or translation;

— Imbues its discourse with sensorial imagery, metaphoric indirection and the centrifugal allusiveness of symbol;

— Ignores the standard journalistic and historical taboo against irony, sarcasm, satire, puns and outright comedic laughter; and

— Relies on structuration of the discourse to simultaneously withhold and multiply meanings, thus forcing the reader to participate in making the discourse; the chronicle may foreground the narrative constructedness of historical time by presenting events in a paradoxically antichronological order.

crónica vs. essay

Perhaps more than any other of its traits, the crónica's aggressive artistic play can dupe readers into believing or at least wondering whether they are reading a work of fiction. It is also the textual marker that most overtly distinguishes the chronicle from the straightforward essay, history account or news article. A brief textual sample here may help us appreciate differences between essay and chronicle, in particular, for these are the hybrid genres most routinely read as synonymous. We will look at contrasts in discourses of Monsiváis and a contemporary of his, Néstor García Canclini, also known for his studies of culture.

In one sober-toned essay on culture and consumerism in Mexico City today, García Canclini mentions the country's "crecimiento poblacional incontenible" [uncontainable population growth] before citing some numbers (Consumo cultural 47); in a crónica on the same topic, Carlos Monsiváis blends his own voice with that of the average upper middle class citizen who shrieks in horror: "Eramos tantos que ya no había dónde peinarse . . . El Diluvio Poblacional!" [We were so numerous there was no longer room even for a place to comb our hair . . . The Population Flood!] (Escenas 198). On another topic, while García Canclini gravely laments the dearth of methodologically rigorous research on the consumption of popular cultural artifacts (15), Monsiváis inserts himself for long periods in the nightlife of Mexico City's poor urban youth and lets us extract from his I-was-there reportage the theoretical conclusions that his immersion method constructs for our apprehension. Specifically, on a common cultural theme, García Canclini tells us that television soap operas recruit most of their viewers from among poorly educated young women (73); Monsiváis shows the reasons why by dramatizing his documented reportage with scenes of teenaged girls reaching to touch a rock idol backstage or ironing shirts in front of the TV. One of his messages is that statistics alone are a poor transmitter of cultural truths and that Mexican policymakers and powerbrokers must get inside the skin of the poor urban girl, so to speak, in order to truly understand why this sector of Mexico's population clings to and is immobilized by her dependence on melodrama (Escenas 141–60). Further, while García Canclini scrupulously avoids telling us how the citizens he analyzes think and feel, Monsiváis will brazenly step inside the mind of his subjects. He tells us, for example, that the governor of Durango defends his brutal actions against peace-and-freedom demonstrators in his region with "la conciencia tranquila" [a tranquil conscience] (Días 39) and that "sólo lo pone nervioso el esfuerzo de los demás por averiguar de qué modo oculta su nerviosismo" [the only thing that makes him nervous is how hard others try to discover the way he hides his nervousness] (38).

Cronistas are well aware of the difficulties that arise when they cross "literary class lines" in these ways (Wolfe, "New Journalism" 40), but they do it anyway. In spite of and perhaps because of what Monsiváis irreverently dubs "la Enemistad Prestigiosa" [Prestigious Hostility] ("Alabemos" 200), contemporary writers of crónica share the belief of historians of classical antiquity that, by encasing the unmediated real within the precise ambiguity of artistic expression, the experiential world can acquire meanings beyond the contingent import of its events (Shotwell 2). The crónica's verbal play is a defining characteristic and not merely what may be seen as self-indulgence, narcissism or incompetence.

This misplaced aesthetic idea shouts its presence precisely in order to shake the reader up. The chronicle's combined attack on the artistic and social fronts is aimed in part at overturning conventional acceptance of traditional journalism's "objective" language, in part to pit its "very watchable" prose (Weber, "Artistic" 21) against television's audiovisual appeal and, in large part, to begin the macrostrategy of changing society's attitudes with a micro-assault on the individual consciousness of each reader. Neither the immediate nor the long-range effectiveness of this intangible aspect of the crónica's functional form can be objectively assessed, of course. But I believe it reasonable to surmise that Tom Wolfe, for instance, could assume his readers as susceptible to the emotional impact of his writing as *he* was: Nobody entertained Tom Wolfe like Tom Wolfe in the act of creating his trademark brand of pyrotechnical journalism, which amazed and infuriated in collections like *The Kandy-Kolored Tangerine-Flake Streamline Baby* (1963), *The Electric Kool-Aid Acid Test* (1968) and *Radical Chic and Mau-Mauing the Flak Catchers* (1970). Captivated by the entertainment and shock values of the chronicle, our emotions are awakened and we are more likely to perceive within the discourse's referent its less evident but *real* meaning.

humor's critical role

Humor plays a big role in this dynamic process of meaning production. Internally, satire, parody and irony produce their effects in the way I have described the interaction between form and function in the chronicle, in the gap between outward sign and inward meaning. The dualistic chronicle attracts opposites in order to explore the tension between them and, sometimes, to resolve their incongruities by marrying them in unconventional ways. Cronistas are especially fond of vesting humor with this authority.

Irony can be used to disarm resistance to hard truths (Hutcheon, *Irony's Edge* 33–35), for example, while satire, an omnipresent impulse in transitional cultures (Scholes and Kellogg, *Nature* 113), corrodes the herd instinct cultivated by the hegemonic ideology and exposes the incongruity of rhetoric and reality. A raucous street demonstration acted out through the crónica's vividly iconic prose will more readily acquire depth of meaning if it is presented as a satire of the collective refusal to conform to social order that in Mexico may be termed "relajo" or "desmadre" (Portilla 19–25). This form of passive resistance satirizes Authority's solemn calls for orderly conformism, and inspires humorous aspects of the crónica's brand of literary "desmadre," or refusal of formal limits. As Monsiváis puts it: "Mi adolescencia y mi juventud fueron etapas diezmadas, secuestradas por la estupidez, la solemnidad, la pompa de tanto cretino con poder. . . . Me implantó un rencor que debía desahogar. . . . No puedo evitar la impunidad económica, no puedo evitar la impunidad política. . . . Pero el lujo de burlarme, en mi modestísimo grado de acción, de la estupidez del poderoso, eso sí me anima" [My adolescence and youth were decimated, kidnapped, by the stupidity, solemnity and pomp of so many cretins in power . . . . This instilled in me a resentful malice I had to relieve myself of. . . . I cannot prevent economic or political impunity. . . . But the luxury of making fun, my very modest kind of activism, of the idiocy of the powerful—that surely does lift my spirits] (*Debate Feminista* 46–47).

In discourse, satire models the modern, secular, individual and autonomous mindset (Kahler 72), precisely the psycho-intellectual orientation that the cronista wants to foster throughout society. Monsiváis indicates irony as the overriding element of modernity in Salvador Novo's innovative mid-century chronicle; his malicious views of Mexican society in the 1950s, seeking a corresponding skepticism in the reader (Monsiváis, "De la Santa Doctrina" 766), affirms a gap between the narrator and his material that, for example, a preliterate culture cannot tolerate (Ong, *Interfaces* 299). The humor that may be found in a contemporary chronicle challenges us to read against expectations in order to uncover a "real" person behind the authorial narrator, a presence who serves as an additional extratextual assurance that we are being told a truth we can apply to our own lives. Because irony engages our humanity (Booth 33), it figuratively loops an arm around our shoulder, offers a joke to break the ice and then recruits us to help the author take apart and reassemble the world we both inhabit.

From the critical discourses of Bernal Díaz, Cabeza de Vaca, Acosta, Clavijero and Servando Teresa de Mier onward, the Mexican chronicle was developing a modern language of paradox and irreverence to express its generic will to celebrate multiplicity and provisionality, discursive traits today described as postmodern (Seidman 17–18). This admirably pluralist spirit is one of the chronicle's most recognizable assets. To exploit the polysemous force of its voice, however, this genre must cling to its (factual) chronicity and avoid crossing over into (fictional) mimesis. The challenge is to keep its artistic play from "disappearing" the referent, whose perception as an uninvented and verifiable aspect of the experiential world is essential to the crónica's very being.

the reality of the real

As we prepare to identify the markers of factuality that a chronicle *must be seen to possess,* we need to dispense, first, with recent theoretical assertions that no outside referent can exist or be perceived in a text because nothing we may call "reality" can be ascertained in the first place. Semiologists have demonstrated that human consciousness (language) automatically transcodes raw experience into metaphor, metonymy and synecdoche: I think, therefore I fictionalize. The narrative mode has accommodated this instinctive mix of the fictive and the real since the first fabulous histories configured lived experience, history and fictional time into discourse (Ricoeur, *Time* 2: 156).

On the other hand, deconstructionists have extrapolated from this basic effect of language a hyperreal scenario in which all is imitation, nothing is verifiable, truth is nonexistent and life itself is a textual construct. This "exacerbated textocentrism" (Prince, "Narratology" 545) invites amused disregard. Abrams, for example, has observed that, if deconstructionists were right about the disappearance of authors and worlds, no one would be able to perceive, much less understand, the self-eliminating theories they describe (272). In straining to deter the search for meaning, these writers betray their own human eagerness to find it, despite having lapsed into "a negative theology that revered the signifier hovering over the abyss of absence" (Yúdice, "Postmodernity" 22). "It is . . . a theoretical mistake and a practical blunder to collapse the distinction between representation and reality," even while recognizing that "we cannot keep them isolated from one another" (Greenblatt 7). All history is somewhat untrue and all fiction relies on fact, but the absence of polar purities does not weaken reality's claim to being: There really is a real world reflected in the made world of the text (Ricoeur, *Time* 1: 79). Notwithstanding the work of the imagination in configuration, it is *not* a synonym of fiction, nor are attempts to classify a text as fiction or nonfiction "byzantine."

If, however, fictionality and historicity in discourse cannot be detected in language itself, then the determination of a text's fictional or factual status must be based both on how language is used within the text and, at the same time, on data that are external to it (Schmidt 170). There being nothing in words as such to prove that their signifieds represent real-world truths or an invented world, we are compelled to search for markers of veracity in how words are configured and displayed on the page, and how the text is offered to the reader.

It is especially important to read such conventional, or generic, signals correctly in the crónica, for therein lies the possibility of *perceiving* the realness of the real in the discourse (Iser 12). The referent itself must be a phenomenon that pertains to the public domain outside the text. Typically, it will be fresh in the reader's mind for having occurred or attracted public notice in the recent past, a factor of immediacy that ties the chronicle to journalism more than to history. So long as the public can be assumed to recognize it, the journalistic object can be any observed, recorded or documented detail(s) referring to people, objects, events, traditions, customs, fashions, ideologies or states of mind which, as already-known historical, cultural and social facts, will inherently possess an aura of authenticity. If it can be found in a document in the library, seen on television, researched in a book, magazine or newspaper, observed in a museum, public plaza or boxing ring, purchased in a store, and so on, then the referent is fair game to the cronista. Put another way, a putative chronicle cannot, finally, be accepted as a true account if none of the people, places or events can be tied to an independently verifiable—and public—source. "El lector, las más de las veces, *ya ha visto* las noticias importantes y ha padecido el adelanto de la TV; conviene ahora nombrar, ofrecer una conciencia lingüística de lo visto" [Most of the time, the reader *has already seen* important news items and has suffered TV's advance notice; now is the time to name, to offer a verbal consciousness of, what has been seen] (Monsiváis, *A ustedes* 206).

All that I have just said might be applied, as well, to the "undergirding of documentation" that could be found in any novel. The question is: What must a narrator do to preserve perceivable "trace" elements of the experiential referent in an otherwise narrativized discourse? The answer is to be found in two kinds of proofs, one extratextual and one textual. As are other dualities fused in the crónica's discourse, the categories are interdependent although, as we shall see, the latter is finally the more binding.

prior proofs of nonfictional status

Documentation and other sources of independent verification are the most reliable form of proof, and can be perceived both outside and inside the text. Monsiváis may rely on the expandable reference of poetic language to create meanings larger than life, so to speak, but he must finally restrain his discourse with the concreteness of facts such as those gathered for a 1994 crónica—"En Chiapas mueren al año 15.000 personas de enfermedades que son curables, se da el 90% de los casos de tracoma en el país (focalizados en el municipio de Ocosingo), hay un 50% de analfabetismo, un 34% de las comunidades carece de energía eléctrica, hay un médico por cada 1.500 habitantes . . . " [In Chiapas, 15,000 people die every year of curable diseases, ninety percent of the country's trachoma cases occur there (concentrated in the municipality of Ocosingo), the rate of illiteracy is fifty percent, thirty-four percent of towns lack electricity, there is only one doctor for every 1,500 inhabitants . . .] (Monsiváis, "Milenarismos" 179). Related to such material proofs of factualness is a series of extradiscursive structures that predispose the reader to a particular attitude about the work's truth-claims.

A work's pretextual credentials may include the quality of the book itself (hardcover or paperback, cover design, use of color, legibility of the print, quality of the binding and so on); title of the work; name and fame of the author; preface; publisher's blurbs; overt claims to generic status; epigrams, dedications and other optional addenda; any known facts regarding existing or expected public reception of the work, dates and, in the case of the journalistic chronicle, the reputation of the newspaper or journal in which the text appeared, as well as that of the publishing house that may later issue a collection of crónicas. All these factors, which a reader evaluates before reading a single word of the text, create an image of the "implied author," or public narrator (Lanser 138), and affix a provisional judgment regarding the authority of both the facts soon to be consumed and the credibility of their purveyor.

Previously, when I was describing the unique authority with which Carlos Monsiváis speaks in his crónicas (chapter 1), I pointed out that the narrator of a genre offered as assertive is, by convention, understood to be the same as the real-life author who gathered the true information that his textual voice is conveying. If the author, who is believed to be the same as the person speaking in the text, is considered trustworthy and professionally competent, his or her perceived intent is more likely to be accepted up front. An author's promise to tell the truth is not, in fact, sufficient proof of genre, but it does at least impose a prior restraint on "the free play of the *intentio lectoris*" (Collini 9), or what may be construed as an irrelevant or arbitrary imposition of meaning on a text (Lanser 72). Granted, authorial intention is difficult to detect and frequently irrelevant, but the relationship between the producer of the text and his or her reader is important in determination of genre, especially when a text asks its readers to interpret figurative language (Siebenschuh 112–13). The author-reader contract, as an implicit agreement representing a negotiation of "the rights of texts and the rights of their interpreters" (Eco, *Interpretation* 23), provisionally assures us that, if the author says the work is true, we can probably give him the benefit of the doubt.

An example: Before we turn to the first page of the first text of Monsiváis's *Escenas de pudor y liviandad*, we are already predisposed to accept the discourse as true. The book-as-object, although paperback, has a high-quality, glossy four-color cover and, on my copy, boasts of being the eighth edition, an advertisement for the book's durable shelf-life and money-earning power (a not-irrelevant factor). This author's words have been subjected to reader skepticism for many years and have stood the test of time. On the back, the content is listed as "la pequeña historia en el México del siglo XX" [An informal history of Mexico in the twentieth century]; specifically, the publisher's blurb announces that readers will find within the covers personalized biographies of screen icons María Félix and Dolores del Río, right along with accounts of gangs and punks, nightclub dancing and pop singer Juan Gabriel. Everybody knows that all those figures are in the news and in the neighborhood.

The book's introductory note consolidates the impression of immediacy and reality; it promises that the book contains only journalistic accounts already published in reputable mass media and that the referent of these self-defined *crónicas* is public and widely recognized: "El tema común es el espectáculo y sus figuras, . . . la mudanza de costumbres a que obligan la época y la demografía, y la cultura popular urbana" [the common theme is the spectacle and its stars, . . . changes in customs as dictated by history and demographics, and urban popular culture]. The last phrase alludes in condensed form to the multifaceted referent of most contemporary Mexican crónica. Absent other proofs to the contrary, we are quite willing to enter into a hermeneutical contract with Monsiváis and judge what he has published in this book as a true reflection of the same real world we both live in.

Place of publication is of particular importance to the perception of the chronicle's generic specificity. A reader may form different impressions about how to read a text according to whether it appears in a newspaper or news magazine, a literary journal or a book. By convention, we expect news media and academic journals to publish true accounts, even when, in the case here of Mexico, we recall that its newspapers are routinely accused of spreading lies and also that, historically, Mexican newspapers have maintained few distinctions among the opinions, fictions and poetry they publish side by side with facts.[15] Notwithstanding this historico-cultural context, conventional rules of reception at least dispose a reader to cooperate by accepting a text that appears in a newspaper as true unless the discourse or some other knowledge contradicts the implied assertion.

However large or small the measure of factual authority ascribed to a chronicle, as an essentially journalistic genre the work risks losing a measure of its perceived trueness as time stretches between its publication in a newspaper and, for instance, its being selected for an anthology. In the days and weeks immediately following the September 19, 1985, earthquake that rocked Mexico City, news consumers would likely demand relatively few visual or textual proofs of the veracity of the reports about miraculous rescues, scandalous revelations, bureaucratic snafus and civilian self-empowerment. Four years later, however, in a book purporting to contain previously published news accounts, a vague allusion to a woman who dies from a fall down an elevator shaft that was "sólo un hueco enorme y espantoso que . . . estaba siendo reparado" [merely an enormous and dreadful hole that was under repair] (Trejo Fuentes, Crónicas 162) cannot credibly be taken as a reference to damage that a building sustained during that 1985 earthquake; the text provides no evidence of that connection. The proofs lacking in this book for the perceivable realness of the earthquake or any other purported external referent are too many to safeguard a claim of historical truth, as I demonstrate elsewhere ("Descronicamiento" 160–70).

Writers who compile anthologies of their previously published newspaper and magazine articles want to emphasize the literary merits of their writing, but they also want to retain the full authority of its factual base. Those who demonstrate awareness of the inherently unstable nature of that truth-claim will commonly fix the original date of publication to each text in the book to reinforce their prefatory assurance to the reader. For example, when Monsiváis transfers the seven chronicles of his *Entrada libre* from the immediacy of periodical media *(Proceso, Cuadernos Políticos* and *El Cotidiano)* to the permanency of a book, he introduces the title of each account with the date of its writing, thus creating, at least provisionally, a reassuring linkage in the reader's mind between the documentary materials worked into his discourses and the prefatory assurance that they were gathered from lived reality by an author who is also the narrator. Guadalupe Loaeza doubly assures by tagging each of the pieces of her *Las niñas bien* with both the date and the original publishing venue.

the competent reader's role

All of which brings another important extra-linguistic element into play: reader competence. When confronted with a discourse presented as truthful, the reader must be skilled enough to detect available traces of the (verifiable) real in the empirical world (Ricoeur, *Reality* 2). The fictive exists because it crosses the boundary of the real, a shifting line of demarcation anchored to the extratextual world (Iser xv). A competent reader will consult internalized conventions of meaning-making, as well as common sense, experience and other media, to recognize both a line and the fact it has or has not been crossed.

If authorial intent and other extratextual markers are designed to limit the possible readings of a work, the skill and sophistication of the reader will determine which readings come to dominate. I agree with Eco that irrelevant or illegitimate interpretations are possible *(Interpretation* 24–25), and with van Dijk that "a knowledge of aspects of the empirical world and the way these are normally described or referred to in different types of texts is essential for the perception of the specific referential character of literary discourses" (337). A competent reader must take the fictive and factual parts of a crónica in the context of the work-as-a-whole, so that the meaning(s) generated in the space(s) between them can be apprehended. To take a particularly fictional-seeming segment as a proof of the whole text's invented nature is potentially to practice what Eco has called "grasshopper-criticism" *(Interpretation* 75). Instead, an effective reader will keep in mind, as seekers of meaning have done since at least the dawn of biblical exegesis, that "any interpretation given of a certain portion of a text can be accepted if it is confirmed by, and must be rejected if it is challenged by, another portion of the same text" (65).

the role of competent writing

Competent reception is inextricably tied to competent telling. As I made evident earlier, a narrator builds his or her credibility on a complex mix of factors. The first of these is a mastery of the targeted subject matter that ranges far abroad of the immediate object of reportage. If a crónica informs (transmits news), it will be as a secondary goal in service to the primary objective: the "reconstrucción *literaria* de sucesos o figuras" [*literary* reconstruction of events or people] in a textual space wherein "el empeño formal domina sobre las urgencias informativas" [the formal, or aesthetic, goal prevails over informational needs] (Monsiváis, *A ustedes* 13). We rely as much on the sophistication of the discourse's configuration as on the knowledge and critical intelligence of the author. The effective chronicler has a double job description, then. As a master of knowledges, he or she must appear to be a conscientious fact-gatherer, articulate reporter, and judicious commentator. At the same time, as masters of narrative art, cronistas build public confidence in their trustworthiness on the intangible but no less important authorial assets we can call talent and competence.

Every writer who aspires to produce crónica reaches for a literary effect. Not all succeed, either in entertaining their readers or in creating works of a semantic density, profundity and mystery sufficient to warrant study as good literature. Upon a writer's basic narrative skills, however, may hang a text's very potential to retain its "chronicity." As the external markers of genre I have discussed do not in themselves constitute irrefutable proof of a work's truth-quotient, the writer who-would-be-cronista must manipulate the narrative privilege he or she asserts in such a way as to leave the referent visible as an uninvented reality. The final arbiters of this competency are signals imbedded within the discourse. As the bottom-line textual proofs of generic specificity, these will be the subject of the following chapter.

5

voicing a poetics of the contemporary
chronicle of mexico

After documentable facts, the principal marker of the chronicle's nonfictional status depends on skilled manipulation of point of view and voice. Handled effectively, a fictionalizing posture need not cause the referent to drop out of sight; mishandled, a chronicle's focalization may cause the text's truth-claim to fail. This highly technical function is what will, finally, indicate the generic identity of the crónica. Its essential role must be demonstrated before a poetics of the contemporary chronicle of Mexico can be delineated.

As with almost every other identifying trait of the crónica genre, its narrator's most typical point of view is a dualism that seamlessly fuses two apparently incompatible perspectives: a first and a third person. The cronista's voice of choice might be characterized as an "omniscient I" or autobiographical editorialist. In this hybrid posture, the chronicler reveals a traditional preference for the authority that naturally inheres in the testimony of an eyewitness. A reader of classical histories, Bernal Díaz del Castillo certainly understood the advantages of narrating events of the conquest of Mexico as a participating eyewitness. In the first lines of his *Historia verdadera de la conquista de la Nueva España,* he firmly asserts that "lo que en este libro se contiene es muy verdadero, que como testigo de vista me hallé en todas las batallas y reencuentros de guerra; y no son cuentos viejos, ni Historias de Romanos de más de setecientos años, porque a manera de decir, ayer pasó lo que verán en mi historia, y cómo y cuándo, y de qué manera" [what this book contains is wholly true; as an eyewitness I was in all the battles and skirmishes of war. These are not ancient stories, nor Histories of Romans over seven hundred years old; in a manner of speaking, everything you'll find in my history happened just yesterday, and I will tell you how and when and in what way] (1: 66).

Bernal was no theorist but in this statement he gives his readers a rather good description of the generic distinction between the only known truth-genre of his moment—history—and what he had written without yet having a name other than "true history" to give it. Still, he relied on the historiographical demands of his era: that true accounts be told by a well-traveled eyewitness of demonstrable credibility who could, with fact and rhetorical force, give the reader a plausible and enjoyable report of current events (Menéndez Pelayo 1: 673; Nelson 12–27; Ticknor 192).

a reliance on rhetorical excess

The phrase "rhetorical force" is of prime importance for this part of my discussion of genre. First-person narrators of classical and Renaissance histories did not confine themselves strictly to what they could know from an external point of view. Presentation of great political or moral ideas required a rhetorical bravura that permitted the classical writer "a certain sympathetic entering into the thoughts of the supposed speaker, and even a certain realism" (Auerbach 39). From classical antiquity, cronistas have availed themselves of the kind of mimetic omniscience that would come to be called free indirect, substitutionary, multifarious or dual-perspective discourse (Hernadi, "Dual" 32–43) and considered the touchstone of *fictional* writing (Cohn, "Signposts" 785). Neither Bernal nor his historiographical ancestors, however, feared that the authority of their accounts would be diminished by their lapses into rhetorical excess; quite the contrary: "Intelligent historians considered it their duty to make judgments and to speculate as to why things happened as well as to record what had happened" (Nelson 40). Always, in the history of histories, graphic dramatization created a *perceived* aura of credibility that was as important as the naked truth.

107

voicing

a poetics

of the

contemporary

chronicle

of mexico

By the end of the seventeenth century, however, the shifting first-and-third-person point of view was no longer considered acceptable in a documentary discourse. And that is when Bernal's instinctive understanding of the American truth-genre he helped invent began overtly to diverge, first from history, then from essay and news report and, eventually, from short story. Embedded in the heart of the crónica's difference is the still-evident will to exercise the ancient prerogative of choosing to use either the first person or to freely narrate events from the point of view of a historical or journalistic figure.

bernal díaz, a literary role model

On its way to becoming the kind of truth-account that Monsiváis and his contemporaries write, the crónica of Spanish-held America institutionalized the mixed voice. We can compare the way today's chroniclers appropriate the fictionalist's internal point of view to the way ex-soldier Bernal Díaz del Castillo presumes to tell us what his former boss, Hernán Cortés, was thinking. At one point in Bernal's grand chronicle, Cortés and his men are lost in the jungles of (what we now call) Central America. Cortés had just hanged the captured Aztec chief Cuauhtémoc for treason, an indictment Bernal considers was without foundation. He imagines, thus, that guilt put Cortés in a sour mood (2: 278) and, further, that his sore conscience kept him awake, pacing about in a room full of pagan idols. Bernal says Cortés slipped and fell on his head during this insomniac moment, although Cortés said nothing to anyone about the event the next day. Still, the abrasions on his head were visible, and from those and what Bernal knew of Cortés after years of daily contact with the conqueror, the cronista posits an explanation for the injury. He also leaves us with an image of poetic justice meted out by pagan America itself.

In very much this traditional vein, Monsiváis reserves his historic right to insert words in the mouths of his journalistic "characters." This speech-or-thought-assignment is sometimes difficult, sometimes easier, to detect in monsivaisian discourse, but in its intent and effect, his recreation of thought is the recognizable descendant of the many speeches—*arengas*— that Bernal, Clavijero, Acosta and other Indies cronistas put in the mouths of Cortés, Moctezuma and their interpreter Marina: "Nothing could be more unmodern than this device" (Shotwell 175) nor more timelessly current in chronistic discourse.

an historical narrative posture

In its most typical manifestation, the cronista's distinctive I-He stance projects a critical authority that in part fits the classical narrator Scholes and Kellogg call the *histor*. This is an "inquirer" who gathers evidence "to establish himself with the reader as a repository of fact, a tireless investigator and sorter, a sober and impartial judge—a man, in short, of authority, who is entitled not only to present the facts as he has established them but to comment on them, to draw parallels, to moralize, to generalize, to tell the reader what to think and even to suggest what he should do" (*Nature* 265–66). The histor does not simply record or recount but investigates the past "with an eye toward separating out actuality from myth" (242), and in this guise assumes the posture of a disinterested third-person observer. It is a posture only, however. Classical narrators routinely placed their more covert persona, the eyewitness and participant, in the background, but did not entirely erase that real-world presence from the discourse (243).

Taken together, the ancient histor's "discreet" first-person fact-gatherer and his less discreet third-person interpreter have remained fused throughout the evolution of the chronicle. Of the two, the editorializing and selectively omniscient third person is most often in apparent charge of the telling, but the autobiographical witness is the power behind the throne. The author-narrator's own voice and detectable presence are the touchstone that the genre clings to at the last if a work's recreated world seems in danger of detaching itself from its real-life origin. The contemporary crónica may stray out of sight of its "I" but cannot sever its perceptible link to a reality outside the work. The cronista is the critical consciousness whom readers must be able to see at its work of witnessing while it models for them an exemplary mode of participatory—and self-critical—citizenship.

Examples of this *histor*-ic posture are numberless in Monsiváis's decades of publications. I select one at random to illustrate how the mixed first-and-third point of view works in its most typical—i.e., critical—style. As the text we are seeing opens, we perceive Monsiváis in the public space of a stadium, witnessing a boxing match. A temperate editorialist voice concentrates in the beginning on establishing the context and filling it with facts. This narrative persona notes the waving flags, (then) president Carlos Salinas de Gortari's ostentatious photo-ops with the national boxing champ (*Rituales* 25) and dancers bedecked with neo-Mayan masks cavorting around a fake pyramid. Now the third-person narrator begins to interweave commentary in a notably less objective tone. The prehispanic accessories, apparently "inscritos en nuestro código genérico" [inscribed in our genetic code] are hugely enlarged on a video screen to project a version of Mexico that would have existed "si los aztecas hubiesen conseguido patrocinadores" [if the Aztecs had had sponsors] (26). The laser video system is brand new and Mexican promoters are proud to show off the tricks it can perform: "Seamos posmodernos, ahora que hay modo" [Let's be postmodern, now that we can] (26). While the newly acquired technology animates distorted recollections of Aztec gods, the ironic perspective of the meaning-making histor bursts forth in the first-person voice he has been holding in reserve:

109

voicing

a poetics

of the

contemporary

chronicle

of mexico

> Creo hallarme, felizmente, en la Convención Cósmica de Concheros. Algo de pronto, tal vez el ring, me recuerda la existencia del box. . . . Al cabo de dos horas ya nada significó lo que significa, ni las rechiflas, ni los aplausos (inaudibles), ni la Ola (calistenia de masas), ni el boxeo. Aquí no se viene a encumbrar al Famoso [Julio César Chávez], ya lo está en exceso, se viene a reconocerse en algún nivel del éxito. Muy probablemente por eso han pagado lo que han pagado los de Tepito y La Lagunilla y La Merced.[1] (27)

> [I seem to have beamed myself up to the Cosmic Convention of Conch Blowers. Something, perhaps the ring, suddenly reminds me that I'm in fact at a boxing match. . . . Two hours later, nothing means what it had, neither the jeering nor the (inaudible) applause, nor the Wave (calisthenics for the masses), nor boxing itself. No one comes here to exalt the Man of the Hour, because he already is exalted, to excess. You come to know yourself at some level of success. Quite likely, that is why patrons from Tepito and Lagunilla and Merced have paid what it cost them to get in.]

In the first four pages of this crónica (*Rituales* 24–30), the author has flashed a series of self-images for the reader's entertainment, edification and recruitment: The subtle identification of author and reader links the interchange of first and third person projections, at an almost subconscious level, to descriptions of the flashing nationalistic images on the stadium screen. The metanarrative collage finally produces a realization in the reader that this text is only apparently about the history of boxing and a paradigmatic match. It is really about poverty and progress out of it in Mexico. In the long series Monsiváis has given us in his career, it is one more entertainingly graphic dramatization of the uneven entrance into modernity that has cast Mexico before its time into a postmodernity figured as depthless dots on a giant television screen. Homer and Herodotus echo within the modern wit, genius and critical acumen of Monsiváis, a narrator whose old-new society calls forth and amplifies his own inimitable voice.

narrative ventriloquism

The traditional partnership of first and third persons can sometimes be trickier to sort out. The chronicler may violate conventional rules that call for an "enunciado de vanguardia" [vanguard statement] (Bakhtin, *Estética* 280): some kind of verbal or typographical warning to the reader that one speaker is about to cede the floor to another. Monsiváis is especially fond of letting his third-person narrator fall silent and, without warning to either us or his target, sneaking us with him inside the mind of a character. Naturally, we may easily be tricked into thinking this "I" belongs to Monsiváis, when in fact the author is dramatizing an instance of hybridized discourse: the dialogic simultaneity of heteroglossia, or narrative ventriloquism. It takes a vigilant reader to see the author's lips moving when he throws his voice.

An example: The policeman standing guard at the foot of a rock-concert stage is there to keep fans from climbing up to accost Gloria Trevi but she seems unappreciative. Everybody is laughing at him. Up to now, the narrative voice is recognizably Monsiváis's third-person histor. But between the period ending one sentence and the first word of the next statement, Monsiváis seamlessly switches to free indirect discourse to escort us inside the mind of the policeman: "Él es un representante del orden, caramba. ¿Debió decir 'caramba' o 'carajo'? Pero es que estos jovencitos . . . " [He's a representative of the law, damn it. Should he say "darn it" or "hell"? It's just that these kids today . . .] (*Rituales* 176) Like a submarine commander with his eye to the periscope, Monsiváis zeroes in on the consciousness of his target and silently launches a verbal torpedo. The victim has no warning that a bomb is about to detonate *inside* his own subjectivity; simultaneously, the surprised reader detects a sharp burst of humor exploding in the ironic gap between incompatible registers of (Monsiváis's) "high" and (the target's) "low" speech.[2]

111

voicing

a poetics

of the

contemporary

chronicle

of mexico

The sneak-attack strategy best serves Monsiváis's ideological goals when he can let the target of his criticism appear to destroy itself because of its own structural defects. We can see this at work in his coverage of meetings between city officials and young women of the poorest barrios who are just learning how to turn their simple demands for water, electricity and schools into lasting political power. One moment we are enjoying, with Monsiváis's histor, the delicious triumph of change: "¡Ah, el griterío de los desfiles, la impresión nítida de que el gobierno cedería, que ya estaba a punto de instalarse el nuevo poder urbano!" [Ah, the screaming parades, the precise sense that government would be giving up, that a new urban power was on the verge of taking over!] (*Entrada* 243). In the next moment, we have been swept into a long interval of free indirect discourse that situates us without warning inside the thoughts of the city delegate assigned to catch flak from these insistent women:

¿Qué más quieren? Les ha concedido (parcialmente) la titulación, les ha llevado agua (la suficiente), ha negociado con los de las combis para que no cometan tantos abusos y amplíen sus horas de servicio. ¿Qué más quieren? Es una pesadilla, no dejan de exigir, de hacerle mítines enfrente de su ventana. . . . Esos jovencitos, y ahora esas jovencitas tan llenos de datos, y tan enfáticos. . . . Ni modo. Se le ordenó escucharlos con paciencia y negociar, porque en tiempos de calma los apaciguados salen más baratos que los golpeados. (243)

[What more do they want? He has conceded (partially) the land titles, he's brought them (just enough) water, he's negotiated with the gypsy taxis so they don't commit quite as many abuses and will expand their hours of service. What else can they want? This is a nightmare. They never stop demanding, holding rallies in front of his window. . . . Those young men, and now these young women so full of facts and so adamant. . . . Well, never mind. They told him to listen patiently and negotiate, because in times of calm, those you pacify end up costing less than those you beat up.]

We note the self-serving hypocrisy of an authoritarianism that has not yet internalized the changes in attitude that external forces are pressing on it.

We see that *only* the patient insistence of citizens who won't go away and leave the government in peace will prevent a return to violent suppression of dissent. Even as we capture this covert message, however, we are chuckling with Monsiváis, who is humane enough to recognize in the hapless functionary one more victim of the state.

We may also hear an echo of Wolfe's chronicle "Mau-Mauing the Flak Catchers" on the way African Americans first learned political uses of their anger, during the Civil Rights era in the United States:

> When black people first started using the confrontation tactic, they made a secret discovery. There was an extra dividend to this tactic. . . . It wasn't just that you registered your protest and showed the white man that you meant business and weakened his resolve to keep up the walls of oppression. It wasn't just that you got poverty money and influence. There was something sweet that happened right there on the spot. You made the white man quake. You brought *fear* into his face.[3] (*Radical* 119)

The party flunky being "mau-maued" by the women in Monsiváis's crónica grows desperate: "Qué, ¿esto no se acaba nunca? . . . Eso es lo peor, la gente es inagotable" [What?! Will this never end? And the worst part is that people keep coming in an endless stream] (244). Satisfied to have fully revealed the pain of change as it is perceived from inside the System, Monsiváis slips out of the multifarious mode and returns to his own editorialist third person. The narrative adventurism is not mere malicious jest. It illustrates one of Monsiváis's master themes: that social justice and pluralist politics are first a state of mind. The individual consciousness is his narrator's ultimate target. Monsiváis stretches the traditional histor's narrative freedoms in order to show that the long-term goal of democratization results from tactical negotiations that take place between individuals of unlike politics but of like-minded devotion to their own immediate needs and wants.

overt first-person narrators

The histor's muted first-person voice is the most commonly heard, but not the only, among the several "I's" of the literary journalist. As we look at other chronistic variants, we can speak of *overt* and *covert* first-person narrators. Common on the overt side are (1) Menippean Satire's wise fool and common variants, narrators who may pretend to be unreliable, hostile or self-denigrating (parodic); (2) the metafictional metahistoriographical narrator, who may take the form of any of the previously mentioned first persons, and (3) the frankly autobiographical voice. All these points of view have been amply documented as distinctive features of postmodernist literature globally and of Latin America's boom and postboom narrative, both of its avowed fiction and of those texts denominated nonfiction, documentary or testimonial.[4]

In broad terms, we may think of the histor's point of view as "outside" the discourse that is created and then offered as an object to be consumed by a discerning reader. Implicit in the other half of the histor's mixed being, however, is the downplayed "I" that is always poised to break from behind the scenes—and make a scene. This overt voice belongs to a much more in-your-face persona who may choose not only to speak from inside the discourse but to behave so scandalously that we are dragged in there with him. We'll have to chase down meanings right alongside an "I" who challenges our expectations for success at every turn.

carnival's wise fool

This is the Wise Fool of the seriocomic genre called Menippean Satire, itself a "subgenre" of the umbrella concept of "carnival" (Bakhtin, *Problems* 110–20, 316). We can see Menippean Satire in the carnivalized cronista's taste for theatrics, the eccentric, the scandalous, the intertextual and the multifarious hybridity that can be detected in bilingualism, insertion of extraneous genres, clashing verbal registers and so on. Students of the contemporary chronicle of Mexico will recognize, as well, carnival's broader theoretical attributes, all of them implicit or explicit in the crónica's Wise Fool. As a sociological detective on the trail of change, this chronistic "I" incarnates: dualities, androgyny, unity, inversion, reversal, renewal, decay, transgression, ambivalence, heteroglossia, hybridity, polyphony, mask, festival, spectacle, paradox, polemic, "popular laughter," parody,

113

voicing
a poetics
of the
contemporary
chronicle
of mexico

irony, travesty, enigma, play, ritual, multiplicity, orality, circularity, aperture, abundance, incompleteness, contest, emancipation, truth-seeking, rebellion, antiauthoritarianism, democracy and utopia (Bakhtin, *Rabelais*).

The first piece of Monsiváis's first collection, *Días de guardar* (1970), features the exuberantly carnivalized narrator of "5 de enero de 1969: Con címbalos de júbilo" (20–27). The report's action takes place on the margins of Mexican geopolitical space, in the tourist-dominated port of Acapulco, and inside the Aquarius Theater, "un jacalón restaurado" [a remodeled hovel] (20) that eventually comes to represent a ramshackle Mexican society getting itself remodeled along U.S. lines. Monsiváis is in this symbolic space to observe Mexicans watching the debut of the scandalous U.S. musical *Hair,* whose title song touts the (New) Age of Aquarius. The setting is perfect for Monsiváis's "fool" of a journalist, who borrows rhetorical props from Carnival to stage a dual drama. The first represents the globalized clash between a nakedly postmodern U.S. mindset and the still largely feudal mentality of the Mexican middle class; the secondary plot concerns a national clash, only months after a rebellious sector of the populace confronted Mexican rulers in Tlatelolco Square, between those who can afford tickets to see radical new art in the flesh, and those outside who wave placards begging the well-to-do not to forget October 2, 1968.

Hair's self-conscious nudity and obscenity are themselves an emblem of the grotesque lower-body materialism of carnival; Monsiváis's treatment of the topic mirrors that indecorous shock effect. First, he verbally undresses theater patrons with a parodic commentary on fashion that bares a department-store sensibility hidden under Pucci gowns (22); then he converts the private, closed-loop experience of reading into a scandalous spectacle with anti-alphabetic techniques that include an ample use of white space and ellipses. In those discursive fissures he inserts a meaningless chant that turns the bakhtinian concept of grotesque realism's "lower material bodily functions" into an audiovisual trope: "FUCK-FUCK-FUCK-FUCK . . . " (23). At this moment and throughout the crónica, the narrator-as-master-of-ceremonies subjects us to the constant movement and swirling reversals of carnival's liminal terrain. We sense that we are in the middle of portentous change, but we cannot fix its meaning. The Fool has left us between signifieds with an exit line for theater patrons who wonder about airline departure times for Miami (27).

the unreliable witness

Sometimes the satirist assumes a pose of unreliability, another of the cronista's overt first persons. In the chronicle we have just seen, Monsiváis deliberately presents himself as ignorant so that he can slip his insights past the defenses of a reader who belongs, with him and the other targets of his parody, to a middle class that is just beginning to take baby steps into true modernity: "El reportero—o sea, quien esto escribe y que así se sueña—lamenta muchísimo su ignorancia de la Buena Sociedad Mexicana y del Jet Set, lo que provoca su indiferencia ante los Ilustres Apellidos congregados y lo que le impulsa a revisar . . . la variada falta de imaginación que organiza la vestimenta" [The reporter—that is, he who writes this and imagines himself to be a reporter—greatly laments his ignorance of Good Mexican Society and the Jet Set, which fact explains his apparent indifference to the Illustrious Names gathered here and which moves him to survey . . . the diverse lack of imagination that has assembled their outfits] (21). He aims his cruel "ignorance" toward the stage, as well. We have to laugh at his description of the stilted way *Hair*'s actors move "en ánimo estatuario, morosamente" [morosely, in statuary spirit], like pillars of salt (23): "Al cabo de cinco minutos, ya incluso el reportero (tan preocupado por su crónica que no capta nada de lo que ve) se ha percatado de que *no* contempla una obra tradicional" [After five minutes, even the reporter (so busy with his crónica that he grasps nothing he sees) has noticed that this is not a traditional theater piece].

By stripping himself of his credentials as a gatherer of reliable information, Monsiváis disrobes fixed notions of knowledge and perception. He puts himself, right next to the reader, on a metatheatrical stage where both will rehearse, like Hamlet, a way to emerge from layers of deception to arrive at a reliable understanding of the play *(Hair)* within the comedy (the Jet Set in Acapulco) within the tragedy (Tlatelolco 1968).

a "dunce" as decoy

Another "unreliable" narrator among the overt "I's" is the one who beats up on him or herself. Because the posture of self-parody usually provokes a laugh, readers are cajoled into self-criticism through a kind of positive psychology. A good cronista is almost inevitably going to be asking readers to swallow hard truths, probably about people they can iden-

115

voicing
a poetics
of the
contemporary
chronicle
of mexico

tify with, and to shoulder unpleasant responsibilities. An example: Elena Poniatowska, who wants us to help the poor of Mexico City, will sometimes disarm her implicit criticism of our self-centeredness by modeling the ridicule we deserve. Having elsewhere characterized herself as a writer who keeps safe in "la tranquilidad de mi casota bien burguesota a la cual no le falta nada" [the peace and quiet of my roomy, super-bourgeois house, where nothing is lacking] (*Fuerte* 165), she lets us see her as a careless employer who forgets to pay the Indian girl who works as her maid (15). The self-parody compresses a vast discourse about the casual cruelty suffered by domestic servants.

Similarly, Monsiváis is more likely to persuade with humor than with overt anger. He may choose to appear as a biblical prophet crying in the wilderness about soccer fans who pay no attention to what he has preached at them "repetidas veces desde mi atalaya editorial" [time after time from my editorial pulpit] (*Entrada* 222). Even when he grows desperate to make his readers heed his warnings against looking for self-esteem in an athletic team's win-loss record, he directs his hectoring tone metachronistically back at himself: "Os lo advertí, daos tiempo y leed mis sesudas reflexiones. No digáis que en esto (como en todo) no fui intelectual orgánico de la prevención apocalíptica" [I warned you, take the time to read my wise thoughts. Don't say that in this (as in everything) I was not an organic intellectual dedicated to the prevention of apocalypse] (222).

Even had his readers—of whom some may in fact be soccer fans—heeded his call, they would just as likely have rejected the advice he offers in his "croniquitas" [insignificant little articles] (*Escenas* 199) and bashed him besides for being a "Prejuiciado Autor" [Prejudiced Author] (*Amor* 204). He does not hold this against his readers, for he is the first to recognize his deficiencies. From his first collection of chronicles, Carlos Monsiváis has observed himself with as much critical rigor as he has his fellow citizens. His frequent self-parody, sometimes merely a one-line chuckle slipped between parentheses, helps keep him honest. His assessment of the people he observes is almost always critical, and his self-mocking humility reminds him and us together that he is as fallible as we are.

the reporter at work

Implicit in all of the overt first-person narrators we have been listening to is the metafictional stance, which among nonfiction authors

takes the form principally of those who allow us to see them at work, gathering, evaluating and fitting facts together in words. Not infrequently, we are allowed to witness interviewees and other characters reacting to the journalist, as we are in a recent chronicle by Monsiváis on the impact of Madonna on Mexico; a man approaches him: "Si usted quiere mi testimonio se lo doy con gusto, aunque no trae grabadora ni se le ven deseos de entrevistarme. Pero . . . usted es periodista y debe tener, aunque escondido, algún amor a la verdad" [If you want my opinion, I will gladly give it to you, even though I see you have no tape recorder nor any apparent desire to interview me. But you're a journalist and you ought to own, though you hide it, some love of truth] (*Rituales* 197–98).

117

voicing

a poetics

of the

contemporary

chronicle

of mexico

Theoretically, the reader can critically assume his or her own discrete relationship to this process when able to observe interchanges between the fact-gatherer out in the field and then watch over the writer's shoulder to see how those bits of reality are sorted and ordered on the page. Ultimately, the metafictional trope demonstrates that the significance of the described objects depends upon our individual perception of them and, because the narrator-character also reveals much of his own personality, the reader can identify precisely the consciousness which has shaped the experience within the text. We can then choose whether to agree. In the case of the crónica, the metajournalistic trope of the Reporter at Work strengthens the referent's perceived realness.

From the beginning of his career, Carlos Monsiváis has installed his Reporter at Work in countless crónicas. In 1968, crushed among the hysterical fans of Raphael, we meet his Teórico Súbito, the "wise fool" who is not merely a reporter but a critic, an on-the-spot analyst who turns cultural trivia-as-it-happens into understandings we can hang onto: "Y entonces el Teórico Súbito explicaba el hecho como consecuencia de la realidad del pueblo de México: oír a Raphael gratis era vengarse o recobrarse del cerco de una burguesía exclusivista" [And then the Instant Analyst explained the fact as a consequence of Mexican reality: to hear Raphael for free was to avenge oneself or somehow slip past the guard of an exclusivist bourgeoisie] (*Días* 47). In another text, a year after one Mexican president sponsored the massacre of Tlatelolco, Monsiváis's notably Maileresque reporter takes us to a convention where everyone present in the (ironically appropriate) Sports Arena will pretend that the next president has to campaign to win.[5] The cronista's first words in the resulting report (*Días* 307–20) are: "'Me

llamo Carlos Monsiváis. No pertenezco a ningún partido político.' En el trayecto hacia el Palacio de los Deportes perfecciono y modulo la frase: 'Me llamo Carlos Monsiváis. No . . . ' Ni afirmo mi identidad ni intento conmover a un próximo jurado popular. Inicio la redacción ideal de una crónica; necesito convencerme de que la escribiré" ["My name is Carlos Monsiváis. I do not belong to a political party." On the way to the Sports Palace I test and tighten the phrase: "My name is Carlos Monsiváis. I don't . . . " I neither affirm my identity nor try to influence public opinion. I begin wording a model crónica; I have to convince myself that I will in fact write it] (307).

We share the metajournalist's angst as he struggles to reconcile the irreality of the real-world event he will observe with the reality of its historical context (Tlatelolco, 1521, 1968). By juxtaposing, at the outset, a pair of naked facts he presumably would not falsify—his name is Carlos Monsiváis and he is politically independent of the power structure—to the swirl of events that will not be facts until he reports them, he emphasizes the constructed nature of *all* facts, including the seemingly irrefutable. He forewarns us that even if he decides to write this report, and in it honestly convey events he observes with his own eyes, he will not necessarily have told the reader the truth, for in 1969, Mexico's entire "democratic" process is the mask of an empty ritual: "Favor de agitar la banderita cuando llegue el Lic. Echeverría y mantener tres minutos el aplauso" [Please wave your little flags when Mr. Echeverría arrives and maintain your applause for three minutes] (310). In the first two years after his 1970 "election," president Luis Echeverría will vigorously talk about democratic reform; in June 1971 paramilitary goons working for the government will wound and kill student demonstrators. Sadly, Monsiváis already "knows" this as he covers the election convention but, as his metahistoriographical persona tells us: "Un cronista honesto revisa y comprueba todos sus prejuicios" [An honest cronista tests and confirms all his prejudices] (309). He will observe and listen, but he will not go along just because someone in the power structure tells him to wave a little flag.

the frankly autobiographical "i"

I have said that Monsiváis and other effective chroniclers exploit the power of fact in nonfiction to model for readers an exemplary stance to take in the face of society's challenges. The metadiscursive narrative aids in this goal by replacing traditional notions of Truth with a new paradigm of trustworthiness: that of the sincere, moral, fallible "I" engaging readers, asking them to judge whether an opinion offered "desde mi punto de vista" [from my point of view] (Monsiváis, *Entrada* 254) is worth sharing and, ultimately, being acted upon in public spaces. To display the discerning individual consciousness, cronistas will sometimes entrust readers with frankly autobiographical revelations. In tone, this overt first-person narrative posture may range from the matter-of-fact confidence to the angst-ridden confessional.

119

voicing
a poetics
of the
contemporary
chronicle
of mexico

We detect several ironic effects, for example, in Guadalupe Loaeza's autobiographical recreation of a visit to a bookseller in the flea market. She exploits traditional notions about macho men and weak women in order to give her persona a "masculine" composure that will help her beat down the price of a magazine set. The inspired bargaining that comprises the entire discourse of "Un domingo en La Lagunilla" (29–31) serves as pretext for the charming retrospective we can review with Loaeza as the bookseller tempts her with hints about the contents of the magazine. Between Mr. Olmedo's arguments and her autobiographical rejoinders, we extract an understanding of the negotiations that a place like La Lagunilla institutionalizes between upper and lower classes. In this exchange, the monied class builds its cultural products with raw materials that the working class provides.

Rarely used among the many first-person postures available to any chronicler, the autobiographical pose is especially hard to detect in Carlos Monsiváis's works. Even if he concedes a glancing view of his own true self, he makes us work hard to coax it from hiding. That process of persuasion turns the moving personal drama of "Yo y mis amigos" [I and My Friends] (*Días* 65–77) into a compelling public affirmation. It begins with a challenging mystery: Who is the speaker who opens the text with the assertion, "Yo real, yo inevitable, yo convencional" [real I, inevitable I, conventional I] and who is it that responds, "Yo y mis amigos"? Who ends this enigmatic opening exchange with the announcement: "Y lo que sigue es una vasta, arrogante confesión de inmadurez" [And what follows is a vast, arrogant confession of immaturity] (65)? Already, the discourse demands re-reading, and it will require strict vigilance throughout.

In particular, it demands our willingness to accept the semantic values invested in typographical signifiers such as capital letters, italics, paragraph insets, parentheses, white spaces, punctuation marks and the strange black hand with a pointing finger. Eventually we realize that this icon signs a warning: *Reader, this is now the Lying Nationalistic Government System speaking; this is the brute ideology that killed hundreds of innocent citizens at Tlatelolco and told you to believe it was the fault of outside agitators.* It also functions as a sign that the first-person consciousness in the discourse is about to let the Opposition speak. By juxtaposing the Otherness of State rhetoric with his Self, our narrator's individuality coalesces.

We can now see that the enigmatic opening had been a dialogue between "others" arguing inside the confused consciousness of Carlos Monsiváis, who is here dramatizing his state of mind (after the divisive shock of October 2, 1968) as a split personality. To find a new unity of thought, the autobiographical "I" of Monsiváis consciously seeks alignment (through intertexts) with the thinking of great writers and the wisdom of popular tradition to be found in songs, as other sources of *perspective*. Bolstered with the strength of these external "others," the narrator can begin answering with confidence when the Finger-Pointing Hand of State Ideology interpellates him. He grows in maturity and confidence, speaks now as "Yo teórico, yo doctrinario" [theoretical I, doctrinaire I] to reject Hegemony's invitations to conform (71); as "Yo testigo, yo aliado silencioso" [Witnessing I, I the silent ally] when inspired by the courageous citizens who risked death to weld idea to action in Tlatelolco Square (72); and as "yo que recapitula" [I who recapitulate] when he recalls his life before 1968 (74). Finally, he can claim as independently his the truth that "después de una desgracia injusta, irreparable, impune como la matanza de Tlatelolco, las cosas no vuelven a su lugar. La certidumbre desaparece" [after an unjust, unfixable and unpunished tragedy such as the massacre of Tlatelolco, things don't return to their place. Certainty disappears] (76).

Self-pity is tempting, but he rejects it, together with fear and defeatism: "La autocompasión nos despoja de la libertad penosamente adquirida; el miedo nos obliga a prescindir de la inteligencia; el escepticismo se confunde con el cinismo que se mezcla con el abandono que se contamina de la indiferencia que se entrevera con el letargo" [Self-pity robs us of a freedom painfully obtained; fear obliges us to do away with intelligence; skepticism is confused with cynicism which becomes one with giving up which becomes tainted with indifference which slides into lethargy] (76). What can "yo y mis amigos en 1969" (76) do in light of these realizations? The answer comes clearly from an author and narrator who have gotten their act together: Be optimistic and make common cause with those who languish in prison for their courageous resistance to the blandishments of "National Unity" (76–77).

121

voicing

a poetics

of the

contemporary

chronicle

of mexico

From the confession of credulity it projects at the start to the optimism born of disillusionment that it reveals at the end, "Yo y mis amigos" is the textual mirror image of the private-to-public progression that for Monsiváis is the way a member of plural society should examine her or his conscience before inserting it into the body politic. When we recognize that Gramsci's lectures on the relations between people and power form part of the way Monsiváis's own "I" examined his position in post-Tlatelolco Mexico (76), we can see "Yo y mis amigos" as the dramatization of a process by which the model citizen negotiates a measure of autonomy in a nationalistic medium. "¿Por qué anteponer el yo a las situaciones? ¿Por qué enfatizar el imposible egocentrismo?" [Why put the "I" before circumstances? Why emphasize an impossible egocentrism?] he began by asking (65). Now he answers: Because democracy "happens" one changed mind at a time; this is how I did it, and because I am now different, my society will also change. If enough of us wrestle like this with our consciences, Tlatelolco will never happen again.

covert first-person narrators

Despite initial doubts about the realness of the "I" who inaugurates "Yo y mis amigos," we soon firm up a perception that Carlos Monsiváis is that first-person narrator. Sometimes, however, the chronicler employs a more *covert* first person, seriously challenging the reader to locate the touchstone of an authorial "I" that connects textual assertions to realities in the world. What happens when the first-person narrator is so covert that we cannot count on it to help us perceive that we are reading a factual account? Let us consider a contrasting pair of texts, keeping in mind that we have now arrived at a juncture where the individual reader's own competencies and experiences gain significant weight as "proofs." I will compare works of approximately the same length by the same author, Carlos Monsiváis. The first, "Dancing: el secreto está en la mano izquierda" (*Escenas* 137–40), carries a tagline saying it was written and/or first published in 1982 and is included in the eighth edition of his *Escenas de pudor y liviandad*. I classify it as crónica. The second, "La hora de codearse con lo más granado:

la pareja que leía ¡*Hola!*" (*Rituales* 178–81), is not dated and appears in the 1995 collection, *Los rituales del caos*. I read it as fiction.

perceiving the real

"Dancing: el secreto está en la mano izquierda" is one of seven pieces in *Escenas* about dance venues and styles—25 percent of the book's twenty-eight texts, which overall reveal the depth of Monsiváis's knowledge of this cultural form. Chronologically, "El secreto" is last in the series of seven dance reports, the others being dated between 1975 and 1978. In the book's organization, it is third in the series and, thus, physically in the midst of six other compositions on dancing whose manipulation of the cronista's mixed voice leaves (in me, at least) no doubt as to their classification as crónica. In each of those other texts, we can easily perceive the author-narrator in the club, observing, eavesdropping on or interviewing patrons. I read "El secreto" in this material context.

Narration is divided among four autobiographical first persons who are explaining their presence in a dance club to a silently listening "you" who says nothing to interrupt. This dialogic presence is easily detected in such clues as one interlocutor's "Mira Mano" [Look, Man] (137) and another's "Fíjate en otra cosa" [Consider this as well . . .] (138). Within the material context I described above, one could quite readily imagine the listener to be Monsiváis-the-reporter who has gathered facts for the other dance texts in the collection. This thought encourages us to look for more clues that could support our desire to believe in the story's true status.

No clue to the identity, real or fictive, of the speakers is to be found in the usual overt functions of discourse. They are distinguished only by the Roman numerals I, II, III, and IV. Their physical appearance is not described but, if the four text divisions in fact represent four distinct voices, we do have the occasional adjective to tell us that three are male and the other probably is (138). We are also led to believe they are all at least as young as the last speaker, who says he is twenty-six (140). No aspect of the material space surrounding these dialogic monologues is evident, but we presume from the title and a few textual hints that all four are engaged in conversation with a curious visitor to a dance salon in one of Mexico City's working-class neighborhoods, perhaps in Colonia Guerrero, Colonia Malinche or Tepito ("que es un barrio que ha tenido influencia en el modo de bailar") [a neighborhood that has had an impact on dance styles] (138). We imagine them poor and perhaps no strangers to hunger. When the last speaker tells us that, although his sister claims not to like dancing, he thinks she stays away because she is so "desnutrida [que] apenas consigue moverse, y en el tumulto no se nota" [undernourished she can barely move, and she gets lost in the commotion] (139), our hearts crack a little.

123
voicing
a poetics
of the
contemporary
chronicle
of mexico

None of the speakers reveals a trace of self-pity or ideology. Their voices seem to float in air, disconnected from devastating absences outside the dance hall: work, food, validation. Inside is another world: "A los salones y a las fiestas se va a vivir la juventud" [You go to dance halls and parties to enjoy your youth] (139). Number IV cheerfully confesses: "Pepe, un cuate mío, es campeón de mambo. Bueno, era. . . . Se fracturó una pierna, y lleva cuatro meses sin bailar. . . . Ora no te digo que los dancings siempre sean divertidos. Hay veces que te aburres pero te aguantas. Yo falto muy pocas veces. ¿En dónde la pasaría mejor? Cuando tienes una buena pareja, es el cielo" [Pepe, a pal of mine, is a champ at the mambo. Or he *was*. . . . He broke his leg and he hasn't danced for four months. . . . I'm not saying that every night out dancing is fun. Sometimes you get bored. But you hang in there. I almost never miss it. When you've got a good partner, it's heaven] (139).

Each in turn individualizes himself to his "confessor," the silent "you" whom they entrust with their vulnerability. One loves the "bien sexy bailar" [really sexy dancing] of the tropical *danzón*. Another, who reveals himself to be an expert, explains how he intuitively analyzed the internal logic of the dance in order to locate its existential center before perfecting the techniques needed to release its psychic and physical energies: "Bailar no es demostrar condición física, sino elegancia, algo así como entrarle al frenesí sin despeinarte" [Dancing isn't about physical prowess but elegance, kind of like going wild without messing up your hair] (139). This articulate young man also explains, with persuasive critical authority and admirable concision, a material meaning of "national"—Cubans shake from the hips up while Mexicans shake from the waist down without moving their shoulders (139)—and of "individuality"—the opposite of "estos payasos que dizque muy modernos, y muy videoclip" [these clowns who think they're so with it, so MTV] (139). The voice positioned last in the series reverberates beyond the text. He says he prefers traditional dances because they require discipline, a lot of work and a spiritual connection between body and soul. They also give him a chance to stand out in a crowd: "A mí lo que me gusta es saber si la estoy haciendo o no, despacito, sin prisas, aunque nadie me pele. . . . Yo

no soy payaso ni farolón pero me gusta que se den cuenta de que la muevo, de que no en balde he ensayado y le he metido ganas" [What I like is to be aware that I'm performing well, take it slow, even when nobody's paying me particular attention . . . I'm no clown or show-off but I do like people to see that I have moves, that I haven't been practicing in vain and that I'm putting my best into it] (140).

These four personal revelations achieve a dual significance. First, they fulfill the journalist's goal of allowing "los sectores tradicionalmente proscritos y silenciados" [traditionally proscribed and silenced groups] (Monsiváis, *A ustedes* 76) to speak, here in a prestigious space that amplifies their voices. Each of the dancers claims a unique personality and projects a complex inner life and critical faculty. At the same time, their conscious individualization is paradoxically juxtaposed with the text's self-consciously generic representation of segments I, II, III and IV. After we learn to respect and sympathize with individuals we might ordinarily ignore or condemn, we are thus encouraged to view them as metonyms of a vast mass of malnourished Mexican people who choose, rather than to go home each day "rendido y golpeado" [beat and beaten] (139), to create an alternative to the misery of their lot in society, finding "heaven" and an earthly validation.

Now I add to the context of my reading the theoretical understandings that I know are implicated in Carlos Monsiváis's authorial intent. One of the most important of these is explicitly enunciated in 1975 by Tom Wolfe in his narrativized poetics of U.S. New Journalism and in 1980 by Monsiváis in his working definition of the chronicle in Mexico. Monsiváis sums it up as the chronicler's right to enter at will into the consciousness of the Other (*A ustedes* 13); Wolfe describes it as the use of "point-of-view in the Jamesian sense in which fiction writers understand it, entering directly into the mind of a character, experiencing the world through his central nervous system throughout a given scene" ("New Journalism" 33). Wolfe distinguishes the New Journalist's use of the internal third-person focus from the fiction writer's by assuring us that a reporter can "accurately penetrate the thoughts of another person" because he has made certain to "interview him about his thoughts and emotions, along with everything else" (47). In his discussion of New Journalism, which includes a thumbnail review of Tom Wolfe's career and works, Monsiváis cites Truman Capote's celebrated *In Cold Blood* as an example of such participatory journalism. He reprises how Capote

invierte seis años en la reconstrucción de los asesinatos de una familia típica en un pueblo de Kansas. Para ello, vive en el pueblo, amista con el sheriff, interroga a vecinos y autoridades, visita con frecuencia en la cárcel a los asesinos Dick Hickock y Perry Smith, asiste a la ejecución. Y surge el relato moroso, "desde dentro" de las víctimas, los criminales, los vecinos, los encargados de la administración de la justicia. A sangre fría es el panorama de mentalidades y comportamientos sojuzgados por la conversión del bien y del mal en utopías banales. (20)

125

voicing

a poetics

of the

contemporary

chronicle

of mexico

[invests six years in reconstructing the murder of a typical family in a Kansas town. To do that, he lives in the town, makes friends with the sheriff, questions neighbors and authorities, frequents the jail to visit the murderers . . . , attends their execution. And out of all that there arises a morose tale "from inside" the victims, the criminals, the neighbors, those charged with carrying out justice. In Cold Blood is a survey of thought processes and behaviors subjugated by the transformation of good and evil into banal utopias.]

It does not require much of a stretch to see a similar reportage strategy at work in the many years Carlos Monsiváis has spent constructing an abundant competency on the subject of Mexico City's many types of dance and its devotees. He has "authorized himself" not only to speak about dancers but, in selective instances, to speak for them and through them.[6] He asks us to believe, for example, that the four monologues in "El secreto" are not invented speech "in the Jamesian sense" but instead part of the rich harvest of truth that can be gathered in the field by an experienced, skilled, ethical and respected journalist who is willing and able to cultivate a subject over long periods of time.

In the end, I run through the possible proofs of genre outside and inside this text and I conclude that "El secreto está en la mano izquierda" is a frame narration that hides a very covert first person narrator who is orchestrating a chorus of journalistic interviews and has not made these speeches up. I feel authorized to read them as chronicle.

losing sight of the real

I cannot say the same about the other monsivaisian piece I mentioned in this connection. In "La hora de codearse con lo más granado," the reportorial "I" is not merely covert; it does not exist to be found. The histor's mixed voice has been monopolized by the "he" of fictional omniscience. "La hora" is one of Los rituales del caos's twenty-four primary texts, which are loosely set off in groups by five satiric "parables" whose periodic appearances serve as metaexegetic guides. This polyphonic collage sets "La hora" in a material context whose assertion of genre is much less emphatically chronistic than the one we just examined for "El secreto." *Los rituales del caos* offers a more eclectic range of topics than *Escenas*; no other piece shares the theme of European aristocracy presented in "La hora."

When we begin to seek proof of its truth-claim within the text, we meet a first-person narrator who initially raises our expectations, but almost immediately the content and tone of the discourse undermine the possibility that this could be a reportorial "I." This narrator assures us that "un inconveniente de las oficinas de gobierno, y lo digo con gran conocimiento de causa, es la obligación de frecuentar desconocidos" [one disadvantage of government offices, and I speak from long acquaintance with the subject, is that they obligate one to associate with nobodies] (*Rituales* 178). Not only has Carlos Monsiváis been self-employed and pointedly distanced from government authority throughout his career, but we doubt, as well, that a coworker of his would make him an intimate confidant upon learning he was a fan of "Joan Collins y Demi Moore" (179). We do hear echoes of our real-life cronista's slicing humor in this narrator's characterization of the protagonists as longtime officemates who, if they communicate at all, conduct arid conversations "donde la inercia del lenguaje hace las veces de la voluntad de las personas" [in which linguistic inertia stands in for personal will] (178). There is also a cruel condensation, here, of the antisentimentalist analysis Monsiváis makes of ranchera singer José Alfredo Jiménez in *Amor perdido*. But such impressions in "La hora" merely point to Carlos Monsiváis as author; they do not confirm him as narrator.

The plot, for example, offers no documentary evidence of a bridge with the world outside the text. True, it mentions the magazine *¡Hola!* and parodies its breathless *National Inquirer*–style gossip about the Jet Set. But none of the names or incidents mentioned are linked concretely to recent news reports. The listed names of highly public figures such as Julio Iglesias, the Emir of Qatar and the "fabulous Kashoggi" (179) are only symbolic of the office worker's pitiable addiction to vicarious enjoyment of the lives of the rich and famous, who shall otherwise forever remain "desconocidos" [unknown] to the unknowns who adore them through their images.

In "La hora," two of those fans, Teresa and José Ignacio, fall in love and marry because of their shared adoration of the glitterati. And when Teresa discovers that the boss's wife also shares her passion, she negotiates a bonus that will take her and José Ignacio to Spain on their honeymoon. "Según me contaron casi a gritos" [according to the story they almost screamed at me], our narrator confides in us, they went to all the best-known places in search of a glimpse of their aristocratic heroes, but "ni vieron ni conocieron a nadie" [they neither saw nor met anyone] (180). A friend of the narrator's, a kind of voyeur who spied on the couple in their home, later told our first-person informant that both Teresa and José Ignacio have decided that having children would consume money they would rather spend on their fantasies of becoming "una foto de verano en Biarritz," "la imagen luminosa de un hall amplísimo," a "poster en la Costa del Sol," or a "video-clip turístico" [a summertime photo taken in Biarritz, . . . the luminous image of a great hall, ... (a) poster of the Costa del Sol . . . (or) tourist commercial] (181).

127

voicing

a poetics

of the

contemporary

chronicle

of mexico

This story's pair of sad little Babbitts could be pursuing their sterile simulacrum of a life anywhere in the world, for nothing in "La hora de codearse con lo más granado" situates them in Mexico. What specifically bars Teresa and José Ignacio from the real world of journalistic report is the absence of irony that would, in a chronicle, indicate the distance that should be evident between the characters and the author-narrator or, in Cohn's phrase, between mimetic and nonmimetic utterances ("Signposts" 798). The malicious bearer of tales in "La hora" reveals himself to be just as addicted to secondhand drama as those whose stories he recounts. Because he does not separate his knower from the known as object, he and those he observes must be perceived to belong to the same homodiegetic space. While "La hora" is grouped with the chronicles of Los rituales del caos, all of which are presented in the publisher's blurb as chronicles of urban characters and beliefs (back cover), it does not share the authority of fact that most of the book's texts can claim. By allowing the purported past event's unique "strangeness" to be lost to sight (Ricoeur, Reality 14–15), the traditional fictional pose of Monsiváis's narrator naturalized what should have remained Other in the discourse. As a result, events and characters became detached from his public personality.

Rare as it is to encounter a work of fiction by Carlos Monsiváis, all but one (Entrada libre) of his five collections of journalism pieces contain one or more works that, in my opinion, do not pass muster as crónica.[8] Surrounded by a preponderance of chronicles, the center of moral gravity in these fictions slips; the impression they make on the reader does not penetrate as deeply as their chronistic companions, and that is perhaps only because we were asked in the first place to read them against the integrity of their discourse.[9]

a poetics of the contemporary chronicle of mexico

I have read slowly through proofs that I consider necessary for a discourse to be classified as crónica. The paradigm I have outlined is a metatext extracted from a diffuse and continually produced "text" whose essence I have tried to document. My readers can perceive, I now hope, an indigenous theory proposed in alignment with Cohn's notion of an "historiographic narratology" ("Signposts" 777). This poetics has emerged not only from its intrinsic reality within the texts we can call crónica, but from an ongoing extrinsic metadiscourse.

Monsiváis himself provided a solid theoretical foundation to elaborate. In 1979, he saw the crónica as a form of advocacy journalism whose added artistic element in no way erodes its factual base (Antología de la crónica 7–8); the next year, his "definición de trabajo" (A ustedes 13) appears to have altered slightly, to privilege the "juego literario" [literary game] over the journalistic function of analysis and criticism (A ustedes 13); by 1987 he sees a virtual balance between the two principal ingredients of this mixed genre ("De la Santa Doctrina" 754); in 1991, he again emphasizes the chronicle's sociopolitical function as a space for resistance to the hegemony ("Ejercicio"); in 1992, he seems to give a slight edge to formal aspects of the genre ("Prólogo" in Nostalgia 15–25). Taken together, his views steadfastly characterize the crónica as literary journalism: reportage of a newsworthy reality and moral force that is narrativized on being refigured.

Building on the same narrative base, I specify that the contemporary chronicle's two defining characteristics are equal and coexistent, and that each in itself is dual, one being ideological and critical, the other aesthetic and emotional. One embodies the genre's intellectual function; its two parts can be seen in the interaction of its real-world historiographical referent and its critical, revisionist ideology. The other embodies the genre's emotive function; its two parts can be seen in the interaction of its symbolic and entertainment values. What I am adding to this descriptive base is a pragmatic dimension that includes prescriptive and proscriptive rules for writing and reading. Elements of this practical dimension include recognition of the chronicle's ironic narrative stance, the emblematic character of its mixed idiom, and its aspiration to an ascending symbolism.

129

voicing

a poetics

of the

contemporary

chronicle

of mexico

an ironic outsider narrates

The "ironic" narrator of the chronicle may, in fact, wish to attach a humorous edge to his discourse. In my view, the critical sharpness of parody, satire and irony are almost identifying features of a truly effective (modern) chronicle. But as a base-level marker of genre, I am using ironic here to mean a narrator who knows him or herself to be independent of any other voice that may be heard in the discourse. Further, this irony must be emitted by an author-narrator whose first-person point of view can be perceived as an incorruptible link with the outside-on-the-ground stuff of the world upon which the chronicle is "signifying," or subjecting to an "ironic reversal" (Gates 630). That "I" may play some games with itself and the reader, but its integrity—as the witnessing and evaluating consciousness of a real person gathering facts from his or her immediate environs—must never be entirely removed from the reach of a reader.

An important part of this narrative irony, or aesthetic distance, is to be detected in the gaps between creation, publication and reception. As they negotiate a definition of the genre they are decoding, readers will grasp for rules to read by in the expectations previously formed by tangible facts such as where, when and how the text is published, as well as assertions made by publisher, editor and author, and such intangibles as the author's perceived competence, talent, morality, and general reliability as a bringer of truth(s). None of these building blocks of genre will stand, however, except upon the foundation of an ironic, self-distancing narrator who textually voices his or her identity with the author.

heteroglossia and represented orality

Competent essayists, historians and news reporters also make it textually clear that they are public narrators. But as a matter of generic convention, writers of these truth-genres, even when pursuing a pleasing aesthetic effect, avoid extremes of narrativization. The chronicle, also as a matter of generic convention, would disappoint expectations if it did not engage in narrative adventurism. This historiographic genre transgresses the usual rules of nonfiction discourse precisely in order to write itself into being. It is contestatory in at least two senses: as compromised art, it argues with power; as a dialogic hybrid, it keeps its semantic options open with a mixed voice that not only interweaves fact and fiction, but also reflects the fused dualisms of human society: writing and orality, word and icon, elite (high) and popular (low), serious and comic, archaic and modern.

The genre's characteristic diglossia figurally reminds us of the way oral speech and written discourse intertwine in our daily lives. At the same time, it reminds us of the conflicts that also arise between modes of representation and thinking that result in empathic and analytical knowledges.[10] The complexity of the writing-orality topic is beyond the point I am making, which is that the chronicle is genetically disposed to express in emblematic style the permanent tension between official and popular idioms, and between writing and orality; it deliberately leaves that conflict in plain view as unresolved ambiguity.

The chronicle's heteroglottic speech creates a lingering perception of the spoken word's ancient authority. It is poetic, musical, theatrical, aphoristic, dialogic, personalized and immediate, situated in a local, concrete space. The literary effects of this representation of orality are felicitous. It is highly entertaining. There is abundant humor, of both the popular spirit's simple irony and the self-conscious intellectual's satire and parody. There is color and movement and sound.

an emblematic appeal to the senses

The chronicle exuberantly embraces literary devices that allow it to introduce the diversity and texture of plastic arts and the fluidity of song and verse into its discourse. These not only reward the reader with their pleasing sensory and emotive effect but they also give the form an emblematic power and depth. In this respect, the oral and visual imagery of the chronicle helps it to materialize its intended aesthetic goals. Where the essay or the news article or the history lesson *tells*, the chronicle *shows*. Rather than appeal solely to our intellect, the chronicle also makes a studied effort to engage our senses and, thus, our emotions. Fusing the invisible and the visible is the crónica's most effective tactic-of-the-real; with the compressed suggestiveness of the cultural icons it sculpts in words, this archaic-modern genre allies itself with Renaissance and Baroque emblem-literatures.

.The emblem, or hieroglyphic, is a hybrid form that typically pairs a verse composition with a graphic drawing. In the emblem the visual and verbal arts are organically linked: The poem's full meaning cannot be grasped without reference to the image it glosses, nor are the image's features to be interpreted without the poetic exegesis. In analogous fashion, the crónica makes its ideological appeal to the reader through the iconic persuasion of its "low" register; its use of that "unliterary" language is justified by the morally superior objective that it serves.[11] Like the emblem, the crónica configures a dynamic message that can be seen and felt as well as apprehended in thought. Its concretized voice infuses ideology with emotion as it gestures below syntax toward intangible realities that can only be appreciated, like irony, in a metaphoric gap between the visible said and the invisible unsaid.[12]

131

voicing
a poetics
of the
contemporary
chronicle
of mexico

The chronicle's ironic and iconic speech is, in final instance, directed at that "other" meaning, the larger, truer and more lasting significance that lies behind the apparent message. In the modern era, especially, the cronista who descends into deep structural meaning takes the form of symbol rather than allegory. The latter is a premodern construct of vertical authority whose Truth descends fully formed upon the unquestioning suppliant, while the symbol's truth ascends from the human world below, from the people and events depicted in discourse (Kahler 57). The crónica's final meanings ought to emerge when we insert our consciousness into the gap that the narrator has purposely left open between iconic referent and poetic discourse.

For my part, I insert these theoretical observations as a provisional utterance into an ongoing dialogue on the identity and functions of the contemporary Mexican chronicle. I will continue to test this theory on the readings I conduct in the remainder of this study. Those analyses are also intended to showcase Carlos Monsiváis's unique manner of writing crónica, and demonstrate that good chronicle is synonymous with good literature.

II

carlos monsiváis
author

6

among DAYS TO REMEMBER, the eclipse of eternity

reading DÍAS DE GUARDAR (1970)

While comets like Carlos Fuentes and Fernando del Paso were burning new paths across Mexico's literary universe, Carlos Monsiváis was patiently assembling the narrative craft that would carry him to fame. *Días de guardar* put before the public in 1970 a concentrated sampling of the revolutionary journalism that Monsiváis had been publishing in Mexico's mass media for over half a decade; now he would assert a claim as well to a unique brand of literature. *Días de guardar's* accounts of concerts, protests and pilgrimages retain much of their recordkeeping function. By now, however, they have gained the greater weight of permanency that canonical writing puts on with each new printing run. A ubiquitous presence in Mexico City bookstores and Monsiváis's most-cited work, *Días* includes twenty-three paradigmatic chronicles among its thirty-three texts.[1]

The prologue ("Primero de enero, Año Nuevo: la inauguración formal") was written two years after the crisis that organizes the discourses of *Días:* October 2, 1968, the most ill-fated of days in modern Mexico's history, a day that breaks the Student Movement's heart and casts hopes for democracy momentarily into frozen space. Among the meanings encrypted within the title of "Days of Observance," one signifies upon the 360-day Aztec solar calendar's five leftover days of nontime associated with bad luck, loss, death and chaos. As with many features of Mesoamerican culture, this meaning is reversible. The lost days link old and new years, inserting life into death. The days Monsiváis keeps in *Días* present "situaciones límite" [threshold moments] (17) that similarly hide signs of hope.

In this respect, the twelve-month cycle of days, implicitly alluded to in *Días de guardar*'s title and explicitly invoked in the subtitles of many of its chronicles, is a ritualized measure of time that ends in the disorder of economic chaos, government waste, corruption, rural misery, electoral absurdity, cowardly unions, massive unemployment, unsolved murders and political prisoners (*Días* 18–19). During the ensuing period of mourning, everything sinks to the ground (19). But in the end ("el día 31 de diciembre de 1970"), this book of days offers its series of sociopolitical and cultural analyses to honor a spirit of optimism (380). With the Beatles for backup and the ghostly Revolution whispering from history's backstage, Monsiváis mounts a hopeful comeback on the final page: "*1970: Let it Be: speaking words of wisdom.* . . . El progreso formal es innegable: la ciudad dispone de metro, la ciudad dispone de nueva Cámara de diputados. Se perfila la existencia de un periodismo crítico y se afirma que todo se olvidará y sin embargo nada se olvida. Entre la pena y la nada, se nos va la última oportunidad de hacer uso del sufragio efectivo" [Undeniably, there is tangible progress: the city's got a subway, a new legislature. A critical kind of news reporting has begun to emerge and it is said that all will be forgotten and yet nothing is forgotten. Between grief and nothing, we are letting our last chance to make effective use of the vote slip away] (19).[2]

Monsiváis's prologue to *Días* narrativizes a metonymic list of the principal subtopics that define Mexico late in 1970: explosive growth in industry and finance; runaway population growth (a tragic icon of poverty[3]); expansion of the middle class; greater economic interdependency with the United States, and a deepening schism between those pursuing the American dream and various subcultures expanding in other directions.

suspended in an archaic "modernity"

Contemplation of these features of Mexico's presumed "personalidad moderna" [modern nature] (15) is initially disheartening. Middle-class hopefuls straining to imitate the North American model in fact barely manage to hide their "caritas sonrientes de la cultura prehispánica" [little smiling faces of prehispanic culture] (16).[4] This insecure sector of the population lives with such a horror of being left out (15) that it can neither support student-led efforts to weaken centralist politics nor protect dissidents from government retaliation. The epochal image of October 2, 1968, "el noble sacrificio" [the noble sacrifice] (16–18), fills the prophetic heart of the prologue and sharpens Monsiváis's criticism of Mexico's "nuevorricracia" [nouveau riche] (135) throughout the book.

Prominently foregrounded is a steadfast preoccupation with language as a medium for transformation of the individual and collective consciousness, where Monsiváis locates the birth of a pluralist, modern state (of mind). In 1966, when he was writing some of the chronicles included in *Días,* he published a groundbreaking anthology of twentieth-century Mexican poetry. In the prologue, the young intellectual states a theory of sociolinguistics and humor that he will dramatize in his metaphoric and often savagely funny reportage:

> En tanto que el español no sea vencido, acorralado, desollado, incorporado para siempre a la sensibilidad profunda de todos los mexicanos, nuestra literatura seguirá siendo . . . inflexible y rígida. . . . Una prueba evidente de este continuo vasallaje a una lengua que, . . . por miedo o timidez o rencor, no nos decidimos a maltratar o poseer, es la ausencia de humor en nuestras letras. . . . El humor que burla con y del lenguaje son signos de madurez y civilización. (*Poesía* 10, 39)

> [So long as Spanish is not conquered, cornered, flayed, absorbed forever into the Mexican's deepest awareness, our literature will continue to be inflexible and rigid. . . . One clear proof of this persistent servitude to a language which, out of fear or timidity or resentment, we still can't make up our minds to mistreat or possess, is the absence of humor in our writing . . . Humor that makes fun of and with language is a sign of maturity and civilization.]

In *Días,* he explicitly links sociopolitical liberation to linguistic revolution in two analyses of the Onda, the hippie subculture that skewered Solemn Mexico's "Vocablos Cruciales" and "Vocabulario Básico" ["Crucial Words" and

"Basic Vocabulary"] with its slang (Monsiváis, "Duración" 37). In contrast, Official Mexico imposes its idiom like a loudmouthed bully; for instance, while campaigning in a village with "un magnavoz impío [que] reconstruye, con redovas y canciones rancheras, el estrépito del sitio de Stalingrado, sin siquiera la esperanza de una bomba vindicadora que lo atempere" [a pitiless loudspeaker that reconstructs, while blaring *norteña* and *ranchera* songs, the din raised by the siege of Stalingrad, but without a hope, even, of an avenging bomb to tone it down] (*Días* 29).

Half a century after the Mexican constitution called for modernized education in the provinces, a gaggle of third-rate politicians descends on the stolid citizens of a communal farm to inaugurate its first school. At one point, an ardent young party member is sent out to soften up the crowd: "En su casa habrá libros (subrayados) de las distintas campañas presidenciales, en su voz hay un trémolo peligroso: allí hay discursos agazapados, emboscados que aguardan el menor descuido del viandante" [At home he no doubt has books, all full of underlining, on the various presidential campaigns. There's a dangerous trembling in his voice: Speeches crouch in there, ready to attack the unwary passerby at the least opportunity] (29). Satire attacks the monoglossia of one-party rule, which reproduces itself to prey eternally on the rural masses.

In *Días*, we observe Official Mexico herding citizens into cultural as well as political conformity with a discourse of melodrama designed to imprison the mass mind. Monsiváis assaults this language with metalinguistic irony. In an analysis of camp sensibility he points out, for example, that the solemn speech of state-controlled movies in the 1940s is no less an invented slang than hippiespeak: Venerated actor Miguel Inclán's "empleo de la voz, bronco, abismal, cavernoso, autoparódico, permite que recobremos una herencia auditiva: así debió hablar Huitzilopochtli" [use of his voice—rough, deep, cavernous, self-mocking—allows us to recall an auditory legacy: That's what Huitzilopochtli must have sounded like] (183). A popular icon thus acquires a sinister aspect associated with the Aztec tradition's cruel sun god, ever hungry for hearts; at the same time, parody shows the omnipotent god to be a method actor in a B-movie. The reader of post-1968 Mexico is left to draw the logical inference: the past is only history. Humor helps Monsiváis's reader put the presumably inviolable mandate of "Vigilopochtli" (40) in perspective through a Miguel Inclán who offers himself conveniently as the "living image" of a false god that Monsiváis sacri fices to his own favorite deities: Antisolemnity and Heteroglossia (not to mention better movies).[5]

When he urges his compatriots to speak a Spanish that has been "deso-
llado" [flayed] (*Poesía* 10), he uses the Mesoamerican's iconic compression to
suggest that Mexicans "sacrifice" peninsular Spanish and wear its "skin" as
a symbolic means of appropriating the power of that sacralized Other. The
Bible-reading grandson of a Nahuatl-speaking woman, Monsiváis writes
within two traditions that place violence and play in ambivalent juncture.
His use of religious humor breaks a taboo based on fear, highlights conflicts
needing resolution and thus contests tragic fatalism. Instead of bowing to
tradition, "la pretendida justificación histórica de la inmovilidad" [the historical justification for immobility] (Monsiváis, *Días* 357), Monsiváis moves
its keepers toward modern thinking. He does this by pairing the inward
world of thought to the outward signs of its power in economics, politics and
social conduct. Such dualities emerge as unstable binary oppositions that
stigmatize the monolithic Otherness of authoritarianism and mark structural change.

Among the dualities Monsiváis most insistently attacks is the archaic
dynamic of center and periphery. He shifts it centripetally, in analyses that
condemn the way all roads in Mexico lead to the presidential palace, and
centrifugally, in chronicles that bring his insights out to the provinces where
farmers, Indians and rural schoolteachers battle for a standard of living
and often for their lives. Other fatal divisions insistently targeted include
Mexico's several racisms,[6] sexism, machismo, and the base of all the other
(sch)isms: class conflicts between "los *happy few*, . . . los Favoritos del Des-
tino" (21) and "El que nace pa' maceta" [the *happy few*, Destiny's Favorites and
those who were born to be flowerpots] (296).

cosmic becoming and
apocalyptic progress

Through the ordinance of time, the book's topical syntax
becomes symbol. The prologue and the brief conclusion are pegged to the
first and last days of a calendar year, while half the collection's works are
fixed to dates between. These attach a sense of cause-and-effect to remind us
that most of *Días*'s texts are historical truth-accounts. As punctuation marking socialized time, the periodicity also sets ordinary time and human events

into the broader arena of cosmic "becoming" (Bakhtin, *Rabelais* 90–92). A certain mythic determinism inheres in the implied cycling of beginnings and endings, but each textual moment also aligns itself with apocalyptic thought, the rectilinear notion of progress toward perfection of human thought and conduct.

Monsiváis's *Días de guardar* is, thus, only *ironically* about traditions as a mythological mode of using the past to design and order the present; from a critical and skeptical point of view, it is *historically* about contemporaneous thought processes, decisions and actions that can be invalidated and updated. In Monsiváis's view, "el tiempo recurrente" [recurrent time] (Monsiváis, *Días* 32) can and must become a broken myth. Like a spiral laid on its side, time in *Días* loops back on itself endlessly while human will propels and pulls its cycles forward: "Los informantes [aztecas] de Sahagún han cumplido con su deber. Allí está su relación de los hechos. El turno corresponde a los nuevos informantes, para que digan de la sustitución del vocerío, el alarido, el clamor" [Sahagún's (Aztec) informants have done their duty. Back there you can find their version of events. It's the new informants' turn, and they must speak of an end to the shrieking, howling and clamoring] (114). The job of new informants, in writings like *Días de guardar*, is to help their society escape the eternal "vuelta de la noria" [turn of the water wheel] (32).

Monsiváis overtly displays his teleological yearning when he casts himself as a neobiblical prophet who signifies on the paratactical inevitability of the word made immortal. Early in *Días*, for example, he reviews a pair of concerts, the first attended by masses of indigenous and working-class poor, the second by the bourgeois elite. The rock star as venerated idol appears in the capital's central park-cum–Great Temple, "el lugar del holocausto, el altar propiciatorio" [the place of the holocaust, the propitiatory altar] (45). Here, amid the poor, as he will later amid fans in the elegant El Patio, his Pop psychologist (47) thinks in terms of *el blasfemo . . . el sacrilegio . . . el rito . . . un charro [que] confesó . . . el ídolo . . . [que] se arrodilló . . . técnicas litúrgicas . . . la bendición* and *el éxodo* [blasphemy, sacrilege, ritual, a peasant confessing, an idol, kneeling, liturgical techniques, blessing and exodus]. The litany of religious concepts extends the narrator's gravely punctuated sentences:

> Y la muchedumbre era un solo cuerpo, una entidad indivisible, . . . y la
> multitud se ahogaba dentro de la multitud y quién te adivinara tan exacto

en tus tesis Gustavo Le Bon y las facciones hieráticas de la serpiente emplu-
mada no impedían que la gente se atropellase y gritase y empujase y pre-
sionase en el esfuerzo desmesurado de salvarse de la gente y ganar ese
lugar imposible, la garantía de la proximidad del ídolo [Raphael], aunque,
con tal de estar cerca del ídolo se evitase la presencia misma del ídolo.
(46)

[And the multitude was a single body, an indivisible entity, . . . and the
multitude was drowning in the multitude and who would have figured you
to be so right, Gustavo Le Bon, and the hieratic features of the plumed ser-
pent did not keep the people from trampling each other and screaming and
pushing and pressing in their boundless efforts to save themselves from
the people and gain that impossible place, a guarantee of proximity to the
idol (Raphael), even if, straining to get near the idol, they should miss out
on the very presence of the idol.]⁷

The title of this report, "10/16 febrero de 1968: Raphael en dos tiempos y
una posdata," emphasizes the split-screen reality Mexico is experiencing in
1968. The plural of "tiempo" [time] can refer to days or epochs. Thus, in one
dimension, the people still cling to a hieratic past—"Tradición es el sentido
del pasado total como 'ahora'" [Tradition is the sense of the entire past as
"now"] (358). In the other time, they rush back to the future to worship new
secular gods.

The urgency of the new presses Monsiváis's discourse forward, from
the ponderous solemnity of polysyndeton (history as context) to the shape-
changing chaos of asyndeton (history-in-the-making):

Naufragaron las jerarquías y devino la confusión sintetizadora de sillas,
brazos, rebozos que flotaban, bolsas que levitaban, manifestaciones fa-
llidas y autoridad, enfermos ambulantes, empujones, desvanecimientos,
codazos, niños encumbrados y promovidos por una cadena de brazos, la
muchedumbre, carteristas, voces y reclamaciones de los organizadores,
empellones, sociólogos que interpretaban todo con rapidez, camarógrafos,
paparazzi que registraban sin fatiga a la misma multitud desplegada pro-
teicamente. (50–51)

[Hierarchies collapsed and there was an orchestrated confusion of chairs,
arms, floating scarves, flying purses, failed attempts at order, the walking
wounded, shoves, swoons, elbows in the ribs, uplifted children carried
along a chain of arms, crushed humanity, pickpockets, shouted demands
of the organizers, jostling, sociologists who were analyzing everything on
the spot, cameramen, paparazzi who tirelessly recorded the multitude in
its protean sprawl.]

Self-styled as the Teórico Súbito (47–48), Monsiváis inserts himself squarely in the center of time-passing and lets us see him both as a journalist surrounded by the cinematographic tangibility of immediate reality and as the "Sociólogo Instantáneo" [Instant Sociologist] (47) who seizes upon "analogías históricas" [historical analogies] (56). Such bifocal vision helps Monsiváis track where Mexico has been and see where it has arrived:

> ¿Cuál es la noción de tiempo en un país en vías de desarrollo? . . . El tiempo del subdesarrollo suele ser, en cuanto a forma, circular, . . . porque los hallazgos son los mismos. . . . El drama de México se localiza en su tiempo histórico trunco: una Independencia que se frustra, una Reforma que no llega a término, una Revolución que llega a su feliz desenlace contrarrevolucionario. La suspensión de las grandes ideas históricas equivale al mito del eterno retorno, que . . . es la precaria y atroz sensación continua que nos informa de que esto ya lo vivimos, de que esto ya lo intentamos, de que esto ya fracasó. (152)

> [What is time in a still-developing country? . . . Time in the underdeveloped society is usually, with respect to its shape, circular, because all discoveries are the same. . . . Mexico's drama is to be found in the fact of its incomplete history: a frustrated Independence, a Reform without end, a Revolution arrived but only—cleverly—at a counterrevolutionary impasse. The suspension of great historic ideas calls to mind the myth of the eternal return, which is the precarious, atrocious and ongoing impression that informs us we have already lived this reality, we have already tried this, this has already failed.]

Dual vision helps him see, as well, where Mexico might go. While reflecting on his nation's ineffectual uses of time in the past, he proposes a utopian use of leisure hours as opportunities for citizens to politicize themselves altruistically (153). As the individual's ethical use of time, politics would produce the "centro de gravedad, . . . ese centro polémico de razón" [center of gravity, that polemic center of reason] (153) needed for an effective historical time in which reform and redistribution of power occur in a continually expanding space.

a narrator of baroque abandon

The sober voice of the histor speaks here, the chronicle's favored editorialist who works to unsnarl myths, unmask power and uncover truth (see chapter 5). But in Días de guardar's exhibitionist boom style, the parodic prophet is a more likely stance for Monsiváis. Indeed, he doubles his voice with baroque abandon in this collection, experimenting with metafictional first persons such as the unreliable narrator, Wise Fool and Reporter at Work. Still another self-reflexive mode is the metalinguistic narrator who talks about language with language about language.

Monsiváis clearly revels in the postmodern carnivalesque's love of word games and other overt invitations to the reader. Interspersed among this book's twenty-three serious pieces are comic interludes that both challenge and reward. In these, Monsiváis gleefully performs as Master of Ceremonies, radio dramatist, cultural anthropologist, game-show host, board-game creator, ethnographer, concert and theater reviewer, biographer, photography and art critic, translator of poetry and stand-up comic.

More on the serious side is the hectoring narrator who attacks readers to their face, a stance Monsiváis generally avoids. In *Días* he tries every narrative posture on for size, however, and unleashes his most furious satirist on those among his regular readers who belong to the power class he dubs the Mexican Establishment (203) or, more nastily, "los gigantes, los invencibles, los Monstruos Sagrados, el Consejo de Notables, los Ancianos de la Tribu" [the giants, the invincible, the Sacred Monsters, the Council of Notables, the Tribal Ancients] (204). He characterizes their self-serving political venality as gluttony: Their big stomachs advertise "lo rotundo de los Hombres Ilustres" [the rotundity of Illustrious Men] (207). These self-declared "democratic" leaders elect themselves in blatant violation of the constitution. The worst of Monsiváis's criticism, though, is implicitly reserved for those who permit this travesty: the rest of his readers (208).

This chronicle aimed at the Mexican government's betrayal of the constitution appears without a calendrical date that could imply an end to the situation; further, the wordplay of its title—"No solamente lo fugitivo permanece y dura" [not only the ephemeral endures]—invokes a temporal paradox that will promptly be explained. The following text is an analysis of the Student Movement's first public demand for "sufragio efectivo" [effective electoral power]. It seems there is, after all, hope that the Sacred Monster's time will one day be "lost" at calendar's end.

1968: the semantic backbone of DÍAS

The book's three chronicles on the Student Movement are not presented as a trilogy, but dispersed among other calendrical moments. Still, the 1968 Movement is the semantic backbone of the book, threading "presentimientos" [premonitions] of its modernity (Monsiváis, "El 68" 155) into virtually every text. In the previous chapter, for example, we examined

in detail the moving autobiographical response to Tlatelolco called "Yo y mis amigos" (*Días*, 65–77). In another crónica, an interview with the Durango state governor reminds us that student-led demonstrations for democracy took place not only in the center but also on the nation's periphery, and that these too were violently stifled. Among the many other texts in which the 1968 theme reverberates in the background,[8] two in particular relate to the group Monsiváis devotes specifically to the Movement. In one, the biographies of three nineteenth-century figures explain historical reasons why the police in 1968 were defenders of only a tiny sector of the public. In the other, a piece apparently focused on the Mexican Revolution, we eventually recognize that the civil war's failed aspirations are directly mirrored in the imprisonment of student dissidents half a century later: "Agonía y sueño [agony and dream]. México 1910–1968" (340).

the silence of complicit fear

The first of Monsiváis's three crónicas on "los vastos, infinitos días de 1968" [the vast, infinite days of 1968] (273) takes us *in medias res* to a situation of worsening tension between university students and Díaz Ordaz's government.[9] The immediate catalyst of the protest march in "Primero de agosto de 1968: la manifestación del Rector" is a military occupation of the university that mocks academic independence and bruises the pride of young men who resent being treated like children (244–45). The Rector's march was more a romantic gesture than a true revolt against authority (252); embodying a deeply patriotic cross-sampling of conservative ideologies, many of the marchers would be incorporated into the System upon graduation (251–52).

More than the march, what interests the sober histor narrating this account is the sociohistorical context. Monsiváis wants his readers to grasp a broader understanding of the issues than the marchers themselves possessed when they set out walking in the rain that August 1 day. He makes us traverse fragments of a text that alternates from past to present and to an implied future. Subheaded sections called "El pasado inmediato" [The Immediate Past] contain most of the journalism: the march itself, together with dates and hours supplied like clockwork to keep returning us to the desired forward movement. Sections titled "Relación de los hechos" [The

Facts] contain the historical background. Briefer subsections provide the aesthetic leavening, zooming in on the actors in what eventually is perceived to be a narrative script. "Imágenes: la asamblea" [Images: The Assembly] give us panoramic shots of the collective enterprise; "Imágenes: el mártir" [The Martyr] provide close-ups of role models, such as martyred farmworker Rubén Jaramillo.[10] The metatextual "voiceover" of "Generalizaciones" [Generalizations] converts raw data into symbolic new historical types.

This text's oscillating fragments ultimately assume a divisiveness as orderly as the men in coat and tie who marched behind the Rector. The text's producer would like to see a full rupture with antidemocratic tradition, but in the gaps between takes, he captures blurred shots of the force that continues to reinforce the authoritarian center: fear. History had taught that to be a hero meant to be in jail or dead (223). Watching students take tremulous steps toward heroism in the summer of 1968, Mexicans wanted to close their eyes and ears out of "el temor de informarse" [the fear of finding out] (223). A silence of frightened lambs engulfed the city, the silence of willful ignorance, the silence of complicity.

the didactic silence of moral resolve

Next in *Días*, "13 de septiembre de 1968: la manifestación del silencio" [September 13, 1968: the silent protest] takes us forward six weeks in history, light years in understanding: "La vigencia de una generación empieza a producirse a través del entendimiento de su pobreza" [the validity of a generation begins to emerge from an understanding of what it lacks] (270–71). In a discourse whose profound fragmentarism now truly projects the rupture long awaited, a third-person narrator speaks for an "Él" [He] whose metahistoriographical consciousness films jerky images of a society coming apart. He flashes back two weeks earlier to the memory of students being bulldozed by tanks from the city's center . . . "Él suspende el recuerdo" [He suspends his memory] (263) . . . He leaps forward to preparations for the Silent March that would soon begin. When the narrator "asume el flash-back" [assumes the flashback mode] again (263), he pans over a remembered scene of panic and records an eyewitness account: "El griterío era interminable, . . . como eso que llaman ruido blanco. La gente se movía de un lado a otro, confusa, como en cine mudo. . . . Era el infierno" [The screaming went on and on, . . . like that thing they call white noise. People moved from one side to the other, in confusion, as though in a silent film

. . . It was hell] (266).[11] Now, however, the silence of panic is accompanied by determined action. As students work past their fears through a night of preparations, "He" speaks for them and himself: "La manifestación será un fracaso. . . . Vamos a ser poquísimos. Es una locura, una provocación" [This march is going to fail . . . We are so few. It's crazy, a huge risk] (259).

But now the Movement has learned to pronounce "las palabras iniciales de un cuerpo colectivo que nunca antes había hecho uso de la palabra" [the first words of a collective body that had never before spoken] (271). While government security forces bludgeon, torture, imprison and kill, the courage of heroism blooms. If Díaz Ordaz won't talk to them, they will turn the silence of impunity against him and march with lips sealed, several hundred thousand strong, to stand beneath his balcony and show him the defiant uses of their theatrical silence.[12] What before was imposed is now assumed, what was traditional is now historical: "La manifestación . . . se multiplicaba con el abandono de los pequeños temores, con la cesión de las timideces, . . . en el reconocimiento de que por fin, . . . ese elemento tan extraño, tan desconocido, ese elemento mítico para las nuevas generaciones de mexicanos, la Historia, desertaba de su condición ajena y abstracta para convertirse en una manera concreta y personal de ordenar, vivir, padecer, amar o abominar de la realidad" [The march grew as small fears were set aside, as apprehension ended, with the recognition that finally, that element so rare, so unknown, that element become myth for new generations of Mexicans, History itself, abandoned its alienated and abstract mode to become a concrete and personal manner of ordering, living, suffering, loving or hating reality] (272–73).

The Zócalo is no longer a mythical seat of unassailable authority, but the place where a fallible power resides to be questioned in the light of candles held high, the joy of "victoria popular y triunfo moral" [popular victory and moral triumph], and the sudden understanding of what André Malraux meant when he said "¿y qué es la libertad del hombre sino la conciencia y la organización de sus fatalidades?" [And what is the freedom of man but conscience and the organization of its destiny?] (275)[13]

In this report, Monsiváis's distanced witness-recorder is observed struggling with his conscience and his fears before deciding, finally, to act on the moral convictions he shares with the students.[14] That inner-outer movement harmonizes with the chaotic swirl of new pairings and inversions figured in this text, both tangibly and intangibly: women, no longer invisible and passive, sharing with men the dangers of public action; paralysis accelerating into movement; the writerly narrator, "con su mentalidad retórica" [with his rhetorical cast of mind] (274), splicing in "un hallazgo muy difundido de Marshall McLuhan" [a very well-known notion of Marshall McLuhan's] (271) and "otra cita citable de Wittgenstein" [another quotable quote of Wittgenstein] (272) into the oral stratum of slogans, testimonies and screams; faith checkmating fear.

In the text's fragmented cosmos of unstable binarisms the consciousness of an individual and a community acquire three-dimensional materiality before a hand-held verbal camera. There are no helpful subtitles here: The fissures this narrator describes are structural and irreversible, finding anchor within the spirit. The silence of the innocent now speaks of moral resolve.

the contrasting silence of misery

Now Monsiváis interrupts the chronological flow of the Movement to insert an invitation to observe a contrasting silence of mute misery. His admiration of the Student Movement is not diminished but enriched because he trains his panoramic intellect on a paradox usually forgotten in elegiac writings about 1968, and this is that the largely middle-class youngsters carrying candles to the presidential palace had not found a voice to speak for the vast masses of Mexico whose silence was still traditional. The folkloric face of poor neighborhoods like Tepito and Lagunilla is in fact the image of Mexican poverty, born of colonial abandon, nurtured by nationalist racism, perpetuated by postrevolutionary betrayal and high birthrates (277). An aphonic Greek chorus encircling the tragic actors of the university and Zócalo, typical Mexico is "el born loser, el nacido para perder, el coleccionista del desastre" [the born loser, a collector of disasters]. While university freedom fighters teach themselves how to win democratic rights, in Tepito, "uno se enseña saber perder" [one learns how to lose] (280–81).

This is the most fatal duality of Monsiváis's Mexico: the "determinismo moral de la pobreza" [moral determinism of poverty] among the vast majority of its citizens (288). As much as the shock of October 2, the existential anomaly of classism is what stopped the overwhelmingly bourgeois Student Movement in its tracks. With this in mind, our reception of the final text in the 1968 trilogy will be more complex.

the silence of a dead tradition

After Cortés destroyed the glory that had been Tenochtitlán, one of its vanquished poets wailed: "Y todo esto pasó con nosotros. . . . Con esta lamentosa y triste suerte nos vimos angustiados. . . . Destechadas están las casas. Enrojecidos tienen sus muros. . . . Golpeábamos en tanto los muros de adobe y era nuestra herencia una red hecha de agujeros. . . . Éste fue el modo como feneció el mexica, el tlatelolca" [And all this happened to us . . . We saw ourselves burdened with this lamentable and sad destiny . . . Our houses are without roofs. Their walls are reddened with blood . . . Meanwhile, we beat our fists upon the adobe walls and our legacy was a net made of holes . . . This was how the *mexica*, the Tlatelolcan nation, came to an end] (Nahuatl testimony, cited in León-Portilla, *Literaturas indígenas* 174).

With its allusion to the well-known lament from the "vision of the vanquished," the title of the third text, "2 de octubre/2 de noviembre: Día de Muertos. Y era nuestra herencia una red de agujeros," guides us inescapably toward a historicist reading that sets the Tlatelolco massacre like a photograph into a brittle family album. A month after the catastrophic end of the Student Movement, Monsiváis joins throngs of Mexicans and other tourists on an annual pilgrimage to Pátzcuaro and Mixquic, peripheral centers of ancestral practices. Monsiváis's photographic trope double-exposes the concept of "observation" and laminates two days of the dead onto a single page in Mexico's ritual calendar: "A principios . . . de todos los meses de noviembre, la celebración del Día de Muertos . . . atrae y sectariza a la fotografía. . . . Las velas enormes y las ofrendas y las costumbres prehispánicas . . . han sido el alimento propicio, propiciatorio de . . . curiosidad . . . México ha vendido el culto a la muerte y los turistas sonríen, antropológicamente hartos" [At the beginning of every November, celebration of the Day of the Dead attracts photographers and gives them something to aim at. . . . Huge candles and ritual offerings and prehispanic customs have been suitable food, the propitiatory curiosity. . . . Mexico has sold its cult of death and the tourists smile, anthropologically satiated] (294).

He narrates as the one who is as featureless as the typical Mexican family members being interviewed and the peasant women and men being photographed (296). He also speaks as a traveler from the capital who notes things that seem out of the ordinary in the midst of the most observed of Mexican rituals: the Zona Rosa habitué who comes to Mixquic "para sen-

tirse lejano, extranjero, *otro*, ante las umbrosas y porfiadas ceremonias indígenas" [to feel distant, foreign, *other*, before the shadowy and persistent
ceremonies of indigenous Mexico] (297); the fact that Mixquic's trafficking
in tradition has robbed the ritual acts of their meaning, leaving behind
empty motions masked in North American Halloween style (297); the surprise inherent in noting that "el underground mexicano, la sección subter-
ránea de una ciudad que no acepta siquiera superficies, aflora en Mixquic:
los hippies y su predilección por la mariguana, los radicales y su desprecio
de la burguesía, los homosexuales y su amor por las apariencias" [the Mexican underground, that subterranean sector of a city that does not accept
even superficial images, flourishes in Mixquic: hippies and their love of
marijuana, activists and their contempt for the middle class, homosexuals
and their love of appearances] (298). Where others might lament the paradox, Monsiváis reminds us that all traditions are programmed to deconstruct over time; why be shocked because in Mixquic theories about the
illicit relationship between Death and Mexico are losing their foundation?:
"El Día de Muertos descansa en paz" [May the Day of the Dead rest in peace]
(299–300).

The traveler returns to Tlatelolco, "el lugar del retorno" [the place of
origin] (300). We flash back to that meeting of a month before, and to the
bitter tones of a biblical prophet who had foretold doom for the students
who planned a provocation that would embarrass the regime ten days before
the nineteenth Olympic Games and Díaz Ordaz's opportunity to show the
whole planet how much Mexico had progressed since Cuauhtémoc shot his
last arrow (301). Monsiváis resets the historical clock, however, because what
the Mexican regime carried out was not an ordained ritual but a deliberate
act demanding accountability:

Y eran las cinco y media y la gente se agrupaba, absorta . . . Y el mitin se
inició . . . Y eran las seis y diez de la tarde y de pronto, mientras el equipo
de sonido divulgaba otra exhortación, rayó el cielo el fenómeno verde emit-
ido por un helicóptero, el efluvio verde, la señal verde de una luz de ben-
gala. . . . desde el reposo de lo inesperado . . . Y se oyeron los primeros tiros
. . . Y el gesto detenido en la sucesión de reiteraciones se perpetuaba: la
mano con el revólver, la mano con el revólver, la mano con el revólver, la
mano con el revólver . . . Y como otro gesto inacabable se opuso la V de la
victoria a la mano con el revólver y el crepúsculo agónico dispuso de ambos
ademanes y los eternizó y los fragmentó y los unió sin término, plenitud
de lo inconcluso, plenitud de la proposición eleática: jamás dejará la mano

de empuñar el revólver, jamás abandonará la mano la protección de la V. . . . Y los tanques entraron a la Plaza . . . Y cesó la imagen frente a la imagen y el universo se desintegró ¡llorad amigos! Y el estruendo era terrible . . . y el llanto diferenciado de las mujeres y la voz precaria de los niños . . . Y los alaridos se hundieron en la tierra preñándolo todo de oscuridad. (301–303)

[And it was 5:30 and the people were milling about, focused on their business . . . And the meeting got under way . . . and it was 6:10 P.M. and suddenly, while the sound system broadcast another speech, a green flash from a helicopter split the sky: a cascading green aura, the green signal from a flare bursting out of the quiet, out of the unexpected . . . And the first gunshots were heard . . . and the gesture frozen in time amid a succession of repetitions was perpetuated: the hand with the revolver, the hand with the revolver, the hand with the revolver, the hand with the revolver . . . And another unending gesture was imposed: the trigger finger formed the V of victory with the revolver and the dying twilight froze both gestures in an eternal pattern, separating and joining them forever in the fullness of an inconclusive moment, of an illusory proposition: the hand will never stop gripping the revolver, the hand will never abandon its protective V . . . And the tanks rolled into the square . . . And image dissolved before image and the universe fell apart; weep, friends! And the uproar was terrible . . . and amid it one could pick out the cries of the women and the fragile voices of the children . . . And the screams sank into the earth, filling all with darkness.][15]

Comparison to sacrifices of innocent citizens in Mexico's past is inevitable: "se renovaba la vieja sangre insomne. Y la sangre . . . sellaba el fin de la inocencia: se había creído en la democracia y en el derecho y en la conciencia militante y en las garantías constitucionales y en la reivindicación moral" [the ancient insomniac blood renewed itself and blood . . . sealed the fate of the innocent [although] one had believed in democracy and in the law and in a military conscience and in constitutional guarantees and in moral vindication] (303). Shaking off fatalistic melancholy, however, the "visitor" draws on the histor's strength to report General Marcelino García Barragán's announcement that his men saved Mexico from *agents provocateurs* and then to set the record straight: It was neither tradition nor foreign agitators but machine guns, bazookas and high-velocity rifles that destroyed our innocence (304), modern weapons of an anachronistic state whose own day of retribution would come. We will not forget, declare mourners at Tlatelolco that November 2, 1968: "La Historia los juzgará" [History will judge them]

(304). With simple realism, "la obsesión mexicana por la muerte anuncia su carácter exhausto, impuesto, inauténtico. . . . En Tlatelolco se inicia la nueva, abismal etapa de las relaciones entre un pueblo y su sentido de la finitud . . . Se liquida la supuesta intimidad del mexicano y la muerte. Más aguda y ácida que otras muertes, la de Tlatelolco nos revela verdades esenciales que el fatalismo inútilmente procuró ocultar" [the Mexican obsession with death announces that its nature is spent, imposed, inauthentic. In Tlatelolco there is begun a new, abysmal stage in the relationship between a people and its sense of the finite . . . The presumed intimacy of the Mexican with death is over. More acute and corrosive than others, Tlatelolco's death reveals essential truths to us that fatalism had unsuccessfully sought to hide] (304–305).

The briefest of the 1968 trilogy's texts, "Día de Muertos" has covered huge distances in geometric strides. On the horizontal plane, dualities that tradition had placed in indivisible contiguity—official and popular languages, prehispanic and Christian beliefs, sacrifice and salvation, life and death, despair and hope, past and present—are now seen as separable entities. Between them open historical gaps that time may fill with change. On the vertical plane, the narrator voyages from the bottom level of Mictlan upward, from the dead foundation of ancient sacrificial ritual through a space of postmodern transformation to a ground-level site of traditional praxis and spiritual renovation. Encircling these axes is a line extending outward from the center to the periphery and back, and another that draws the patterned despair of the Eternal Return inward toward individual pursuits of pleasure, comfort and enlightenment before expanding again in the direction of a newly discovered finitude whose apertures and ruptures permit escape from tradition's clasp. The horizontal helix of monsivaisian time emerges: On October 2, 1968, atavistic authorities "suspendieron y decapitaron a la inocencia mexicana" [arrested and decapitated Mexican innocence] (305); in future, however, if the lessons of history do not this time teach Mexico to demand accountability and end official impunity, the innocent will be guilty of silencing themselves.

"dios nunca muere": a quest for knowledge

Against the fear of knowing that had to be overcome in the 1968 trilogy, "Dios nunca muere" [God Never Dies] (91–114) dramatizes a deliberate quest for understanding, undertaken by the singular consciousness of the metacronista who calls himself the Observer and the collective consciousness of a mosaic of Mexicans who voluntarily gather on the country's western shore to observe an eclipse of the sun in March 1970. The superrealism of Monsiváis's Observer, who compulsively edits a discourse-in-the-making, helps us perceive emergent master tropes. Chief among these are the motifs of breaking out, going inside and searching.

If it is true that, in lieu of a tragic literature, Latin America has "una historia de crímenes" [a history of crimes] that writers explore with a profusely baroque style (Fuentes, "Literatura urgente" 14–15), the neobaroque hermetisim of Monsiváis's "Dios" is a paradigmatic proof. The apparent crime itself is hidden like a sphinx on the distant horizon of the text's interdiscursive landscape, first as a riddle, "las tragedias impunes" [unpunished tragedies] (Días 111), then as a local detail already exported to the universal. On this plane, Mexico's most recent unpunished tragedy—"un general se dispone a partir hacia un mitin estudiantil en una plaza pública" [a general gets ready to leave for a student demonstration in a public plaza]—acquires parity with the U.S. dropping of an atomic bomb on Hiroshima ("un aviador acude a liquidar una guerra en oriente" [a pilot hurries to end a war in the East]) and the assassination of Archduke Ferdinand on the eve of World War I ("un exaltado afina su revólver para aguardar el paso del carruaje de un príncipe [a fanatic aims his revolver as he awaits the passage of a prince's carriage]) (111–12). Its temporal and metaphorical (dis)placement persuades us that the crime in Tlatelolco, elsewhere the ubiquitous source of Días's emotive and prophetic energy, is a metonym for a larger transgression in this crónica's plot of gnoseological sustentation, or mystery.[16]

As detectory readers, we begin our search together with the "angustiado Observador" [anguished Observer] (Días 112) by examining externally visible clues. The Observer, who assures us he is not interested in recording the nation's stupefaction before an eclipse (94), must travel in pursuit of his object from his home in Mexico City to Acapulco and from there to towns of increasing geographic marginality. When he eventually reaches the beach at Puerto Escondido, he scrutinizes every clue to the mystery of "la perdurabilidad de la Gran Familia Nacional" [the enduring strength of the Great National Family] (92) that his centrifugal movement has turned up on the landscape: the caravans of cars streaming westward in another kind of Gold Rush (91); the way hillsides (nature) and church walls (culture) together proclaim the presidential merits of Luis Echeverría while an opposition candidate's name appears on a single, isolated, rock (93); the flora and fauna he

names, including cacti and "esas mujeres que calientan tortillas (al abrigo de
la superstición gastronómica que indica como supremamente deleitoso lo
más barato), . . . esas niñas de ojos interminables fugitivas de un cuadro de
Diego Rivera, . . . esos perros de la desesperanza y ese borracho pintoresco
. . . " [those women who heat tortillas (aided by the gastronomic belief that
holds the cheapest food to be supremely tasty) . . . those little girls of bottomless eyes who have escaped from a Diego Rivera painting, . . . those dogs of
desperation and that picturesque drunk] (93).

An early finding is that atemporal misery is one of "las constantes del
ser colonial" [the colonial subject's permanent traits] (93). Moving ever outward from the centrist capital, he notes that, in Acapulco, nature has been
paved over by neocolonialist commercialization, while Puerto Escondido
has so far been discovered only by the underground tourist (94). Here, on
the edge of Mexican territory, eclipse hunters will congregate.

The Observer has arrived two days before the event, giving himself time
to search everywhere for an understanding of the impalpable but ironclad
strength of Mexican nationalism (92). He spies on the middle class that
has brought its can openers to the beach; and on local Indians; student activists exposing themselves to ridicule and arrest; New Age mystics who brag
they can wilt geraniums with the powers of the mind; gringo tourists; hippies dressed like Tarahumaras; urban Indians (nacos) wanting desperately
to belong but knowing they cannot memorize the English lyrics "You can't
always get what you want," knowing themselves to be "humillados por la
pinche vida" [humiliated by this shitty life] (99). He also observes the impoverished wannabes of surrounding villages such as San Sebastián Ixcapa and
Cacahuatepec who show their local pride by singing regional favorites like
the eponymous "Dios nunca muere" [God Never Dies] (100).

As the Observer tucks away another finding (Mexico is divided into
twenty-nine states, two territories, one Federal District, "y decenas de países
y de épocas históricas" [and many countries and historical eras]) (100), he
advances a theorem: Members of the Onda are by far the most interesting
people gathered at the beach (101), even though, as idealistic nonconform-
ists, they leave much to be desired: Their predictable ideology is uninter-
esting—indeed they are actively unintellectual ("no leen" [they don't read]);
they share the general Latin American notion of art as improvisation; they
are vulgar romantics who believe themselves to be profound (105). Still, the
Observer finds the counterculture instructive: "Lo que separa a la Onda del

resto de este mundo no es, pese a todo, tanto lo que consumen como lo que pretenden evitar" [What distinguishes the Onda from the rest is not, in spite of everything, so much what they consume as it is what they try to avoid] (104). What the hippie avoids is communication based on exhortation, received authority, hierarchy, replication and self-congratulation. At the very least, the Onda must be respected for being "una forma de vida que se aproxima, quizás de modo inconveniente, a la libertad" [a lifestyle that comes close, perhaps in inconvenient ways, to freedom] (105).

change enunciated within

Having inventoried significant facts on the external landscape, Monsiváis moves his investigation of the Mexican National Family to an interior horizon. For the last eleven pages of the text, the Observer's gaze will remain fixed on the scene of his own subjectivity and the collective consciousness of the citizens gathered to watch the eclipse. The quest for understanding is now centered squarely on language: the special slang of the Onda, which the Observer kindly translates for us, and the special speech-thought patterns of the narrator himself. Both dramatize how language structures thought and behavior. We detect an equation emerging, something like a theory of relativity: Language (Idea + Action) = Reality.

To work out a proof for us, the narrator, as an obsessive-compulsive seeker of knowledge and a writer of literary journalism who tries to justify his claim to the name with each paragraph (93–94), sets forth essential data. One fact reveals him to be a city slicker who cannot escape the limitations of his origins (92). As fascinated as he is by the hippie mentality, he is himself "un conformista convicto y confeso" [a hopeless, self-confessed conformist] who internalized the Bible in his Protestant youth (110) and who personally cannot buy into either the philosophy or the lifestyle of the Onda (105). Nonetheless, he envies the hippie's capacity to lose himself in the wordless thereness of being, to escape momentarily the prison of reality-making language and surrender to the found meanings of Nature. He senses that he ought to "ensimismarse, zambullirse en algo, hacia algo" [go inside himself, dive into something, toward something], but, anchored to the world of objectified perception, he can only produce something resembling a crónica (110).

He is compelled in this by the linguistic-literary traditions that shaped his subjectivity. In a section subtitled "Tonatiuh cualo" (alluding in Nahuatl to father sun), Monsiváis braids at least five linguistic registers together while the moon spreads her body over the sun. Citing Aztec speech summons Mexico's precolumbian family members to the beach, perhaps to help the Observer, who stands there "incapaz de entender o vivir el significado de acciones que no comparte" [incapable of understanding or living the meaning of actions he does not participate in] (111), wanting to understand the hippie who says "A mí lo único que me importa es tirar la Onda" [The only thing I care about is going with the flow] (110)—which is essentially what the Aztecs managed to do through a cosmovision that fused time, thought, ideology, physical space and action (Alcina Franch 104–106). From offstage, two voices of historical hegemony chime in: that of Sahagún, the Spanish missionary who translated Aztec testimony about eclipses of the sun for Mexican posterity—*"cuando esto acontece (el sol) se muestra muy rojo; ya no permanece quieto"* (110) *[when this happens (the sun) becomes very red; it is no longer still]*—and that of the biblical King David, who asserted the sun's unassailable authority: *"Del un cabo de los cielos es su salida y su giro hasta la extremidad de ellos. Y no hay quien se esconda de su calor"* [It goes forth from the uttermost edge of the heavens and runs about to the end of it again; nothing is hidden from its burning heat] (111).[17] But these are waning voices. Even as they speak, the power they derive from the sun is being eclipsed: "La tierra está adquiriendo esa frialdad previa . . . que anuncia un estado de ánimo intermedio o nuevo" [The earth is acquiring that preparatory cold which announces an intermediate or new state of mind] (111).

As "la invasión ejercida por la luna se acrece, se extiende, sojuzga" [the invasion commanded by the moon expands, extends itself and subjugates], the often criminal authority of "father sun" is occluded and Mexico seems able now to experience instead the novelty of

> la cualidad evocativa de un momento del día que aún no se inventa, equidistante del amanecer y el ocaso, del mediodía y el anochecer . . . . El eclipse ha descubierto las tonalidades luminosas, el aspecto entre desolado y pletórico, del instante del día en que, idealmente, se cometen las grandes traiciones y se inician las conclusiones de una época. . . . Y durante tres intensos, concentrados, prodigiosos minutos no hay sol. . . . Se va erigiendo la visión definitiva del eclipse, tres minutos quizás que se anardecen hasta la incandescencia. (111–12)

> [the evocative quality of a moment in the day that as yet does not exist, equidistant from dawn and dusk, noon and midnight . . . The eclipse has uncovered the luminous tones—an appearance ranging from desolate to

abundant—of the instant, opportune, in which great betrayals are committed and the end of an era begins . . . And during three intense, concentrated, prodigious minutes there is no sun. The eclipse's definitive image slowly builds, during perhaps three minutes that flame into incandescence.]

The eclipse, which Mayans called the castration of the sun (109), is temporary—God Never Dies—but in the momentary suspension of patriarchal dominance, a renegade language like that of the Onda can effect a pantheistic blending of primordial matriarchy, New Age ritual and postmodern liturgy (109); this new syncretism transforms the popular mindset into an undulating wave of sensation and instinct which, perhaps in accord with the powers of the moon, foments "comunión con las ondas, con la Onda" [communion with the waves, with the Wave (Onda)] (109). The Observer, "tan square" [so irredeemably square] (112), cannot emulate the Onda's apparent ability to turn present time and the eclipse into extensions of their bodies and minds (112). But in the gap between his squareness and their moonlike curves, he can perceive new ways of fitting the past into his present state of mind. In the declared war between Order and Onda, the underdog has begun to win: "Algo empieza a morir: que lo registre esta luz; algo se va a decidir que afectará nuestra existencia: que lo capte y lo difunda este sol humillado" [Something begins to die: Let this light record it; something is going to be decided which will affect our lives: Let this humbled sun capture and disseminate it] (111).

rays of hope, a new dawning

Within the historical criminality of a paternalistic system we have detected hopeful signs of structural change: "La Onda es un chance que sí" [The Onda is a little ray of hope] (106). In this and all of Monsiváis's writings, juxtaposition of the expansive language of metonym, metaphor and symbol to the implosive energy of aphorism creates a kind of stylistic "breathing" akin to the Onda's moon-wave dynamism. Journalistic realities such as the eclipse harbor transcendent implications that Monsiváis helps us detect, even as he steps in with summations that channel us in directions he wants us to go. He especially wants to lead his Mexican readers toward a willingness to act in behalf of all oppressed minorities, who are "el retrato exacto del Sistema que en su afán de evitarse problemas ha pospuesto la creación de ciudadanos para el año 2000" [the spitting image of a System which, in its eagerness to avoid problems, has postponed the job of creating citizens for the year 2000] (124).

With the calendar, human inventiveness did its best to eliminate cosmic surprises. Premodern societies the world over boxed time inside a four-cornered space pulling irresistibly toward the center (Mignolo, "Putting the Americas" 30–31). In Mesoamerica, the resulting quincunx, through "arqueoastronomía" [an architectural astronomy] (Alcina Franch 102), became the pyramid, a triangle set upon a square that locked into its stones the nucleus of Nahuatl thought, belief, ideology and action (Séjourné 101–102). Time meshed with buildings and towns placed on the landscape, forming a spatialized cosmogony based on a highly centralized urban social organization. These were literally embodied in the Great Temple in the center of the city (Tenochtitlán-Tlatelolco) and in the person of the *tlatoani*, the chief warrior priest representing divine and secular power. Time thus imagined did indeed attach certainty to existence, but it also tied the present, the future and all possible truth to the past, thus fettering the very creativity of thought that had first imagined a ritual of days. Built into the calendrical schema were inevitable transgressions such as the little moon's takeover of the sun, but also a mode of *a priori* thinking that greatly weakened society's capacity to think its way out of a quandary. Circular day-keeping was one of the hardest practices to give up when the linear-thinking Christians arrived in the New World (Burkhart 72–86).

To imagine, as Monsiváis does, *structural* changes in centralist, hierarchical, traditionalist Mexico is to shift its *Días de guardar* on the cultural landscape. If with "Dios" Monsiváis celebrates the solar calendar's dethroning, with the whole of *Días* he interrupts the ceremonial calendar's eternal round of sacrifices. Only some of *Días*'s "ritual" texts and none of its festive little jokes involving time—games such as "Necrology" and "Guess Your Decade"—are assigned permanent place-dates. Like the three-minute hole of time during the eclipse, the book's imperfect progression leaves room for the imagination.

The greatest transgression in *Días* is the way it assigns meaning to spontaneous events rather than to cycles of rigidly measured time. An "emotive narrative" (Rader 5) that draws on the creative power of disruption, both as to time and as to historico-journalistic exposition, the calendar in *Días* is based on the critical principle of cause and effect, as shown in the following list:

— The first chronicle (January 5) puts a centralist power on stage with all its inadequacies;

— The second (February 5) dramatizes the effect of the first cause on the stagnated periphery of Mexico;

— The third (February 10, 16) juxtaposes center and periphery to show differences of lifestyle but not of essential mindset;

— The fourth (February 14), in contrast, models the rigorous self-criticism of the modern individual consciousness;

— The fifth, without date, juxtaposes another exemplary intellectual with an oxymoron: a traditionalist intelligentsia;

— The sixth (March 7), moving again from center to periphery, transports all Mexican social types to the western limit of the country and deep inside their collective consciousness;

— The seventh (March 9) returns to the center, where peripheral cultures—hippies and nacos—threaten the status quo;

— The eighth, without date, shows the middle class straining to keep the edges—hippies and nacos—from closing in on the center;

— The ninth (March 21) shows a sycophantic Mexican press conspiring with the middle class to keep the center closed;

— The tenth (May 1) illustrates how the State supports this denial of individual opportunities to acquire a political will;

— The eleventh, without date, again turns back, this time to scrutinize historical roots of today's oppressive centralism and false national unity;

— The twelfth (May 10) links nationalism to cultural oppression, through an analysis that contrasts modern and premodern tastes;

— The thirteenth, without date, focuses on another tradition, an instance of authentic creativity that contrasts with the vulgar "herd" instincts of the previous text;

— The fourteenth (July 2) compares imitative Pop Mexico with a genuinely revolutionary North American cultural production;

— The fifteenth, without date, situates the eternal durability of centralized power within its sacralized government officials;

— The sixteenth (August 1) immediately dramatizes the contrasting public challenge of power's abuses;

- The seventeenth (September 13) intensifies the contrast. This chronicle and the previous one, which reveal the spiritual ascension of 1968, occupy the ordinal and cardinal center;
- The eighteenth (September 15) balances the optimism of the previous chronicles with the admonitory reminder of poverty;
- The nineteenth (October 2/November 2) measures the problem that Mexico's traditional "calendar" presents for solution;
- The twentieth (November 15) points to the monolithic political system as a first place to search;
- The twenty-first (November 20) links that failed democracy to dictatorial impulses that survived the 1910 Revolution;
- The twenty-second (December 12) links those to the "culture of poverty" that is tied to the cult of the Virgin of Guadalupe; and
- The twenty-third (December 25) gives birth to laughter and its power to neutralize unproductive attitudes, cultural weaknesses and political failings.

From first to last, *Días* demonstrates a moral and political use of time. The eighteen dated chronicles perform as "living images" of an eighteen-month Aztec solar calendar ready for sacrifice, while the five without dates, embodying traditions and patriarchal practices that are frequently injurious to modern Mexico, have been cast as "lost days" out of time. The anachronistic square triangle has been weakened by ellipses and spirals and penetrated by radical contingencies and a willingness to accept the unknown. In Monsiváis's *Días*, traditions have become singular events. Yesterday has lost its footing in today and loosened its grip on tomorrow.

7

finding LOVE in all the "wrong" places
reading AMOR PERDIDO

Seven years after Carlos Monsiváis measured Mexico's "dimensiones perdidas" in *Días de guardar* (264), he gathers another twenty-three chronicles that will now somehow meditate on Mexico's *Amor perdido* (1977). Is there a link between the loss in *Días* that alluded to the disillusionment of the 1968 Student Movement and the loss in *Amor* that refers to Mexico as it was in the wake of Tlatelolco (*Amor* 57)? To answer, we begin with the readily evident.

There is no brief introductory text that we might easily understand as a prologue's authorial guide to reading. *Amor* offers us a single pretextual clue: A mortuary voice says, "En tus manos encomiendo el epígrafe" [Into your hands I commend this epigraph]; this is the text of the eponymous popular song, "Amor perdido" [Lost Love]. Loosely paraphrased, the lyrics we have been bequeathed present a speaker who wishes a former lover good luck and adds, with cheerful civility, good riddance: "Por tu parte nunca fuiste mío ni yo para ti" [You were never mine nor I yours]; our whole relationship was a game of chance that I lost; you're better off without me and, frankly, I'm out looking for a new love. Far from the melancholy lamentation one would expect in a song about a lost love, the lyrics suggest a possibly ironic reading not noted in reviews.[1]

The table of contents organizes the crónicas in seven categories with mostly playful subtitles. Title and subtitle of the first text—"Alto contraste (A manera de foto fija)"—do not acquire usable meaning until one begins to read the text. The same is generally true of all the titles; their referents become known only in the readings they introduce. "Yo te bendigo, vida" and "Señores, a orgullo tengo de ser antimperialista" announce analyses of two popular singers and two famous communists; "Mártires, militantes y memoriosos" groups five texts on leftist opposition; "La crema de la crema" examines six aspects of high society; "Mi personaje inolvidable" refers to chronicles on a variety-show host, a labor leader and a beauty queen; "La naturaleza de la Onda" chronicles the Mexican hippie movement; "Que si esto es escandaloso" announces three pieces on public figures with controversial lifestyles. The significance of their order must be discovered in the reading.

The epilogue, "Colofón en modo alguno autocrítico" (347–48), is in fact the book's most helpful prereading guide. Its nine short segments and dated tagline read like anecdotal comments that mourners might offer at a funeral service, an appropriately ironic mode, given that a third of this book's texts originated in reportage on funeral services for public figures. The epilogue provides clues to posthumous understanding of a book that is dead, as it were, or of a play just ended—"muchas gracias por su asistencia . . . gentil auditorio" [Thanks a lot for coming . . . dear audience]. Monsiváis assures us that *Amor perdido* is not a Mexican version of Carlyle's *Heroes*,[2] and that it does and does not intend to be "anotaciones sobre un mundo circular en cuya estabilidad, eficacia y ánimo invulnerables casi todos creían, sin mayores reservas, hasta hace poco tiempo" [notes on a circular world in whose invulnerable stability, efficacy and spirit almost everyone believed, with few reservations, until a short time ago] (347–48). A parody of "la fugacidad de lo eterno" [fleeting eternity] (348) is retrospectively apparent in his inclusion of a chronicle on "el fugaz embajador de México en España (doce días en el cargo)" [the ephemeral ambassador of Mexico to Spain (twelve days on the job)]—this being former president Díaz Ordaz, of Tlatelolco infamy.[3]

He implies that *Amor perdido* participates in Mexico's historical personality cult but adds that "el star system" has been replaced by a new protagonist, "el desempleado, que crece a sesenta minutos por segundo, y bajo cuya invocación catastrófica medran todas las profecías y se van extinguiendo las ilusiones fáciles o matizadas en el progreso" [the unemployed worker, increasing at the rate of sixty minutes per second, under whose catastrophic invocation all prophecies come true, and facile or subtle dreams of progress die away] (348).

He signs this document as one would a last will and testament which, with no small irony, bequeaths the family to the family: "México, agosto de 1977, en el año de la tregua, la confianza serena y la contemplación amorosa de las raíces. C.M." [Mexico, August 1977, in the year of the truce, serene confidence and the loving contemplation of my roots. C.M.] (348).

Mexico in a nutshell

The longest contemplation of his roots comes in the first chronicle, which, if not in name, in fact functions as the prologue. "Alto contraste (A manera de foto fija)" reprises Mexico's cultural history, from the nation's first concerted efforts to modernize (Porfirio Díaz's thirty-four years of dictatorship, 1876–1911) through the Mexican Revolution and the decades of the nationalist state, up to and after the quashed bid for democratic aperture in 1968. The summation would be remarkable alone for fitting in thirty-two pages; it becomes a chronicle for the canon because fact is so seamlessly forged with theory, analysis, drama and baroque virtuosity. Enclosing vast implicit spaces of representation and significance, the dense phrasing impels a pace of reading as slow and gestured as the reality here recreated.

The crónica's title refers to the narrator's contemplation of black-and-white photographs of the Porfiriato and Revolution.[4] In a grave voice that keeps to the background like that of a curator gracing visitors with their personal guided tour, he pastes the tangible photographs of that time a century before in a verbal album displaying Mexico at significant stages in its development, older each time, but always with the same extremely rehearsed gestures (17) in a world inhabited and dominated by purely external sensations

(18), always depicting the same handful of powerful Mexicans (18), always including "un blow-up de nuestro culto a la personalidad" [a blow-up of our personality cult] (19), always posed with sexual repression in the background (20), with the black sheep (abused masses and persecuted rebels) always out of frame (22).

A revolution ought to invert top and bottom of society, and indeed, with the emergence of the woman as camp follower and soldier, the Mexican Revolution of 1910 did allow feminine liberation to draw a short-lived experimental breath (22–24); geographical redistribution of the population revealed many members of the "Gran Familia Mexicana" (*Días* 92, 264; *Amor* 201) that had previously gone unrecognized (24); the opportunism of a new class (25) squeezing itself between the powerful and the persecuted did give the oligarchy something to look at besides itself (24).

The postrevolutionary phase lasts at least through 1958 when, driven by the middle class's avid pursuit of an overwhelming Americanization, a different mentality begins to emerge and loss of the old concept of nation seems to be irreversible (37). Until then, each six-year regime consolidates the foundational blocks of a society Monsiváis insistently characterizes as doubly medieval, imprisoned in the legacies of both feudal Christianity and prehispanic ritualism. Both of these reject possession of an autonomous interior life as an impermissible luxury (18) while defending their centralist authority from behind theatrical gesture and mask (18, 33–34, 46) and with language emptied of any possible signification except the stultification of melodrama and the preemptive authority of myth (38). Not merely patriarchal and sexist, Mexico's leaders are deeply machista, a pathology that Monsiváis perceptively equates with the programmed infantilism, dependency and violence of an impoverished client state (30–32).[5] From the tlatoanis of Tenochtitlán and the Spanish conquistadors on, Mexico's chiefs pursue an inflexible schema for monopolizing power: a paternalistic rule that vests legitimacy in the president as God the Father (33, 36); corruption (which Monsiváis sees as the heart of national life) (34), and conformity: in sum, a monolithic moral and (a)political shield against fissure.

Monsiváis asks: What social and cultural spaces have been made available to Mexican dissidents fighting for democracy or socialism, or for alternative lifestyles? (40). He answers: no space at all. Dissidents have been repressed with jail, murder, censorship, hate campaigns, character assassination, ostracization and relegation to oblivion, as well as cooptation by a

monolithically persuasive system which, by destroying or engulfing opposition, permits "todas las libertades menos una: la libertad de ejercerlas"
[every freedom but one: the freedom to exercise it] (41). This frees the establishment to eternalize its omnipotence through a policy of rapacious capitalism known in Mexico as "desarrollismo" [developmentalism]; Monsiváis
sarcastically calls this a technical term for corruption (34).

the two mexicos, starkly depicted

Overall, the image developed to this point in "Alto contraste"
is starkly black and white. There are two countries, one visible and compact
enough for a photograph, one invisible and too massive to be posed. We
must envision a tiny circle in which, explosively compressed, the nation's
entire treasury of powers is invested to keep at bay "las hordas" [the hordes]
(26) and to suppress any possibility that class struggles (35) on the Periphery
might find a crack through which to penetrate the perfectly enclosed Center.
Collective conformity, obedience and dependency (36) reinforce a powerful
antimodern sentiment (44). Díaz Ordaz's Mexico, "centro del mundo" [the
center of the universe] (43), replicates a belief in Tenochtitlán as *tlalxicco*,
the "center, or navel of the earth" (Moctezuma 56; Broda 168). A palimpsest
underlying the whole of "Alto contraste," the Aztec motif prophetically summons the "world-ending" catastrophe implicated in the sacrifices of Tlatelolco in 1968 (44).

Next to the exteriorized archaism of nationalist Mexico's discourse,
Monsiváis's neobaroque (post)modernity installs aphorism, chiasmus and
cinematic metaphor to develop a "high contrast." Against the sociohistorical prohibition on introspection (i.e., unsupervised thinking), Monsiváis's
psychoanalytic narrator penetrates the subconscious of his subject to expose
reasons why "la verdad es lo social, lo social es la verdad" [truth is the social
and the social is truth] (19); why Mexicans tolerate a situation in which most
of them are "grupos de extras en la película donde un actor único monologa"
[extras in a film with but one speaking part] (19); why "los símbolos de la
grandeza son los manuales del comportamiento" [the symbols of greatness
constitute manuals of behavior] (36); why the loudest disagreements tend to
cover up the real ones (39); why a grinding economic reality spawns a psychology that legitimizes feelings of impotence (44). As in *Días de guardar*,
the primordial theoretical construct underlying his analyses is language:

Employed by the Establishment, it is a prison: the unalterable rhetoric (38) of unilateral power (43). Freed by underground tendencies that erupt into view in 1968,[6] language can be liberating: To demonstrate that the official version of an event is not the only one is to free the mind from myth, melodrama and, at this point in his career, what Monsiváis characterizes as psychoanalysis used by the middle class as another excuse for remaining silent and deaf (41).

Together, the violent dissolution of dissidence and the no less effective repression of difference through language project a disneyesque holograph as nation. After Tlatelolco, the regime's touted democratic opening is the Potemkin-like establishment (46) of one more lie. Hypocrisy frames a failed democracy that asserts itself after independence, again after the Revolution and still in 1968 (45). Ignorance and ego falsely define modernity as the self-indulgent prerogatives of a small class with disposable income (41). Hosting the Olympic Games is not proof that Mexico has reached its first, definitive, maturity when the government's response to an embarrassing announcement that it could be losing a race for power is to kill the messengers, and when the conditioned response of the society at large is to turn a deaf ear to official silence afterward (43). A country obsessed with appearances cannot, however hard it tries, fully mask the drawbacks of being a colonial and, now, "semicolonial" country, especially when it acts these out in inescapable view of the United States and "la falta de admiración o reconocimiento del resto del mundo" [the rest of the world's lack of admiration or recognition] (43).

held back by a premodern dependency

The psychic stresses endured by an essentially archaic culture forced ahead of its time, as it were, into a technological era, which it regards with "una repugnancia profundamente imbuida en la ideología de la Revolución Mexicana" [a repugnance deeply imbued in the ideology of the Mexican Revolution] (44), can be expected to cause depression after a trauma such as the 1968 sacrifice of its adolescent aspirations. Between *Días de guardar* and *Amor perdido*, the middle class, especially, became paralyzed by the defeatist conviction that its doom was foreordained (44). By the November 1976 date attached to this segment of "Alto contraste" (15–49), the Right could no longer disguise its fakery (46), the Left was a powerless mirror image of the Right (46–47) and the Middle contemplated the crum-

bling base of its only consolation—economic ascension—after the 1976
devaluation of the peso (47–48). Between the "foto fija" taken just after the
Revolution and this disheartening portrait of postmodern Mexico, the country has apparently managed only to travel backward to an impasse it had
never escaped.

In the concluding section dated April 1977 (49–57), Monsiváis
unsheathes an aggressively hostile "I" to cover a press conference given
by Gustavo Díaz Ordaz on the occasion of his appointment as Mexico's
first ambassador to Spain since that country's Civil War.[7] The triumphalist
and unrepentant machismo of the architect of Tlatelolco would seem to justify the middle class's regressive state of mind. Entering there, Monsiváis
encounters a catastrophic dependency: "El progreso aún puede aguardar-
nos si nos deshacemos de las pretensiones inútiles, si esperamos de arriba
cualquier buenaventura, si cedemos nuestras manías participatorias" [We
might still achieve progress if we let go of useless pretensions, if we accept
that all good fortune rains on us from above, if we give up our insistence
on participatory governance] (49). The speech echoes those of Aztecs interviewed by Sahagún: "Señor nuestro . . . En vuestras manos me pongo total-
mente porque yo no tengo posibilidad para regirme ni gobernarme . . . ¡Oh,
señor nuestro . . . ! [Mira] su pueblo, . . . huérfanos, que no saben ni entienden, ni consideran lo que conviene a su pueblo . . . Están como mudos. No
saben hablar; están como un cuerpo sin cabeza" [Lord, I put my life in your
hands because I am utterly unable to rule or govern myself . . . Oh, Lord! . . .
(See) your people, orphans who know nothing, understand nothing, cannot
even weigh what would be good for them. They are as mute beings. They
know not how to speak; they are as a headless body] (2: 335–36).

Ancient fears of being abandoned by the Father cluster in the deep
shadows behind the National Family gathered for the photograph that Monsiváis has just shown us. In the nearer background, we can perceive blurred
figures that Monsiváis advises us need longer in the developer to be brought
into clear focus: From 1968 to 1976, "la complejidad del país se acentúa
regionalmente y los intentos de independencia sindical o los esfuerzos orga-
nizativos de los grupos disidentes o la emergencia contradictoria de las colo-
nias populares . . . son fenómenos que en lo nacional ocupan, si acaso,
un segundo plano" [the complexity of the country is accentuated regionally,
and attempts at union independence, or organizational efforts by dissident
groups, or the contradictory emergence of popular neighborhoods, are all

phenomena which, at the level of the national, are of only secondary importance, if that] (47).

Our long look at the foregrounded image we have just scrutinized will inform Monsiváis's study, next, of faces drawing closer to visibility in the snapshot that *Amor* takes just when Mexico is poised to turn.

"Como suele suceder en los países dependientes, la historia de la mayoría de sus figuras emblemáticas es una sencilla y compacta visión del desencuentro y la pérdida" [As commonly happens in dependent nations, the history of the majority of its emblematic figures is a simple and compact vision of disunity and loss] (288). That is true enough for *Amor's* histories; as part of this collection's exploration of mésalliances in the Mexican Family, several notable deaths in the seventies present symbolic opportunities to "sentir la herencia cultural en el contexto de un velorio inolvidable" [feel our cultural heritage through the occasion of an unforgettable funeral] (102). We meet seven of *Amor's* emblematic figures at their burials and two through their memoirs.[8] Most of these funerary pieces are placed in the first half of the book and they are about men. Five of *Amor's* twenty-three chronicles focus on women; the book's last two texts analyze living women.

poking fun at the new power class

In the middle are the six pieces devoted to Mexico's movers and shakers. These call forth the narrator's most derisive tones and are the briefest and least journalistic of *Amor's* discourses. "El proyecto general: atmósferas de alta sociedad" introduces the Nouveau Riche who will misbehave in the following five vignettes. This "crema de la crema" is in fact an "aristocracia pulquera" (156)—a withering judgment that links Mexico's so-called aristocracy to *pulque,* a cheap liquor two steps down from tequila and an emblem of the alcoholic vagrant. These upstarts, who invented themselves during the Porfiriato, are still, in the forties, nothing but "inditos que hace treinta años apenas podían con una carreta de mula y ahora manejan cádillacs" [poor little Indians who only thirty years before were lucky to own a mule cart but now drive Caddies] (159). If they have money it is because, darwinian, they take advantage of institutionalized corruption: Mexico's developmentalism favors those fittest for survival (161); they purloin caché from servile society pages, (162) which speak for a smug minority.

The first individual we meet is "El Self-Made Man," the banker who throws a party to invite envy into his mansion (164). In this satirical fantasy, we are lavished with neobaroque description of glittering possessions and breathless guests—the omniscient narrator suffers "el anhelo de adjetivos contundentes" [a dearth of sufficiently dramatic adjectives] (164); but we also hear, weaving itself through the rooms of the mansion of this man who, "sin ayuda de nadie, se hizo a sí mismo" [made it all by himself] (163), the ironic leitmotiv of a mariachi whose plaintive song brings the impoverished masses on which the banker's fortune rests right inside his sanctuary. The splendor of this palatial house testifies to the banker's investment in the valuation of appearances and links him to the conquered Aztecs who also believed life was defined by the erection of monuments to their own glory (164). The banker's mausoleum presents a provocative target for contemporary descendants of the Aztecs, the hordes of poor crammed into the slums of Ciudad Netzahualcóyotl (164) who, all the guests fear, "acabarán por devorarlo todo. ¡Qué fauces! Se multiplican al mil por uno. Donde había un miserable ahora hay una colonia" [will end up devouring everything. What gaping maws! They multiply like rabbits. Where before there was one miserable wretch there's now a whole neighborhood] (165).

In this and each of the "Crema" pieces, Monsiváis unfurls *Amor perdido*'s most experimental narrator and trespasses on fictional omniscience. The merciless fun he pokes at these bourgeois arrivistes deconstructs their pretensions to modernity. The confused patrons of a benefit ballet featuring "Nureyev en Bellas Artes" don't know when to applaud (171); watching dancers who move in incomprehensibly suspect ways, the men wonder if they are risking their manhood; in fact, is it possible that "¿este Nureyev es un fraude? No será la primera vez que nos tomen por subdesarrollados y nos den lo que les antoje" [this Nureyev could be a fraud? It wouldn't be the first time we were treated like third-world peons who have to take whatever's foisted on them] (170). Having read promotional promises that Nureyev floats they expect him to fly over the stage, not to stay close to the floor with little controlled movements (172): "Es sensacional, pero ¿por qué no quiso bailar para nosotros? ¿Qué, nos habrá visto inditos?" [He's terrific, but why does he refuse to dance for us? What, does he think we're just a bunch of poor Indians?] (172)

porfirio díaz lives on

The savage humor in "Nureyev" is inverted in "La vieja usanza: Genaro Fernández Macgregor." The pages analyzing the epitome of Establishment Power between 1920 and 1960 occupy the exact center of the book and, by metonymic extension, represent the most authentic animus of a Mexico ferociously machista and violently afraid of dissidence (178–79). Fernández Macgregor is the emblematic Mexican Gentleman: honorable, Catholic, sentimental, apolitical and decent (173). He is Porfirio Díaz living on into postmodern times, opposing signs of restlessness with an archaic language employed like a walled compound (175). But, while he believes language and reality are identical (175), the younger generation of the next text, "El 'disidente' (Radical Chic): los burgueses con corazón de masa," demonstrates how the power class's rhetoric fails to apprehend or adjust to facts.

mexico's radical chic

Monsiváis overtly signifies on Tom Wolfe's *Radical Chic,* which Monsiváis characterizes as the description of a soirée in the condominium of Leonard Bernstein and his wife Felicia (180), a party given so that the oligarchy can dramatize a politically correct interest in the masses (181). Like Bernstein's theatrical "solidarity" with the Black Panthers, the pity that is acted on by a Mexican Felicia, who will go to a poor neighborhood to raise the consciousness of the masses (182), is the stylized act of a "dissident" who enjoys playing at revolution "sin que intervengan ni las consecuencias ni el temor a las consecuencias" [without risk of either consequences or the fear of consequences] (181). While the narrator does not doubt her sincerity or cynically take her radical chic for terror of the inevitability of change (182), her bid to "desclasar" [un-class-ify] the poor is more adolescent rebellion than revolution (183).

a cosmetic self-confidence

Monsiváis completes his review of the illegitimacy of bourgeois centrality when he invades the consciousness of one of the Beautiful People attending a star-studded fashion show for which guests come dressed as their favorite actors. Most of these are Hollywood celebrities, and we see that Mexico's power class has put on an assumed self-confidence that masks an historical inferiority complex (187). Using money as the minimum compensation possible for being condemned to live in Mexico (188), the bourgeoisie is here a child with its nose pressed to the glass of a store stocked with enchanting foreign goods. This small middle-class island of discourses sits like froth atop the surface of *Amor*'s other discourses. These break in waves on the tiny bourgeois enclave and patiently extend the book's sustained tropes of Inside-Outside and Center-Periphery.

The first to undermine the literate class's master narrative is the vulgarity of popular song. "El bohemio mexicano del siglo XX" (76), Agustín Lara in "El harem ilusorio" refunctions the excruciating elitism of modernist poetry to create a repertoire of torch songs celebrating society's double standard in sex: decency at home and delight among the twelve percent of women who have registered as prostitutes with the government, which supervises brothels as containment devices (66). The theatrical hypocrisy of the bolero, whose vulgar exaggeration is meant to effect an appreciation of the sublime (86), acquires another dimension in the following text on José Alfredo Jiménez. We saw in chapter 3 how the exaggerated machismo of this ranchera singer symbolizes a culture of poverty whose manipulation by government is mirrored outward in Mexico's self-presentation as a mistreated dependent in the global market. Read against each other, the "low-class" art of Lara and Jiménez and the "high-class" art of bourgeois at the ballet depict the same anachronistic contrast.

true believers and martyrs

The archaic paternalism of Fernández MacGregor and Radical Chic's false conscience are next contested in seven chronicles about the left intelligentsia, stalinist true believers and martyred activists. Famed muralist David Alfaro Siqueiros is the ambivalent iconoclast of Mexico's Old Guard communists. As a persecuted critic of government and bourgeois elitism (105) and also a victim of the Communist Party, which expelled him for having an extramarital affair, he is a complex icon of difference: a power-wielding cacique, a stubbornly independent thinker, an artistic pioneer, an insider on the outside and a maker of myths. In his same class, and subject of the next crónica, novelist José Revueltas is less enigmatically dissident. Fifty-four in the summer of '68, Revueltas has survived several imprisonments by the time he serves as elder statesman for the youths launching themselves against the Center's arrogant paternalism (124). Throughout his exemplary life, he acts selflessly (124) and, unlike so many beaten down over time, he keeps alive a sense of joy in his inexhaustibly militant activism (125).

In sharp contrast, an unflattering portrait of "La vieja izquierda" (126–32) [The Old-Guard Left] shows Latin American stalinism to be a self-righteous, prudish and corrupt institution with no real political power (127). The Party becomes another "visión de los vencidos" of self-destructive sentimentalism and melodramatic defeatism (129–30). Then, in the ebb and flow that structures these short texts, Benita Galeana is praised as an exemplary communist and, as well, a heroine of women and the poor. Brutalized by men in her childhood, she was a rural immigrant who learned very early how to survive in the dog-eat-dog urban world, a militant communist jailed fifty-eight times and, overall, an untutored but indomitable opponent of governmental paternalism and persecution by her macho comrades. She remains an icon of the best moral tradition of the Mexican Left (137). Following her example, rural educator Joel Arriaga is honored in a mortuary piece for his irreducible courage and honesty (142) in the face of persecution by Catholic Puebla's Moral Majority (140). He was assassinated for his trespasses, but, in Puebla, "en medio de la estrepitosa y aullante reacción que juzga idénticas todas las formas de vida marginal (del comunismo al consumo de mariguana, del ateísmo al lesbianismo), transcurre una juventud educada . . . para la cual ahora el fin primero es norteamericanizar al medioevo . . . La Puebla tradicional se desmorona" [in the midst of a rabid reactionary group that considers all minority lifestyles to be identical (from communism to marijuana use and atheism to lesbianism), an educated youth appears, for whom the primary goal now is to Americanize the Middle Ages. . . Traditional Puebla begins to crumble[9] (143). The Establishment has not given up believing in its absolute right to impunity before the law (144), but it is being knocked over by the dictates of the Hit Parade (143).

The distinction is as yet very subtle, however. Elsewhere in Puebla, Ramón Danzós Palominos, leader of a farm union, is arrested for inciting workers to seize lands. Thanks to Monsiváis's in-depth reportage, we can peek inside the prison at the inner workings of a sham justice system that jails the father of a large family for ten months, after refusing to allow the man's lawyer to speak for him (145–48). A following report, "Las ganas de vivir," demonstrates anew how a corrupt system safeguards its impunity.

Communist Hilario Moreno Aguirre, a provincial schoolteacher, is accused of terrorist sympathies and later dies in jail, despite news accounts attempting to extend a shield of public light on his case (149).

Colonized voices of the mainstream

The appalling injustice of this death crashes up against the chronicles on middle-class frivolity. On the other side of this island of discourses, three other sets flow outward like a riptide: The first is a trio of texts embodying the weight of mainstream masses, the second brings the Onda's complexities to bear, the third hails three exemplary dissidents.

Raúl Velasco emblematizes a relationship between Mexico City's rapidly growing population and television, here seen as a hegemonic tool to neutralize mass culture's liberating potential. The variety-show host's cultivation of archetypes promotes false democracy by depoliticizing the mass mind and trivializing the lower middle class's latent power (195). This text's hectoring narrator says, "mira, Velasco, sucede que tú eres un vocero de las modas sin riesgo" [See here, Velasco, you're nothing but a mouthpiece for conformist fashions] who ratifies programmed behavior (193). Equally an obstacle to modernity, labor boss Fidel Velázquez is an "enforcer" for the regime who counters the union's oppositional power and domesticates its "indios fieles" [obedient Indians] (198). Velázquez is observed at a nationally televised labor convention held in a movie theater, an irony that constructs the figure of a televisual democracy enclosing its own dissidence: The beginning of the end of "charro" (macho) unionism is seen in the power of video (203), a technology that may one day expose union protections as lies and show Velázquez as "la permanencia en el control y el control de la permanencia" [permanence in control and control of permanency] (210).

The same chiastic duality also obtains in "Miss México," in which the national beauty pageant is seen to be simultaneously a monument to the power class's legitimacy (212) and a reversible sign of women's liberation. Because Mexico's young womanhood unwittingly objectifies herself while seeking her fifteen minutes of fame (217), the beauty contest is a particularly egregious form of sexism. Still, this false sharing of male power is based on the authentic liberation of women's sports, which weakened prejudice against women baring their legs in public (221).

the counterculture: a deficient dream

These colonized voices of the mainstream Mexican masses are immediately answered in "La naturaleza de la Onda," Monsiváis's most often cited analysis of the meaning of the counterculture. Here, as we saw in the previous chapter, the Onda is presented as a postcolonial bid for modern autonomy whose dictatorial imposition of a dissident slang became neocolonialist self-subjugation (236–37). Now Monsiváis specifies, in order to diversify, his reader's understanding of this group's nonconformity. Styled on North American popular culture, the Onda is a utopian enterprise aimed at creation of a nation within a nation and, as the primordial enabler of the fantasy, a language that diverges from the standard idiom (230). In keeping with that pluralist project, Monsiváis subtitles a series of sections that individualize divergent aspects of the movement. These include its anticolonialist ancestors (bohemian artists of the Romantic and Modernist schools) (231–34), the mainstream hippie culture on display in "La nación de Avándaro" (247–55) (an analysis of the Mexican "Woodstock" concert) and the young man with a brilliant future (259–62) who, because he prefers his technocratic training to the government's traditional ranchera image, gives the center a facelift; he does not, however, repair the sagging musculature: the ages-old practice of Mexico hating Mexicans (262).

The sub-subsection titled "Los nacos en Avándaro" (252–53) explicitly dwells on the overwhelmingly middle-class character of the Onda and opposes its desire to act out against the Father to the evident desire of the marginalized popular classes to learn a language that will help them acquire a visible presence in the National Family Portrait. This is finally Monsiváis's harshest critique of the Onda. It frittered away its potential because it was not an ethical—i.e., political—use of dissident energy. Hippies were not trying to find a way into a center whose authority they could modify and share; all they wanted was out. They are therefore, as Monsiváis already observes in *Días de guardar*, valuable most as a negative example.

novo: another waste of potential

In a sadder way, Salvador Novo also dissipates his contestatory potential. In the first of three close-ups at book's end, Monsiváis meditates, after this man's death, on the life of a homosexual who was famously "outed" in an era when nationalist machismo infused society with toxic levels of testosterone. The trajectory of Novo's responses to being marginal-ized descends from the satiric high road (277–79) to a self-pitying and the-atrical conformity (284–90). He blazed pioneering trails as an avant-garde poet and the immediate predecessor of contemporary cronistas, most par-ticularly, Monsiváis, but was finally defeated in his lifelong struggle to find acceptance despite his alternative lifestyle. "No obstante su numeroso poder de atracción . . . Novo nunca dejó de ser un outsider" [Despite his consider-able popularity, Novo never escaped his outsider status] (296). An intruder in the Gran Familia, he died alone at the end (296).

As if to his rescue, Irma "La Tigresa" Serrano now appears, like a "venus de fuego" [Venus of fire] (297). Nightclub performer, composer and singer of popular songs, actress and entrepreneur, Serrano trades sexual favors for their value as entertainment, protection, financial gain and notori-ety. Utterly transgressive, Serrano marginalizes marginalization itself, using her stage popularity to turn sexist objectification against men (298).[10] Unlike the "Self-Made Man" we saw above, Serrano is truly a self-made woman, a multimillionaire who markets scandal like computer components. She is public, aggressively active, antimaternal, loud, coarse and irreverent. Her vulgarity "es una atmósfera vasta y legítima, la oscura y poderosa sensación colectiva de que el buen gusto sigue siendo galardón de una minoría intoler-able" [is a vast and legitimate cosmos of feeling, a dark, powerful and collec-tive impression that good taste is still the reward of an intolerable minority] (310). She is the perfect dissident in the pluralist society Monsiváis is design-ing and she is joined by the burlesque actress Isela Vega in "¡Viva México hijos de la decencia! (Del nuevo status de las 'malas palabras')."

Vega's stage act impersonates the theory that Mexicans will not live democratically until they learn to violate the father-god's "lenguaje sagrado" [sacred language] (Paz, Laberinto 67). The most guarded of Mexico's "pal-abras prohibidas, secretas" [forbidden, secret words] (67) is "chingar," a complexly nuanced word, roughly equivalent to English "fuck," which Carlos Fuentes intertextually comments on in 1962, in La muerte de Artemio Cruz (143–47). It is already significant that this "four-letter" word turns up in the most canonical (and machista) of the nation's elite literature; that it should be appropriated by a woman who shouts it out as she struts about in vari-ous stages of undress on stage is to expand 1968's language of modernity so that it includes Mexico's historical outcasts. Tagged unacceptable by their indecent use of language, these date from the street vagrant of colonial days

(*Amor* 322) through the illiterate mestizo's rejection in the nineteenth century (323) and up to 1977, by which time even the upper classes admit bad words into their discourse. The hegemony's use of "el Perfecto Decir" [Perfect Speech] (323) as a way of marginalizing undesirables has been broken down; it is naive to think—to have ever thought—that "la Pureza Idiomática nos preservará de las invasiones de los enemigos" [Linguistic Purity will preserve us from enemy invasion] (324), that a prohibition on pornography could be the shield of a monolingual society that hoped to keep Isela Vega from ever exercising her freedom of speech in a public forum. But here she is, brandishing the forbidden word with great good humor as "un desafío político, la bofetada en el rostro del Sistema" [a political challenge, a slap in the System's face] (343).

Bad language is part and parcel of a general disrespect for sacred cows that from about the mid-sixties on began to surface as a fashionable antisolemnity (321). Historical Eternity leaned desperately against the tide, but by now, forces for change were swimming in postmodernist eclecticism and electronic invisibility, and the power class found itself unable to check the invasion. It could not even see or identify, much less control, the diffuse, anonymous hordes who, in pursuit of pleasure and permission to speak their mind freely, began slipping in:

> Venga a nos el Día de Hoy: el pluralismo político/ la desaparición de los caciques/ las prácticas democráticas en la vida sindical/ la industrialización del campo/ la erradicación del patrioterismo/ la reconciliación con el lenguaje cotidiano. Lo que—en buena y mala hora—quiso lograr la Apertura Democrática (mayúsculas de necrofilia) fue la modernización exigida por los contingentes del 68, por los manifestantes del 10 de junio de 1971. (321)

> [Come, Modernity: political pluralism / no more local bosses / democratic action in the labor unions / an industrialized countryside / eradication of jingoism / acceptance of everyday speech. For better or worse, what the [1970s] Democratic Opening (Necrophiliac capital letters) tried to achieve was a modernization demanded by the troops of '68, and by the demonstrators of June 10, 1971.]

At book's end, Isela Vega's idiomatic freedom (321) enlarges the frame of the Family Portrait in "Alto contraste" by making room in the album for a previously hidden mass of desire, will and capacity. If these can be helped to make the best use of themselves in society, Mexico will gain an exemplary kind of delinquent democracy, the hardy sort born of dissident desires and behavior (237) and strengthened by the obstacles and distances it has had to cross in getting to its rightful place.

The abstraction may obscure a point of fundamental import, which is that the eclectic array of types in *Amor perdido* illustrates not dissidence but heterodoxy. A system perceived externally as pluralist can only manifest that multivalent character if first, in the "darkroom" of its collective mind, a throng of individualists develops several languages of desire. Carlos Monsiváis went to a press conference in April of 1977 armed with a barrel of ink and his desire to deconstruct the "Único Responsable" [the Only One Responsible] (57) for Tlatelolco. When he was through pitting his brand of "libertad idiomática" against Gustavo Díaz Ordaz's macho bluster, the monster had defanged himself. You cannot demonize a man who reveals himself to be as much a victim of the Porfiriato's infantilizing custody as were the citizens victimized by Díaz Ordaz's homicidal tantrum. *Amor perdido* constructs many icons of resistance to overprotection, building tropes of tension and trespass, as well as violence and revolt. All of these signify a young society, torn between obedience and independence, suspended between poles of machismo and feminine abnegation, acquiring words and courage at last to say good-bye to daddy and find a new love better suited to its needs.

SCENES of massive transformation

reading ESCENAS DE PUDOR Y LIVIANDAD (1981)

Critical commentary about works of Carlos Monsiváis, scant
and superficial in general, is virtually nonexistent for his third collection,
Escenas de pudor y liviandad (1981, 1988).[1] The nude woman on the book's
cover could suggest that Monsiváis was indulging his ludic temperament,
and I am supposing most readers have assumed as much. The woman who
has turned from her dressing-room mirror to strike a coquettish pose before
the camera illustrates the subject of many of this book's twenty-eight pieces
on public women and scandalous entertainments. However, even if the
chronicle genre itself did not already direct us to perceive a moral and critical function in these dramatic accounts of strippers, film icons and indigenous beauty queens, a significant contrast between the frivolity of the

subjects and the sustained gravity of the narration makes a curious reader wonder what this book is really about.

The selections were written or first published between 1975 and 1987, from two years before *Amor perdido* appeared until the year Monsiváis's next collection, *Entrada libre,* came out. This notable temporal continuity is reinforced by semantic sequencing. On *Amor perdido*'s last page, Monsiváis prompts us to consider whether the "star system" that privileges an elite minority can survive in Mexico when the desperate worker without a job is the most visible citizen who, in massive numbers, is foreclosing the nation's options on a future (348).

He issues this hyperbolic warning on December 31, 1977. Sometime in the new year, he finds himself in a fetid bar, observing a series of tragic figures act out the drama of slow suicide with "carencia de miedo, acciones mecánicas, vetas simbólicas. Con ustedes el desempleado profesional, agresivo, tenso, irritado" [fearlessness, robotic acts and rich symbolism. Here you are, readers: the full-time unemployed man: truculent, tense and angry] (*Escenas* 200). This character may well illustrate the future that awaits the thousands of young men who congregate in dance dives catering to Mexico City's underclass. Week after week these youngsters come, "deseosos de soltar vapor. En la semana los regaña y friega el agente de tránsito, los maltrata el maestro del taller o el gerente del almacén, los fastidian en su casa porque no consiguen chamba, los insulta la novia porque no tienen dónde" [anxious to let off steam. During the week they get hassled on public transport, mistreated by the workshop teacher or store manager, nagged at home because they don't have a job and insulted by their girlfriends because they can't even get a place for them to be together] (237).

a doomsday report

Through frequent repetition, a series of descriptive phrases characterizes the mass Mexico (279) of *Escenas de pudor y liviandad.* This society features anonymous urban agglomerations (185) that silently forge new trends in mass culture amid "el apretujamiento" [the crush] (236) of "la gleba" [the rabble] (24, 55) and a lack of space (236, 288). This seething mass (241), which grew from a multitude-in-the-making (78), submits to the dictates of mass-mediated sensations (274). Unable to resist the provocations that come of being pressed up next to densities of human flesh (242), soci-

ety transforms the scandalous sexuality of the pre-electronic era (317) into the promiscuity that results when sex, now massified (253), proves unable to abridge the "kilómetros y kilómetros de soledad aglomerada" [endless stretches of solitude] (336) that "la explosión demográfica" [the population explosion] (56) opens up. Far from an account of fun and games in a liberated modern society, *Escenas de pudor y liviandad* is a report on apocalypse now.

Overtly New Historicist in his pursuit of the psychosocial truths that might be discovered in these "excavaciones de arqueología cultural" [excavations of cultural archaeology] (321), Monsiváis's narrator, a kind of social Peeping Tom (346), here combines traits of the anthropologist, psychologist and professor who conducts extensive documentary and field research on controversial and highly topical subjects in a local milieu. His thick descriptions, akin to those of a cultural anthropologist, align him not only with new historicists but also with cultural materialists like Raymond Williams. Bakhtin, Freud, Jung and Lacan speak between every line.

Seemingly to entertain us, Monsiváis directs our attention to picturesque topics such as turn-of-the-century postcard pornography (23–24) and the enthusiasm in popular barrios for jolts of electricity sold by ambulant child vendors (203–204). Then we realize he has brought us these scenes to disturb our notions of quaintness among "typical" Mexicans. In the first chronicle's genealogical survey of Celia Montalván, for example, he places the famous burlesque performer of the 1920s and 1930s in a direct historical line leading to Isela Vega, the stripper we saw in the last piece of the previous collection. From this (con)textual vantage, Monsiváis observes that a vedette like Montalván reveals in her contemplated flesh the enjoyment of a popular culture that does not realize it is popular, and that she exemplifies a deification of woman that is nothing like the true place she is assigned by machismo (44). The latter mindset he dramatizes in a 1985 piece set in an old-fashioned dive. The bumping and grinding of stripteasers cause effects among the audience whose details the squeamish imagination wants to erase (246). Between Montalván's stage act on turn-of-the-century vaudeville stages and Isela Vega's in the monstrous megalopolis, "hay un camino donde la intensidad quizá no varíe pero en donde la *conciencia mítica* está cada vez más informada de sus mecanismos y procedimientos. De una latría inocente a una latría computarizada y fallida. . . . La relatividad de la conducta, la relatividad de la culpa, la contraposición de lo urbano y lo parro-

quial" [there is a venue where the intensity is perhaps the same but in which the *mythical consciousness* is increasingly aware of its own mechanisms and procedures. (We've gone) from an innocent form of worship to a computerized and frustrating worship, to the relativity of conduct and guilt, the contrast of urban and parochial] (44).

Cumulatively, historicist exchanges such as these shift the center of society off its presumed traditional base. The resultant dislocations are seen to emerge from the psychiatric examination that Monsiváis conducts. The profound economic crisis of the 1980s directs his selection of subjects, as well as the tone and style of his questioning. This psychologist-narrator observes ordinary citizens having fun—at a quinceañera party, on the dance floor, telling off-color jokes—and interviews them in their own environments. Because these sessions could lead to a program of therapy requiring his elite readership's cooperation, we are dragged with him into clubs, stadiums and bars. When we end up in a strip joint where teenagers in the balcony and the sexually deprived express their cultural tastes in ways we don't want to know about (251), we feel like going home.

But the frontal nudity of Celia Montalván sticks in our consciousness. We cannot avoid looking at the information she imparts. The narrator, who may well be thinking of Paul's exhortation in Romans 12:16 to not be haughty, but associate with the lowly, wants us to identify with his persona, a critical Outsider who stoically explores places where his elitist class has cast its unwanted members. We find it shocking that anyone could calmly endure its squalor, much less the millions upon millions forced to adapt, just like the young man in the dancehall bathroom who lingers before the mirror, combing his hair while "su olfato tolera y vence cualquier conspiración úrica y fecal" [his nose accepts and conquers uric and fecal assaults] (189). Occasionally, we enter a place so bestial that our guide puts on the protective coloration of self-criticism before natives who must be thinking him a "pinche clasemediero" [fucking middle-class snob] (202).

libidinal strategies

Among the meanings divulged by these chronistic counseling sessions, sexuality and the sex act are a ubiquitous concern; the book's title already warns us that its content may slide over into the explicitness of "impudicia . . . escénica" [graphic immodesty] (319). Virtually every one of the twenty-eight pieces treats issues arising out of relationships between the sexes: machismo, sexism and homosexuality. The libido, or Id, is the psychic locus Monsiváis must visit to apprehend the forces that naturally drive cultural formation and overwhelm Power's capacity to direct them. In *Escenas*, the hegemony is a distant superegoistic influence which, for being self-consciously constructed, is inherently less stable than instincts that propel the masses toward satisfaction of their desires.

In this scenario, the narrator is the executive force of the ego, the conscious mind in contact with the real world and possessed of the information and critical capacity to direct energies of both the id and the superego into socially accepted patterns, or at least to suggest a program of action for the fledgling civil society. In this context, "civil society" is the collective ego with the will and capacity to impose checks and balances on power and to treat its less fortunate members with pragmatic compassion. That sector is not in evidence in *Escenas;* tension is instead sustained by libidinal strategies. The narrator who can interrupt his discourse to command: "Reloj, no marques las horas porque voy a teorizar" [Clock, stop marking time because I'm about to theorize] (176), is one who understands that the narrative impulse tolerates digression as a technique to sustain excitement and direct its ultimate discharge.

Escenas's narrator employs other interruptive tactics, most notably of the semiotic language that Kristeva relates to the pleasure and play of the Imaginary. This unruly speaker enjoys breaking the Symbolic order's conventional rules of discourse with such staples of monsivaisian style as song lyrics, puns and fragments of poetry, all speech effects from the oral dimension that configure the fluid image of a subject who is "in process/on trial" (Kristeva 17). They also assign a concrete meaning to the phrase "developing nation" and, most significantly in this book, they construct nondiscursive statements about a society caught between acts, as it were, naked in the dressing room.

a book of emblems

In this context, the nude lady on the cover poses as the frontispiece of an emblem-book, a disturbing and titillating icon whose polysemous signification is encoded in its relationships with visual and verbal images of the book's two-tiered symbolic space. Here, mass society is an emblem-theater in which this narrator's subjects perform their meanings so that he can devise a portfolio of Rorschach images. These exploit the crónica genre's emblematic reliance on both dramatic scene (visual icon) and metaexegetical commentary (verbal interpretation). The cultural traditions Monsiváis most frequently draws on for construction of his visually intended imagery—medieval biblical symbolism and the complex narrative iconography of prehispanic paintings and sculpture—direct him to an "emblematic world-view . . . based on the emblematic mode of thought" (Daly 168).[2] Monsiváis's strong visual imagination and deep appreciation of pictures and similitudes are facets of the emblematist's "controlled associative thinking" (60), which tends to seek transcendent meanings in ordinary things.

In *Escenas,* Monsiváis's inclination toward pictorial association links the linguistic theatrics we have already observed in his writing to images of provocative women's bodies distributed throughout the book and a ubiquitous insistence on photographic, televisual and filmic image. Many chronicles direct us toward an emblematic reading with such overt references as the assertion that Pancho Villa is an emblem of machismo (105) or that the distinctive clothes of the pachuco are "nuevos emblemas del ascenso del ego en medio del descenso de los recursos" [new emblems of the ego's ascent in the midst of descending resources] (286). Other texts focus the narrator's ideographic vision through a posture called camera (Friedman 163) or the lens of the compiler-activator (Beverley, *Against* 76–77). Several can be read as oral histories whose effaced narrator silently frames an iconic discourse.[3]

In support of these tactics, Monsiváis routinely deploys (here and throughout his *oeuvre*) a version of the "backstroke" sentence common among postmodernist writers (McHale 155). Exploiting possibilities of Spanish grammar, Monsiváis routinely enunciates the object before the subject and verb, thus freezing action in a kind of snapshot syntax (which in English is rendered in the passive voice): "A *lo tropical* lo afianza un dato inmutable" (192), "a su rostro no lo transfiguran las lágrimas" (198); "al personaje lo movilizan la exaltación y las iluminaciones de la sensualidad" [*The tropical* is reinforced by an immutable fact; her face is not transfigured by tears; the character is motivated by the exaltation and enlightenment of sensuality] (218).

Although the manner of communication between the pictures and words that compose emblems is connotative rather than denotative (Daly

8), the emblem's polysemousness must be based concretely on essential qualities of the thing pictured. Thus, we are constrained to see in Celia Montalván's naked pose meanings related to the human body, sex(uality), performance, lewdness, social convention, transgression and so forth. Until we read—both literally and abstractly—the series of word-emblems in the discourse, we will not know how to characterize their relationship to the frontispiece or to the book's other visual devices: the seven postcard images that mark sectors of the book, the cluster of actual postcards in the center that can be torn out and used by the book buyer, a highly iconic textual organization, and the many disruptive subtitles that fragment images called to mind by the main titles. If we consider the emblem's three parts—a brief motto *(inscriptio)* alluding enigmatically to the icon, the visual graphic itself *(pictura)* and the verbal explanation, often in the form of an epigrammatic poem *(subscriptio)*—*Escenas*'s antic subtitles work as *inscriptios* inviting us to a carnival where we can see and hear the cultural forms that pose for us in this book.

mainstream culture's cursi taste

Perhaps we already know that the polysemous concept of cursi calls to mind such things as "el Cristo de mirada móvil que venden en los atrios de los templos, los restos de la oratoria sacra y de la oratoria patria, la emoción de oír 'bien declamado' un corrido" [the Christ with eyes that move who is sold on church steps, vestiges of sacred and patriotic oratory, getting choked up on hearing a corrido sung beautifully] (186), and that it is often synonymous with the kitsch sensibility which, in a mass culture, wants to be taken for a valid aesthetic experience (Eco, *Open Work* 185): "el snobismo de masas" [the snobbery of the masses] (*Escenas* 186). We cannot know, however, until we connect the title and subtitles to the discourse, that Mexico's *cursilería* taps into that country's nineteenth-century poetic sensibility, which ran across all class lines (176). The punning subtitle, "Y en un vaso olvidado se desmaya un país" [And in a vase, forgotten, a country wilts] would very likely make even Monsiváis's elitist readers smile nostalgically as they recall having once memorized part or all of Rubén Darío's exaggeratedly elegant (i.e., cursi) "Sonatina," in which the lonely little princess wilts in her chair while "en un vaso olvidada se desmaya una flor" [in a vase, forgotten, a flower wilts]. Despite being attacked by a trendy "pogrom"

(183) against cursilería, these educated readers secretly cheer the narrator's defense of their enjoyment of such cultural artifacts and to take deep pleasure, as Monsiváis evidently does here, in declaiming a string of recitable poems (181–83).

Because this aesthetic was and remains identified with the premodern society of cursilería's classic space—the province—antivulgarity snobs who hunt down *cursis* (180) are doing hegemony's work (184). Defiantly enamored of cursi audiovisual effects, Monsiváis insists that, "en el trayecto de una sociedad semifeudal a una semimoderna, se reafirma el amor por las palabras sin las cuales los objetos languidecen y las situaciones se esfuman" [as we travel from semifeudalism to semimodernity, we reaffirm our love of words, without which objects languish and realities fade away] (177).

A writer who sits at the very pinnacle of elitist intellectualism in Mexico, Monsiváis is perhaps most widely known among the capital's newspaper readers for his maliciously antihegemonic column called "Por mi madre bohemios." In *Escenas*, he tells us that the poem "El brindis del bohemio" [The Bohemian's Toast] (from which he took his column's title) is one of the most maligned by "anti-cursis" (183). The revelation juxtaposes the image of an intellectual who toasts his mother among his peers—a gesture of perfectly cursi camp—to a dialogic word-emblem depicting an assault on the gesture by culture police who are then counterattacked by an elite journalist who honors his mother. We have to laugh, although we do not know at (or with) whom. In linking this text's metonymic lists, ideographic poetry, iconic descriptions and epigrammatic commentary, we construct a multifaceted emblem of unfinished meaning.

spatial and numerological structuration

The openness of *Escenas*'s discourses is enclosed in a rigid architecture that divides twenty-eight texts into sequences of four under generic mottoes that repeat themselves seven times. In each group, the first text is categorized as Instituciones and is followed by one labeled Dancing, then one called "Mexicanerías" [Typical Mexican Things] and finally by one classified as a "Crónica de sociales" [Society Column]. At the start of each quartet, the photograph of a seductively posed vedette carries an inscriptio consisting of lines of sentimental and erotic modernist poetry and a Roman numeral indicating the section's place in the sequence. Trundling the reader's attention back and forth among thematic blocks is inefficient; this structure must therefore signify on another plane, perhaps "a deeper and more diffuse cultural level, . . . based on subconscious or only partially conscious presuppositions, such as . . . the idea of the analogy between cosmic, religious, and political hierarchies" (Ginzburg 67).

Mesoamerican and medieval European thought are fraught with numerical preoccupations. In the first place, these serve to spatialize time: lock it in a jail, so to speak, to make sure it does not escape the cosmos (a dreaded possibility suggested by millenarian panic on both sides of the Atlantic during the Middle Ages). Further, in terms of European symbology, the repetition of sets of four could represent a trinity-plus-one: masculine father, son and holy spirit, and a virgin mother who plants seeds of dissent in the middle of the paradigm. In Mesoamerica, as in archaic cultures everywhere, grids that plot space are based on four cardinal points (a square) with a fifth point in the center: the pentacle or quincunx. A fifth point in *Escenas de pudor y liviandad* can be seen in the photographs placed between the sets of four and in the dead-center placement of the usable postcards, the "mercadotecnia de la época" [marketing technique of the day] in the still-feudal Mexico of 1910 (*Escenas* 43). All these images are of vedettes who, in postrevolutionary Mexico, planted seeds of dissent in the middle of the patriarchal paradigm. The postcards themselves illustrate the book's major thematic categories, listed above.

After the number three, whose magical properties are implicated in the tripartite emblem's metonymic and symbolic structures, seven is the most significant sacred unit. It alludes to the twenty-eight-day moon cycle divided by four.[4] Distributing *Escenas*'s twenty-eight chronicles into seven groups of four suggests, then, the tetradic cosmology enclosing ancient Mexico's divine center (Tenochtitlán) and the heavenly Jerusalem of the Book of Revelation. Both of these *axes mundi* were meant to fix an eternal Symbolic order against the instability of ungovernable natural and psychic forces. The *axis mundi* implied in *Escenas*'s emblematic organization must similarly be understood in relation to the verbal discussions that illustrate the destabilizing forces of desire, pleasure, hate, frustration, rage and fear.

The middle of twenty-eight is thirteen and fourteen. Text number thirteen corresponds to the mainstream aesthetic of "Cursilería," which, as we saw above, justifies the absorption of orality into writing while discussing

hierarchical privilege within an orderly protocol of consent and dissent. This chronicle's partner, text number fourteen, spins us off to the margins of national taste and prerogative, where the physical senses still rule, where inchoate dissent is not a recognized concept, where hierarchical judgment is enforced by police, where eroticism is not at all the sculpted nudity of a couple gazing into each other's eyes in the exquisite instant before kissing (see the photograph introducing the section in which this chronicle finds itself, page 169). This is a text about the two thousand or twenty-five hundred couples per night (190), most of them unemployed youths, who congregate each ritual Sunday (189) in "El California Dancing Club" to let off steam.

Crushed together, sweaty body to sweaty body amid "la densidad oleoginosa [de] un apiñamiento donde ni siquiera caben las miradas" [oleaginous density of a jam-packed crowd where not even a glance can find room], they would not appreciate the caption for the image preceding this text, Luis G. Urbina's poetic allusion to "un cautivo beso enamorado" [a captive kiss of love] (169) between a couple taking advantage of its privacy. Despite their nudity, the postcard couple's bodies, scarcely touching and in frozen attitude, refer antiseptically to an incipient sexuality. The California Club's couples, on the other hand, understand that "la cópula imita al dancing" [copulation imitates dancing] and that one makes love without delay, even while dancing, because "la distinción entre baile y coito equivale a lo que la vida prometió esta tarde y lo que la vida les cumplirá" [the difference between dancing and intercourse is like the gap between what life promised in the afternoon and what life will in fact deliver] (194). The girls are the daughters of poor workers, prostitutes, servants, urban immigrants and unemployed mothers. Subjected to the rules of working-class machismo (196), these young women, either because of "el efecto del sudor" [the effect sweat has on them] or because they simply need a place to sleep that night, will first perform a vertical sex act on the crowded dance floor (190), and then move on to a horizontal space (196). For these, among other, complex reasons, "La población aumenta de modo geométrico mientras la prostitución apenas crece aritméticamente . . . En el apremio, se disminuyen los controles morales . . . ni quien se muera por tener varios hijos de padre irreconocible, o por abortar para no tener ninguno, o por fingirse doncella con tal de negociar" [the nation's population grows geometrically while prostitution scarcely increases arithmetically. Under unbearable duress, moral

controls subside. No one cares if a woman has several children by unknown fathers, or aborts so as to have none, or fakes being a virgin to boost her price] (190–93).

In this scene of *liviandad* [lewdness], the *pudor* [modesty] of the police is risibly ineffectual (191) and the measuring gaze of hegemonic culture (the writing-culture narrator) is literally an outsider who can borrow only a few inches of space while he takes a quick peek inside the world in which the unemployed, the abandoned and the despised rule. The true authority in this alternative Paradise (191) is the pursuit of instantaneous happiness and the satisfaction of fleeting desire, ambulant truths we capture in our study of the emblem Monsiváis constructs from the leitmotiv of hair-combing (189, 191, 193–95, 197, 198). Repeated viewings of this graphic are interspersed with metatheoretical analysis and heavily accented irony—"Guías para entender lo evidente" [Guides to Understand the Obvious] (196). Subtitles functioning as stage directions move our attention back and forth between the visual and the verbal: "Fíjense en esta escena" [Note This Scene] (police expel a young woman for drinking alcohol) fugues into a meditation on this crowd's motives for being present; "Regresen a la escena" [Go Back to the Previous Scene] returns us to the dramatized action (190); ordered back to the same young man from the first scene, we reenter the bathroom, where we can now see the young man's struggles with his hair as contours of an icon.

"Reflexión para darle tiempo al galán de que vuelva a su lugar" [Pause for Thought to Give the Guy Time to Get Back to His Place] (191) appends the significant fact that these thousands of teenagers, multiplied in dance places throughout the capital, are laying their claim to a unique cultural identity based on the anachronistic allure of 1940s tropical dances like the danzón: "Ni Travolta en su momento, fíjense. Aquí nada vale el chantaje de onda moderna" [Not even Travolta was as popular in his time, you know. They can't seduce *us* with any of that modern hippie stuff] (192). Here in plain view is the next generation of Mexico's cursi trendsetters, consciously choosing to belong; in this and two other chronicles on dancing, "El Hoyo Fonqui" (233–43) and "El Hoyo Punk" (285–99), we obtain visual proof that the monstrously "other" Mexicans of spiky orange hair, Indian facial features and baggy pants are not candidates for demonization. Punkers too have moms who come out at night to introduce their offspring to the reality principle (296), and outlandishly dressed pachucos, cholos and chicanos who effect a rebellious rejection of mainstream culture have in fact based their difference on the aesthetic institutionalized by middle-class pretensions to culture (290–98). Even the implacably resented, dark-featured "naquiza" practices the same cursi cultural forms as everyone else (238).

an icon of consent and dissent

The icon of hair comes to signify both belonging and dissent; inside the bathrooms of shabby clubs, its visual features give the Youth Culture a face in a (post)modern wasteland here characterized as both mass-mediated and massive. As an image of individual identity combed from meager resources, the hairdo is a uniquely styled technology of the self: The Jovenazo's "manejo virtuoso del peine" [exemplary handling of the comb] (195) wins him a measure of agency ("equilibrios del copete" [ways to balance a crest of hair]) which, however fragile ("el cabello se resbala" [his hair is slipping]), represents a precious sensation of distinction in a medium that strips him, even, of a name; of individual worth in a society that utterly devalues his being and potential; of privacy in an environment crowded with unfulfilled desires; of confident manhood in a personal space from which classism's authoritarian impulse to "incarcerate" the masses has excluded itself. Here the young man feels both safe and competent to know the procreative joy of culture formation and its rhythmic "cortejo y consumación, vente, aléjate, regresa, apriétate, apártate, júntate hasta que desaparezcas" [courtship and consummation: Come over here, move away, come back, press up tight, pull back, join your body to mine until you dissolve] (194).

Coursing in sync with the iconic message, the verbal text enters and leaves the grotesque realism of the bathroom to alternately watch and hide its eyes from the carnivalesque dance floor where "¡El Diluvio Poblacional!" covers every inch of available space, flowing out in "la esperma [que] crece al ritmo de los tambores" [sperm that swells in sync with the rhythm of the drums], while "miles y millones de niños se gestan, se plasman en los arrebatos de la música, los niños que demolerán los últimos resquicios de cordura y civilización. ¿Qué no habrá quién extermine la orquesta?" [thousands and millions of kids are conceived and brought into being in the ecstasy of the music, children who are going to demolish our last slight chance to achieve wisdom and civilization. My God, is there no one who will kill the orchestra?] (198) Locked in passion's grip now, the narrator cannot restrain his tumescent imagination. He shouts at us:

Obliguen al Jovenazo a continuar peinándose. . . .
Que no vuelva a la pista a restregarse, y si lo hace, apaguen ese sonido, vil afrodisíaco, comparsa del suicidio colectivo. . . . Paren ese danzón, quiten la cumbia, eternicen el uso del peine. . . . Ya no los inciten, la miseria y el robo nos acechan y estos tipos siguen bailando, cada vez más juntos, empalmados, fundidos, frotándose como cerillos, enardeciéndose a la primera rozadura. . . . Cada semana, los jóvenes sufren amnesia patria al bailar . . . (198)

[Make that young man keep on combing his hair. Don't let him go back to the dance floor to rub himself up against someone else, and if he does, turn off that sound, that vile aphrodisiac, that nonspeaking extra in the mass suicide scene. Stop that danzón, take the *cumbia* away, make the hair-combing last forever. Don't excite him any more; already, misery and robbery stalk us and these guys keep on dancing, each time closer, skin to skin, welded together, scraping like matchheads that burst into flame on the first strike. Every week, all these young people lose their patriotic memory as soon as they start to dance . . .]

The narrator is losing control, now. Imprisoned in the steamy beat of the danzón, his apocalyptic imagination bursts from its metatheoretical confines to engender an end-of-the-world scenario: *"¡¡¡La Explosión Demográfica, carajo!!!" [The Population Explosion!!! Fuck!!!]* (198). Pausing momentarily, the Young Man, before asking his companion of the moment to seduce him, "se peina una vez más" [combs his hair one more time] (198). But we know that the pause is cosmetic. The young man's thrusting tower of hair asserts a promise that his cultural logic compels him to keep.

emblems of a regressive order

The overall logic of *Escenas de pudor y liviandad* becomes clearer now. Monsiváis has organized his thematic nodules (Institutions, Dancing, Things Mexican, Society Pages) as emblems of a regressive order:

— The seven pieces classified as "institutions" analyze cultural preferences established between 1900 and the 1950s. An emblematic reading yields collective meanings of *openness, becoming, transformation, emer-*

gence, transgression, border-crossing, fusion, liminality, feminization and *power-sharing.* These are associated with illusory freedoms after the Revolution, and with postmodern displacement of Mexico's geopolitical margins.

— The seven "Dancing" pieces focus principally on loci where social outcasts immerse themselves in alternative dance styles. Collectively, their emblems speak of *privatization, individuation, expansion, seeking, legitimation, multiplication, pluralization, dissent* and *copulation.*

— The seven "Mexicanerías" are, as their name implies, about "typical" cultural forms and practices: a beauty pageant for copper-skinned girls of a far-flung Mexico City suburb that itself is an icon of the Aztec past (59); the (un)changing face of machismo; heart-breaking limitations imposed on economically disadvantaged young women; alcoholism; burlesque; sexist and racist humor. Collectively, these emblems compress five hundred years of negativity in their motifs of *exclusion, marginalization, oppression, suffering, destruction, stagnation, pain, death, want* and *absence.*

— The seven "Crónicas de sociales" are about middle-class nostalgia for a Golden Age, exemplified predominantly in film and other mass media. From these chronicles emerge bourgeois emblems of *denial, negation, pretense, hierarchy, escapism, artifice, repression, degradation, obsolescence, sterility, abandonment, authority* and *power.*

In each four-part segment, time marches from past to present while spiritual development, or social consciousness, retreats from open to closed. Thus, instead of seeing an *evolution* toward democratization, the ritualized cycles are seen to stagnate, building up a head of potentially *revolutionary* psychic steam.

Let us recall that, toward the beginning of *Días de guardar,* published nearly two decades earlier, a Raphael concert was presented in two parts: the first was outdoors in the park and offered free of charge to Mexico City masses as a gift from the city fathers; this audience was seen as unruly and violent, and reminded the narrator of the storming of the Bastille. That was followed by the more controlled indoor half of the idol's visitation: among the rich, well-dressed and conventionally behaved elite. Now, at the last of *Escenas de pudor y liviandad,* a star named Emmanuel will also sing twice, but this time the first to hear him will be the rich, seated at tables indoors.

This is an elite audience so disciplined that it seems nearly comatose, utterly out of touch with its Id. The second concert is again given to the poor as a gift, outdoors and in the capital's central square, boxed in by the national church and the government palace. Eyewitness to history, the narrator is sandwiched amid seething masses paying raucous homage to their Id. The ruling class's management of the event is so inept that a riot ensues. The narrator himself panics as hordes of youths crush each other in an effort to break through a fence that stands between them and the object of their desires (Emmanuel: "God is with us"—Isaiah 7:14). The Idol flees before them.

Escenas ends abruptly here, without epilogue, discharging its cumulative verbal energy into a void where

> Emmanuel deja trunca "Toda la vida" . . . y la batalla por el espacio vital se intensifica . . . La infame turba de nocturnos fans derriba un costado de la cerca de alambre, que defendía a Emmanuel de la impávida idolatría, y los policías se lanzan a la pedagogía sanguinolenta. . . . El orden con sangre entra. Durante unos minutos se prodiga el uso del cinturón y de la macana, los alaridos mezclan dolor e insultos, y luego todo vuelve a su sitio, o a su falta de sitio. (354)

> [Emmanuel breaks off "All My Life" . . . and the battle for space to breathe grows more intense. The infamous rabble of nocturnal fans tears down one side of the wire fence, the one that had been shielding Emmanuel from the fearless idolaters and police officers leap into the fray, dispensing bloody lessons. . . . Blood's arrival brings order. For a few minutes, swinging belts and clubs are used without restraint, while screams of pain and insult rise, and then everything is back in place—or in its lack of place.]

mass-ive, uncontainable desire

A chronotope of carcelary ritual that is sustained over seven decades (1910s–1980s) seems reinforced with unyielding rigidity. But, down in society's collective Id, and in the ironic gap between extratextual structure and textual discourse, desires for independence and change are gathering themselves to become demands. This civil war is utterly unlike the stylized "revolution" of 1910, in which social equals of Porfirio Díaz enlisted the help of the ignorant poor to clone him and, thus, assure the unruffled continuity of Power over People. In *Escenas*, the revolution is, indeed, more like the storming of the Bastille. Unruly, undernourished and untutored, "una muchedumbre ignorante de sus propias dimensiones" [a crowd unaware of its own dimensions] (353), it does not know how to contain the measure of its gestating power.

Escenas de pudor y liviandad disrobes Mexico's repressed desires, at first coyly and then brazenly, to expose the society's Real order, that reality least accessible to the country's willfully blind leaders: the scores of millions of anonymous masses whose plurisignification breaks free of narrative restraint. Swept upon a tidal wave of panic, anger and frustrated desire, the narrator abandons these scenes of control and license, helpless to do more than hold a graphic mirror up and pray that Mexico's Superego will break its frozen attitude and finally embrace its Id. "Hicieron mal, Monseñor, en menospreciar el infierno. Aún se requieren escenografías persuasivas, tridentes y llamas espectaculares" [They did wrong, Monseigneur, when they scoffed at hell. There is, after all, still a need for didactic spectacle, for tridents and dramatic flames] (247). Elsewhere, Monsiváis irrepressibly documents his optimistic belief that civil society will come of age in Mexico. Here, he reminds us that it can be born rationally—or it can abort itself in an explosion of fury.

While 1968 does not explicitly colonize the consciousness of this book, as it did in *Días de guardar* and *Amor perdido*, it is present in an implicit contrast between the concern of those books with the violent suppression of democracy and the concern of this book, which is the violent eruption of demography amid the sweaty, fecal, sexually promiscuous *production* of mass society. That population is seen here to be growing out of control, in both senses of the word. The material one makes the narrator break out in a cold sweat. The second gives him courage to venture into the company of the least among Mexican citizens. An elite Insider swallowed by an historical Outsider, he excavates from within that layered space a durable icon showing Mexico's popular consciousness to be "growing out of control." There is as yet no sign that this "presencia masiva que ya define al Distrito Federal" [massive presence, which by now defines the nation's capital] (241) is growing *toward* any particularly productive uses of its freedom. But the energy is there and, in part fueled by the mathematics of birth, it has begun an uncontainable process of fission. Readers who cooperate with government in historical schemes to keep the common people from participating in political decisions are sentenced in *Escenas* to face the naked body of truth posed before Celia Montalván's mirror.

9

FREE ADMISSION to democracy

reading ENTRADA LIBRE (1987)

Narrative continuity among Carlos Monsiváis's books is especially striking between the third and fourth in the series. The closing image
of *Escenas de pudor y liviandad* easily superimposes itself on the inaugural
vision of the roughly concurrent *Entrada libre: crónicas de la sociedad que se
organiza* (1987)[1]; a yoked reading magnifies their independent significance.

On *Escenas*'s last pages, we recall, working-class fans cram themselves
into Mexico City's Constitution Plaza, to enjoy a free but poorly managed
concert sponsored by the government. Anxious and enraged, the massive
crowd riots before breaking down fences to escape. A parody of grotesque
realism's liberating potential, this explosion of energy from the compressed
center of the nation's political and religious core demonstrates what Monsiváis explicitly says in *Entrada libre:* "el paternalismo es fórmula cada vez

más inerte de control social" [paternalism is an increasingly obsolete form of social control] (211). The panicked crowd disappears into the night (*Escenas* 354). At virtually the same historic moment, *Entrada libre* opens on a parallel scene: Masses on capital streets flee in terror from a world that is falling down around them (17). But this time, we will not be told that, after the initial burst of panic, "todo vuelve a su sitio, o a su falta de sitio" (*Escenas* 354). Instead, at multiple points throughout the city, citizens will restrain the centrifugal impulses of fear and fatalism; their autonomous acts of reconstruction after the earthquake of 1985 contribute to nothing less than a "reordenamiento social" [reordering of society] (*Entrada* 34). Many reject government patronage, electing to pay, at great personal cost, for admission to a future rebuilt on more rational foundations.

Dynamic public scenes such as these structure an expanding semantic universe at this juncture in Monsiváis's project. Traditional and historical elements of the sociopolitical space realign themselves to admit a primordial innovation: a people who want to organize a civil society for themselves (76). To a star-gazing hopeful like Monsiváis, detection of a new constellation of democratic behaviors comes as a shock: "¡Detente reportero! Has caído en el universo de la autogestión, y la desconfianza orgánica ante el gobierno" [Stop, Reporter! You have just fallen into a world of self-empowered agency and the natural distrust of government that goes with it] (112). Despite official moves to contain it, the spirit of a different city materializes amid the debris of a disaster which, if first felt as a crushing material weight, almost simultaneously releases psychic energies; these begin to undermine a monumental authoritarianism that has drawn its strength from a body politic that historical handicaps weakened:

> El cascajo, la selva de objetos ya sin dueño, los refugiados en la calle, la tragedia que sustituye a la desolación de todos los días, hacen evidente el desastre social que anticipó la furia geológica. Tras medio siglo de permanecer virtualmente intocadas, sobre las zonas del centro desciende una claridad inexorable, que disipa en minutos la confusión ancestral entre miseria y pintoresquismo. . . . Se origina una nueva conciencia, cuya esencia es la relación distinta con el gobierno, ya no desde las posiciones del mendicante y el "menor de edad" civil. (106–107)

> [The rubble, a jungle of objects no longer owned by anyone, the homeless in the streets, the tragedy that has replaced everyday desolation—all reveal a social disaster preceded by the geological storm. After a half century in

which they remained virtually untouched, an inexorable clarity of vision falls upon zones in the city's center, and in only minutes dispels an ancestral confusion between blatant misery and picturesque reality. A new awareness is born whose essence feeds a different relationship with government, which no longer emanates from a vision of citizens as beggars and "minor children."]

Entrada libre's narrator, whose customary focus is on the ancient epicenter of Mexico's cultural, political and economic power, now extends his gaze to slums on the fringe of the megalopolis, north toward the U.S. border and south into the previously intractable otherness of indigenous territory.

watching democracy happen

The moral tone of this collection is explicit, introduced from the prologue's first sentence—"¿Cuánto falta en México para el pleno ejercicio de la democracia?" [How much longer will Mexico wait for true democracy?] (*Entrada* 11)—and its impact is undiluted: Previous collections contain dozens of chronicles; *Entrada* admits but seven, all of them focused on the emotional, intellectual and pragmatic *processes* of self-governance. The prologue announces essential themes of what readers will experience as a kind of textual "street theater" organized in seven acts (11–15). We will watch as Mexicans in public places assess evidence that government does not, after all, possess all the answers nor wield inexhaustible powers. Sometimes we share a wry laugh with Monsiváis's ironic metajournalist; it can be funny to watch unpracticed democrats struggle with the traps of self-governance. Mostly, however, we share his pride in citizens who have donned white hats and ridden to their own rescue.

Many of the new heroes taking center stage in *Entrada libre* come forth during "Los días del terremoto" (17–122), an unusually long chronicle (105 pages) devoted to a meticulous but highly selective account of the devastating earthquake and aftershocks of September 1985. Rarely does Carlos Monsiváis permit himself the luxury of unrepentant emotion, but here, without a hint of lachrymose melodrama, he is deeply moved to observe that citizens suddenly understand the benefits of disinterested solidarity; to note that, without prior warning, spontaneously and on the run, brigades of twenty-five to a hundred individuals organize small armies of volunteers who are ready for both physical effort and psychic transformation; an unprecedented outpouring of heroism has allowed human life to obtain an absolute value (19). Monsiváis sets aside large pages to record the sound of buildings toppling, the sight of shoes and lamps on sidewalks, the smell of decomposing bodies, the taste of tainted air, the feel of a hand clasped deep under a tomb of rubble, the euphoria of saving even a single life (21). These minute gestures profile a new protagonist (33), the ordinary citizen willing to make personal sacrifices for the good of strangers, brave enough to confront an inept government with civil disobedience (34), determined to carry out self-empowering acts (40) and to renounce defeatism, because "la sumisión no es el camino" [giving up is not an option] (115).

"La primera y más decisiva respuesta al terremoto es de índole moral. . . . Cada persona que se extrae de túneles y hoyos es epopeya compartida de modo unánime. Nunca en la capital han sucedido tantos fenómenos tan dramáticos ni respuestas tan emotivas. Como en muy escasos momentos de México, la vida humana se eleva al rango de bien absoluto" [The first and most decisive response to the earthquake is of a moral character . . . Each individual pulled out of tunnels and holes is a national epic that everyone, without exception, shares in. Never in the capital have there occurred events so dramatic nor reactions so deeply emotional. This is one of the rarest of times in Mexico: Human life has appreciated to the point of becoming an absolute asset] (32).

the conscious construction of change

One can almost sense the reporter holding his breath, however, in the months after the "acción épica" [epic action] (32). He wants to see if the altruism inspired by the urgency of disaster takes root as a *structural* change in the collective civic mind, because Mexican cities urgently need long-term policies and rational administration within a democratic system (32).[2] The best pages of *Entrada libre* are those that sit us down with him in *ad hoc* town halls throughout the nation, between 1983 and 1987, and make us stay awake through the tedious ticking of hours as brand-new democrats practice the mind-numbing give-and-take of pluralist dialogue. The kind of transformations Monsiváis seeks to document cannot be found in ordinary news reports, nor can they simply be asserted as true. They have to be lived through, observed over long periods of reportorial immersion, "constructed" by a consciousness that performs a service for readers who cannot or will not, like him, spend months gathering visual memories, personal impressions and disparate facts with which to assemble an apprehensible viewpoint. In *Entrada libre*, for example, Monsiváis assigns himself to

— Show up at a meeting of volunteers planning strategies to counter government opposition to the first-ever union of sweatshop seamstresses (101) ("Los días del terremoto");

— Attend a meeting of low-income residents who are planning how, despite their exceedingly modest resources, they can elude government obstructionism to finance and rebuild their own homes (114) ("Los días del terremoto");

— Testify to the relegation of indigenous residents on the outermost edges of the capital, martyred when government and private sector indifference for human life (139) results in a horrific explosion of poorly supervised federal gas storage facilities built next to a massive agglomeration of immigrants; to glimpses of a civilian solidarity that, however short-lived, overrides racist contempt for San Juanico's indigenous slum dwellers; and to the fact that, before the disaster, San Juanico had no neighborhood organization. Three days after the explosion, popular assemblies begin to meet (142) ("San Juanico: los hechos, las interpretaciones, las mitologías");

— Be present in southern Mexico at a heated confrontation between local citizens agitating for an autonomous municipal government and federal party hacks who stubbornly insist on retaining control of the politics of patronage (153, 159–60) ("Juchitán: *¡Ay zapoteco, zapoteco, lengua que nos das la vida!*");

— Devote nine days to reporting the tactics of rural teachers opposing centralist caciquismo's denial (at times murderously) of their right to unionize independently (182) ("La disidencia magisterial: los apóstoles se cansaron de serlo");

— Travel to a provincial jail to interview seven imprisoned dirt farmers allied with striking teachers, criminalized for pressing the government on price supports (185) "La disidencia magisterial: los apóstoles se cansaron de serlo");

— Make the wearisome trek to one of the "lost cities" clinging by hope alone to the outer fringes of the sprawling capital in order to watch how the slow burn of historical relegation finally ignites in a provincial immigrant woman the capacity to publicly demand that the government provide her neighborhood with water service (240) ("Viñetas del movimiento urbano popular");

— Endure the screaming frenzy of World Cup Soccer fans in both the capital and Monterrey, to witness an alternative form of "democracy" in a space for letting off steam that a paternalistic government allows the masses ("¡¡¡Gooool!!! Somos el desmadre");

— Attend months of stultifying meetings of student groups and university officials as they debate a plan for cogovernance of the institution; nearly 20 years after the marches of 1968, Monsiváis again weighs the democratizing merits of strikes and marches organized by student activists ("¡Duro, duro, duro! El CEU: 11 de septiembre de 1986 / 17 de febrero de 1987").

Sequencing of these texts emphasizes the emergence of independent social movements (15). The prologue's didactic title, "Lo marginal en el centro" [the margin in the center], reflects organization of the chronicles. The first, as we have noted, contains nearly a third of the book's pages and serves as the narrative epicenter, much like the capital city, whose massive population and rapidly expanding territorial mass ripple outward.³ Monsiváis follows that path into unexplored democratic territory.

san juanico: indifference for human life

The first stop on his outward migration is the slum of San Juanico, a densely populated center of the demographic, political, economic and social periphery of the nation where former farmland is subjected to "el crecimiento desenfrenado, producto de la necesidad de vivir lo más cerca que se pueda del Gran Surtidor de Empleo, la capital" [uncontrolled growth, the outcome of being compelled to live as close as possible to the Great Provider of Jobs, the capital] (129). The report of the November 1984 Pemex explosions foreshadows the next year's more generalized disaster. The gas explosions kill at least 2,000 outright (134) and send half a million souls fleeing into the early morning streets, "semisdesnudas, descalzas, llagadas, gritando, rezando . . . obsesivamente" [half-naked, barefoot, wounded, screaming, praying obsessively] (126–27). While Monsiváis notes the stirrings of a democratizing instinct (128) and a hint of the compassion that would notably characterize civilian responses to the earthquakes ten months

later, he also shows that San Juanico's victims met a stone wall of bureaucratic resistance (142–43). What mainly emerged from San Juanico were
proofs of collusion between government and private investment (129–39)
(which became a motivating issue with victims of substandard buildings
that collapsed in 1985); impunity for a criminal act of negligence (139), and a
flare-up of cruel disaster jokes which, although quickly extinguished ("¿Por
qué pasaron de moda los chistes de San Juanico? R: Porque se quemaron
muy rápido" [Why did San Juanico jokes go out of fashion? A: Because they
burned up really fast]) (143), emphasizes the racist and classist bias underlying this neighborhood's failure to wrest concessions from authorities. If
anything, he says, the so-called accident revealed the country's characteristic
lack of solidarity or concern for human life (129).

juchitán women help build unity

Indigenous migrants in the capital come predominantly
from homelands in the south (García Canclini, *Consumidores* 60), so it is
natural that Monsiváis's next stop will be Juchitán, a Zapotec municipality
that is by now a household word among Mexicanist scholars, to whom Juchitán signifies cultural resistance, political dissent and strong women who
dominate in a matriarchal society.[4] To Monsiváis, the Juchitec women who
arm themselves with sticks to fight alongside their men for communal lands
and local control (153) are evidence that "las mujeres (felizmente) dejarán de
ser el paisaje de la voluntad patriarcal" [women (fortunately) will stop serving as mere background scenery for patriarchal dramas] (160–61). Women
like these will move Mexican society an essential step closer to a truly democratic weal: Women comprise a new kind of popular power that, while not
yet autonomous, is no longer silent and segregated, he notes (164–65).[5]

teachers link center and margin

Entrada libre's middle chronicle historicizes a decades-long
struggle of rural schoolteachers and farmers for independent union protections, wage increases and price supports in states encircling the capital and
extending out to the national limits. Activists among these, dissenting from
the government-backed national teachers union, "ya enclave feudal" [still
a pocket of feudal power] (169) and a mirror image of the PRI's paternalistic hierarchy, are murdered or threatened, as though the national union
were Hernán Cortés and those dissenting from its point of view were Tlax-

caltec natives: "Pediremos que les corten las manos por meterlas en nuestro organismo" [We will demand that their hands be cut off for having stuck them in our business] (174).[6] Significantly, the maltreated periphery brings its complaint to the center and, indeed, to the very heart of Mexican authoritarianism: the Metropolitan Cathedral, which faces the National Palace in the capital's Zócalo. While one contingent of professors carries out a hunger strike in the cathedral, another does the same in front of the Government Palace in Oaxaca, symbolically realigning civic powers along a decentralized axis.

the false unity of soccer madness

"¡¡¡Gooool!!!" strikes an almost vulgar contrast with these epic accounts of brave citizens battling against natural, political and social forces of destruction. Monsiváis's mordant satirist makes his most pointed appearance in *Entrada libre* precisely here in order to emphasize the difference between citizens who "take the streets" in the texts bracketing this one, and the televisual demonstrations of hysterical soccer fans dancing on the hoods of automobiles (215–17). The chronicler now takes backhanded swipes at centralist authorities whose inadequacies he attacks more frontally in other parts of the book. For example, we had just met Agricultural Secretary Eduardo Pesqueira in the previous chronicle, as one of many government powers who conspire to keep dissenting farmers and teachers in prison (195); now we see him making a Wave in Estadio Azteca, rising with his arms in the air beside the next president of the Republic (Salinas de Gortari) (203). The corrosive satire directs us to read with skepticism everything this chronicle says about freedom, solidarity, "national unity" and patriotism (208–20). The civil disobedience of jailed activists is rational and altruistic; the barbaric democracy (210) of fanatic fans screaming for the national soccer team (213) is an irrational form of liberation: "el desmadre menor que no deja ver el Gran Desmadre de todos los días, la toma de la calle que es la revancha por el despojo de las economías" [public disorderliness of a minor nature hides the Great Incivility of daily national life, and taking the streets is a way of getting revenge for being ripped off by a rapacious economy] (216). Sympathetic as Monsiváis is to desperation masked as savage joy, he notes that government sells the masks: Its equation of soccer and patriotism (204) promotes a false unity that will dissolve the minute Mexico loses a match (231).

consciousness-raising in the slums

Against the manipulated patriotism of athletic spectacle, Monsiváis now sets the scene—which no television station wants to film—in which political and evangelical activists perform the difficult, patient and anonymous work of politicizing rural immigrants in the outlying slums of the capital (239). In "Viñetas del movimiento urbano popular" Monsiváis dramatizes what García Canclini has described as "de-urbanization" from the extreme limits of the capital (*Consumo cultural* 48). Every day, whether Mexico wins or loses soccer matches against Bulgaria, true believers clinging to their convictions on the margins of national politics invest their idealism in a cause aimed at decentralizing power and bringing some of its basic privileges out to the ignored citizens of the capital's "lost cities." Here, grassroots organizations turn "emoción utópica" [utopian fervor] (Monsiváis, *Entrada* 243) into down-to-earth programs of civic self-help that slowly make gains against government stonewalling (243–45). They do so with the significant help of those who inherited 1968's "mito esplendente" [shining dream] (249), volunteers who, directly and indirectly, sponsor consciousness-raising in unlikely places:

> *Causa directa*: los estudiantes indignados deciden actuar en medio del pueblo. *Causa indirecta*: el sacudimiento nacional ante las manifestaciones y la matanza es la certeza confusa pero inerradicable de una crisis política. Ya es hora de que el PRI no nos maneje como niños. . . . De modo paulatino, una segunda generación estudiantil interviene, ya no lacerada psíquicamente por el 68, ya no ansiosa de redimir en una sola asamblea al pueblo de México. . . . El fervor cede el paso a una comprensión más detallada de los procesos urbanos, al estudio de los pasos específicos. (241–42)

> [*Direct Cause*: indignant students decide to take their activism to the masses. *Indirect Cause*: the psychic jolt Mexico suffered from marches and the massacre (of October 1968) is certain, if confusing, proof of an ineradicable political crisis. It is past time for the PRI to stop treating us like children. . . . Very gradually, a second generation of student activists comes onto the scene, not suffering the psychic wounds of '68, not needing to redeem all of Mexican history in a single rally. Fervor gives way to a more detailed understanding of urban processes, and to study of specific strategies.]

Instructed in the pragmatics of the game—inform yourself, show up at meetings, be persistent—women in particular advance the struggle. Their presence in offices of municipal service providers multiplies, "y es ya política el uso de su paciencia" [and their historic patience is now a political weapon] (245).

1968 replayed by different rules

The closing chronicle leads us back to the site of "el férreo centralismo" [ironclad centralism] (209), where we began *Entrada libre*'s search. After moving outward through the ring of surrounding slums to the provinces, we passed back into centralist territory by way of another fringe of oppression. Now we complete the loop. Significantly, this closure will open a gigantic democratic space: a public dialogue with national university appointees that culminates in negotiated power-sharing with students and faculty. The symbolic linkage of this event with the proximate causes of violence in 1968 is immediately evident; what is not so easy to see is the overwhelming transcendence of the deal worked out over painful months of grappling in packed auditoriums. The issues are custom-ordered soporifics: years to degree completion, graduation requirements, faculty size, tuition rates and so forth (248). Further, the initial response of a small group of student activists almost imperceptibly evolves from the question of admissions into an issue of vastly more lasting reverberation: how reform should be achieved—democracy as process rather than product.

An additional complication is the fact that the discussion is far from dualistic; here and throughout *Entrada libre*, the struggle is not between "good" and "bad" actors but among a plurality of interests which, one by one, elect to join the debate. The leading group of activists is shortly opposed by students of the ultra-radical left (298); official arguments are countered by respected public intellectuals; sectors of the faculty eventually ally themselves with student demands for shared governance, and even television, always before opposed to student movements (269), decides to broadcast portions of the ongoing debate: "O el país se democratiza, o los programadores de Televisa ya no saben cómo llenar el tiempo" [Either the country is becoming democratic, or Televisa is at a loss to fill air time] (270). This is not entertaining footage of soccer fans tearing up the town but far more exciting stuff: a rational decision of 250,000 citizens to "hacer del espectáculo de la disidencia el ejercicio de la ciudadanía" [turn the spectacle of dissidence into an act of civic duty] (271).[7]

This time, taking the streets does not mean, as it did in 1968 or 1971, physically battling police but instead a possible victory over the apathy of millions of anonymous citizens (271). Student leaders conduct to the Zócalo a generation that had never before made a political journey to the famous seat of Mexican power (272). The sprawling all-inclusiveness of the Universidad Nacional Autónoma de México (UNAM) symbolically holds a door open onto modernity (255). Whether a student manages to overcome economic privation or other obstacles in order to graduate is here symbolically beside the point. An open-admissions policy means "free entry" to a place where the Periphery can learn a language of democracy and experiment with civil liberties from within the Center: "Estos chavos ven en la UNAM literalmente la nación que les corresponde, y tienen la 'ciudadanía universitaria' que (esperan) les servirá para escapar de la pobreza, y no deteriorarse como sus padres. La UNAM: la red del conocimiento masificado que es para millones de jóvenes la síntesis del país que los admite" [These kids see in the National University a nation that literally belongs to them; it gives them a "university citizenship" that (they hope) will help them escape poverty rather than go down the tubes like their parents. The UNAM: a massified network of contacts that is, for millions of young people, a microcosm of the country that grants them admission] (273).

Consequences of this reform radiate from the seat of intellectual privilege—the center of the Center—throughout the nation on a horizontal plane: geographical strings that untie the compact of power held in the capital and distribute its prerogatives to the four corners.

breaking out, climbing up

Opposition to the archaic quincunx's enclosing impulse is, however, not as definitive as movement along a vertical axis that passes through a series of inversions. These lend themselves to a before-during-after sequence reflecting each text's chronotopical elements (reprisal of causes, recreation of immediate reality, analysis of change).

Before (Causes). Because a centralist culture balances national life on a precariously small base—"somos millones viviendo y bailando en un solo ladrillo" [we are millions living and dancing on a single brick] (38)—immobility answers an endemic fear of falling. Sahagún first exposed this communal dread in the words of an Aztec father to his child.[8] Monsiváis exposes it in the words of various speakers. A seamstress: "Nosotras sólo sabemos que se nos niega lo prometido, y la única persona capaz de resolver este problema es el Presidente, sí sólo él" [The only thing we

205
reading
ENTRADA
LIBRE

women know is that they withhold from us what we were promised, and the only person who can solve this problem is the President, only he] (104). The father-president (Miguel de la Madrid) to the child-nation: "Sé muy bien que en estos casos hay el peligro de la anarquía . . . de la iniciativa espontánea de la sociedad. Al gobierno le corresponde evitar que ocurra esta anarquía ya que es el representante global de la sociedad" [I know very well that in cases like this there is danger of anarchy brought on by society acting spontaneously, on its own] (79). The president again: "¿por qué ahora le llaman sociedad civil a lo que antes se decía lisa y llanamente pueblo?" [why do they now call it civil society, when before they simply called it The People?] (80). Government: "no se muevan" [Don't move] (33), "somos la permanencia" [We are permanence] (183). The president again: "Yo no veo . . . un deseo de cambio fundamental de nuestra estructura política" [I see no desire for fundamental change in the way our political system works] (64–65).

Paralysis unwinds a fatal sequence: atrophy, rot, death: "Los profesores hemos comprobado que en el estado donde se pone un dedo sale pus. El sistema está putrefacto" [We teachers have demonstrated that wherever you touch the State, pus runs out. The system is rotten] (190). Inverting expectations, the earthquake heals by airing the gangrenous lie of Mexico's post-Revolutionary "National Unity." *Entrada libre* opens on a scene of incongruous immobility. The dangerous world has just shoved the balance off-center and, for two and a half pages, the discursive cosmos freezes into a nearly verbless atavism. First, "el miedo. . . . (e)l miedo . . . el pánico . . . su pánico, el miedo . . . su miedo . . . el pavor" [fear . . . fear . . . panic . . . their panic, fear . . . their fear . . . terror] (17). Then, piles of nouns, adjectives and gerunds fix consciousness on the grotesque material body: "en la exacerbación olfativa hay pánico, sospecha de hedores inminentes, certeza de que . . . la ciudad no es ya la misma, porque uno está consciente, ávidamente consciente de la terrible variedad de sus olores" [panic enters through the nose with strong smells and the fear of imminent new stenches, with the certainty that the city is not as it was, because one is aware, powerfully aware, of the awful variety of its smells] (19).

Physical exhaustion, thirst and hunger reign during the most urgent hours and days of attempts to battle the earthquake's immediate effects (35–36). So also do losses in that battle. "Atrapado entre . . . cadáveres . . . que se descomponían" [Trapped next to decomposing cadavers] (64), a victim buried in rubble emblematizes the descent to death required before "el regreso a la vida" [being returned to life] (64). As though debriding a deep wound, *Entrada libre*'s first half insists on the dismembered social body, giving us unflinching realism also in San Juanico, where horrified witnesses testify: "advertí que era un cuerpo en la banqueta y sentí que olía a carne quemada" [I realized that was a body on the sidewalk and I detected the smell of burned flesh] (124); "las teas humanas . . . se revuelcan en la calle sin que nadie pueda auxiliarlas" [human torches writhe in the street and there's nothing to be done for them] (125); "fue pavoroso ver cómo se revolvían cadáveres de animales y humanos. . . . ver aquel cuadro de brazos y piernas. . . . Había huellas de sangre por todas partes. . . . El lodo estaba revuelto con sangre y había cuerpos tirados por todas partes" [it was dreadful to see how animal carcasses and human corpses were all tangled up together, to see that arrangement of arms and legs. . . . There were bloody footprints everywhere . . . The mud was mixed with blood and bodies were strewn everywhere] (126).

Religion is aligned with death, suffering and immobility in *Entrada libre*, here dramatized in the popular sector's hysterical appeals to God and the Virgin of Guadalupe as "la técnica favorita de neutralización de fuerzas naturales" [the favored technique for neutralizing natural forces] (30) and also in Church spokesmen who blame the victims, thus reinforcing the people's historic belief "que somos dueños de nada" [that the only thing we have ever owned is nothing] (31).

These reactions call to mind the compensatory sacrifices of prehispanic society which, in *Entrada libre*, are figured in post-Revolutionary Mexico's iron-fisted insistence on conformity to centralist authority. The earthquake caused huge losses in provincial cities as well, but the government pays no attention to those losses (28), in a sense sacrificing the needs of ninety-nine percent of the country's territory to the demands of the one percent occupied by capital residents (41). Fighting for its share of governing power, Juchitán has seen itself subjugated: "ha contemplado el sacrificio de sus líders" [it has witnessed the sacrifice of its leaders] (162), while, for the farmers of Chiapas, "el Centro es la concentración del poder que se opone a la repartición de sus beneficios. Ellos viven el atraso educativo, la falta de comunicaciones . . . , las demoras eternizadas" [the Center is the accumulation of power that opposes the just distribution of its benefits. They live with educational backwardness, a lack of communication, and other eternal postponements] (187). Thus forced to subsidize all of Mexico (192), starving farm families are driven toward a Center so overcrowded that, as man-made and natural disasters show, it cannot keep its balance on the capital's compacted pyramid of goods, services and people (42).

In the midst of the earthquake's revelations of corruption, torture, ineptitude and cynicism (244), state television assures listeners that World Cup Soccer will not be affected (89). The subliminal message is that those dead in the earthquake—the "more than three thousand" mentioned, Monsiváis says, could as easily mean ten or twenty thousand (119)—are acceptable losses that should not slow ticket sales for the international soccer matches to be proudly hosted in Mexico. Monsiváis wants us to see a parallel with the sacrifice of students in 1968 for the foundational act of hosting the Olympic Games. The more things change, the more they stay the same where power is concerned: "En México sólo interesa lo que sucede en el Estadio Azteca" [In Mexico, the only thing that matters is what happens in Aztec Stadium] (189), which, significantly, was constructed on top of communal farmlands (204). The sports arena here is a degraded Templo Mayor where promoters regret that, unfortunately, the sacrifices must be only symbolic (233) and civilian aspirations to upward mobility die so that power's ego may live on (205). Indeed, the one uncontested aspect of culture available to the government for melodramatic glorification are prehispanic themes which, by default, come to represent a unanimous National Identity (235). Sharp as an obsidian knife, satire cuts to the heart of this lie and metaphorically kicks its corpse down the steps of Aztec Stadium (236).

During (Present Reality). *Entrada libre*'s parodic sacrifice of cultural conformity establishes conditions for a carnivalesque opening of the body politic. As a first step toward revival, citizens must overcome historic and natural fears. In both disaster chronicles, the paralyzing horrors of grotesque realism are followed immediately by reports filled with dynamic verbs describing frenetic comings and goings (19), decisions taken, acts begun, things improvised and solutions invented by human chains who collectively "rescatan . . . entregan . . . alejan . . . abren . . . sostienen. . . trepan . . . instalan . . . cuidan . . . remuevan . . . aguardan . . . izan . . . enfrentan" [rescue, hand over, take away, open, support, climb, install, take care of, remove, await, raise, confront] (19–20). Shaking off the torpor of surprise, individuals mobilized by television and radio (127) throw themselves into actions whose cumulative energy pulls steadily, powerfully, against the downward press of death and despair and, startlingly, against the suffocating immobility of government and big capital.

Monsiváis's understanding of modernity is sharply etched in his persistent scrutiny of exemplary individuals—heroes of democracy—as models for "el poder de la razón" [the power of reason] (295) that guides civic activism and "la demanda moral, sin la cual ningún movimiento existe verdaderamente" [moral imperative, without which there can be no true movement] (257). Their civil insurrection (50) constructs didactic images of a new, antipatriarchal, David and Goliath: individuals who defy police orders to sit in government shelters, women who throw rocks at bulldozers crushing buildings where survivors may still cling to life, women who assault government arrogance with sticks, a volunteer who thrusts his skinny body into a "mole hole" to tunnel down to survivors. Heroic risk-taking is here essential to calm fears of the masses, stir their imagination and press against their resignation.

Clear-thinking volunteers, who know themselves to be models for the masses (283), seize control of circumstances to demonstrate how all of society might subordinate its fears to the novel sensation of a new work ethic and learn the potential benefits of altruism (34). It is no small risk to oppose society's customary immobility, Monsiváis observes at one point (247). But he shows, time and again in *Entrada libre*, how individuals armed with facts (243) and authorized by an active sense of morality (242) can invert the traditional order. Figured as worker-ants whose collective strength is sufficient to undermine obdurate towers of oppression, Monsiváis builds upon "las inmensas ruinas de Tlatelolco y sus hormigueros humanos" [the immense ruins of Tlatelolco and its human ant hills] (52) an epic vision of reconstruction from below, of young rescue workers who "se distribuyen en los niveles de las ruinas como en una pirámide" [spread out on every level of the ruins as in a pyramid] (53). Every life extracted from a tunnel because of the self-sacrifice of moral individuals is an epic feat shared by all (32). What had been urban chaos (211) gives birth to a desperate life force (212) that topples archaic structures of control and rebuilds a moral Mexico (243) nourished by anonymous acts of love (128), supported by critical rage and anchored by knowledge.

After (Change). Classism and racism survive this "reordenamiento social" (148–51, 205, 228–29, 302), and nothing in Monsiváis's unabashed admiration for heroic acts is meant to obscure that fact. On the contrary, he depicts individual and collective bildungsromans as Mexico's only hope of ever treating its outcast citizens with justice. Left to its own devices, government clings adamantly to dehumanized and inhumane power, moved to concede some of it only when individuals acting with a social conscience assert the rights of many. Against a discriminatory status quo, Monsiváis gives us promising ruptures: the spontaneous organization of decentralized governing bodies, the cacophony of an unprecedented one-for-all-and-all-for-one mentality speaking itself into being and—a portentous innovation—the awakening of the margins to their dormant powers of protest and self-governance. Women, indigenes and discriminated citizens of every class unite with other apprentice democrats to extract themselves from the fallen structures of tradition and, both literally and metaphorically, illuminate a well thought-out path to their society's Zócalo, "lugar de las apoteosis" [the site of glorified ideals] (276).

Carlos Monsiváis has always spoken with a Christian voice; in *Entrada libre* his faith in the perfectibility of his society, unshaken by political catastrophes in 1968 and 1971 or natural disasters in 1984 and 1985, puts finishing touches on a trope of the biblical Fall that he had been narrating since *Días de guardar*'s chronicles about violations of trust, loss of innocence and historical separations. *Amor perdido*'s biographies of the misuse and re-use of cultural canons pointed a way out of the living hell that National Unity's unbreakable commandments created for vast sectors of Mexico's people. *Escenas de pudor y liviandad*'s descent into the despair of those condemned masses illuminated the psychosomatic effects of domestic exile on a repressed people. *Entrada libre* finds constructive outlets for pent-up desires through redemptive acts of anonymous love, self-criticism and ratiocinative sacrifice.

Rather than lead Mexican society, like Joseph, back to Unity or, like Adam, to any proximation of Paradise, this moral journey has consciously directed people away from that primitive space and upward, to a mature sphere of action where "el poder acumulado de las fuerzas sociales trasciende enormemente las debilidades de los discursos, o lo esquemático de las consignas" [the accumulated power of social forces greatly transcends the weakness of the speeches and stilted slogans] (277). Democracy in the flesh looks awkward and exhausting (306), seemingly conceived to expel from its followers all but the most stout-hearted seers: "Si un movimiento sobrevive a sus asambleas, sobrevivirá sus enemigos" [If a movement can survive its rallies, it can outlive its enemies] (113). What invests it with a grandeur that shines even in shabby meeting halls is the quality of gnostic enlightenment that inheres in conscious flights from bodily fear and "force-jeos" [grappling] (278) toward exemplary "figuras que ascienden" [ascendant figures] (278) and salvific unification through uses of speech and opinion (289). Mexican civil society's heroes and grassroots organizations are not only moral but expressly rational counterforces to bureaucratic sequestration of authority and the inertia of hedonism. Where *Escenas de pudor y livi-andad* emphasized the solitude of Mexico's "naked" body politic, *Entrada libre* pays homage to the spirit now issuing from its bruised flesh to effect a new unity that is first human, then local and finally national.

10

making sense of CHAOS

reading LOS RITUALES DEL CAOS (1995)

There is a piece in *Los rituales del caos* that reminds me of that man the Kingston Trio sang of, the one who went down into the subway with his brown bag one day and whose fate is still unknown, for he "will ride forever 'neath the streets of Boston; he's the man who never returned." Fifteenth of thirty pieces in this book, "El metro: viaje hacia el fin del apretujón" [The Subway: Journey toward the End of the Crush] (111–13) puts Carlos Monsiváis's sweating narrator in the suffocating middle of five million subway riders, "en batalla álgida por el oxígeno y el milímetro" [in feverish battle for oxygen and a millimeter of space] (111). As depicted on the collection's cover, he is packed inside one of the train's cars, from where his hyperbolic humor reaches our ears like the sound of whistling in the dark. Punning, he says the "metro cuadrado" [square meter/subway] (113) he occupies is so stuffed with the materiality of pluralism amid Mexico City's massive populace that New Age notions of transcorporality appeal (111–12)—a single new thought can crush you against your neighbor and the struggle here is not for life but simply to find space within space (111). On the heaving back of a vast multitudinousness, the ritual of traveling to work is eternally about to fail in its job of ordering chaos. Similarly, the narrator who has been asserting metaphysical order upon Mexico's diverse cultural practices since 1970's *Días de guardar* is, at almost every moment in 1995's *Rituales,* a baroque dialectician whose conclusions are forever provisional.

That he should "fail" to understand what his culture's new relationships signify at century's end is an ironic indication of success. We recall that in *Entrada libre,* he had applauded hints of a shift from a focus on power-grabbing toward emergent concerns about ecology, education, women's and minority rights and the quality of urban life (*Entrada* 14). Significantly, ordinary people make these advances from anonymity, the most propitious terrain, Monsiváis believes, for seeing with greater clarity the way democracy functions in a global society (14). In *Entrada libre,* authority was wrested from a hostile government in the presidential palace. In *Rituales,* Big Brother has been assigned standing room only in a back corner of the subway car.

the freedom in overcrowding

From that vantage, we can appreciate the ubiquitous pressure that has shoved government-enforced "unity" into the background. This is humanity's sheer corporeal excess. A persistent monsivaisian theme of ambivalent *noir* tone, overpopulation is here the nightmare that arises from the child-bearing sector's incontinence—"¡Cómo se multiplican!" [How fast they multiply!] cries the bourgeoisie (*Rituales* 35). Like a subway window, the front cover of *Rituales* allows us to peek from a distance at a profuse society that overflows boundaries of the train and the book. On the back cover, this surplus of meaning is announced with an "approximate language" (Fox 15) that unfixes concepts of ritual and chaos and, as well, what we have come to expect regarding Monsiváis's attitudes toward cultural diversity, permanence and national unity.

What, exactly, does it mean to say that the increased diversity to be revealed in the book "apunta al caos, en esta oportunidad no la alteración de las jerarquías sino la gana de vivir como si las jerarquías no estuviesen aquí, sobre uno y dentro de uno" [points toward chaos, in this context not the alteration of hierarchies but the desire to live as though hierarchies did not exist on and inside of us]? How shall we understand the apparent paradox in the assertion that, "aunque no se perciba, en las grandes ciudades las jerarquías se mantienen rígidas y, al mismo tiempo, las jerarquías pierden su lugar y se deshacen" [although one may not be aware of it, hierarchies remain rigidly in place in big cities and, at the same time, lose their grip and dissolve]? Against this evocation of a world wobbling on its axis, order is either inevitable or desired: "Son los rituales, esa última etapa de la permanencia, los que insisten en la fluidez de lo nacional. En la más intensa de las transformaciones concebibles, las ceremonias, objeto de estas crónicas, aportan las últimas pruebas de la continuidad" [Rituals, the last stage of permanence, are what guarantee the nation's viability. Within the most intense transformation conceivable, ceremonies—the object of these chronicles— are the ultimate proof of continuity] (back cover).

a ritualized disorder

The container of these unstable binarisms—*Los rituales del caos*—is itself a ritualized disorder. Self-defined as "estas crónicas" (15), *Rituales* in fact presents an interdiscursive mix of genres and registers. As do his previous collections, this one includes emblematic photographs, for example. Each of these sixteen images can be easily made to correlate with following texts in *Rituales,* but as a group they also form an autonomous discourse on multitudes and singularities, exterior and interior orders, and the tension between body and spirit. Here also, some of the primary texts slip over into fictional territory; I consider three to be short stories.[1] Unique to this book, however, are six quasifictional parables, microtexts that resemble *Nuevo catecismo*'s satirical fables; both draw on medieval comic literature's mixture of the sublime and the low.[2] The narrator of the parables speaks from a more godlike position—and with notably more angst—than the voice who observes and analyzes in the chronicles-proper.[3]

The first parable floats without page number between the prologue and the black and white images that precede the first chronicle. Its title ("Parábola de las imágenes en vuelo" [Parable of Images in Flight]) suggests it should be read as a photo caption; its millenarian tone is suggestive of a sermon about a crouching horde of dehumanized beings whose number threatens to dissolve the cosmic order. Their propagation—direct consequence of those mandated in *Genesis*—pushes the world headlong down "el perpetuo Camino del Exceso" [the perpetual Road of Excess] toward a (self)destructive imbalance: "la implosión de recursos y la explosión de familias" [the implosion of resources and the explosion of families]. The other five parables, inserted throughout the book, sustain this focus on chaos as massive population growth.

Notable repetitions in the other five parables work against the surging energies they enunciate. For example, each is inserted with meaningful periodicity in a "subplot" called "Parábolas de las postrimerías" [Parables of the End of Time].[4] The apocalyptic narrator of these minitexts views impersonal statistics with alarm while lamenting that privacy and uniqueness have been swept away by the demographic explosion (38). Dreamscapes such as Borges would imagine are "el único y último territorio liberado de la multitud que contiene a una multitud que encierra a una multitud" [the only and the last free territory for a multitude that contains a multitude that encloses a multitude] (110).

regressive and progressive time

Parable time in *Rituales* advances from creation through a disorderly peripheral period and toward an apocalypse that seems to have already taken place. On a parallel textual plane, chronicle time ticks with greater immediacy; the words "La hora de . . . " [The Hour/Time of . . .] introduce twenty of the twenty-three main titles. As a sense-making device, this time relies on *kairos*, a fullness of time, more than on *chronos*, a waiting or empty time (Kermode 47). Monsiváis's ritualistic consciousness establishes concord, with titles such as "La hora de la pluralidad" or "La hora del lobo," between a topic selected from reality (a concert, a religious rite, a boxing match, sex in the nineties) and the meaningful finish revealed at the end of its time on the page. The other three chronicles, subheaded "Protagonista," analyze an exemplary life that inserts itself into a vast sociocultural subtext.

An implicit directive issued by Monsiváis helps organize an excavation of that subtext. In the prologue he characterizes culture as a Medusa-like figure of tangled forms, a shape-changing confusion of "multitudes que se hacen y rehacen cada minuto, carnavales previstos e imprevistos" [multitudes that form and reform every minute, carnivals foreseen and unforeseen] (15). While this appears to confirm what he alludes to as Mexico's much-cited "feroz desorden" [savage disorder], or desmadre, he refutes the stereotype with precise suggestiveness: "Si esto alguna vez fue cierto ya ha dejado de serlo. Según creo, la descripción más justa de lo que ocurre equilibra la falta aparente de sentido con la imposición altanera de límites. Y en el caos se inicia el perfeccionamiento del orden" [If this was once true it no longer is. As I see it, one could most aptly describe what's happening as a balance between apparent senselessness and the dogmatic imposition of limits. Chaos gives rise to the perfection of Order] (15). Appearances deceive. Further, the issue is not perfect order, such as that pursued by post-Revolutionary governments, but evolution of an unfixed form: order as the place "donde concurren las variedades del caos" [where varieties of chaos converge] (15), *Rituales del caos* being a textbook illustration of the theory.

a dramatization of chaos theory

The chaos that orders *Rituales* is characterized as traditional and prescientific (15). Given the biblical and prehispanic substrata of his discourse, one exegetical guide can be found in religious thought. In that arena, one view sees chaos as an "empty, formless reality" (Metzger and Coogan 105) where nothing is in its proper place (Armstrong 268), a vision recalling Greek mythology's pre-Creation storms and wars (Hamilton 79–85) and the everlasting darkness before the dawn of both Judeo-Christian and Nahua thought (Fox 16–18; Burkhart 35). As a "presagio de la tierra desordenada y vacía antes del Principio o del Apocalipsis" [portent of the formless and empty earth before the Beginning or the Apocalypse] (*Rituales* 48), chaos is seen in *Rituales*'s "tempestades demográficas" [demographic storms] and the tumult and whirlwinds (17) associated with a "población monstruosa cuyo crecimiento nada detiene" [monstrous population whose growth has become uncontrollable] (21).

A variant on the theme inverts the *pre*order perspective and adds a judgmental moral dimension: chaos as *dis*order, or loss of a prior discipline because of some irrational or eccentric otherness requiring control (Armstrong 92; Burkhart 46, 58–60). This chaos is an essentially secular, instinctual space that is evil by virtue of its excess (Burkhart 28)—"el caos en una cáscara de nuez" [chaos in a nutshell] (*Rituales* 111); the overpowering weight of religion felt amid the crush of parishioners in the cathedral (48); a girl attacked by a gang because there are "demasiadas manos, demasiadas excitaciones" [too many hands and too many arousals] (36); the dissolution of tradition itself: "Hay que dejar de creer para volver a creer" [One must stop believing in order to believe again] (90).

The last statement's progressive movement relates to a favored aspect of chaos in *Rituales:* the destruction of order that is considered a necessary "prelude to a new creation" (Armstrong 268), as well "an ongoing activity" (Metzger and Coogan 105). Although the Aztecs thought of the disorderly gap between states of being as dangerous and immoral, it was not an inherently bad thing but a component of cosmic dynamism, time and human life (Burkhart 35–39). If the parables of *Rituales* suggest an atavistic emotional response to forces beyond rational control (such as we saw depicted in *Escenas de pudor y liviandad*), they are bracketed by the more deliberate mood of the primary texts, which pull the discourse back toward an "ethos of moderation" (Burkhart 168), prized in both precolumbian and Christian value systems. If the postmodern era's fascination with electronic media potentially turns these into "manuales del sojuzgamiento" [manuals for subjugation] (16), one must balance this ideological view, says Monsiváis, by taking into account the self-liberating experience of genuine entertainment that escapes control. Rock fans do not imagine a hidden hegemonic force wanting to brainwash them (16).

a discourse of abundance

Against a discourse of scarcity that enumerates the "nacidos-para-perder" who escape poverty through sports, Monsiváis posits a discourse of abundance that imagines the transcendent import of an individual who autonomously inscribes himself as a free agent in the order that emerges after capitalist consumerism weakens statist controls (28). If the chaos of too many people breaks down traditional liturgical discipline, an "eclesiogénesis" (self-renewing dogma) from below introduces heterodox rites that attract more devotees (47–48). When the corporeal massification of society flattens rigid barriers, social classes mingle in newly opened spaces (78). If loud music destroys ambient peace, it also creates a bubble of "outer" space into which the individual can retreat to think (118). Lest we forget to balance all this solemnity with humor, Monsiváis also reminds us that sometimes, the actual destruction of bodies is required to create new role models out of "héroes cuyo público anterior fue un pelotón de fusilamiento" [heroes whose previous audience was a firing squad] (135).

The figure standing like a statue before the firing squad and eventually being cast into bronze emblematizes a cosmology which, like that of ancient Greeks and Mesoamericans, does not wish to arrive at an unchanging universe such as that which ideological uniformity hardens into public monuments ("La hora cívica") (*Rituales* 135–53) but instead to create a material world in which opposing impulses are "eternally engaged in a dialectic movement of desired instability" (Russell 56). In such a world, a soccer critic may observe that the city has achieved an optimum disorderliness ("desmadre óptimo") (*Rituales* 33) while the diversity of Virgin worship in the late or postnationalist era teaches that licentious abandon ("relajo") and respect for order are inherently equal forms of transcendence (52). Instances of this sort of dialectic compromise are so numerous in *Rituales* as to constitute the discourse, even down to the controlled chaos of its language: baroque poetry serving prosaic goals. Its metonymic and metaphoric displacements, paradoxical ironies and antithetical unions begin to explain the ambivalent terms of engagement with which we began our reading.

keywords redefined

Keeping in mind Monsiváis's perennial focus on the problems inhering in Mexico's late entry into modernity, let us consider the surprisingly positive tone in which words such as "permanence" and "continuity" were pronounced in prefatory texts. Logically, one would condemn, as Monsiváis has, the rigid postcolonial mentality that enforces unchanging values of a hieratical colonial tradition. Yet, the piece on Jesús Helguera, "El encanto de las utopías en la pared" (65–71), tenderly enumerates the charms of a genre of lowbrow calendar art that idealizes the culture of poverty, colonial Mexico's most oppressive legacy. The exaggeratedly romantic Aztec figures painted by Helguera, now considered vulgarly kitsch (67), are here rescued from modernity's rubbish pile and hung in a gallery of remembrance. Then it occurs to us that an individual's talent is the *objet d'art* being honored. Only in the hands of a Jesús Helguera is it worth preserving a style that immortalizes the national mania for myths (71). And besides, there remains the implication that we are, after all, talking about an aesthetic that Monsiváis has just put in a museum.

"Unity" is another monsivaisian keyword whose definition acquires additional usages in *Rituales*. Perhaps the most indissoluble unity in Mexico's history has been its adherence to Catholicism. In previous works, Monsiváis has discoursed at length and from a sophisticated theoretical posture on popular Catholicism (see my analysis of *Rituales*'s chronicle on Boy Fidencio in chapter 3); although his approach is more subtle than most, he agrees with scholars who see nothing "alternative" about the notably pagan form of Christianity practiced by the masses. Now, when he goes to a mountain in Los Tuxtlas, with "los crédulos, los incrédulos y esa mezcla cabal de ambos, los reporteros" [the credulous, the incredulous and that exact mixture of both: reporters] (72), to await an appearance of the Devil, he is plumbing the depths of a spiritual diversity grown ample enough to permit, even in Mexico, the alternative cult of an aggressively marketed Satan-worship. With a seriocomic tone in "La hora de las convicciones alternativas: ¡Una cita con el diablo!" (72–92), he reports heterodox behaviors that nonetheless do not entirely obscure their basis in the old orthodoxies. In the way that science fiction's distortions provide an accurate negative depiction of reality, the studiously inverted rituals of these anti-Christians betray a passion for the Virgin of Guadalupe that is out of place (73). What attracts Monsiváis in this media event is precisely the fact that such a blasphemous departure from National Unity caused few ripples because, apparently, a new, more broadminded nation is able to naturalize, or at least tolerate, anomalies.

The foregoing is a fair description of the way ritual is seen in this book to work within and around chaos in order to contain it, in the multiple task of controlling it, giving it meaning and rechanneling its creative force. With respect to traditional religion, Burkert observes that it develops around an unseen that cannot be verified empirically (5) and exists to provide "orientation within a meaningful cosmos" (26). Gravitating to the political elite, it tends to use power and, even, violence to suppress dissident or rival religions (14). When religions sense themselves to be endangered, they defend with isolation and procreation (Burkert 14).[5] In either a sacred or secular context, rituals are meaning-containers and shapers which serve to minimize the dangers of change (García Canclini, *Consumidores* 47).

These parameters can also apply to the secular ceremonialism highlighted in *Rituales*, which recognizes organic links among politics, entertainment and religion. In Monsiváis's synthesizing view, religion is at work in the individualists who cultivate their "know-how dancístico" (115), TV-wrestling's cruel spectators who shout "'¡Queremos sangre!' tal vez para imaginarse los sacrificios en el Templo Mayor" ["We want blood!" perhaps to imagine they are witnessing sacrifices in the Great Temple] (126); civic statuary enunciating state ideology through its rigid messages (138); the "vasallaje ígneo" [flaming servitude] of candle-holding concertgoers paying homage to First World music's symbology of success (186); the "cuatro palabras cabalísticas" [four cabalistic words] that singing idol Luis Miguel repeats while his audience assumes the ritualized movements of a pagan celebration of U.S. music deities (195); the religion of success practiced at a sales seminar where competitive zeal reaches mystical heights (214), or converts to the artistic creed (240) whose obsessive addition of pieces to their collections establishes a new religion and cosmic order (241–43).

the virgin of guadalupe is no exception

A persisting example of the symbiosis between state ideology and social psychology is the cult of the Virgin of Guadalupe. If she represents religious life's most prodigious sign in Mexico (39), it is in large measure because she is symbolic on so many planes of consciousness: as religious doctrine and national identity, as comfort to the multitudinous miserable, as the safety of belonging to local worship groups. Mostly, however, when the Basilica of Guadalupe in the nation's capital overflows with pilgrims on the eve of her December 12 feast day, the ritual of bloodied knees brings out for display what cannot be seen the rest of the year: a Mexico for whom entry to modernity is barred (39). But then, noting how pilgrims today play up their suffering for "la Máquina Inmortalizadora" [the Immortalizing Machine] (59), Monsiváis observes that television has stripped the Guadalupan cult of much of its historical fervor: "Lo cierto es que, apretujado en la nueva Basílica, soy testigo del escamoteo: a la piedad que observa la sustituye la piedad que se siente observada" [What's certain is that, crammed into the new Basilica, I am witness to a vanishing act: Piety observed is replaced by a piety that knows itself to be under observation] (46).

While Monsiváis acknowledges those who hold spectacle to be a hegemonic strategy to control potential disorder (15–16),[6] the Basilica scene is perforated with avenues of escape. If official culture disciplines the masses by promoting entertainment events, the people who take advantage of such cultural capital will invest it as they choose: "La diversión genuina (ironía, humor, relajo) es la demostración más tangible de que, pese a todo, algunos de los rituales del caos pueden ser también una fuerza liberadora" [Authentic entertainment (irony, humor, joking around) is the most tangible proof that, despite everything, some rituals of chaos can also be liberating] (16).

the traditions of postmodernism

This brings us to the book's main thrust, an exploration of the heterodox ways that a postmodern "chaos" of factors inverts or revises traditional forms, and how, in the free-form gap between past and future, the masses acting against the guardians of order (or disorder) devise new rituals (35). Population's monstrous excess in the parables is now a force that necessitates and energizes transformation. In this enterprise, the birth rate's partners are the mass media; an economy that persistently disappoints desires; the Mexican government itself (whose negative example inspires on many levels) and, insistently throughout *Rituales,* U.S. cultural, economic and sociopolitical models.

Congenitally indisposed to fatalism, Monsiváis labors to identify "las ventajas de la desventaja" [the advantages of disadvantage], especially with respect to the overcrowding that results when rural migrants jam themselves into slums (18). Giving way before the incoming tide of poor Mexicans, the power class retreats to ghettos of privilege (23). On the urban stage now monopolized by the masses, the most dramatic change is a loss of concern for what the neighbors might be thinking (21–22). Freed of carcelary notions of an unattainable upper-class demeanor, the underclass and middle classes are also liberated, paradoxically, through the democratization forced by sheer proximity to vast numbers of others (113).[7] In an environment overcrowded with differences, the dance hall is a habitat in which couples move as though transported in a time machine to a personal universe. In this microcosm, televisual homogenization helps society sweep aside the unrealistic luxury of obsolete mindsets and concede a place where even homosexual cross-dressers can gain marginal acceptance (115), and statues of fieldworkers resemble Ninja Turtle warriors (152).

In the context of such reshuffled expectations, pairs of chronicles negotiate meaning production across an intratextual bargaining table, so to speak. For example, juxtaposing "La hora de la tradición" and "La hora de las convicciones alternativas" isolates these texts in a cultural dialogue which, on the reportorial level, is about contrasts between the Virgin of Guadalupe's cult and those dedicated to Satan-worship and other nontraditional creeds; on the theoretical level, the textual pair speaks of intellectual conformity and pluralism and the implications of (in)dependent thinking on quality of life. Further, on a more universal level, it seems significant that kneeling devotees of the Virgin are mainly young men of the popular classes (39), while followers of witchcraft are mainly middle-class women (76, 79). Monsiváis goes out of his way to make these observations; he leaves their interpretation up to us.

These contrasts sharpen in another semantic pairing, this time between a fictional satire, "La hora de la pluralidad," and the chronicle that immediately follows, "Protagonista: el Niño Fidencio." In "Pluralidad" Monsiváis pokes fun at urban New Age mysticism, not least for its historical amnesia. The following chronicle reveals that particular New Age ritual's forgotten links to the religiosity of the rural poor, which we see in the tragicomic figure of the provincial miracle worker. Thought and gender relations oscillate ironically between continuity and rupture in both texts. Characterized as a domineering female, the fiction piece's Alicia ends her sexual relation with Luis because he is abnormally attached to traditional thinking and conduct: "No eres normal . . . Acéptalo. . . . Desde hace años, y ahora más aceleradamente, todos se han afiliado a otras creencias . . . Se van corriendo a reuniones de estudios de textos sagrados, . . . experimentan con el grito primordial de la raza, acatan las órdenes de la Naturaleza tal y como las apresa una maceta en un corredor" [You aren't normal . . . Believe me . . . For years, and especially now, everybody has taken up different belief systems. They're all running off to study sessions on sacred books, experimenting with primal screams and obeying the laws of Nature exactly the way a flowerpot in the hallway tells them to] (95).

Ironic plays on meanings of "traditional" and "new" show New Age beliefs to be as rooted in the primitive past as the openly traditional cult of the 1920s witch doctor. Further, while the inverted New Age hierarchy problematizes relations between the sexes, Boy Fidencio and his heretical faith-healing are associated with a complex mix of ambiguous sexualities (98–100). What does emerge as new in these reports is posttraditional religion's explicit refusal to ritualize the sacrificial magic of suffering.

the religion of success

The amplified meanings that issue from these yoked readings extend their significance when we link them to the pair that ends this series of chronicles, "La hora del ascenso social" and "La hora de las adquisiciones espirituales."[8] By virtue of their posterior location, these works place historical notions of religiosity in dialectical opposition to (post)modern acceptance of secular routes to the inward order of being.

At the start of "Ascenso," the cronista is covering a company convention in Cuernavaca. The training rituals for door-to-door cosmetics sales act out a plethora of national themes. The old ones include the inferiority complex of the "pobretón" [poor wretch] (215–16) and learning English as the language of material success (213). New themes are more numerous. The first one forms the narrative backbone of both this text and the entire book (Monsiváis's inaugural assertion: consumption is central (15).[9] The capitalist motif develops interrelated ideas about the imperialism of appearances (not for nothing did Monsiváis select a *cosmetics* company to market his symbols); the mystical properties of competition (213–14), whose intensely personal, self-authorizing orientation is related to U.S.–style Protestantism's eternally optimistic can-do faith (218–19), and the hope of "making it" on which capitalism's universal appeal is based (220–23). There is also proof that this is an equal-opportunity ethos that sells its seductions even in the provinces (225).

As a part of the overall book's patient refunctioning of cultural capital, "Ascenso" fabricates its meanings through a process of self-improvement (15) that is here pegged to three temporal stages: the 1970s, 1980s and 1990s. Notions of self-help germinate close to the ground in the 1970s, when "Atrévate a ser grande" [Dare to be great] then meant touting high-heeled shoes as a way of uplifting the colonized mentality of a people persuaded to think of itself as "la raza 'bajita'" [a race of short people] (212). Light sarcasm adds encouragement to entrepreneurial novitiates who are perfecting their faith: "La competencia. El aturdimiento inducido, el ritmo detonante. 'GO, GO, GO, GO, GO, GO . . .' . . . Táctica azteca: Si uno dice muchas veces una palabra en inglés la nacionaliza. (A cambio de Texas y California les hemos ido arrancando a los gringos su vocabulario.) Ve, sigue, prosigue, continúa. GO" [Competition. The induced giddiness, the explosive rhythm. "GO, GO, GO, GO, GO, GO . . . " Aztec tactic: If you repeat an English word enough times you nationalize it. (In exchange for Texas and California we've been stealing the gringo's vocabulary). Come on, keep it up, keep going, don't stop. GO] (213).

The ironic inversion—Mexico conquering U.S. language and social practices—suggests that it is possible, after all, to decolonize a fatalistic mentality. The emphasis here is on a yearning for radical individualism (20), as well as a pursuit of abstraction that results from an intense desire to *subtract* oneself from the human conglomerate. In varied contexts, these *forward, inward* and *upward* tendencies begin to favor the incorporeal side of the body-mind dialectic in *Rituales*. Detours from historical habit produce the internal changes on which any possible external transformation is predicated. In "Ascenso," individuals brag that they have gotten rid of their "español-de-pobre"—Poor Man's Spanish—and criticize their elders for having brought them up to accept a habit of deprivation (213). They study English because it is the language of the present and the future, they plan trips to "los esteits" [the States], not to pick lemons but to pick up computer science skills that they can bring back to Mexico and invest in their own businesses. They speak without embarrassment of cultivating their "preparación espiritual" [spiritual development] with the help of New Age self-esteem gurus (215). They assign themselves the job of learning, in short, a new way to relate to power. As one seeker of autonomy tells Monsiváis: "Las puertas al poder son la confianza en ti mismo y el deseo de no quedarte nunca donde estás. *Poder* es lo obvio: el chorro de tarjetas de crédito y el rumbo que aleje a tus hijos del naquerío y los viajes y lo que quieras, pero—antes de nada— *poder* es una decisión interior que se consigue entrenando el espíritu" [The doors to power are confidence in yourself and the desire to never get stuck where you are. *Power* is the obvious: a pile of credit cards and a road that takes your kids out of the ghetto and travel and whatever else you want, but—above all—*power* is an internal decision that you arrive at by training your spirit] (216).

Even during the disastrous eighties, a growing cadre of can-do citizens summoned a will to believe in the symbol of a friend who struck it rich. "Si el ejemplo cunde, la mentalidad cambia" [Multiply the example, mutate the mind] (219), Monsiváis quips. Listening to the salesman who dreams of rising to the top of his company, he adds: "Como todas las religiones, la del Éxito también empieza de casa en casa, ganando adeptos, iluminando semblantes" [As with all religions, the one called Success also starts by going door to door, gaining converts and illuminating countenances] (219).

A significant detail: These converts seek inspiration through reading, here a sacred literature that includes testimonies republished in *Selecciones del Reader's Digest,* Dale Carnegie's gospel of success and Norman Vincent Peale's explicit parables (220–21). A lightly satirical tone warns against fanaticism, but the details tell an undeniably upbeat tale of Mexicans, with "la vista al infinito" [their gaze fixed on Eternity] and infused with faith in "la Voluntad Individual" [the Will of the Individual] (221), working to pull themselves up by their bootstraps. Capitalism as a ritual naturally invites derision, but this chronicle also shows it to be a ticket out of misery for a number of exemplary individuals who motivate masses. Deceitful as "la ideología del Optimismo" [ideology of Optimism] (221) may be for most who hope to get rich, it is better than the litany of compensations waiting in heaven that the Church promises; better also than the socialist creed's promise of compensation for everybody—in some impossibly far-off future (221). A steely eyed, softhearted reporter may warn them against disappointment, but "nada los detendrá en su anhelo, ni el pesimismo atávico, ni que les recuerden los 'fenómenos de clase'" [nothing will stop their yearning, neither atavistic pessimism nor being reminded about the hard realities of classism] (225): "Les costó mucho adquirir un punto de vista y no lo abandonarán antes de que sus hijos vayan a Disneyworld, antes de asemejarse a los símbolos externos y ser tan eficaces como un automóvil o un refrigerador" [It cost them a lot to acquire this point of view and they will not give it up until their children have seen Disney World, until their own lives begin to resemble all the visual symbols of success and become as efficient as a car or a refrigerator] (231).

A generation of Mexicans is now willing to risk pursuing a future that only their great-grandchildren will be alive to enjoy (225). They have undergone what we see here to be a genuine "remodelación interior" [internal remodeling] (229), a spiritual alignment facilitated by computerized technology and divested of pessimistic moralizing.

The chronicle I have paired with "Ascenso" documents a view from inside the pot at the foot of the rainbow. In "La hora de las adquisiciones espirituales: el coleccionismo en México," the protagonists are the Mexicans cronistas usually love to hate: the Very Rich (241). Here, however, Monsiváis desists from elite-bashing so that we can see one of the more uplifting uses to which capitalism's rewards may be put: the acquisition of fine art, which does not always remain only in private collections. Often enough, wealthy

Mexicans will lay out great sums at New York auctions to acquire pieces of art that have ended up out of the country; they may eventually donate an entire museum for public enjoyment (243–45). Monsiváis explores the spread of art collecting in Mexico principally through ideas that Walter Benjamin, whom he characterizes as perhaps the most astute theorist on the subject (235), gathered from his study of a European collector at the turn of the century (234).

Updating Benjamin's view of the collector's passion as a dialectic tension between extremes of order and disorder (235), Monsiváis suggests that collectors be seen as treasurers of the finest that tradition has produced (236–37); creators of a unique cosmos, complete with its own mythology (241–43); beneficiaries of international models who in turn inspire new creation of domestic arts (243); and, most significantly, as another sector of the citizenry that contributes to the individuation, privatizing and spiritualization that are hallmarks of a modern cast of mind.[10]

a form of gnostic ascension

That Carlos Monsiváis has ended one of his collections by acknowledging a meritorious aspect of the Very Rich is not merely novel. In *Los rituales del caos*, it seems the logical conclusion to reach at the end of a twenty-three-text progression that advances slowly but surely in a forward direction, away from the limiting aspects of institutionalized religious suffering and toward a more humane secularism, away from poverty and toward material well-being. Further, the progression takes us inward, away from public spheres of action and increasingly into the mind, a shift that also implies a voyage from multitudes to individuals. And throughout, even in texts firmly anchored in the material body of indigent masses, the semantic trajectory is ascendant.

Snippets of interviews conducted with sexually active young people for "La hora del lobo: del sexo en la sociedad de masas" (163–65) compress the progressions I have just described. A sampling shows, for instance, that virginity today has gone past being an anomaly to becoming a girl's chosen *"claim to fame"*; safe sex is every day less an exception; book-learning sometimes seduces more than intercourse; orgies can be boring; masturbation gains a measure of Retro chic; abstinence can add to one's vocabulary; women reserve the right to judge a man by the shape of his behind; pornographic videos can be as effective as a cold shower. We may laugh at some of these anecdotes (and we are supposed to), but they encapsulate displacements that proceed in *Rituales* from an oppressive disorder tied to the material Body toward the orderly chaos of "solitary confinement" within the unsupervised Mind.

Ihab Hassan's characterization of "The New Gnosticism" can be illuminating at this juncture. In the context of a technologized postmodernism, the Body-Mind division, which is also a (re)union, progressively opens up in *Rituales* to reflect several aspects of the intellectual mysticism that Hassan depicts as "convergences that are silently altering the definitions of culture" (76). Specifically, the so-called new gnosticism breaks with traditional Christianity (146) by focusing on *consciousness* per se rather than on faith (62, 70–71, 123). It eludes "distinctions of the old mind, seeking yet unknown synergies" (64), and can be detected in a gradual "process of 'ephemeralization'" aimed at "regenerating *metaphysically* a *physically* decaying universe" (70).

I note in the previous chapter that the heroic individuals of *Entrada libre* exemplify a moral and spiritual ascension toward rational consciousness and autonomy. *Los rituales del caos* shows a similar democratic illumination, but here much larger sectors of the populace are shown thinking with a changed mind. A further difference: This book's "heroes" are not self-sacrificing political activists bent on stirring multitudes to slay dragons, but "selfish" individuals struggling to get ahead financially. Monsiváis does not censure these social climbers. He may subject their rituals to light satire, but he leaves essentially alone the creative heart of their enterprise, the surging desire that drives them to give meaningful form to their personal lives. A chaos of eclecticism, *Los rituales del caos* testifies to one man's durable faith in the Mexican people's will and capacity to prosper.

conclusions

The five books that are the principal basis of this study tell a story of ever-renewing suspense. We cannot know "the end" until Carlos Monsiváis is through constructing his literary project, and that conclusion promises to be long deferred. Still, his work between 1970 and 1995 documents real finds in his search for causes, effects and deconstructions of historical obstacles to Mexico's passage into modernity. For Monsiváis, modernity is a state of mind, a (self)critical consciousness synonymous with attitudes that include morality, accountability, tolerance, fairness and optimism. These are the mental patterns this cronista would make the basis of political, economic and social structures presently under construction: concrete institutions meant to equip all Mexican citizens with opportunities to build a better standard of living for themselves and a civil society whose liberties and causes for hope their grandchildren may inherit.

Without (perhaps inevitably) blood, sweat and tears, this blueprint would remain but an architect's dream. From *Días de guardar* through *Los rituales del caos*, Monsiváis's crónicas recruit active optimists whose nation-building skills include the hands-on variety that can lead marching citizens in the path of tanks or risk assassination to organize a farm union or defy a bulldozer to pull a loved one's body from a collapsed building. A kleptomaniac of culture, Monsiváis steals from the forms of ritual and chaos that daily life in Mexico places within reach of his eye, ear and metaphoric imagination. In these he finds proof of a spreading will to disbelieve—and disobey—archaic institutions of authority: to resist structures of oppression where they still stand.

Modeling foundational attitudes, Monsiváis remains tirelessly indignant when tyranny causes death, machismo abuses, racism wounds, bigotry attacks, or intolerance anywhere of any kind limits an individual's freedom to choose his or her lifestyle. He never wearies of explaining how an historical dearth of options in spheres of autonomy stunts democracy's growth. He applauds every sign of a citizenry now willing to step around an obsolete paternalism and create its own options.

Founded on fact and rising upon art's figuration, the chronicle form is made to order for the story he tells. With writers like Monsiváis and Poniatowska, Mexico's historical chronicle has become a mature form that daily remakes itself from a dynamic eclecticism. The result is an emblem of Mexican literary discourse: a gestural, iconic, disputatious union of oral and written idioms. The contemporary Mexican chronicle, durably and elegantly practiced by Carlos Monsiváis, is a complete discourse, a democratic genre, a form that mirrors its content.

For the exuberant stylistics of *Días de guardar* and *Amor perdido*, Monsiváis has been situated with other boom writers. These books appeared to attract the notice of serious readers at the same time that other Latin American giants were fashioning the boom's extemporaneous identity with critical ideologies, international commercialism and narrative pyrotechnics. However, the boom admits subgenres of experimental writing, one of which—the neobaroque's semantically arid antinarrative—I would not choose to associate with Carlos Monsiváis's hypermeaningful works, which never let the richness of their language get in the way of the story they tell. I place his works within postmodernist terrain, which accommodates his varied modes: carnival's liberation theology, Menippean satire's utopian realism and the baroque's dialectic ambiguity.

If his ideological stance is postmodern, the form of his arguments is baroque. The prelude to his decision to develop a career in journalism was a long apprenticeship in poetry. That figural substratum tones the referential assertiveness of his discourse, giving it music and flexible muscle. Its fusion of fact with poetic speech produces a rhetorical register of seductive, and often aggressive, complexity. Monsiváis's language is centrifugal, expanding outward in measured circles of import from the pregnant detail to the exemplary metonym to the transglobal metaphor. At the same time, it is centripetal, pressing inward toward the atomic core of the alephic aphorism's ungovernable signification. Exquisitely elite, raucously popular, convex and concave, upright upon storied allegories, recumbent upon concatenations, or doubled over with irrepressible antisolemnity, monsivaisian speech breathes, flexing to accommodate the expanding universe of observations that it represents.

As a self-fashioned outsider who invades the home territory of Mexico's elite and popular sectors, Monsiváis knows that his narrative stance is both suspect and potentially misleading (Monsiváis, "Idolos" 48). While he cannot fully overcome the unbridgeable gap between his own and the consciousness of those others, he carefully positions himself metajournalistically as "other" to all, the better to point out the similarity of their separate claims to legitimacy. When Monsiváis plans an incursion into orality's terrain, he steps as far into narrative invisibility as he can without implying he possesses the omniscience of God. In the end, we can just make him out in the shadows: the ethnologist being instructed by the "other" he has come to study. He doesn't try to hide his own bourgeois formation, tastes and preferences. The fact that he criticizes power's aristocracy from within its keep complicates his relationship with authority and the way others perceive him. That complex public presence sometimes brings accusations that he has sold out to power or become a tyrant.[1]

Despite the perils implicit in either his own conscience or among his sociocultural peers, he persists in carrying out work that must surely cause pain in some part of the world he pokes about in for traces of Mexico's historically most estranged Other: the modern, secular mentality. His self-deprecating narrator-hero is a mask for the Nahua *tlamatini*, "the one who knows something" (León-Portilla, "Sabios" 254), the Greek histor, the twentieth-century newsman who engages with "la eternidad del minuto" [the eternity of a minute] (*Días* 122) to coax from it a portentous sign. Over a career of some forty years, Monsiváis has been turning life's small epiphanies into tools of self-empowerment that he hands to his countrymen, with "prophetic confidence of renovation" (Kermode 99).

At one such moment, in *Amor perdido*, he bares himself in a vulnerable attitude, of the sort that one would naturally assume upon the death of a cherished friend. He is clearly moved by the unrepentant idealism of José Revueltas, who was in his fifties when he served as guru to the young students marching in 1968 against strongman politics and in support of a system based on the law. Revueltas, who stood by his convictions even after they locked him in jail, is to Monsiváis a shining example of civil disobedience; to me, he is a reflection of Monsiváis's own conscience. Thirty years after the Movement, the cronista still thinks like one of the student brigadistas who improvised sidewalk theater in their effort to politicize citizens who may have ignored the way Díaz Ordaz's government was endangering their civil liberties. He said, in 1998, that "cuando en la Cámara de Diputados se opone a declarar el 2 de octubre día de luto nacional, merece una movilización de la sociedad civil" [a vote in the Chamber of Deputies against declaring October 2 a day of national mourning is cause for a public demonstration in behalf of civil society] (Ponce 16). In the last year of the millennium, he copublished a book on the Student Movement (*Parte de guerra*, with Julio Scherer). Carlos Monsiváis: unrepentant brigadista.

The emotional subtext of his work supports his existentialist aim of linking idea to action and—just as important—action to idea. Speaking once of railway activist Demetrio Vallejo's willingness to spend long years in prison for his militant demands for government respect of the worker, Monsiváis once pointed out to Elena Poniatowska that the measurable gravity of Vallejo's political convictions—his years in jail—had carried him far beyond symbolic status: "En Vallejo el acto ha sido más importante que su verbalización y en eso le ha ganado de mano a todos, ha sido un pionero" [In Vallejo, action has mattered more than his speeches and that's why he has surpassed everyone, why he has become a pioneer] (cited in Poniatowska, "Monsiváis: cronista" 4).

Nonetheless, like many postcolonial writers, Monsiváis understands that power is prescribed through language; he understands oratory's persuasive resources. Fundamental to the chronicle's *literary* nature is the emotion it enlists to carry its critical thought, both of which are powered by utopian yearnings. During the marches of 1968, his narrator consciously decided to "reconocer la gana que el pueblo tiene de creer en el pueblo, el ávido

indescriptible deseo de soñar que alguien, al fin, actuó con generosidad, pro-
cedió con amor" [acknowlege the people's desire to believe in itself, the avid,
indescribable desire to imagine that someone, finally, had acted out of self-
less generosity, had been moved by love] (*Días* 269). He had to wait nearly
twenty years for a replay of that inspirational exhibit of selflessness, but by
the time he stood watching his compatriots make sacrifices for strangers
amid the rubble of 1985's earthquakes, he might well have recalled the metaphor he released above the candlelit sea of optimism that filled the Zócalo
during "los vastos, infinitos días de 1968" (*Días* 273): "con su mentalidad
retórica, él hubiese designado toda la jornada con una expresión del tipo de
'Paraíso Recobrado'" [with his rhetorical mind, he would have labeled the
whole day's journey as a kind of "Paradise Regained"](274).

"Eden and Utopia, the first and last perfection" (Hassan 125), are nothing less than Carlos Monsiváis's desire: a social order, here and now and
documentable, based upon ethical choices and moral action in every material and spiritual sphere of influence. He openly articulates his utopian ideology in a recent article on millenarian thinking in Mexico. For him, utopia
is a fleeting quality that he glimpses "a ráfagas, por instantes" [in brief
flashes of inspiration] when civil society mobilizes ("Milenarismos 176), and
in "enclaves," a term that calls to mind radical groups like the one formed
by initiates of Jesus's cabalistic teachings and didactic miracles. For Monsiváis, utopia is a language that translates desire for action into reality, while
teaching patience and reason: "Según creo, lo utópico no radica en las inten-
ciones, por loables que sean, sino en la articulación del lenguaje. . . . Cada
utopía es una hipótesis sobre el comportamiento humano, que se esfuerza
por ser objetiva, y por no alejarse de la realidad, ya no dimensión inexorable, sino concatenamiento de hechos" [As I see it, utopia does not reside
in intentions, however laudable these may be, but in their enunciation in
language. Every utopia is a hypothesis about human behavior that tries to be
objective and—so as not to be too unrealistic about it—is not a result of any
single factor but, rather, of a concatenation of facts and events] (174).

Utopia's is a language which, like the Word said to have created a
cosmos, can bring about genuine transformation in the world (175) through
its "vigor demiúrgico" [demiurgical vigor], which is to say, the power of its
thought to inspire a civilizing project in individuals who feel compelled
to organize their indignation and, with realistic expectations and resolve,
achieve a desired ethical rectification (176). Utopia: an optimism some

233
conclusions

might call romantic but which continually rebuilds itself upon reality's demand for reform (175).

Without perhaps intending to, Carlos Monsiváis sums up the purpose and spirit of his own life's work in the final words he writes about civilian idealism in "Milenarismos":

> ¿Por qué subrayo las cualidades utópicas de estas acciones y este pensamiento? Porque el deseo de felicidad en esta época, la proyección del hoy sobre el futuro, se ha ampliado y se ha reducido. Fuera del espacio religioso (y aun allí con demasiadas modificaciones) el reino milenario se aleja. Y lo que debe seguir ahora es un ámbito donde esté en manos de todos el rechazo de la injusticia. Sin necesidad de aclaraciones teológicas, el papel del pecado le corresponde ahora a la impunidad.
>
> Al margen, insisto, de los contenidos religiosos, tan determinantes en las utopías marxistas, se produce la secularización de la utopía, centrada en la distribución equitativa del derecho a la esperanza. De nuevo, . . . lo real es racional y lo racional es real. (176)

> [Why do I call attention to the utopian aspects of these acts and this thinking? Because today, the desire for happiness right now, as well as the tendency to project forward into the future, has both expanded and diminished. Outside of religion (and even within, albeit with too many exceptions) the millenarian kingdom has receded into the distance. And what ought to be realized in the present is a space in which the elimination of injustice becomes possible for all. I make no theological statement when I say that the role of sin now belongs to impunity.
>
> To repeat: outside of religion—so decisive in marxist thought—utopia is becoming a secular force centered on the equitable distribution of the right to hope. Once again, the real is rational and the rational is real.]

Creator of a kind of salvation history, Monsiváis drafts a blueprint for the national character by reading his society's myths, not only to delineate their structures but also to assess their moral content. He finds, as does a noted scholar of sacrifice, that "a society whose solutions are provided by fear and despair is headed for tyranny and cruelty" (Maccoby 181). In Mexico, from precolumbian society until as recently as the 1996 national elections, omnipotent authority of a tlatoani-president posed a danger that could be fatal to rebels and, less obviously, to passive followers of his will. Fortunately, "killing the father" in the presidential palace is today a less scandalous proposition than the "crime" of figuratively murdering the habit of depending on him. The messenger who brings that item to attention risks taking the president's place as the sacred scapegoat who carries communal fears and guilts. One wonders whether this subtle psychology explains why some of Monsiváis's readers seem to want to kill the messenger (see, for example, José Joaquín Blanco's attack on a Monsiváis clearly presented as a father figure, in Villarreal). What we can ascertain from close reading of his works is that Monsiváis does assume the guise of the intimidating Trickster of Carnival, who in turning the world upside down, commits an awesome crime under cover of humor.

The disturbing union of laughter, fear and outrage in his writing is not to be found in the more rhetorically placid essay and is one explanation for the chronicle's remarkable durability in the history of Mexican letters. It also argues for its greater diffusion in literature departments. A poetics of the genre, perhaps one such as I have argued for in this study, may help in that promotion. Outside of Mexico, at least, the chronicle remains a vast underground literature whose study will continue to be limited or distorted if more university-trained readers do not take a critical look at the way this narrativized journalism nimbly captures the unique character of socioeconomic and cultural realities in Mexico and elsewhere. A canon of chronicle works, apart from the writings of the conquest and colony, awaits formation. There lies a fertile ground for primary research, for much potentially canonical crónica is housed in periodical archives. A search for further gems of Carlos Monsiváis's daily literature would reward, for, like the Nahua poet, he is "él mismo escritura y sabiduría" [himself the embodiment of writing and wisdom] (León-Portilla, "Sabios" 254):

Suya es la sabiduría trasmitida, él es quien la enseña, sigue la verdad.
Maestro de la verdad, no deja de amonestar. . . .
Pone un espejo delante de los otros, los hace cuerdos, cuidadosos; hace que
    en ellos aparezca una cara.
Se fija en las cosas, regula su camino, dispone y ordena. Aplica su luz sobre
    el mundo.

[His is the wisdom that is communicated, he is the one who teaches, who
    follows after truth.
Master of truth, he never fails to counsel . . .
He places a mirror before others, he helps them be prudent and careful; he
    helps them to acquire a face.
He notices things, he walks a temperate path, he arranges and puts things
    in order. He focuses his light on the world.]

notes

introduction

1. Respectively titled: *Lo fugitivo permanece: 21 cuentos mexicanos* (1989), *La poesía mexicana del siglo XX (Antología)* (1966) and *Por mi madre, bohemios, I* (1993), first of a projected series to publish selections of the eponymous column.

2. *Parte de guerra: Tlatelolco 1968* (1999), by Julio Scherer García and Carlos Monsiváis.

3. His many prologues and explanatory texts for books of cartoons and comics include "Dispositivos para identificar a la gente famosa" and "Hagan su contrajuego, señores" (both on the political cartoons of Rogelio Naranjo); "Posada: el repertorio de las emociones" (on nineteenth-century cartoonist José Guadalupe Posada); "La ingenuidad no existe, Yolanda," an introductory text for *La comedia del arte* (celebrating Abel Quezada's satirical cartoons).

4. Enrique Krauze divides Mexican culture production of the twentieth century into four "generations": 1915 (born 1891–1905); 1929 (1906–1920); mid-century (1921–1935), and 1968 (1936–1950). Monsiváis was born in 1938; the events leading up to and encompassing the traumatic Student Movement of 1968 form the heart of his sociopolitical project. I agree that Carlos Monsiváis could be considered the Godfather of the Generation of '68 (155).

5. Unless otherwise noted, all translations are my own.

6. See Antonio Marimón's gleeful report on the "camp" presentation of *Por mi madre, bohemios*, in which Monsiváis participated like a stand-up comic in a parody of the usually quite solemn cultural custom in Mexico known as The Book Presentation. See also the two-part interview prior to the event in Andrés Ruiz.

7. In 1993, Monsiváis's career would have spanned closer to forty years. In an unpublished paper on "El ejercicio de la crónica," he says he published his first chronicle on a political protest in 1954 (p. 2 of the conference paper he delivered at the III Congreso de Mexicanistas, Mexico City, April 1–5, 1991; Hernán Lara Zavala kindly provided photocopies of all the papers presented at that meeting). Javier Aranda Luna includes anecdotal reference to that 1954 inaugural crónica in a 1995 interview with Monsiváis.

8. "La de México sigue siendo básicamente una cultura oral, que pese a la alta tecnología y pese a lo que se diga, estamos viviendo una cultura oral" [Mexico's is still an essentially oral culture; despite high technology and in spite of what may be claimed, we are living in an oral culture]. Interview with Carlos Monsiváis, in *Confrontaciones* (36).

9. See my doctoral dissertation, a distant starting point of this writing: Linda Egan, "'Lo marginal en el centro': las crónicas de Carlos Monsiváis" (1993); also, my "Crónica y periodismo" and "Descronicamiento." I will use the Spanish terms *crónica* and *cronista* interchangeably with the English chronicle and chronicler.

10. I propose not to theorize nonfiction in general, but, specifically, the contemporary chronicle of Mexico.

11. Salvador Novo (1904–1974) was Mexico's Cronista by virtue of journalistic essays such as "Nuestra ciudad mía," in which he sings homeric praise of the capital (*Toda la prosa* 97–100) and "Nueva Grandeza Mexicana," in which he reveals the enthusiasm of a tour guide for the sites of developing modernity in a city that in his lifetime had begun a process that would soon turn it into an urban megacenter (457–535). Novo revolutionized Mexican newspeak by combining the richness of oral tradition with new languages of modernity, such as psychology, anthropology and the mass media, which, in the twenties and thirties, had scarcely caught the attention of less perceptive analysts of Mexican culture. Novo's early formation as a poet of the Estridentista school gave him a flexible language that reveled in combinations of scientific jargon, traditional idiom and cosmopolitanism (the injection, for example, of bilingual phrases, especially those taken from the exemplary modernity of the Anglo world). In precociously "postmodern" style, Novo turns his private life into public art, making his literary persona an icon of change, his consciousness a mirror of modernity's angst, his intimate knowledge of local custom a window through which Mexico could contemplate the evolution of its being from within and without. Anticipating the ambivalence of the poststructuralist era, Novo wanted Mexico to Americanize itself even as he lamented that Mexico was de-Mexicanizing itself (33), thus bequeathing to contemporary Mexican cronistas one of their most persistent and complex themes. Novo's conservative politics would be abandoned by the generation of '68, but in the ways he used language to make daily life a literary art form, Novo figures among the tutors Monsiváis consulted as he launched his own journalism career. For Monsiváis's view of Novo as an icon of exemplary difference, see, especially, his *Salvador Novo: lo marginal en el centro* (2000), or his earlier, briefer crónica in *Amor* 265–70; for a more strictly literary analysis, see his "Santa Doctrina," especially pages 765–70. See also my dissertation, pages 601–20, especially. For other detailed discussions of the historical predecessors of today's cronistas, see elsewhere in that same thesis, in particular, the four hundred pages of its chapter 3.

12. Among a few essays on the technical aspects of Monsiváis's works, an example is the narratological analysis of one of his texts and another by a newswriter. The schematic comparison demonstrates much lesser discursive complexity and stylistic hybridity in the news article (Pescador 67–68).

13. Monsiváis has been investigating the nation-in-the-process-of-articulating-itself since 1954, decades before Homi K. Bhabha promotes "narrating the nation" in the name of postcolonialism ("Narrating the Nation" 3). While Bhabha may obfuscate with metamystifying prose (see example, p. 4), Carlos Monsiváis clarifies in his entertaining crónicas. Where, for example, Monsiváis will allude to the nationalist government's empty rhetoric with a self-explanatory term such as "verbomanía," Bhabha adopts Derrida's "the irreducible excess of the syntactic over the semantic" (4). Monsiváis has read Derrida, no doubt to his benefit. He sees no merit in speaking like Derrida.

14. Spanish American and peninsular *modernismo* (end of the nineteenth, beginning of the

twentieth centuries), was followed by a brief and stylistically chaotic "postmodern" period before fuguing into the *vanguardia* or avant-garde, which would correspond to the English-speaking world's concept of Modernism. From a strictly Mexican perspective, postmodernism as Linda Hutcheon or Andreas Huyssen understand it might be conceived of as a kind of *neovanguardism*. Today in Mexico, the term and concept of postmodernism have converged in notable multinational style to coincide with European and North American usage. See, for example, Jorge Ruffinelli's interrogation of Latin American premodernism, modernism, antimodernism and postmodernism, in "Los 80."

15. *Aires de familia*'s seven pieces will not be examined here, in part because their intended perspective is more regional than local (Mexican) but mainly because, as I read them, they are essays rather than chronicles.

16. For a prime example of the angst-ridden discourse Docker and I allude to, see Meaghan Morris's "On the Beach." It is a dramatic illustration of thinking "sous rassure."

17. From his earliest publications, Monsiváis stamped as his the English-language phrase "last but not least." This lexical trademark is a reminder of his bilingual perspective, an instance of his neobaroque playfulness, a sign of his carnivalesque devotion to the colloquial and, last but not least, a logical outgrowth of one of his most recognizable stylistic tools: the catalogue or enumeration, what Severo Sarduy calls the proliferation (170–72) and I simply call The List.

chapter 1

1. In this context, I do not refer to any "authority to speak" that government or other agencies may concede to a writer; I do not, in other words, allude here to any possible censorship or threat, perceived or real, to the writer.' The historical relationship between intellectuals and power in Mexico is an important topic that is not an emphasis in this study. My focus is upon the *reader's* perception of the cronista as a well-informed, ethical and competent writer of documentable truths; the concern, in other words, is for the literary journalist's credibility, as a component of what will be set forth as a theory of the contemporary chronicle.

2. "Mi imagen de mí misma es de una gente muy aloof, muy retirada, muy distanciada, que no concede y por lo tanto no espera demasiado de los demás" [I see myself as a very aloof person, quite shy and distant, who neither gives to nor, as a consequence, expects much from others], he has said (Egan, "Entrevista" 18).

3. A homework assignment sent seventeen-year-old Carlos Monsiváis, enrolled at the National Autonomous University, out in the field to gather (wo)man-in-the-street views about the impact of the newly granted women's vote (Monsiváis, "Día de la primera votación"). Forty-six years later, in the first election that the ruling party had lost in seventy-one years, Monsiváis notes that "en el año 2000 la participación femenina ha sido extensa.... Se extingue la antigua subordinación.... Las mujeres políticas son ya el hecho a partir del cual se construye la novedad llamada cambio histórico" [in the year 2000, women's participation in the vote was considerable ... The old subordination is over ... Women in politics are now a fact on which the novelty known as historical change is being built] (Monsiváis, "Viaje de un largo día").

4. Monsiváis and Pacheco made a pact never to expose their early poetry-writing efforts (J.E. Pacheco 39). The young Monsiváis's interest in verse extended to a first critical coup: the 1966 anthology of Mexican poetry he edited, with a brilliant prologue. From 1960 to 1970, Monsiváis directed programs for Radio Universidad, including "El cine y la crítica" [Film and Criticism], a laboratory in which he discovered the power of parody "en un país barroco" [in a baroque country] (*Monsiváis* 38). For a year (1962–1963), Monsiváis was a scholarship student sponsored by the Centro Mexicano de Escritores. Pacheco, Pitol and Poniatowska severally recall a story published by Monsiváis in 1957, "Fino acero de niebla." It was a tour de force of the Mexican hippiespeak called *la Onda* (literally, "the wave"), and quite possibly had an influence on the novelists of the Onda (José Agustín, Gustavo Saínz, et al) who would publish throughout the sixties and seventies.

5. Monsiváis was executive editor from 1972 to 1987.

6. Denouncing the press is a Mexican national pastime and Monsiváis is a devoted player. Among his criticisms of newspapers and state-owned television, an eloquent example is his acceptance speech on receiving a national journalism prize. See his "Premio Manuel Buendía."

7. José Agustín recalls that Carlos Monsiváis, in 1969, joined with Alfonso Arau to write ironic and funny song lyrics for the rock group The Tepetatles, predecessor of Botellita de Jerez of the eighties (1: 267).

In 1969, Monsiváis teamed up with Carlos Fuentes and others to read *Todos los gatos son pardos*, an experimental historical play in which Fuentes links the 1968 Student Movement massacre to the Conquest of Mexico and the colonial era. The play was read in the Teatro Universitario de la Avenida Chapultepec, and, according to Fuentes, the audience held as many government spies as genuine theater patrons (*Ceremonias* 8).

8. He has written often on the chronicling of crime by newspapers, novelists and moviemakers. He considers the super-popular U.S.–style thriller to be the international genre par excellence, "omnipresente, revelador, que al hacer del crimen un componente esencial de lo moderno y de lo posmoderno, se acerca a las imágenes esenciales de una sociedad" [omnipresent and revelatory, which, by making crime an essential component of modernity and postmodernity, comes close to capturing society's basic character] (Monsiváis, "El crimen" 69).

9. Of an extensive bibliography on the political upheavals of the 1960s, Todd Gitlin's *The Sixties* remains an excellent reference for the U.S. situation in relation to Europe and Mexico.

10. Huberto Batis includes two lists of members of the intellectual-literary mafia of the early sixties (112–13, 177). He mentions Monsiváis in only one of them.

11. The Contemporáneos, a group of cosmopolitan avantgardists from the twenties and thirties, took their name from the literary magazine *Contemporáneos* (1928–1931). Jaime Torres Bodet and Salvador Novo are among writers usually placed in this group.

12. Trejo Fuentes is by no means alone. Other voices decrying a lack of critical professionalism include Monsiváis citing Jorge Cuesta ("Notas" 363); Carlos Fuentes telling an interviewer that Mexican writers in general have to wait until their books are published outside the country to get objective criticism, which is the kind he considers "good" because "me ha iluminado, me ha enseñado algo, aun cuando el libro no le haya 'gustado' al crítico" [it has enlightened me, shown me something I didn't know, even if the critic has not particularly "liked" the book] (Fortson 19); Octavio Paz denouncing the "aullidos de . . . chacales" [howls of jackals] ("Veo" 8); Domínguez Michael on the "chantaje" [blackmail] that passes for criticism (*Antología de la narrativa* 2: 514); Jorge Aguilar Mora on "diatribas envidiosas e intransigentes" [envious and intransigent diatribes] (13); and Aníbal González wishing for "more solid scholarship" ("After 1992" 48).

13. Another critic uses similar imagery to describe Monsiváis as a cannibal who destroys others (L.J. Mier and Carbonell 112).

14. In an historical look at "Literary Theory and Criticism" in Mexico, Daniel Altamiranda's short list begins with Alfonso Reyes, includes Octavio Paz, Carlos Fuentes and José Revueltas, and culminates with Carlos Monsiváis.

15. Another notable case: Jaime Giordano's recent survey of the contemporary Latin American essay seems to catalog all the actively producing essayists, including Gabriel Zaid and Elena Poniatowska. But Giordano does not mention Carlos Monsiváis, not even to explain why he has left his name off the list.

16. Ejército Zapatista de Liberación Nacional, or EZLN, alludes to the folk hero Emiliano Zapata, who gained immortal symbolism as a freedom fighter who, in the Mexican Revolution, fought for the return of stolen lands to Indians. He alone among numerous heroes of the Revolution (who included Pancho Villa) did not appear to sell out his principles. The January 1, 1994, rebellion in Chiapas, where a significant portion of Mexico's remaining Indian population is concentrated in economic and existential misery, symbolically takes up again the original Zapatista struggle for social justice.

17. Recall that Subcomandante Marcos has always appeared in photographs and descriptive narrative in a ski mask; perhaps in the beginning of the military phase of the rebellion

the mask served to protect Marcos's life, but by now his iconic "invisibility" has assumed mythical value: Marcos remains masked *because the Mexican people want him to maintain his mystique.* See Monsiváis's reportage of this significant anecdote in the second of the pair of crónicas I am examining, on the Convention itself ("Crónica de una Convención" 323).

18. A younger member of Mexico's cadre of quality cronistas, Guadalupe Loaeza, gives us a tongue-in-cheek characterization of the spoiled upper middle class young woman as someone who reads newspapers without understanding Carlos Monsiváis (*Niñas bien* 10).

19. Jorge G. Castañeda, in *Utopia Unarmed,* consciously presents Cárdenas as the political incarnation of Monsiváis's theoretical and political evangelizing (224–25). After a defeat for the presidency in 1988, a loss widely attributed to fraud, Cárdenas and his supporters regrouped, in no small measure aided by the kind of enthusiasm that Monsiváis's charismatic thought and figure could increasingly foment. The July 1987 elections catapulted Cárdenas to the most significant oppositional victory that, at the time, republican Mexico had witnessed: mayor of Mexico City, center of a centralist sociopolitical system. Monsiváis openly spoke then of an end to Mexico's concentration of power in the person of the president (presidencialismo) ("Después del 6 de julio").

Still, it was the conservative PAN party's Vicente Fox who became the first candidate to wrest the presidency from PRI's hands, as a result of elections July 2, 2000. For the first time in 71 years, voters assigned the top government job to someone other than the outgoing PRI president's hand-picked successor. A split among liberal intellectuals contributed to Fox's win; Castañeda is among those who elected to swing their vote toward Fox, in the pragmatic interest of ousting the PRI. Monsiváis, however, did not consider his "losing" vote for Cárdenas, who gained only 17 percent of the vote, to be impractical: "es urgente preservar los espacios de una izquierda democrática, crítica, generosa y solidaria" [it's important to keep alive a democratic left that is critical, tolerant and solidarian]. See Juan Jesús Aznárez, "Fuga de intelectuales mexicanos hacia el candidato conservador Fox."

20. For an exquisitely detailed view of the painful process of democratization from within, see Monsiváis's eyewitness report on the post-1968 Student Movement of 1986–1987 (*Entrada* 246–306).

21. This text first appeared in the Mexico City news weekly *Proceso,* on August 15, 1994. I will cite from its reprinted version in the book that Monsiváis coauthored and edited to bring together the documents and communiqués issued between January and August of 1994 by the Zapatista rebels. See ("Crónica de una Convención" in *EZLN* 313–23).

chapter 2

1. For anecdotal testimony on the guerrilla war fought for study of popular culture, see Ray B. Browne's *Against Academia;* Grossberg, Nelson and Treichler's introduction to *Cultural Studies;* and Stuart Hall's "The Emergence of Cultural Studies" and "Cultural Studies and Its Theoretical Legacies."

2. Among Benjamin's best-known works, see "Unpacking My Library" (58–67) and "The Work of Art in the Age of Mechanical Reproduction" (219–53).

3. In *Masse und Macht* (1960), Canetti analyzes the priestifying of power, a metaphor of recurring use in Monsiváis. In one text, the Mexican theorist "prays" to Elias Canetti for guidance in his analysis of Mexican soccer frenzy (*Entrada* 202).

4. See Fiske's overview in Allen of British Cultural Studies and Alan O'Connor on the importance of Williams's work for Latin American theory (61). Besides occupying, as Monsiváis has throughout his career, a kind of "academic border country" (Morgan and Preston 1), the British critic also cultivated ambivalence and "an openly conducted inner conflict" (3) over the paradoxes of modernization (McGuigan 182).

5. On New Journalism and its practitioners, see Hellman, *Fables* and "Postmodern Journalism"; Hollowell; Weber, *Literature of Fact* and *Reporter,* and Zavarzadeh.

6. On this ambivalent and cautiously affirmative view of external influences on a domestic cultural milieu, see "Las ceremonias de Durango" (*Días* 65–77); "Notas sobre el Estado" (1981); "Lo popular en el espacio urbano" (1984); "De algunos problemas del término 'Cul-

tura Nacional" en México" (1985); "Civilización y Coca-Cola" (1986); "Para un cuadro de costumbres" (1989); "No con un sollozo" (1989) and "Duración de la eternidad" (1992). (An English translation of "Civilización y Coca-Cola" is available as "He Wagered His Heart and Lost It to Coca Cola.")

7. Of course, notions of orthodox and heterodox are relative and time-sensitive; the ages-old ascendancy of pagan pluralism had first been brought low by an annoying bunch of new-age purists calling themselves Christians.

8. For a detailed look at this mechanism at work, see Lawrence Levine's enjoyable read on cultural differentiation with respect to Shakespeare in the nineteenth and early twentieth centuries, in *Highbrow/Lowbrow: The Emergence of Cultural Hierarchy in America.*

9. See, for example, the "Editors' Letter to Future Contributors" that precedes each issue of *Studies in Latin American Popular Culture,* as well as Browne, "Popular Culture as the New Humanities" and "Popular Culture: Notes Toward a Definition," and Hinds, Jr., "Popularity." For a helpful discussion of the problematical definition and position of folklore, see Rowe and Schelling (3–6).

10. See, for example, Barkin (Dependency Theory); Bonfil Batalla, *Culturas populares* and *México profundo* (Anti-Western restoration of indigenous hegemony); Brito García (traditional cultures privileged); Déleon Meléndez (foregrounding diversity of popular cultures, including folklore); Stavenhagen (threatened indigenous cultures) and Ramiro Beltrán (U.S. cultural imperialism).

11. The trend toward a universal technical language of culture theory can be seen, for example, in Néstor García Canclini: "Cultura transnacional"; *Culturas híbridas; Consumo cultural; Consumidores y ciudadanos* and *Transforming Modernity* (García Canclini closely follows Monsiváis); Raúl Ávila; Jesús Martín-Barbero (who also relies heavily on Monsiváis), Celeste Olalquiaga; Jorge Klor de Alva; Roberto Schwarz and Hernán Vidal.

12. See also a five-point definition of urban popular culture in Isaac León and Ricardo Bedoya's interview with Monsiváis (71–72), as well as Alan O'Connor's reprise of a typical monsivaisian discussion of the evolution of popular culture in Mexico from the late nineteenth century through the fifties (62–63).

13. *Fotonovelas* are illustrated adult comic books whose storylines typically run parallel to those of televised soap opera.

14. The original version of "Landscape" is "No te me muevas, paisaje."

15. The *quinceañera* refers to a girl's fifteenth birthday party, a rite of passage in popular Mexican culture when a child becomes a young woman. The event is celebrated as with as much showy elegance as a family's means permit.

16. Monsiváis identifies four levels of camp in Mexico: (1) the High Camp of the Palace of Fine Arts, "donde Tláloc y Tiffany's se dan la mano" [where the rain god Tlaloc and Tiffany's shake hands] (*Días* 183); (2) the Middle Camp of the heart-of-gold prostitute or those who want to turn Nahuatl into the national language: beings who teeter between awareness and ignorance (186); (3) the Low Camp of people who have no idea they are making a spectacle of themselves—choral poetry groups or people who sing songs of political protest in nightclubs (188), and (4) Inferior Camp, which Monsiváis cruelly assigns to the Mexican film industry, so perfectly bad "que no hay siquiera lugar para la crítica" [so perfectly awful it leaves no room for criticism] (189).

17. In this politicized view of popular culture's "innocent" artifacts and "objective" impacts, we can intimate the sort of psychosocial dynamic that might lead a society to fragment into militantly guarded enclaves of "cultural identity," such as those currently influencing public life in the United States.

18. The literature on prehispanic Aztec and other Amerindian cultures is extensive and growing. But see, for points of departure: Burkhart; Clendinnen; Fagan; Labbé; León-Portilla, *Antiguos mexicanos* and *Toltecáyotl;* Sahagún, Séjourné and Townsend.

19. Intertextual reference to the conquest as described by the conquered Indians (León-Portilla, *Visión de los vencidos*).

20. Léopold Sédar Senghor, president of Senegal from 1960–1980, wrote—in French—about the traditions of his country. He contributed to development of the concept of *negritude,*

an affirmation of black African culture. Monsiváis reminds his readers that, although Senghor's consciousness had been "colonized" by the French language, he was nonetheless capable of constructing his own cultural identity.

21. Reyes Matta's assertion that news in Latin America is defined by transnational agencies, for example, is not atypical. See also Ramiro Beltrán and Fox de Cardona on how the United States dominates Latin American media.

22. Citing Roger Rouse's study of the inhabitants of the Mexican village of Aguililla (the same one whose immigrant citizens Mexican journalist Teresa Gurza interviewed in the series published in Mexico in 1991), García Canclini notes that, since the 1940s, Aguililla's tradition is to send all its members to live in the United States. Most congregate in Redwood City, in California's Silicon Valley. Aguililla survives because of its dependence on the personal dollar exports of its emissaries in the North, creating a part of what García Canclini calls "economías cruzadas" [crossbred economies] of the transglobal space (*Culturas híbridas* 190–91).

23. Monsiváis integrates into his theories a series of provocative analyses of the cultures of chicanos, *cholos, pachucos, pochos* and other transculturated Mexicans. See, for example, his "Cultura de la frontera," "De México y los chicanos, de México y su cultura fronteriza," "Éste es el pachuco, un sujeto singular" and "Es el pachuco un sujeto singular: Tin Tan" (English version in *Mexican Postcards* 106–18).

24. Patrick Oster refers to Mexico's "cultural self-hate," an inner-directed racism that "runs so deep that many Mexicans feel the ideal of beauty is the physical opposite of an Indian: a blue-eyed child" (249). I recently observed columns of black-eyed, black-haired, brown-skinned tots filing through the doorway of a Mexican daycare facility that advertised itself from the rooftop with the huge cut-out figure of a blond, blue-eyed child.

25. Monsiváis highlights women's issues in each of his five collections of chronicles devoted to Mexican topics, spanning the years 1968–1995. His attention to feminist concerns is in fact interwoven throughout all his discourse. For explicit reflections on the feminine outside of his books of chronicles, see: *El género epistolar* (31–41), "No te fijes en lo que ves, sino en tus reacciones moralistas" (*Rituales* 155–17), "Nueva salutación del optimista," "Sexismo en la literatura mexicana," "La mujer en la cultura mexicana," "Lo vi tan cerca, que me pareció de carne y hueso" (revised and expanded in *Escenas* 119–20), "Mi oficio es el de comunicador," "'¡No queremos 10 de mayo. Queremos revolución!!': sobre el nuevo feminismo," "A mi mamacita en su día," "De la construcción de la 'sensibilidad femenina,'" "El amor en (vísperas eternas de) la democracia," and "La Malinche y el Primer Mundo." Also significant are his statements on the painter Frida Kahlo: *Frida Kahlo: una vida, una obra*, "De todas las Fridas posibles" and "El fin de la diosa arrodillada."

chapter 3

1. "Excorporation," as used here, is characterized as the conscious or unconscious taking out of (excorporation) the dominant culture a practice or artifact that is then "refunctioned" or "incorporated" into the popular cultural repertoire. Excorporation is a form of cultural redefinition and recycling.

2. An English version of this chronicle is available in *Mexican Postcards* (119–28).

3. Rowe and Schelling provide a compendium of popular (i.e., archaic-pagan) Catholicism's characteristics (68–70). For a more complex understanding of Mexican popular religion, see Louise Burkhart on Catholicism's attempts to get inside the mind of conquered Amerindians in order to grasp how their metaphors and other meaning-making tropes functioned at the time when paganism's polytheistic matriarchy prepared to absorb, by transforming it, Christianity's masculine monotheism.

4. Monsiváis draws on a biography of the healer; movies; popular songs; a classic commentary on popular mysticism (William James's 1907 *The Varieties of Religious Experience*); parapsychology and popular medicine texts; archived news accounts; a relevant literary cousin of real-life *fidencismo* (Juan Rulfo's story, "Anacleto Morones") and his own reporting: a healing pool of water in which Fidencio bathed is still in use today (101); in his heyday, a visit from Fidencio was anticipated like the Second Coming (98).

5. The corrido is a popular song form rooted in the medieval Spanish ballad, itself derived from epic narrative compositions. Vestiges of its former usage can be perceived in the corrido's preference for singing the praises of local popular heroes, who usually suffer imprisonment, torture, tragic loss, exile or death, most often in times of privation, repression and war.

6. The Cristero War, or *Cristiada*, 1926–1929, sparked by government programs to implement secularizing articles of the postrevolutionary Constitution of 1917. In an important sense, the Revolution and the Cristiada represent elements of a single conflict. They embody the very dualism Monsiváis dramatizes in the Boy Fidencio story: how poverty, social disenfranchisement and spiritualism transport Mexico on its rough road to modernity.

7. Sahagún notes with disgust how Christianized Indians parroted newly learned Catholic words and gestures, while in the secrecy of their hearts—and mountain caves—they continued to worship their old gods. Eventually redefined as the expressly Mexican Virgin of Guadalupe (the Dark Virgin, *la morenita*), she is a symbol capacious enough to have absorbed qualities and functions of most of Mexico's prehispanic goddesses (2: 808–809).

8. *The New Collegiate Latin and English Dictionary* lists meanings of religion, cult, mode of worship and object of veneration for *religio* and meanings of to tie up and to moor for *religo* (265).

9. Monsiváis, an avid collector of rare photographs of popular subjects, has done much to turn photography into an object of elite study in Mexico. His texts on this subject include "Los testimonios delatores, las recuperaciones estéticas" and "Los hermanos Mayo"; prologues to books such as *Cien retratos por Daisy Ascher, The World of Agustín Víctor Casasola, Un día en la gran ciudad de México*, and *Foto estudio Jiménez: Sotero Constantino, fotógrafo de Juchitán;* "Posada: el repertorio de las emociones."

chapter 4

1. Elsewhere I have elaborated on the "great divide" that opened in the nineteenth century between fictional and empirical literatures (Egan, "Lo marginal en el centro" 24–28 [1993 dissertation] and "Crónica" 304–306). The question of the textual and extratextual qualities that will grant a text admission to the literary canon has been explored long and deeply and with little practical result. I will return to the topic of the chronicle's claim as an aesthetic object later in this chapter.

2. What Ronald Weber says of New Journalism applies as well to the Mexican crónica: "What [New Journalists] are up to is neither exactly literature [i.e., fiction] nor exactly journalism but a rough mixture of the two—and that's the heart of the critical problem. It can be argued that it misses literary quality because it remains bound to fact. . . . But it likewise can be argued that the New Journalism lacks real journalistic quality because in the very imaginative artistry it *does* employ it leaves itself suspect as solid reporting ("Artistic" 23).

3. The verses are from *Los senderos ocultos* (1911) by the Mexican modernista, Enrique González Martínez.

4. I doubt anyone would take seriously an assertion that it simply doesn't matter whether one reads Juan Rulfo's eccentric *Pedro Páramo* as a novel-length work of fiction, as a confused philosophical statement on life and death, or as a badly assembled set of autobiographical notations. *Pedro Páramo* remains a discourse of seemingly boundless—and canonically precious—mystery precisely because it is understood to be fiction rather than fact.

5. It may be that the crónica has suffered a deficit of critical attention because narratologists have ignored the behavior and objects of nonfictional narrative as a whole (Genette, "Fictional Narrative" 755) and, when these have been examined, without looking to the discipline that has dug most deeply into the ground of narrative itself (Cohn, "Signposts" 775). Paul Ricoeur calls for "historiography and literary criticism . . . together to form a grand narratology, where an equal right would be given to historical narrative and to fictional narrative" (*Time* 2: 156).

6. Those who coincide with this view include Beardsley 174–75; Eagleton 1–2; Hernadi, *What*

Is Literature? 20; Mignolo, "Entre el canon" 27 and "Sobre las condiciones"; Scholes and Kellogg, *Nature* 248, and Searle 319–21.

7. Among minimum conditions of straight news reportage, the reporter's own voice is suppressed so as to create a perception of disinterested objectivity and evenhanded fairness.

8. Scholars typically emphasize the essay's moderate language, expository formality, didacticism and alliance with philosophy, metaphysics and confession (Core; García Monsiváis; Gómez-Martínez; Martínez, *Ensayo;* Oviedo; Scholes and Klaus, *Elements;* Skirius, *Ensayo;* Stabb, "The Essay"). In general, extant descriptions of the essay fail to distinguish the form from the chronicle and, even when a distinction is asserted, the implicit difference is not demonstrated.

     For a detailed reading that demonstrates textual differences between essay and crónica, see my forthcoming chapter article, "Play on Words: Chronicling the Essay," to appear in an anthology on the chronicle edited by Beth Jorgensen and Ignacio Corona and to which Monsiváis has also contributed.

9. Elena Poniatowska's *La noche de Tlatelolco* is perhaps the most celebrated text frequently cited as testimonial literature in Mexico; this and her *Nada, nadie,* on the 1985 earthquakes that shook Mexico, are made almost entirely of interview materials.

10. The growing bibliography on testimonial literature includes a rich vein tapping into Latin American narrations produced cooperatively by (1) a witness (presumably "subaltern" and "postcolonial," incapable of writing his or her memoirs independently) who dictates life experiences of sociopolitical and cultural significance to (2) a recorder or arranger of the testimony, someone with access to publishing power in the developed world. The testimonio form's nonauthorial, nonelaborated nature, its deliberate "naturalness" and "oralness" and its conspicuously antiliterary form (Beverley, *Against* 130) situate this discourse 180 degrees distant from the crónica's self-conscious artifice.

11. For a case in point, see Emiliano Pérez Cruz's *Noticias de los chavos banda:* a jarring mix of generic elements—scholarly citations from myriad documentary sources, a scrupulously external, fictionalizing third-person narration and long stretches of dialogue presented without hint of a first person who could literally embody the real-world gatherer of information—that drains an inherently dramatic and critical subject of its potential literary life.

12. On the highly condensed literary evolution I have just summarized, see Goic 33; Pupo-Walker 12–24 and 192; Blanco, *Esplendores* 255–70; McLean 130; Jiménez, "Ensayo" 540 and "Teoría" 81; Ramos 91; Luna 1–21, and Monsiváis, "De la Santa Doctrina" 765–70.

13. The parallelism, for Mexicans, was so clear that virtually none could resist allusions to what was alternately perceived as the Aztec curse or the subjugated Mexican's eternal cross to bear. In his 1970 *Posdata,* a "postscripted" essay to his classic 1950 psychoanalysis of the Mexican character, Octavio Paz equates the tragedy of 1968 with the sacrificial authoritarianism of imperial Aztec Mexico, a "pasado que no hemos sabido o no hemos podido reconocer, nombrar, desenmascarar" [past we have been unable to understand or acknowledge, mention or reveal] and which is "el tema central y secreto de nuestra historia" [the central and secret theme of our history] (40).

14. On narrative techniques that produce literariness or fictionality in a chronicle, see Foster, *Alternate* 22; Hellman, *Fables* 13–15; Hollowell 22–30; Monsiváis, *A ustedes* 13; Rader; Siebenschuh 48–52 and Weber, *Literature of Fact* 19.

15. Mexican news media provided from their inception in the eighteenth century a relatively inexpensive and accessible publishing venue for poems, short stories and serialized novels. With no overt signals to help a reader sort among hard news reportage, chronicles of manners, literary criticism or outright fiction, Mexico's mixed newspaper discourse problematized—and continues to destabilize—expectations that, merely because it appears in a newspaper, it is true (Carter 75–77; Dallal 155–62; González 2–18).

chapter 5

1. Poor neighborhoods in Mexico City.

2. Tom Wolfe claims to have initiated this new-journalistic technique: "I switched back and

forth between points-of-view continually, and often abruptly, in many articles I wrote in 1963, 1964, and 1965" ("New Journalism" 33): "A reviewer called me a 'chameleon' who instantly took on the coloration of whomever he was writing about. He meant it negatively. I took it as a compliment" (33).

3. Monsiváis openly dialogues with Wolfe's 1970 *Radical Chic* in his 1973 chronicle, "El 'disidente' (Radical Chic): los burgueses con corazón de masa" (*Amor* 180–83, written in 1973). For more on this, see chapter 7's discussion of *Amor perdido*'s crónicas on the nouveau riche in Mexico.

4. Recent discussion of the boom, which Angel Rama situates without any great conviction between 1958 and 1972 ("El *boom*" 275, 289), gives fairly equal credence to the opinion that it represented an extratextual function of globalized marketing and arose out of regional literary impulses. Whatever its genesis, its onset and products are widely held to be part of the postmodernist literary phenomenon. See, for example, Sommer and Yúdice's "Latin American Literature from the 'Boom' on." However, see also Ruffinelli's strong argument against the logic of applying postmodernist theoretical constructs to the developing post-colonial cultures of Latin America (32).

5. Norman Mailer is the single literary journalist Monsiváis mentions in the theoretical preamble to his anthology of Mexican chronicles (*A ustedes* 13). Mailer's *Armies of the Night* is the work Monsiváis then had in mind to illustrate the crónica's deliberately subjective reportage, but in the context of the presidential campaign he covered in 1969, he may well have had in mind Mailer's 1968 chronicles on the Republican and Democratic campaigns, *Miami and the Siege of Chicago*.

6. Monsiváis is reputed to have said that "un porvenir que me interesa, cuando muera, es que dispersen mis cenizas por el California Dancing Club para que sobre ellas bailen un conmovido danzón" [one thing I want when I die is for my ashes to be strewn over the California Dancing Club's floor so that a heart-wrenching danzón can be danced over them] (cited in Poniatowska, "Monsiváis: cronista" 5). His passion for dancing is surpassed only by his love for Mexican popular song. Poniatowska told an audience in the capital's Palace of Fine Arts in the autumn of 2000 that Monsiváis sings so well he can give Mexico's most famous crooners a run and that his musical and lyrical talents are such that he can make up songs "en el aire" [in the air] (6).

7. These include the demographics of Mexico City, analyses of boxing, soccer and wrestling, as well as popular religion, nineteenth-century literature, the mass media, musical kitsch, calendar art, New Age religions and other fads, dancing, the underground economy, civic monuments, sexual liberation, rock concerts and collecting.

8. Besides those already cited in *Los rituales del caos*, see, for example, in *Días de guardar:* "Incitación a la vida productiva: parábola del banquero y el jazz" (61–64), "Homenaje al espíritu lúdico de una década [Del Camp a la Trivia]" (143–44), "Necrología de la tradición: catálogo de instituciones mexicanas recientemente fenecidas" (254–57), "Informe confidencial sobre la posibilidad de un mínimo equivalente mexicano del poema *Howl* (El aullido) de Allen Ginsberg" (290–94) and "Adivine su década" (321–27). In *Amor perdido*, "El Self-Made Man: sin ayuda de nadie, se hizo a sí mismo" (163–68). In *Escenas de pudor y liviandad*, "Crónica de sociales: es muy molesto / tener que llegar a esto / tener que menear el tiesto / para poder mal vivir" (205–10). And, for a delightful piece of fiction outside of his collections, see "Tres nichos sin retablo."

9. It is not uncommon for fiction to be mislabeled as chronicle. In addition to the previously cited *Crónicas romanas* by Ignacio Trejo Fuentes, see, for example, most of José Joaquín Blanco's *Un chavo bien helado*, and virtually all the pieces reprinted in Cristina Pacheco's *El corazón de la noche, Para mirar a lo lejos, Para vivir aquí, Sopita de fideo, La última noche del "Tigre"* and *Zona de desastre*. As I read Pacheco, only her *Cuarto de azotea* is, as claimed, a collection of chronicles. I elaborate on this point in my "Cristina Pacheco" and "Sound of Silence."

10. Writing interiorizes consciousness and perception such that predominantly chirographic cultures develop modes of thinking and meaning- making that differ radically from those of oral cultures, according to Walter Ong. The difference in thought processes, or mental-

ity, is the principal mark of distinction between archaic and modern societies (*Interfaces* 290).

11. If only metaphorically, many of the emblem's traits can be seen to operate in the chronicle: poetic language to unite the visual and the verbal, as well as the sensory and the conceptual (Dieckmann 5); language combining iconic and discursive aspects; reliance on metaphors that please, move and persuade (Moseley 7); polysemous images of multivalent meanings (3); dramatic compression, especially in order to relate ideas to objects (which are frequently icons of popular culture) (5); the seriocomic potential to amuse and instruct simultaneously (28).

12. Carlos Monsiváis's whole *oeuvre* is notably emblematic. His collections typically include reprinted news photos and other images which can be seen as icons "explained" by his texts. In the mass media, his pieces are routinely accompanied by cartoons and other graphics; both his bibliography and his library attest to the way he has reached many of his deepest insights by wrapping his highly chirographic intellect around the iconic substance of comics, caricature, painting, film, photography, song, dance and other concrete expressions of his society's soul.

chapter 6

1. Excepting the prologue, the others fall outside the definition of chronicle established in the previous chapter. Two, "Parábola del banquero" and "Confesión de un triunfador," are vignettes approaching fiction; one is a verse "translation" of a poem; two are satirical anecdotes; one is a "colofón" or afterword, and three are games involving aphoristic riddles.

2. "Sufragio efectivo" alludes to the motto of revolutionaries in 1910 who campaigned against Porfirio Díaz for a chance to turn Mexico's fixed elections into true contests.

3. Monsiváis speaks persistently of Mexico's poverty-driven population growth, a theme related to delayed democratization that Carlos Fuentes also emphasizes (in *Tres discursos* 64–65, for example). Links between endemic poverty and high birth rates are documented worldwide. On the situation in Latin America, see Calvert and Calvert 194. On ties between the demographics of poverty and sociopolitical and economic conditions, see Castañeda (219).

4. These faces may refer to the enigmatic figurines of joyful expression discovered at the Mesoamerican site of Remojadas (300–900 A.D.) in what is now the state of Veracruz.

5. See Clendinnen (73, 75, 99, 101, 105–10, 147–48, 157, 201, 248–49, 251, 261–62) for detailed explanations of the "living images" (god-presenters or god-representations), most typically slaves or captive warriors. These sometimes participated for extended periods in elaborate rituals before being sacrificed.

6. Monsiváis addresses the European's hatred of the "barbaric" native; the rising middle class's abhorrence of Indian immigrants in the capital; Mexican hatred of U.S. gringos, and a form of victimology arising out of identity politics that is said to produce a type of autoracism or self-hatred (Aínsa 10).

7. Gustave Le Bon (France, 1841–1931), a founder of social psychology, was marginalized in the academic community for his politically unpopular thinking during the rise of world socialism, which he described as a new religion that could not fulfill its promises but would lead to collectivism and terrorism. His best-known work, *The Crowd: A Study of the Popular Mind* (1895), includes a chapter on "A Religious Shape Assumed by All the Convictions of Crowds" (72–78).

8. In the first chronicle of *Días*, the biblical intertext of the title ("Con címbolos de júbilo" [With Cymbals of Joy] is a line from Psalm 150) ironizes the "modernity" of a middle class brave enough to stare at naked actors while, outside the theater, those who might truly appreciate the modernity of *Hair* hold placards exhorting patrons to remember October 2 (24); during a Raphael concert, no one believes the Student March for Freedom will endanger anyone's authority (57). This is the elegant Mexico of "Cuevas en la Zona Rosa" that refuses to see reality: "¿Cuál desastre? ¿De qué 1968 me hablan?" [What disaster? What 1968 are you talking about?] (90). It is the complacent middle class that ignores the youths of "Dios nunca muere" who demonstrate for "Freedom to Political Prisoners" (101). In

"Para todas las cosas hay sazón" [For Everything There Is a Season], The Byrds come to Mexico to sing a message whose words (from Ecclesiastes 3) are obsolete even before the Student Movement (123). While World Cup Soccer monopolized the attention of the *entire* city, the Student Movement stirred up only parts of it (161). And, because he knows that "sick jokes proliferate after social tragedies" (Herzog and Bush 323), Monsiváis entertains readers who may be feeling disheartened with a medical quiz in the 1960s section of "Adivine su década": "¿Asocias la palabra 'grandadero' con la idea de 'hospital'?" [Does the word "police" make you think of "hospital"?] (*Días* 326). Students quelled by Díaz Ordaz's paramilitary riot force frequently ended up in worse places than the hospital.

9.   For historical reprises of the Movement's inception, objectives and development, see, especially, Monsiváis's indispensable 145-page reflection on "El 68" (118–264), in *Parte de guerra*, a book he coauthored with Julio Scherer García in 1999. See also Carr 257–66; Poniatowska, *Fuerte* 34–77 (or her separately published "Movimiento"), Ramírez, and Zermeño.

10. Rural activist Jaramillo and his family were assassinated on May 23, 1962, in Morelos.

11. The narrator is recalling the August 27, 1968, march and the gathering the next day of an estimated 500,000 people in the Central Plaza (the Zócalo), the largest antigovernment rally in Mexican history. Late the following night, government tanks and armored cars broke up the gathering.

12. Thirty years after this writing, Monsiváis recalls the dramatic March of Silence, with its "sustrato poético" [poetic foundation] and 200,000 to 300,000 participants, as the most eloquent event of the Movement ("El 68" 206–207). He places the September 13 march at the literal and figurative center of his *Días* trilogy, for he saw in the *symbolic* use of such massive self-discipline an expansive poetic vehicle.

13. André Malraux (France, 1901–1976) was a fervent anticolonialist and advocate of social change whose novel, *L'Espoir* (translated *Days of Hope* in England, *Man's Hope* in the United States), and whose celebrated history of art, *Les Voix du silence (The Voices of Silence)*, can be seen as implicit intertexts from first to last of this chronicle and perhaps, as well, of all of *Días de guardar*.

14. Monsiváis served on the board of directors of the Asamblea de Intelectuales, Escritores y Artistas that supported the Student Movement. Others on the board included Juan Rulfo and José Revueltas (Monsiváis, "El 68" 193).

15. Meyer and Sherman (669) report that army and police units arrived at 6:30 p.m. in tanks and armored vehicles. "What happened next will never be completely clarified": The Mexican press blamed terrorists firing on police from apartment buildings. Thousands of innocent people were caught in the crossfire between army units and snipers, under the light of flares dropped by helicopters. Government spokesmen admitted "first eight, then eighteen, and finally forty-three deaths, but few knowledgeable Mexicans accepted mortality figures under three or four hundred." Over two thousand participants were jailed. Mexican writers emphasize that, by the next morning, blood splatters and empty shoes were all that remained in the square. The conditions for denial were in place.

16. Tzvetan Todorov defines as "gnoseological" or "epistemical" a type of narrative organization in which the unfolding argument is based upon a "sustentation" of interest that makes the reader want to discover information and meaning. This is a narrative "in which the event itself is less important than our perception of it, and the degree of knowledge we have of it" (*Genres* 31). Monsiváis's "Dios nunca muere" conforms to the type of narrative that Todorov characterizes as "the quest for the Holy Grail: the mystery, or detective story," in which the reader must establish a relationship between "the story of the crime, which is missing, and the story of the investigation, which is present, and whose only justification is to acquaint us with the other story" (33).

17. For the Aztec intertexts, see Sahagún 2: 478–79. For the biblical intertexts, see Psalms 19: 2–6.

chapter 7

1.   See Blanco, "Aguafuertes" 36; Cossío 138; Gustavo García, "Monsiváis."

2.   Thomas Carlyle (Scotland, 1795–1881), a critic of sham, hypocrisy and materialism, as well

as mob politics, is best remembered for works on the power of the individual, especially the heroic leader, in such books as his three-part *The French Revolution* (1837) and *On Heroes, Hero-Worship, and the Heroic in History* (1841).

3. The chronicle he refers to is printed without title or subtitle as the last section of the book's first text, "Alto contraste." See pages 49–57. Our only clue to the separateness of his discussion of a Díaz Ordaz press conference are the two dates printed at the end of the text: "Noviembre de 1976 / Abril de 1977."

4. For a review of this collection in English, see *The World of Agustín Víctor Casasola (1900–1938)*, a text produced for the exhibition of Casasola's archive in 1984, in Washington, D.C.

5. For another discussion of the links between politics, religion and the psychodynamics of machismo, see Carroll, especially chapters 2 and 3, pages 22–74.

6. This section of the historical prelude to *Amor perdido* closes with a magnificent retrospective view (42–47) of the upheaval of 1968, here depicted as the government's use of violence to affirm the impossibility of democracy and the Student Movement as "una espléndida toma de conciencia moral, política y social" [a splendid inventory of moral, political and social conscience] that results in "la manufactura de una historia pública y la forja de una historia verdadera" [the manufacture of a public history and the forging of a true history] (44).

7. Díaz Ordaz's presidency ended in 1970. Luis Echeverría's spanned 1970–1976. This press conference occurs in the early days of José López Portillo's six-year reign.

8. These are Agustín Lara (d. 1970); José Alfredo Jiménez (d. 1974); David Alfaro Siqueiros (d. 1974); José Revueltas (d. 1976); Joel Arriaga (d. 1972); Hilario Moreno Aguirre (d. 1975); Salvador Novo (d. 1974); Benita Galeana (her autobiography of 1940) and Genaro Fernández MacGregor (his memoirs; he died in 1959).

9. The verb, "se desmorona," is the same as that which Rulfo uses to describe the death of the antihero in *Pedro Páramo* (195), a novel about the crumbling of rock-hard traditionalism in provincial areas like Puebla.

10. She eventually conquers the Mexican male in the very center of his lair; although a bid for the national senate was unsuccessful, in 1994 she won a seat in the chamber of deputies. She has also published serial volumes of a testimonial autobiography. See Castillo, especially pages 194–214.

chapter 8

1. I refer to criticism that goes beyond the summary statement, such as Jean Franco's brief observation at the end of an article otherwise focused on literary criticism in the era of Cultural Studies ("Ocaso"). Franco cites *Escenas* as an illustration of a new antiacademic form of critical treatise; she says Monsiváis's book demonstrates the gap between academic criticism and an emergent culture, in which *Escenas* implicitly offers a nontraditional kind of criticism (20).

   John Kraniauskas translated three of *Escenas*'s pieces for his English anthology: "El Hoyo Fonqui" (*Escenas* 233–43; *Postcards* 48–56), "Dolores del Río" (213–32; 71–87) and "Cantinflas" (77–96; 88–105). In his introduction, Kraniauskas briefly alludes to "The Funky Dive" (xii) and mentions the Cantinflas chronicle in the context of commentary on humor (xiii).

2. Peter Daly emphasizes throughout his study of *Literature in the Light of the Emblem* that medieval biblical exegesis and allegorical interpretation were the foundation of emblematic modes of thinking and representation in the sixteenth and seventeenth centuries, especially in baroque art. Elsewhere I have emphasized Carlos Monsiváis's predilection for biblical registers, baroque expression and theatrical and photographic imagery.

3. See "Crónica de sociales: Cinco cenas de amor" (119–23); "Instituciones: La nostalgia. La mano temblorosa de una hechicera" (127–36); "Dancing: El secreto está en la mano izquierda" (137–40) and "Crónica de sociales: ¿Qué le vamos a tocar?" (257–62).

4. Sources on the symbology of numbers are vast. For convenience, I have consulted a *Dictionary of Symbolism* (Biedermann 143, 302–303, 318–20).

chapter 9

1. The last text of the second edition of *Escenas de pudor y liviandad* (1988) focuses on an event that bridges New Year's Eve 1986 and the inaugural days of 1987. The first text of *Entrada libre* (1987) is based on events of September through November 1985.

2. Still, in 1998, Monsiváis sees government as dangerously self-congratulatory and incapable of managing society to the benefit of its citizens: "¿Cómo es posible que un gobierno al frente de la catástrofe económica se considere el último depositario de la autoridad moral? Ante esto mantengo una hipótesis. La ineptitud de los funcionarios es tan pasmosa, que si no se muestran coléricos e intransigentes, deben asumir los resultados de su propio comportamiento. Su intransigencia es un método de ocultamiento de la torpeza" [How is it possible that a government faced with economic catastrophe can be considered the ultimate repository of moral authority? About this I have a theory. The ineptitude of our civil servants is so astounding that, if they didn't act mad or stubborn, it would force them to accept the consequences of their behavior. So their mulishness is a cover for their incompetence] (cited in Ponce 15).

3. García Canclini reports that Mexico City is literally (territorially) one hundred times larger than it was a century ago (*Consumidores* 61) and that between 1940 and 1980 the metropolitan area's population increased from 1.64 million to 14.4 million; by the end of the twentieth century, the capital (one percent of the nation's land mass) was projected to hold twenty-five percent of the nation's people (*Consumo cultural* 45). A 1993 *Time* magazine report on megacities of the world cites a United Nations population estimate of 15.3 million for Mexico City, with a projected 16.2 million for the year 2000 (Linden 36). A Washington Post article of October 1999 lists the country's population at 98.5 million. A world population Web site last updated Dec. 19, 2000 (http://www.citypopulation.de) gives Mexico City's population as 19.2 million, or approximately 20 percent of the nation's total.

4. For a particularly beautiful and entertaining evocation of this image of Juchitán, see Elena Poniatowska's "Juchitán de las mujeres."

5. Juchitán's resistance is widely held as a model of nongovernmental organizations ("organizaciones no-gubernamentales," or ONGs), key signs of emergent autonomy among politically active sectors of the country. See Jorge Castañeda's summary of these grassroots groups (202–36).

6. See Bernal Díaz del Castillo (1: 254; chapter 70) on the first hugely epic battle of the conquest. The intertext implies that federal mandates are foreign invaders violently imposing an alien will upon a local region's natural autonomy.

7. The breakdown of center-periphery/us-them poles is a significant leitmotiv seen, for example, in the three-way debate involving government, local townspeople and the national intelligentsia in the report on teacher strikes in Tuxtla (193–94), and, most dramatically, in the complex of perspectives on the situation of the seamstresses, "epifoco moral del sismo" [the moral epicenter of the quake] (92), which points of view include seamstresses, entrepreneurs, welders, feminists and government functionaries allied with factory owners. At one hilariously liberating moment, owners leap out their office windows to escape the seamstresses—"La toma de la Secretaría del Trabajo (Los patrones por las ventanas)" (101–103).

8. "Acá en este mundo vamos por un camino muy angosto y muy alto y muy peligroso, que es como una loma muy alta, y que por lo alto della va un camino muy angosto, y a la una mano y a la otra está gran profundidad, hondura sin suelo. Y si te desviares del camino hacia la una mano o hacia la otra, cayerás en aquel profundo. Por tanto, conviene con mucho tiento seguir el camino [Here in this world we walk along a very narrow and high and dangerous road, which is like a very high hill with a very narrow road winding on top of it; on one side and the other the road drops off steeply to a bottomless depth. And if you stray from the road toward one side or the other, you'll fall into that bottomless hole. Therefore it behooves us to step with extreme care along that road] (1: 372).

chapter 10

1.   One of these we have seen in detail (see chapter 5's analysis of "La hora de codearse con lo más granado") (*Rituales* 178–81). Another, "La hora de la pluralidad" (93–96), shares with others in this book a parodic biblical tone, here ironizing New Age solemnity. The third, "La hora del consumo de emociones" (32–37), employs a self-satirizing technique, mentioned elsewhere in connection with the burlesque sociologist Laura ("Crónica de sociales," *Escenas* 205–10), which inserts Monsiváis's analytical observer inside the consciousness of a rabidly fanatic soccer fan who now, with an "alien brain," finds himself unable to stop thinking about the Freudian and religious meanings of the game he takes as the center of his existence (*Rituales* 31–36).

2.   See Auerbach 143–73, on biblical satire's mixed style; also Bakhtin, *Rabelais* 13–15, on the *coena Cypriani*, a popular genre that parodies official religious rituals in medieval Europe.

3.   Part or all of many of the chronicles in *Rituales* are fragments of a major cultural survey published two years earlier as "Los espacios de las masas," a chapter in volume 1 of *México a fines de siglo* (Blanco and Woldenberg 1: 267–308). Most of the fragments appear in *Rituales* in revised and expanded form; ten carry the same subtitles as used in "Espacios."

4.   "Meaningful periodicity" alludes to the way each parable's place of insertion expands its own significance and that of neighboring pieces. An example: the second parable of "las postrimerías" locates the source of overpopulation in the countryside and in poverty (109). It is preceded by analysis of a rural miracle worker with twenty-four siblings who represents the culture of poverty. The parable is followed by the previously cited subway piece's alarmed reaction to the overcrowding that results when poverty and traditional mindsets transfer high birth rates from the periphery to the center.

5.   A curious fact: There was a Jewish population explosion in Hellenistic times when anti-Semitism was gaining force (Burkert 14). A provocative observation: Both Catholicism and Islam oppose birth control, and Burkert wonders if this could be due to a "selfish gene" connected to oppression and survival instincts.

6.   See, for example, Eco's contention that bakhtinian theories of transgression are "unfortunately false" because power has historically used carnival "to keep the crowds quiet" ("Frames" 3).

7.   Fiske says something similar about the unbearable "density" of the materially packed cultural space of poverty. An academic observer operates there like a tourist who can scarcely understand the "texturing" of the setting. About this type of ethnographic cultural study, Fiske is adamant: "Our thinking about . . . rural or folk culture should not be nostalgically romantic—it was a culture of deprivation, oppression, or slavery, which is why its popular creativities of making do with limited resources transfer so readily to contemporary conditions" ("Cultural Studies" 158).

8.   These are the last of *Rituales*'s primary works. The text that ends the book is the fifth parable, whose narrator complains that he has lived his life as a good guy in expectation of Judgment Day, when the bad guys would get theirs, but it seems to him that the apocalypse already happened and he wasn't even invited: "la pesadilla más atroz es la que nos excluye definitivamente" [the worst nightmare is the one that completely shuts us out] (250).

9.   Whereas here he is inclined to seek out the positive potential that accompanies capitalist consumerism's negatives, five years later, in *Aires de familia* (2000), Monsiváis seems clearly disheartened before the onslaught of neoliberalism's homogenizing and destabilizing forces.

10.   In August 1998, Monsiváis made a selection of one hundred eighty images of his Mexican photography collection available to the public, on loan to the Mexican Centro de la Imagen.

conclusions

1.   For a recent example, see Rogelio Villarreal's "El lado oscuro del buen *Monsi* . . . " [The Dark Side of "Good *Monsi*"]. Although it was published in one of Mexico City's most

respected newspapers, this essay betrays a notable lack of professionalism and journalistic balance, a judgment I feel should precede citation of any part of the unsubstantiated rumors it purveys, all without evident attempt to include a comment from the object of its vituperation. Villarreal passes on accusations from some in the intellectual community that Monsiváis has shown himself to be "más interesado . . . en las relaciones públicas, la política y sus intrigas, que en la difusión de la cultura" [more concerned about public relations and politics and its intrigues than in the diffusion of culture], and that, "maquiavélico" [Machiavellian], he manipulates young writers, cultivating them to be a domesticated cadre of sycophants (4). One spectacularly unwarranted innuendo even suggests that Monsiváis's critical comments about aspects of the Mexican counterculture "orientaron" [aimed] repressive actions of Díaz Ordaz's administration, which culminated in the October 2, 1968, massacre (5). That, as Monsiváis once said in another context, is giving the chronicle and the writer too much credit for influence and is, besides, an egregiously churlish summation of Carlos Monsiváis's contributions to civic consciousness in Mexico.

works cited

by carlos monsiváis

Monsiváis, Carlos. "A mi mamacita en su día," *La Cultura en México* 21 Sept. 1983: 52–53.

————. *Aire de familia. Colección de Carlos Monsiváis.* Mexico: INBA and Pinacoteca Editores, 1995.

————. *Aires de familia: cultura y sociedad en la América Latina.* Barcelona: Editorial Anagrama, 2000.

————. "Alabemos ahora a los hombres famosos (Sobre el Nuevo Periodismo norteamericano)," appendix, 1st ed., in *Antología de la crónica en México.* Mexico: Universidad Nacional Autónoma de México, 1979.

————. "El amor en (vísperas eternas de) la democracia," *Debate Feminista* Mar. 1980: 236–39.

————. *Amor perdido.* Mexico: Era, 1977.

————. "La aparición del subsuelo (Sobre la cultura de la Revolución Mexicana)," *La Cultura en México* 1122 14 dic. 1983: 36–42.

————. *A través del espejo: el cine mexicano y su público.* Prólogo Carlos Bonfil. México: Ediciones el Milagro, 1994.

————. *Carlos Monsiváis.* Nuevos escritores mexicanos del siglo XX presentados por sí mismos 776. Mexico: Empresas Editoriales, 1996.

———. *Celia Montalván: te brindas, voluptuosa e impudente*. Mexico: Martín Casillas Editores: Cultura/SEP, 1982.

———. "La ciudad de México: un hacerse entre ruinas," *El paseante* 15–16 (1990): 10–19.

———. "Civilización y Coca-Cola," *Nexos* 9, no. 104 (1986): 19–29.

———. *Confrontaciones: el creador frente al público*. Colección Laberinto 6. Azcapotzalco, Mexico: Universidad Autónoma Metropolitana, 1984. Group interview of the author.

———. "El crimen, si evidente, dos veces ambiguo," *Nexos* (1990): 69–71.

———. "Crónica de una Convención (que no lo fue tanto) y de un acontecimiento muy significativo," in EZLN. *Documentos y comunicados 1º de enero / 8 de agosto de 1994*. Prologue Antonio García de León. Texts by Carlos Monsiváis and Elena Poniatowska. Mexico: Era, 1994, 313–23.

———. "Crónica de San Juanico: los hechos, las interpretaciones, las mitologías," *Cuadernos Políticos* 42 (1985): 87–101.

———. "La cultura de la frontera (lado mexicano)," in *Conference on Contemporary Dilemmas of the Mexican–United States Border*. Mexico: Departamento de Investigaciones Históricas, El Colegio de México, 1975, 1–23.

———. *Cultura urbana y creación intelectual: el caso mexicano*. Japan: The United Nations University, 1981.

———. "De algunos problemas del término 'Cultura National' en México," *Revista Occidental* 2 (1985): 37–48.

———. "De las ciudades que se necesitan para construir una casa," in Skirius, *Ensayo*, 587–600.

———. "De cómo un día amaneció Pro-Vida con la novedad de vivir en una sociedad laica," *Debate Feminista* 3 (1991): 82–88.

———. "De la construcción de la 'sensibilidad femenina.'" *Fem* 10, no. 49 (1987): 14–18.

———. "De cultura y política," *Memoria de Papel* 1, no. 1 (1991): 70–72.

———. "De la Santa Doctrina al espíritu público," *Nueva Revista de Filología Hispánica* 35 (1987): 753–71.

———. "De las relaciones literarias entre 'alta cultura' y 'cultura popular.'" *Texto Crítico* 7, no. 33 (1985): 46–61.

———. "De todas las Fridas posibles," *Nexos* 169 (1992): 69–70.

———. "Después del 6 de julio," *Vuelta* 248 (1997): 27–29.

———. "El día de la primera votación," *La Jornada* 21 Oct. 1993: 1, 12.

———. *Días de guardar*. Mexico: Era, 1970.

———. "Duración de la eternidad," *Nexos* 172 (1992): 37–45.

———. "El ejercicio de la crónica," in *La crónica de la época de indias a nuestros días*. Unpublished papers of the III Congreso de Mexicanistas, held in Mexico City April 5, 1991.

———. *Entrada libre: crónicas de la sociedad que se organiza*. Mexico: Era, 1987.

———. "Es el pachuco un sujeto singular: Tin Tan," *Intermedios* 4, no. 1 (1992): 6–13.

———. *Escenas de pudor y liviandad*. 8th ed. Mexico: Grijalbo, 1988.

———. "Los espacios de las masas," in *México a fines de siglo*. Vol. 1 of 2. Eds. José Joaquín Blanco and José Woldenberg. Mexico: Fondo de Cultura Económica, 1993, 267–308.

———. "Éste es el pachuco, un sujeto singular," in *A través de la frontera*. Mexico: CEESTEM, 1983, 83–90.

———. "Estética de muchos, consuelo de monopolios," *La Cultura en México* 19 Jan. 1983: 2–8.

———. "El fin de la diosa arrodillada," *Nexos* 170 (1992): 79–81.

———. "Fino acero de niebla," *Estaciones* 8 (1957): n.pp.

———. *Frida Kahlo: una vida, una obra*. Mexico: Consejo Nacional para la Cultura y las Artes; Era, 1992.

———. "Fuegos de la nota roja," *Nexos* 176 Aug. 1992: 27–35.

———. *El género epistolar: un homenaje a manera de carta abierta*. Mexico: Servicio Postal Mexicano, 1991.

———. "He Wagered His Heart and Lost It to Coca-Cola: On the Happy Forever-after of Civilization and Barbarism," in *Bordering Difference: Culture and Ideology in 20th Century*

Mexico. Ed. Kemy Oyarzún. Riverside, Calif.: University of California, Riverside, 1991, 21–48. (Translation of "Civilización y Coca-Cola," above)

———. "Los hermanos Mayo: . . . Y en una reconquista feliz de otra inocencia," *La Cultura en México* 12 Aug. 1981: 2–8.

———. "Idolos populares y literatura en América Latina," *Boletín Cultural y Bibliográfico* 21, no. 1 (1984): 47–57.

———. "La ingenuidad no existe, Yolanda, o al menos, está tan contaminada de malicia que uno no confía tanto en ella," in *La comedia del arte*. Abel Quezada. Mexico: Fondo de Cultura Económica, 1985, 11–13.

———. "'Landscape, I've Got the Drop on You!' (On the Fiftieth Anniversary of Sound Film in Mexico)," *Studies in Latin American Popular Culture* 4 (1985): 236–46.

———. "Léperos y catrines, nacos y yupis," in *Mitos mexicanos*. Ed. Enrique Florescano. Mexico: Aguilar, 1995, 165–72.

———. "Lo popular en el espacio urbano," *La Cultura en México* 18 Jan. 1984: 42–45.

———. "Lo vi tan cerca, que me pareció de carne y hueso," *Proceso* Dec. 1980: 56–57.

———. "Los de atrás se quedarán (I) (Notas sobre cultura y sociedad de masas en los setentas," *Nexos* 3, no. 26 (1980): 35–43.

———. "Los de atrás se quedarán (II) (Cultura y sociedad en los 70)," *Nexos* 3, no. 28 (1980): 11–23.

———. "La Malinche y el Primer Mundo," in *La Malinche, sus padres y sus hijos*. Ed. Margo Glantz. Mexico: Universidad Nacional Autónoma de México, 1994, 139–47.

———. "La mano temblorosa de una hechicera," in *Agustín: rencuentro con lo sentimental*. Ed. E. M. Mexico: Editorial Domés, 1980, 63–77.

———. *Mexican Postcards*. Trans. and intro. John Kraniauskas. London and New York: Verso, 1997.

———. "Mi oficio es el de comunicador," *La Cultura en México* 995 22 Apr. 1982: 2.

———. *Los mil y un velorios: crónica de la nota roja*. Azcapotzalco, Mexico: Alianza, 1994.

———. "Los milenarismos," in *Las culturas de fin de siglo en América Latina*. Ed. Josefina Ludmer. Rosario, Argentina: Beatriz Viterbo Editora, 1994, 164–83.

———. "Muerte y resurrección del nacionalismo mexicano," *Nexos* 10, no. 109 Jan. 1987: 13–22.

———. "La mujer en la cultura mexicana," in *Mujer y sociedad en América Latina*. Ed. Lucía Guerra-Cunningham. Universidad de California, Irvine; Editorial del Pacífico, 1980, 101–17.

———. "¡¡No con un sollozo, sino entre disparos (Notas sobre cultura mexicana 1910–1968)," *Revista Iberoamericana* 55 (1989): 715–35.

———. "'No queremos 10 de mayo. Queremos revolución!!': sobre el nuevo feminismo," *La Cultura en México* 1088 13 Apr. 1983: 2–5.

———. "No te me muevas, paisaje: sobre el cincuentenario del cine sonoro en México," *Aztlán* 14 (1983): 1–19.

———. "Notas sobre la cultura mexicana en el siglo XX," in *Historia general de México*. Mexico: El Colegio de México, 1976, 303–476. Vol. 4 of 4.

———. "Notas sobre cultura popular en México," *Latin American Perspectives* 5, no. 1 (1978): 98–118.

———. "Notas sobre el Estado, la cultura nacional y las culturas populares en México," *Cuadernos Políticos* 30 (1981): 33–43.

———. "Nueva salutación del optimista," *Fem* 9 (1978): 17–19.

———. *Nuevo catecismo para indios remisos*. Mexico: Siglo XXI, 1982.

———. *Nuevo catecismo para indios remisos*. Mexico: Consejo Nacional para la Cultura y las Artes, 1992. (Ten new texts added)

———. "Para un cuadro de costumbres: de cultura y vida cotidiana en los ochentas," *Cuadernos Políticos* 57 (1989): 84–100.

———. "Penetración cultural y nacionalismo," in *Culturas populares y política cultural*. Ed. Guillermo Bonfil Batalla. Mexico: Museo de Culturas Populares, 1982, 79–99.

———. *Por mi madre, bohemios I*. Comentarios y alabanzas de Carlos Monsiváis, selección de textos de Alejandro Brito, ilustraciones y cuidado ornamental de Rafael Barajas (El Fisgón). Mexico: La Jornada Ediciones, 1993.

———. "El Premio Manuel Buendía, una razón contra la cultura de la impunidad," *Proceso* 6 June 1988: 14–16.

———. "Respuesta de Carlos Monisváis a *Marcos*," *La Jornada* 27 July 1994: 1, 16.

———. *Los rituales del caos*. Mexico: Era, 1995.

———. *Salvador Novo: lo marginal en el centro*. Mexico: Era, 2000.

———. "El 68: las ceremonias del agravio y la memoria," in *Parte de Guerra: Tlatelolco 1968*. Julio Scherer García and Carlos Monsiváis. Mexico: Nuevo Siglo Aguilar, 1999, 119–262.

———. "Sexismo en la literatura mexicana," in *Imagen y realidad de la mujer*. Ed. Elena Urrutia. Mexico: SEP/Diana, 1979, 102–25.

———. "Los testimonios delatores, las recuperaciones estéticas," *La Cultura en México* 12 Jan. 1983: 2–4.

———. "Tres nichos sin retablo," *Nexos* 150 (1990): 72–75.

———. "Variedades del México Freudiano," *Nexos* 1, no. 12 (1978): 10–15.

———. "Las vísperas del pasado: es pues la fe la substancia de las cosas que se esperan," *La Cultura en México* 24 Nov. 1982: 2–3.

———. "Viaje al corazón de Monsiváis," Interview. Cayuela Gally 6.

———. "Viaje de un largo día hacia la transición," *El mundo* 4 July 2000 (n.p.).

works coauthored by carlos monsiváis

Monsiváis, Carlos, Héctor Aguilar Camín, Jorge Alcocer, and Rolando Cordera. "México ante la adversidad," *Nexos* 197 (1994): 30–35, 37–39.

Monsiváis, Carlos, José Emilio Pacheco, and Elena Poniatowska. *El derecho a la lectura*. Mexico: El Colegio de México, 1984.

Monsiváis, Carlos, and Julio Scherer García. *Parte de guerra: Tlatelolco 1968: documentos del general Marcelino García Barragán. Los hechos y la historia*. Mexico: Nuevo Siglo Aguilar, 1999.

Monsiváis, Carlos, Arsacio Vanegas Arroyo, Adrián Villagómez L., Francisco Díaz de León, Luis Cardoza y Aragón, Antonio Rodríguez, and Fernando Benítez. "Posada: el repertorio de las emociones," in *Exposición-Homenaje: José Guadalupe Posada*. Mexico: Instituto Nacional de Bellas Artes, 1980, 35–37.

prologues by carlos monsiváis

Monsiváis, Carlos, prologue. "El caso del horrorosísimo hijo que con tal de no matar a su horrorosísima madre leía la horrorosísima nota roja," in *Fuera de la ley: la nota roja en México 1982–1990*, by Antonio Arellano, et al. Mexico: Cal y Arena, 1992, I–XXXI.

———, prologue. "Como se lo iba diciendo, el caudillo ni se dio por enterado," in *Antología de la crónica en México*. 1st ed. Mexico: Universidad Nacional Autónoma de México, 1979, 9–36.

———, prologue. "Daisy Ascher: de semejanzas y distanciamientos," in *Cien retratos por Daisy Ascher*. Mexico: Instituto Nacional de Bellas Artes, 1981, 9–11

———, prologue. "De México y los chicanos, de México y su cultura fronteriza," in *La otra cara de México: el pueblo chicano*. Ed. David R. Maciel. Mexico: Ediciones "El Caballito," 1977, 1–19.

———, prologue. *Un día en la gran ciudad de México*. Mexico: Grupo Azabache, 1992 (n.p.).

———, prologue. "Dispositivos para identificar a la gente famosa a simple vista," in *Elogio de la cordura: para un retrato de la clase gobernante*. Rogelio Naranjo. Mexico: Era, 1979, 9–27.

———. "Prólogo," in *El fin de la nostalgia. Nueva crónica de la ciudad de México*. Eds. Jaime Valverde y Juan Domingo Argüelles. Mexico: Nueva Imagen, 1992, 15–25.

———, prologue. *Foto estudio Jiménez: Sotero Constantino, fotógrafo de Juchitán*. 1st reimp. Mexico: Era; H. Ayuntamiento Popular de Juchitán, 1984, 7–16.

———, prologue. "Guillermo Prieto: cuadro de costumbres," in *Obras completas* de Guillermo Prieto. Vol. 2 of 2. Mexico: Consejo Nacional para la Cultura y las Artes, 1992, 13–36.

————, prologue. "Hagan su contrajuego, señores," in *Los reyes de la baraja*. Rogelio Naranjo. Mexico: Siglo XXI, 1980, 5–9.

————, prologue. *The World of Agustín Víctor Casasola*. *México: 1900–1938 / El mundo de Agustín Víctor Casasola*. Washington, D.C.: The Fondo del Sol Visual Arts and Media Center, 1984–1987. Museum exhibition catalog.

————, prologue. "Y yo preguntaba y anotaba, y el caudillo no se dio por enterado," in *A ustedes les consta: antología de la crónica en México*. Rev. ed. Mexico: Era, 1980, 15–76.

editions by carlos monsiváis

Monsiváis, Carlos, ed. and prologue. *A ustedes les consta: antología de la crónica en México*. Rev. ed. of *Antología de la crónica en México*. Mexico: Era, 1980.

————, ed. *Antología de la crónica en México*. 1st ed. of *A ustedes les consta*. Mexico: Universidad Nacional Autónoma de México, 1979.

————, ed. and prologue. *Fuera de la ley: la nota roja en México 1982–1990*. Mexico: Cal y Arena, 1992.

————, ed. *Lo fugitivo permanece. 21 cuentos mexicanos*. Mexico: Cal y Arena, 1989.

————, ed. and prologue. *La poesía mexicana del siglo XX (Antología)*. Mexico: Empresas Editoriales, 1966, 9–72.

other works cited

Abrams, M. H. *Doing Things With Texts: Essays in Criticism and Critical Theory*. Ed. Michael Fischer. New York: W.W. Norton, 1989.

Acosta, José de. *Historia natural y moral de las Indias*. Ed. José Alcina Franch. Crónicas de América 34. Madrid: Historia 16, 1987.

Aguilar Camín, Héctor, and Lorenzo Meyer. *A la sombra de la Revolución Mexicana: un ensayo de historia contemporánea de México 1910–1989*. 10th ed. Mexico: Cal y Arena, 1993.

Aguilar Mora, Jorge. *La divina pareja: historia y mito. Valoración e interpretación de la obra ensayística de Octavio Paz*. Mexico: Era, 1978.

Agustín, José. *Tragicomedia mexicana. La vida en México de 1940 a 1970*. Vol. 1. 3rd reimp. Mexico: Planeta, 1991. 2 vols.

————. *Tragicomedia mexicana. La vida en México de 1970 a 1982*. Vol. 2 of 2. Mexico: Planeta, 1992.

Aínsa, Fernando. "The Antinomies of Latin American Discourses of Identity and Their Fictional Representation," in Chanady 1–25.

Alatorre, Antonio. Rev. of *A ustedes les consta* by Carlos Monsiváis. *Vuelta* 5, no. 53 (1981): 37–41.

Alcina Franch, José, Miguel León-Portilla, and Eduardo Matos Moctezuma. *Azteca-Mexica: las culturas del México antiguo*. Barcelona and Madrid: Lunwerg Editores, 1992.

Allen, Robert C., ed. *Channels of Discourse, Reassembled: Television and Contemporary Criticism*. 2nd ed. Chapel Hill and London: University of North Carolina Press, 1992.

Altamiranda, Daniel. "Literary Theory and Criticism," in *Mexican Literature: A History*. Ed. David William Foster. Austin: University of Texas Press, 1994, 341–63.

Anzaldo, Sergio. "El costo de la entrada." Rev. of *Entrada libre* by Carlos Monsiváis. *Revista Mexicana de Ciencias Políticas y Sociales* 34, no. 132 (1988): 178–80.

Aranda Luna, Javier. "Entrevista con Carlos Monsiváis: el carnaval como desquite," *La Jornada Semanal* 6 Aug. 1995: 10–11.

Arendt, Hannah. "Walter Benjamin: 1892–1940," in Benjamin 1–55.

Argüelles, Juan Domingo. "Letras insomnes: el ensayo literario en México," *Memoria de Papel* 3, no. 5 (1993): 4–36.

Armstrong, Karen. *A History of God: The 4000-Year Quest of Judaism, Christianity and Islam*. New York: Alfred A. Knopf, 1993.

Ashcroft, Bill, Gareth Griffiths, and Helen Tiffin. *The Empire Writes Back: Theory and Practice in Post-Colonial Literatures*. London and New York: Routledge, 1989.

Ashcroft, Bill, Gareth Griffiths, and Helen Tiffin, eds. *The Post-Colonial Studies Reader*. London and New York: Routledge, 1995.

Auerbach, Erich. *Mimesis: The Representation of Reality in Western Literature*. Trans. Willard R. Trask. Princeton: Princeton University Press, 1968.

Ávila, Raúl. "El español es nuestro . . . y el inglés también." Coords. Aralia López González, Amelia Malagamba y Elena Urrutia. *Mujer y literatura mexicana y chicana: culturas en contacto 2*. Mexico: El Colegio de México, El Colegio de la Frontera Norte, 1990, 159–66.

Avilés Fabila, René. "México 68. Veinte años después de 'El gran solitario de Palacio,'" in *Literatura mexicana hoy: del 68 al ocaso de la revolución*. Ed. Karl Kohut. Frankfurt am Main: Vervuert Verlag, 1991, 93–106.

Aznárez, Juan Jesús. "Fuga de intelectuales mexicanos hacia el candidato conservador Fox," *El País* 25 June 2000 (n.p.).

Bakhtin, Mikhail. *The Dialogic Imagination: Four Essays*. Trans. Caryl Emerson and Michael Holquist. Ed. Michael Holquist. Austin: University of Texas Press, 1981.

———. *Estética de la creación verbal*. Trans. Tatiana Bubnova. Mexico: Siglo Veintiuno, 1982.

———. *Problems of Dostoevsky's Poetics*. Ed. and trans. Caryl Emerson. Intro. Wayne C. Booth. Minneapolis: University of Minnesota Press, 1984.

———. *Rabelais and His World*. Trans. Hélène Iswolsky. Bloomington: Indiana University Press, 1984.

Barkin, David, et al. *Las relaciones México–Estados Unidos. 1*. Mexico: Universidad Autónoma Nacional de México, Nueva Imagen, 1980.

Barthes, Roland. *Image-Music-Text*. Trans. Stephen Heath. New York: Hill and Wang, 1977.

Batis, Huberto. *Lo que "Cuadernos del Viento" nos dejó: memorias de la revista literaria publicada en México de agosto de 1960 a enero de 1967*. Mexico: Diógenes, 1984.

Baudrillard, Jean. *America*. Trans. Chris Turner. London and New York: Verso, 1991.

———. *Selected Writings*. Trans. Jacques Mourrain. Ed. Mark Poster. Stanford: Stanford University Press, 1988.

Beardsley, Monroe C. "Aesthetic Intentions and Fictive Illocutions," in Hernadi, *What Is Literature?* 161–77.

Benítez, Fernando. "¿Quién es Carlos Monsiváis?" Cayuela Gally 4.

Benjamin, Walter. *Illuminations*. New York: Harcourt, Brace and World, 1968.

Best, Steven, and Douglas Kellner. *Postmodern Theory: Critical Interrogations*. Houndmill, Basingstoke, Hampshire, and London: MacMillan, 1991.

Beverley, John. *Against Literature*. Minneapolis and London: University of Minnesota Press, 1993.

———. "Cultural Studies," *Latin American Literary Review* 20 (1992): 19–22.

———. "'Through All Things Modern': Second Thoughts on Testimonio," in *Critical Theory, Cultural Politics, and Latin American Narrative*. Notre Dame, Ind., and London: University of Notre Dame Press, 1993, 125–51.

Bhabha, Homi K. "DissemiNation: Time, Narrative, and the Margins of the Modern Nation," in *Nation and Narration*. London and New York: Routledge, 1990, 291–332.

———. "Postcolonial Authority and Postmodern Guilt," in Grossberg 56–68.

Bhabha, Homi K., ed. "Introduction: Narrating the Nation," in *Nation and Narration*. London and New York: Routledge, 1990, 1–7.

Biedermann, Hans. *Dictionary of Symbolism*. Trans. James Hulbert. New York: Facts on File, 1992.

Blanco, José Joaquín. "Aguafuertes de narrativa mexicana, 1950–1980," *Nexos* 5, no. 56 (1982): 23–39.

———. *Un chavo bien helado: crónicas de los años ochenta*. Mexico: Era, 1990.

———. *Crónica de la literatura reciente en México (1950–1980)*. Mexico: Instituto Nacional de Antropología e Historia, 1982.

———. *Esplendores y miserias de los criollos: la literatura en la Nueva España 2*. Vol. 2 of 2. Mexico: Cal y Arena, 1989.

Blanco, José Joaquín, and José Woldenberg, eds. *México a fines de siglo*. Mexico: Fondo de Cultura Económica, 1993. 2 vols.

Bonfil Batalla, Guillermo, ed. *Culturas populares y política cultural*. Mexico: Museo de Culturas Populares, 1982.

———. *México profundo: una civilización negada*. Mexico: Grijalbo, 1987.

Boorstin, Daniel J. *The Image, or What Happened to the American Dream*. New York: Atheneum, 1962.

Booth, Wayne C. *A Rhetoric of Irony*. Chicago and London: University of Chicago Press, 1974.

Brémond, Claude. "The Logic of Narrative Possibilities," *New Literary History* 11 (1980): 387–411.

Brito García, Luis. "La identidad de América Latina a través de su cultura popular," *Folklore Americano* 44 (1987): 37–51.

Broda, Johanna, David Carrasco, and Eduardo Matos Moctezuma. *The Great Temple of Tenochtitlan: Center and Periphery in the Aztec World*. Berkeley, Los Angeles, and London: University of California Press, 1987.

Brooke-Rose, Christine. "Whatever Happened to Narratology?" *Poetics Today* 11 (1990): 283–93.

Browne, Ray B. *Against Academia: The History of the Popular Culture Association/American Culture Association and the Popular Culture Movement 1967–1988*. Bowling Green, Ohio: Bowling Green State University Popular Press, 1989.

———. "Popular Culture as the New Humanities," *Journal of Popular Culture* 17 (1984): 1–8.

———. "Popular Culture: Notes Toward a Definition," in *Popular Culture and Curricula*. Eds. Ray B. Browne and Ronald J. Ambrosetti. Bowling Green, Ohio: Bowling Green University Popular Press, 1972, 3–11.

Burke, Peter. "The 'Discovery' of Popular Culture," in *People's History and Socialist Theory*. Ed. Raphael Samuel. London: Routledge and Kegan Paul, 1981, 217–26.

Burkert, Walter. *Creation of the Sacred: Tracks of Biology in Early Religions*. Cambridge, Mass., and London: Harvard University Press, 1996.

Burkhart, Louise M. *The Slippery Earth: Nahua-Christian Moral Dialogue in Sixteenth-Century Mexico*. Tucson: University of Arizona Press, 1989.

Cabeza de Vaca, Alvar Núñez. *Naufragios y comentarios*. Ed. Roberto Ferrando. Crónicas de América 3. Madrid: Historia 16, 1984.

Calvert, Peter, and Susan Calvert. *Latin America in the Twentieth Century*. London: MacMillan, 1990.

Canetti, Elias. *Masse und Macht*. Hamburg: Classen, 1960.

Carballo, Emmanuel, prologue. *Carlos Monsiváis* by Carlos Monsiváis. Nuevos escritores mexicanos del Siglo XX presentados por sí mismos 776. Mexico: Empresas Editoriales, 1966, 6–10.

Carballo, Emmanuel. *Notas de un francotirador*. Villahermosa, Tabasco, Mexico: Gobierno del Estado de Tabasco, 1990.

———. "El Sabio Monsiváis," *El Financiero* 14 Aug. 1994: 43. One of a regular column called "Diario Público."

Carpentier, Alejo. "La novela latinoamericana en vísperas de un nuevo siglo," in González Echevarría, *Historia* 19–48.

Carr, Barry. *Marxism and Communism in Twentieth-Century Mexico*. Lincoln, Neb., and London: University of Nebraska Press, 1992.

Carroll, Michael P. *The Cult of the Virgin Mary: Psychological Origins*. Princeton: Princeton University Press, 1986.

Carter, Boyd G. "Revistas literarias hispanoamericanas del siglo XIX," in Iñigo Madrigal 2: 75–86.

Castañeda, Jorge. *Utopia Unarmed: The Latin American Left After the Cold War*. New York: Alfred A. Knopf, 1993. (Spanish version: *La utopía desarmada*, Mexico: Joaquín Mortiz and Planeta, 1993)

Castañón, Adolfo. "El ensayo en México a fin de siglo: brevísima relación de los que ensayaron y sobrevivieron," *Cuadernos Hispanoamericanos* 549–550 (1996): 65–81.

———. "Un hombre llamado ciudad," *Vuelta* 163 (1990): 19–22.

Castillo, Debra. *Easy Women: Sex and Gender in Modern Mexican Fiction*. Minneapolis and London: University of Minnesota Press, 1998.

Cayuela Gally, Ricardo. "Carlos Monsiváis: retrato para armar," *La Jornada Semanal* 6 Aug. 1995: 4–6.

Chanady, Amaryll, ed. *Latin American Identity and Constructions of Difference*. Minneapolis and London: University of Minnesota Press, 1994.

Clavijero, Francisco, Javier. *Historia antigua de México*. Ed. R. P. Mariano Cuevas. 2a ed. Mexico: Porrúa, 1968.

Clendinnen, Inga. *Aztecs: An Interpretation*. Cambridge, England, and New York: Cambridge University Press, 1991.

Cohn, Dorrit. "Signposts of Fictionality: A Narratological Perspective," *Poetics Today* 11 (1990): 775–804.

———. *Transparent Minds: Narrative Modes for Presenting Consciousness in Fiction*. Princeton: Princeton University Press, 1978.

Collini, Stefan. "Introduction: Interpretation Terminable and Interminable," in Eco, et al., *Interpretation* 1–21.

Collins, Jim. "Television and Postmodernism," in Allen 327–53.

Connor, Steven. *Postmodernist Culture: An Introduction to Theories of the Contemporary*. Oxford: Basil Blackwell, 1989.

Core, George. "Stretching the Limits of the Essay," in *Essays on the Essay: Redefining the Genre*. Ed. Alexander J. Butrym. Athens and London: University of Georgia Press, 1989, 207–20.

Cortés, Hernán. *Cartas y documentos*. Intro. Mario Hernández Sánchez-Barba. 1522, 1523, 1525. Mexico: Porrúa, 1963.

Coser, Lewis A. *Men of Ideas: A Sociologist's View*. New York: The Free Press, and London: Collier-Macmillan, 1965.

Cossío, María Eugenia. "El diálogo sin fin de Monsiváis," *Hispanic Journal* 5 (1984): 137–43.

Cuéllar, José Tomás de. *La linterna mágica*. 12 vols. Ed. Mauricio Magdaleno. Biblioteca Universitario 27. Mexico: Universidad Nacional Autónoma de México, 1973.

Dallal, Alberto. *Periodismo y literatura*. Mexico: Universidad Nacional Autónoma de México, 1985.

Daly, Peter. *Literature in the Light of the Emblem: Structural Parallels between the Emblem and Literature in the Sixteenth and Seventeenth Centuries*. Toronto, Buffalo, and London: University of Toronto Press, 1979.

Davis, Robert Con, and Ronald Schleifer, eds. *Contemporary Literary Criticism: Literary and Cultural Studies*. 2nd ed. New York and London: Longman, 1989.

de Certeau, Michel. *The Practice of Everyday Life*. Trans. Steven Rendall. Berkeley, Los Angeles, and London: University of California Press, 1984.

Debate Feminista. "Un diálogo (¿o dos monólogos?) sobre la censura," *Debate Feminista* 5, no. 9 (1994): 25–50. Edited by Marta Lamas.

Déleon Meléndez, Ofelia Columba. "Criterios fundamentales para la comprensión y valoración de la cultura popular o culturas populares," *Folklore Americano* 43 (1987): 5–13.

Derrida, Jacques. "Structure, Sign, and Play in the Discourse of the Human Sciences," in Davis 230–48.

Díaz del Castillo, Bernal. *Historia verdadera de la conquista de la Nueva España*. Ed. Miguel León-Portilla. Crónicas de América 2a–2b. Madrid: Historia 16, 1984.

Dieckmann, Liselotte. *Hieroglyphics: The History of a Literary Symbol*. St. Louis: Washington University Press, 1970.

Docker, John. *Postmodernism and Popular Culture: A Cultural History*. Cambridge, England: Cambridge University Press, 1994.

Dolezel, Lubomir. "Mimesis and Possible Worlds," in *Poetics Today* 9 (1988): 475–96.

Domínguez Michael, Christopher, ed. *Antología de la narrativa mexicana del siglo XX*. Mexico: Fondo de Cultura Económica, 1989. 2 vols.

———. "Treinta años de crítica," in Martínez and Domínguez Michael 262–71.

Duncan, Ann J. *Voices, Visions, and a New Reality: Mexican Fiction Since 1970*. Pittsburgh: University of Pittsburgh Press, 1986.

Eagleton, Terry. *Literary Theory: An Introduction*. Minneapolis: University of Minnesota Press, 1983.

Eco, Umberto. "The Frames of Comic 'Freedom,'" in *Carnival!* Ed. Thomas A. Sebeok. Berlin, New York, and Amsterdam: Mouton, 1984, 1–9.

———. *The Open Work*. Trans. Anna Cancogni. Intro. David Robey. Cambridge, Mass.: Harvard University Press, 1989.

Eco, Umberto, with Richard Rorty, Jonathan Culler, and Christine Brooke-Rose. *Interpretation and Overinterpretation*. Ed. Stefan Collini. Cambridge, England, and New York: Cambridge University Press, 1992.

Egan, Linda. "Cristina Pacheco: nómada entre géneros," in *El cuento mexicano: homenaje a Luis Leal*. Ed. Sara Poot Herrera. Mexico: Coordinación de Difusión Cultural, Dirección de Literatura, Universidad Nacional Autónoma de México, 1996, 459–79.

———. "Crónica y periodismo: 'el género Carlos Monsiváis,'" in *Tradición y actualidad de la literatura iberoamericana. Actas del XXX Congreso del Instituto Internacional de Literatura Iberoamericana*. Vol. 1 of 2. Ed. Pamela Bacarisse. Pittsburgh, Penn.: University of Pittsburgh, 1995, 303–10.

———. "El 'descronicamiento' de la realidad: el macho mundo mimético de Ignacio Trejo Fuentes," in *Vivir del cuento (La ficción en México)*. Ed. Alfredo Pavón. Mexico: Universidad Autónoma de Tlaxcala, 1995, 143–70.

———. "Entrevista con Carlos Monsiváis," *La Jornada Semanal* 26 Jan. 1992: 17–22.

———. "'Lo marginal en el centro': las crónicas de Carlos Monsiváis." Dissertation. University of California, Santa Barbara, 1993.

———. "'Mechicanos' al borde del cambio en el valiente mundo nuevo de Carlos Monsiváis," *Revista de Literatura Mexicana Contemporánea* 1, no. 3 (1996): 72–80.

———. "The Sound of Silence: Voices of the Marginalized in Cristina Pacheco's Narrative," in *The Other Mirror: Women's Narrative in Mexico, 1980–1995*. Ed. Kristine Ibsen. Westport, Conn., and London: Greenwood Press, 1997, 133–46.

Escarpeta-Sánchez, José Angel. "Carlos Monsiváis y sus croni-ensayos de *Amor perdido*," *La Palabra y el Hombre* 88 (1993): 158–64.

EZLN. *Documentos y comunicados 1º de enero / 8 de agosto de 1994*. Prologue Antonio García de León. Texts by Carlos Monsiváis and Elena Poniatowska. Mexico: Era, 1994.

Faber, Sebastiaan. "La metonimia en una crónica de Carlos Monsiváis. Hacia un periodismo democrático," *Literatura Mexicana* 10 (1999): 249–80.

Fagan, Brian. *From Black Land to Fifth Sun: The Science of Sacred Sites*. Reading, Mass.: Helix Books, 1998.

Ferman, Claudia. "México en la posmodernidad: textualización de la cultura popular urbana," *Nuevo Texto Crítico* 7 (1991): 157–67.

Fishkin, Shelley Fisher. *From Fact to Fiction: Journalism and Imaginative Writing in America*. Baltimore and London: Johns Hopkins University Press, 1985.

Fiske, John. "British Cultural Studies and Television," in Allen 284–326.

———. "Cultural Studies and the Culture of Everyday Life," in Grossberg 155–73.

———. *Reading the Popular*. London: Unwin Hyman, 1989.

———. *Television Culture*. London and New York: Methuen, 1987.

———. *Understanding Popular Culture*. Boston: Unwin Hyman, 1989.

Foley, Barbara. "Fact, Fiction, and 'Reality.'" *Contemporary Literature* 20 (1979): 389–99.

———. *Telling the Truth: The Theory and Practice of Documentary Fiction*. Ithaca, N.Y., and London: Cornell University Press, 1986.

Fortson, James R. *Perspectivas mexicanas desde París: un diálogo con Carlos Fuentes*. Mexico: Corporación Editorial, 1973.

Foster, David William. *Alternate Voices in the Contemporary Latin American Narrative*. Columbia, Mo.: University of Missouri Press, 1985.

———. "On the Study of Popular Culture in Latin America," in *Contemporary Latin American Culture: Unity and Diversity*. Ed. C. Gail Guntermann. Tempe, Arizona: Center for Latin American Studies of Arizona State University, 1984, 27–43.

———. "Popular Culture: The Roots of Literary Tradition," in *Imagination, Emblems, and Expressions: Essays on Latin American, Caribbean, and Continental Culture and Identity*. Ed. Helen Ryan-Ranson. Bowling Green, Ohio: Bowling Green State University Popular Press, 1993, 3–27.

Fox, Robin Lane. *The Unauthorized Version: Truth and Fiction in the Bible*. New York: Alfred A. Knopf, 1992.

Franco, Jean. "Marcar diferencias, cruzar fronteras," in *Las culturas de fin de siglo en América Latina*. Comp. Josefina Ludmer. Rosario, Arg.: Beatriz Viterbo Editora, 1994, 34–43.

———. "El ocaso de la vanguardia y el auge de la crítica," *Nuevo Texto Crítico* 7, no. 14–15 (1995): 11–22.

Friedman, Norman. "Point of View in Fiction: The Development of a Critical Concept," in *The Novel: Modern Essays in Criticism*. Ed. Robert Murray Davis. Englewood Cliffs, N.J.: Prentice-Hall, 1969, 142–71.

Frith, Simon. "The Cultural Study of Popular Music," in Grossberg 174–86.

Frow, John. *Cultural Studies and Cultural Value*. Oxford: Clarendon Press, 1995.

Fuentes, Carlos. *Ceremonias del alba*. Madrid: Mondadori, 1991.

———. *Cristóbal Nonato*. Mexico: Fondo de Cultura Económica, 1987.

———. "Una literatura urgente," in *Latin American Fiction Today*. Ed. Rose S. Minc. Takoma Park, Md.: Hispamérica; Upper Montclair, N.J.: Montclair State College, 1979, 9–17.

———. *La muerte de Artemio Cruz*. Mexico: Fondo de Cultura Económica, 1962.

———. *La nueva novela hispanoamericana*. Mexico: Cuadernos de Joaquín Mortiz, 1969.

———. *La región más transparente*. Mexico: Fondo de Cultura Económica, 1958.

———. *Tiempo mexicano*. Mexico: Cuadernos de Joaquín Mortiz, 1972.

———. *Todos los gatos son pardos*. Mexico: Siglo Veintiuno, 1970.

———. *Tres discursos para dos aldeas*. Buenos Aires: Fondo de Cultura Económica, 1993.

———. *Valiente mundo nuevo: épica, utopía y mito en la novela hispanoamericana*. Mexico: Fondo de Cultura Económica, 1990.

García, Gustavo. "México bien vale una crónica," *Revista de la Universidad de México* 33, no. 11 (1979): 41–2.

———. "Monsiváis: los rostros evanescentes y entrañables," *Revista de la Universidad de México* 32, no. 6 (1978): 29.

García Canclini, Néstor. *Consumidores y ciudadanos: conflictos multiculturales de la globalización*. Mexico: Grijalbo, 1995.

García Canclini, Néstor, coord. *El consumo cultural en México*. Mexico: Consejo Nacional para la Cultura y las Artes, 1993.

García Canclini, Néstor. "Cultura transnacional y culturas populares en México," *Cuadernos Hispanoamericanos* 431 (1986): 5–18.

———. "Cultural Reconversion," trans. Holly Staver, in Yúdice, et al., *On Edge* 29–43.

———. *Culturas híbridas: estrategias para entrar y salir de la modernidad*. Mexico: Grijalbo, 1991.

———. *Transforming Modernity: Popular Culture in Mexico*. Trans. Lidia Lozano. Austin: University of Texas Press, 1993.

García Monsiváis, Blanca M. *El ensayo mexicano en el siglo XX: Reyes, Novo, Paz. Desarrollo, direcciones y formas*. Iztapalapa, Mexico: Universidad Autónoma Metropolitana, 1995.

García Scherer, Julio, and Carlos Monsiváis. *Parte de guerra: Tlatelolco 1968: documentos del general Marcelino García Barragán. Los hechos y la historia*. Mexico: Nuevo Siglo Aguilar, 1999.

Garibay, Ricardo. *De lujo y hambre*. Mexico: Nueva Imagen, 1981.

Gates, Henry Louis, Jr. "The 'Blackness of Blackness': A Critique of the Sign and Signifying Monkey," in Davis 629–58.

Gelpí, Juan G. "Paseo por la crónica urbana de México: Carlos Monsiváis y José Joaquín Blanco," *Nómada* 3 (1997): 83–88.

Genette, Gérard. "Fictional Narrative, Factual Narrative," *Poetics Today* 11 (1990): 755–74.

———. *Narrative Discourse: An Essay in Method*. Trans. Jane E. Lewin. Ithaca, N.Y.: Cornell University Press, 1980.

Gerard, Philip. *Creative Nonfiction: Researching and Crafting Stories of Real Life*. Cincinnati, Ohio: Story Press Books, 1996.

Ginzburg, Carlo. *Myths, Emblems, Clues*. Trans. John and Anne C. Tedeschi. London: Hutchinson Radius, 1986.

Giordano, Jaime. "El ensayo hispanoamericano de las últimas generaciones," *Mundo, problemas y confrontaciones* 1 (1987): 73–79.

Gitlin, Todd. *The Sixties: Years of Hope, Days of Rage*. New York: Bantam Books, 1987.

Godzich, Wlad, and Nicholas Spadaccini, eds. *Literature Among Discourses: The Spanish Golden Age*. Minneapolis: University of Minnesota Press, 1986.

Goic, Cedomil, ed. "Temas y problemas de la literatura hispanoamericana colonial," in *Historia y crítica de la literatura hispanoamericana I: época colonial*. Vol. 1 of 3. Barcelona: Editorial Crítica, 1988, 23–48.

Gómez-Martínez, José Luis. *Teoría del ensayo*. 2nd ed. Mexico: Universidad Nacional Autónoma de México, 1981.

González, Aníbal. *La crónica modernista hispanoamericana*. Madrid: Porrúa, 1983.

———. "After 1992: A Latin American Wish List," *Latin American Literary Review* 20 (1992): 46–50.

———. *Journalism and the Development of Spanish American Narrative*. Cambridge, England: Cambridge University Press, 1993.

González Echevarría, Roberto, ed. and prologue. *Historia y ficción en la narrativa hispanoamericana*. Caracas: Monte Avila, 1984, 9–13.

González Echevarría, Roberto. *Myth and Archive: A Theory of Latin American Narrative*. Cambridge, England, and New York: Cambridge University Press, 1990.

González Irigoyen, Julieta. "Periodismo literario," in *Mujer y literatura mexicana y chicana: culturas en contacto*. Eds. Aralia López González, Amelia Malagamba, and Elena Urrutia. Mexico: El Colegio de México, El Colegio de la Frontera Norte, 1990, 201–204.

Goody, Jack. *The Interface between the Written and the Oral*. Cambridge, England: Cambridge University Press, 1987.

Greenblatt, Stephen. *Marvelous Possessions: The Wonder of the New World*. Chicago: University of Chicago Press, 1991.

Grossberg, Lawrence, Cary Nelson, and Paula A. Treichler, eds. *Cultural Studies*. New York and London: Routledge, 1992.

Gruzinski, Serge. *The Conquest of Mexico: The Incorporation of Indian Societies into the Western World, 16th–18th Centuries*. Trans. Eileen Corrigan. Cambridge, England: Polity Press, 1993.

Guillén, Claudio. *Literature as System: Essays Toward the Theory of Literary History*. Princeton: Princeton University Press, 1971.

Gurza, Teresa. "Los Angeles, ciudad de mexicanos, latinos y negros," *La Jornada* 10 July 1991: 1, 14.

Gutmann, Matthew C. *The Meaning of Macho: Being a Man in Mexico City*. Berkeley, Los Angeles, and London: University of California Press, 1996.

Hall, David. "Introduction," in *Understanding Popular Culture: Europe from the Middle Ages to the Nineteenth Century*. Ed. Steven L. Kaplan. Berlin, New York, and Amsterdam: Mouton Publishers, 1984, 5–18.

Hall, Stuart. "Cultural Studies and Its Theoretical Legacies," in Grossberg 277–94.

———. "The Emergence of Cultural Studies and the Crisis of the Humanities," *October* 53 (1990): 11–23.

Hamburger, Kate. *The Logic of Literature*. 2nd rev. ed. Trans. Marilynn J. Rose. Bloomington: Indiana University Press, 1973.

Hamilton, Edith. *Mythology*. U.S.A.: Little, Brown and Co., 1942.

Hassan, Ihab. "The New Gnosticism: Speculations on an Aspect of the Postmodern Mind," in *Paracriticisms: Seven Speculations of the Times*. Urbana and Chicago: University of Illinois Press, 1984, 121–47.

Hellman, John. *Fables of Fact: The New Journalism as New Fiction*. Urbana: University of Illinois Press, 1981.

———. "Postmodern Journalism," in McCaffery, *Postmodern Fiction: A Bio-Bibliographical Guide* 51–61.

Hernadi, Paul. "Clio's Cousins: Historiography as Translation, Fiction, and Criticism," *New Literary History* 7 (1976): 247–57.

———. "Dual Perspective: Free Indirect Discourse and Related Techniques," *Comparative Literature* 24 (1972): 32–43.

———, ed. *What Is Literature?* Bloomington and London: Indiana University Press, 1978.

Herzog, Thomas R., and Beverly A. Bush. "The Prediction of Preference for Sick Humor," *Humor* 7-4 (1994): 323–40.

Hinds, Harold E., Jr. "Latin American Popular Culture. A New Research Frontier: Achievements, Problems, and Promise," *Journal of Popular Culture* 14 (1980): 405–12.

———. "Popularity: The Sine Qua Non of Popular Culture," *Studies in Latin American Popular Culture* 9 (1990): 1–13.

Hirsch, E. D., Jr. *Validity in Interpretation.* New Haven and London: Yale University Press, 1967.

Hollowell, John. *Fact and Fiction: The New Journalism and the Nonfiction Novel.* Chapel Hill: University of North Carolina Press, 1977.

Huerta, David. "Transfiguraciones del cuento mexicano," in *Paquete: cuento (La ficción en México).* Ed. Alfredo Pavón. Tlaxcala, Mexico: Universidad Autónoma de Tlaxcala, Instituto Nacional de Bellas Artes, 1990, 1–15.

Hutcheon, Linda. *Irony's Edge: The Theory and Politics of Irony.* London and New York: Routledge, 1995.

———. *A Poetics of Postmodernism: History, Theory, Fiction.* New York: Routledge, 1989.

Huyssen, Andreas. *After the Great Divide: Modernism, Mass Culture, Postmodernism.* Bloomington: Indiana University Press, 1986.

Íñigo Madrigal, Luis, coord. *Historia de la literatura hispanoamericana.* Madrid: Cátedra, 1982. 2 vols.

Iser, Wolfgang. *The Fictive and the Imaginary: Charting Literary Anthropology.* Baltimore and London: The Johns Hopkins University Press, 1993.

Jameson, Fredric. "Postmodernism and Consumer Society," in *The Anti-Aesthetic: Essays on Postmodern Culture.* Ed. Hal Foster. Port Townsend, Wash.: Bay Press, 1983, 111–25.

Jiménez, José Olivio. "El ensayo y la crónica del modernismo," in Íñigo Madrigal 2: 537–48.

———. "Teoría y práctica de la crónica en José Martí," *Insula* 92 (1990): 81–94.

Johnston Hernández, Beatriz. "En México, la tortura sigue; los torturadores, impunes; la CNDH, limitada," *Proceso* 13 July 1992: 28–29.

Kahler, Erich. *The Inward Turn of Narrative.* Trans. Richard and Clara Winston. Princeton: Princeton University Press, 1973.

Kaplan, Robert D. "History Moving North," *The Atlantic Monthly* Feb. 1997: 21–22, 24, 31.

Kermode, Frank. *The Sense of an Ending: Studies in the Theory of Fiction.* New York: Oxford University Press, 1967.

Kipnis, Laura. "'Refunctioning' Reconsidered: Towards a Left Popular Culture," in MacCabe 11–35.

Klor de Alva, Jorge J. "Colonialism and Postcolonialism as (Latin) American Mirages," *Colonial Latin American Review* 1, no. 1–2 (1992): 3–23.

Krauze, Enrique. *Caras de la historia.* Mexico: Cuadernos de Joaquín Mortiz, 1983.

Kristeva, Julia. *Revolution in Poetic Language.* Trans. Margaret Waller. New York: Columbia University Press, 1984.

Labbé, Armand J. *Religion, Art, and Iconography: Man and Cosmos in Prehispanic Mesoamerica.* Santa Ana, Calif.: Bowers Museum Foundation, 1982.

Langley, Lester D. *MexAmerica: Two Countries, One Future.* New York: Crown Publishers, 1988.

Lanser, Susan Sniader. *The Narrative Act: Point of View in Prose Fiction.* Princeton: Princeton University Press, 1981.

"Latin American Discourses of Identity and Their Fictional Representation," in Chanady 1–25.

Lentricchia, Frank, and Thomas McLaughlin, eds. *Critical Terms for Literary Study.* Chicago: University of Chicago Press, 1990.

León, Isaac, and Ricardo Bedoya. "Cultura popular y cultura masiva en el México contemporáneo: conversaciones con Carlos Monsiváis," *Contratexto* 3 (1988): 71–72.

Leonard, Irving. *Books of the Brave: Being an Account of Books and of Men in the Spanish Conquest and Settlement of the Sixteenth-Century New World.* Cambridge, Mass.: Harvard University Press, 1949.

León-Portilla, Miguel. *Los antiguos mexicanos a través de sus crónicas y cantares.* Mexico: Fondo de Cultura Económica, 1961.

———. *Literaturas indígenas de México.* 1st reprint. Mexico: Fondo de Cultura Económica, 1995.

———. "Sabios y poetas," in *Azteca-Mexica: las culturas del México antiguo*. José Alcina Franch, Miguel León-Portilla, and Eduardo Matos Moctezuma. Barcelona and Madrid: Lunwerg Editores, 1992, 253–63.

———. *Toltecáyotl: aspectos de la cultura náhuatl*. 2nd reimp. Mexico: Fondo de Cultura Económica, 1987.

———. *Visión de los vencidos: relaciones indígenas de la Conquista*. 12th ed. Mexico: Universidad Nacional Autónoma de México, 1989.

Levine, Lawrence. *Highbrow/Lowbrow: The Emergence of Cultural Hierarchy in America*. Cambridge, Mass., and London: Harvard University Press, 1988.

Lienhard, Martín. *La voz y su huella: escritura y conflicto étnico-social en América Latina 1492–1988*. Hanover, N.H.: Ediciones del Norte, 1991.

Linden, Eugene. "Megacities," *Time* 11 Jan. 1993: 28–38.

Loaeza, Guadalupe. *Las niñas bien*. Mexico: Océano, 1987.

Luna, Andrés de, comp. and intro. "Introducción," in *Martín Luis Guzmán*. Mexico: Senado de la República, 1987, 9–28.

Lyotard, Jean-François. *The Postmodern Condition: A Report on Knowledge*. Trans. Geoff Bennington and Brian Massumi. Foreword Fredric Jameson. Minneapolis: University of Minnesota Press, 1984.

MacCabe, Colin. "Defining Popular Culture," in *High Theory/Low Culture: Analyzing Popular Television and Film*. Manchester, England: Manchester University Press, 1986, 1–10.

Maccoby, Hyam. *The Sacred Executioner: Human Sacrifice and the Legacy of Guilt*. London: Thames and Hudson, 1982.

Mailer, Norman. *The Armies of the Night. History as a Novel. The Novel as History*. Reprint. New York: Signet, 1968.

———. *Miami and the Siege of Chicago*. New York: Signet, 1968.

Marimón, Antonio. "*Monsiváitis* aguda, el mal del día," *La Jornada* 31 Aug. 1993: 1, 8.

Marsal, Juan F. *Los ensayistas socio-políticos de Argentina y México (aportes para el estudio de sus roles, su ideología y su acción política)*. Buenos Aires: Instituto Torcuato di Tella, Centro de Investigaciones Sociales, 1969.

Martín-Barbero, Jesús. *De los medios a las mediaciones: comunicación, cultura y hegemonía*. Mexico: Ediciones G. Gili, 1987.

Martínez, José Luis, ed. *El ensayo mexicano moderno*. Mexico: Fondo de Cultura Económica, 1958.

Martínez, José Luis, and Christopher Domínguez Michael. *La literatura mexicana del siglo XX*. Mexico: Consejo Nacional para la Cultura y las Artes, 1995.

McCaffery, Larry, ed. *Postmodern Fiction: A Bio-Bibliographical Guide*. New York: Greenwood Press, 1986.

McGuigan, Jim. "Reaching for Control: Raymond Williams on Mass Communication and Popular Culture," in Morgan and Preston 163–88.

McHale, Brian. *Postmodernist Fiction*. New York and London: Methuen, 1987.

McLean, Malcolm D. *Vida y obra de Guillermo Prieto*. Mexico: El Colegio de México, 1960.

McLuhan, Marshall. *Understanding Media: The Extensions of Man*. New York: Mentor, 1964.

McRobbie, Angela. *Postmodernism and Popular Culture*. London and New York: Routledge, 1994.

Menchú, Rigoberta. *Me llamo Rigoberta Menchú y así me nació la conciencia*. With Elisabeth Burgos-Debray. Barcelona: Argos Vergara, 1983.

Menéndez Pelayo, Marcelino. *Historia de las ideas estéticas de España*. 4th ed. 1883. Madrid: Consejo Superior de Investigaciones Científicas, 1974. 2 vols.

Menéndez-Pidal, Ramón. *Romancero hispánico (Hispano-Portugués, americano y sefardí): teoría e historia*. Madrid: Espasa-Calpe, 1953. 2 vols.

Menocal, Nina. "Carlos Monsiváis," in *México: visión de los ochenta*. Mexico: Editorial Diana, 1981, 11–26.

Menton, Seymour. *Latin America's New Historical Novel*. Austin: University of Texas Press, 1993.

Merrell, Floyd. *Pararealities: The Nature of Our Fictions and How We Know Them*. Amsterdam and Philadelphia: John Benjamin's Publishing Company, 1983.

Metzger, Bruce M., and Michael D. Coogan, eds. "Chaos," in *The Oxford Companion to the Bible*. New York and Oxford: Oxford University Press, 1993, 105.

Meyer, Michael C., and William L. Sherman. *The Course of Mexican History*. 4th ed. New York and Oxford, England: Oxford University Press, 1991.

Mier, Luis Javier, and Dolores Carbonell. *Periodismo interpretativo: entrevistas con ocho escritores mexicanos*. Mexico: Trillas, 1981.

Mier, Servando Teresa de. *Memorias*. Ed. Antonio Castro Leal. Mexico: Porrúa, 1946. 2 vols.

Mignolo, Walter D. "La colonización del lenguaje y de la memoria: complicidades de la letra, el libro y la historia," coord. Iris M. Zavala, in *Discursos sobre la "invención" de América*. Amsterdam and Atlanta, Ga.: Rodopi, 1992, 183–220.

———. "Entre el canon y el corpus," *Nuevo Texto Crítico* 7, no. 14–15 (1995): 23–36.

———. "Introduction," in *Loci of Enunciation and Imaginary Constructions: The Case of (Latin) America, I*. Special issue of *Poetics Today* 15 (1994): 505–21.

———. "El metatexto historiográfico y la historiografía indiana," *Modern Language Notes* 96 (1981): 358–402.

———. "Putting the Americas on the Map (Geography and the Colonization of Space)," *Colonial Latin American Review* 1, no. 1–2 (1992): 25–63.

———. "Sobre las condiciones de la ficción literaria," *Escritura* 6 (1981): 263–80.

Moctezuma, Eduardo Matos. "The *Templo Mayor* of Tenochtitlan: History and Interpretation," in Broda, et al. 15–60.

Mora, Juan Javier. "El recuento de los daños de *Los mil y un velorios*," Rev. of *Los mil y un velorios* by Carlos Monsiváis. *La Palabra y el Hombre* 94 (1995): 230–2.

Morgan, John W., and Peter Preston, eds. *Raymond Williams: Politics, Education, Letters*. London: St. Martin's Press, 1993.

Morris, Meaghan. "On the Beach," in Grossberg 450–78.

Moseley, Charles. *A Century of Emblems: An Introductory Anthology*. Hants, England, and Brookfield, Vt.: Scholar Press, 1989.

Navarro, Desiderio. "La novela policial y la literatura artística," *Texto Crítico* 6, no. 16–17 (1980): 135–48.

Nelson, William. *Fact or Fiction: The Dilemma of the Renaissance Storyteller*. Cambridge: Harvard University Press, 1973.

Novo, Salvador. *Toda la prosa*. Mexico: Empresas Editoriales, 1964.

Ochoa Sandy, Gerardo. "Y cuando ocurrió el *big bang*, Monsiváis ya estaba ahí." Rev. of *Los rituales del caos* by Carlos Monsiváis. *La Jornada Semanal* 6 Aug. 1995: 7.

O'Connor, Alan. "The Emergence of Cultural Studies in Latin America," *Critical Studies in Mass Communication* 8 (1991): 60–73.

Olalquiaga, Celeste. *Megalopolis: Contemporary Cultural Sensibilities*. Minneapolis and Oxford: University of Minnesota Press, 1992.

Ong, Walter J. *Fighting for Life: Contest, Sexuality, and Consciousness*. Ithaca, N.Y., and London: Cornell University Press, 1981.

———. *Interfaces of the Word: Studies in the Evolution of Consciousness and Culture*. Ithaca and London: Cornell University Press, 1977.

———. *Orality and Literacy: The Technologizing of the Word*. London and New York: Routledge, 1982.

Ortega, José. *La estética neobarroca en la narrativa hispanoamericana*. Madrid: Porrúa Turangas, 1984.

Ortega, Julio. *La contemplación y la fiesta: ensayos sobre la nueva novela latinoamericana*. Lima: Editorial Universitaria, 1968.

Oster, Patrick. *The Mexicans: A Personal Portrait of a People*. New York: William Morrow, 1989.

Oviedo, José Miguel. *Breve historia del ensayo hispanoamericano*. Madrid: El Libro de Bolsillo, Alianza Editorial, 1991.

Pacheco, Carlos. *La comarca oral: la ficcionalización de la oralidad cultural en la narrativa latinoamericana contemporánea*. Caracas: Ediciones la Casa de Bello, 1992.

———. "Sobre la construcción de lo rural y lo oral en la literatura hispanoamericana," *Revista de Crítica Literaria Latinoamericana* 21, no. 42 (1995): 57–71.

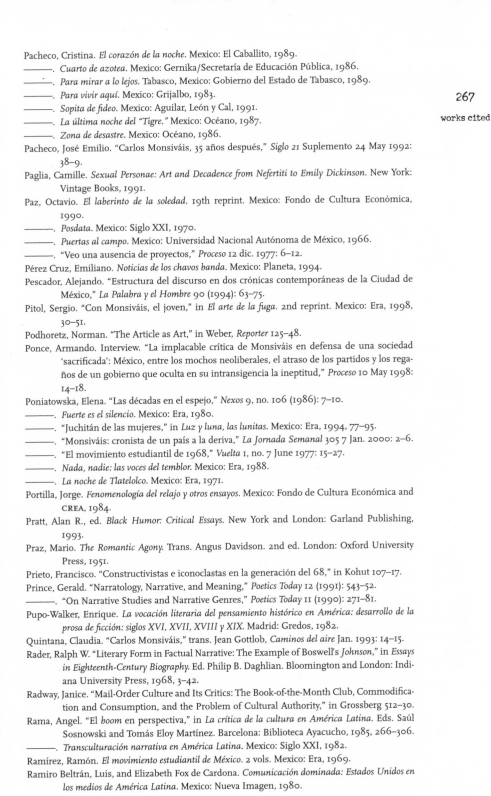

Pacheco, Cristina. *El corazón de la noche*. Mexico: El Caballito, 1989.

———. *Cuarto de azotea*. Mexico: Gernika/Secretaría de Educación Pública, 1986.

———. *Para mirar a lo lejos*. Tabasco, Mexico: Gobierno del Estado de Tabasco, 1989.

———. *Para vivir aquí*. Mexico: Grijalbo, 1983.

———. *Sopita de fideo*. Mexico: Aguilar, León y Cal, 1991.

———. *La última noche del "Tigre."* Mexico: Océano, 1987.

———. *Zona de desastre*. Mexico: Océano, 1986.

Pacheco, José Emilio. "Carlos Monsiváis, 35 años después," *Siglo 21* Suplemento 24 May 1992: 38–9.

Paglia, Camille. *Sexual Personae: Art and Decadence from Nefertiti to Emily Dickinson*. New York: Vintage Books, 1991.

Paz, Octavio. *El laberinto de la soledad*. 19th reprint. Mexico: Fondo de Cultura Económica, 1990.

———. *Posdata*. Mexico: Siglo XXI, 1970.

———. *Puertas al campo*. Mexico: Universidad Nacional Autónoma de México, 1966.

———. "Veo una ausencia de proyectos," *Proceso* 12 dic. 1977: 6–12.

Pérez Cruz, Emiliano. *Noticias de los chavos banda*. Mexico: Planeta, 1994.

Pescador, Alejando. "Estructura del discurso en dos crónicas contemporáneas de la Ciudad de México," *La Palabra y el Hombre* 90 (1994): 63–75.

Pitol, Sergio. "Con Monsiváis, el joven," in *El arte de la fuga*. 2nd reprint. Mexico: Era, 1998, 30–51.

Podhoretz, Norman. "The Article as Art," in Weber, *Reporter* 125–48.

Ponce, Armando. Interview. "La implacable crítica de Monsiváis en defensa de una sociedad 'sacrificada': México, entre los mochos neoliberales, el atraso de los partidos y los regaños de un gobierno que oculta en su intransigencia la ineptitud," *Proceso* 10 May 1998: 14–18.

Poniatowska, Elena. "Las décadas en el espejo," *Nexos* 9, no. 106 (1986): 7–10.

———. *Fuerte es el silencio*. Mexico: Era, 1980.

———. "Juchitán de las mujeres," in *Luz y luna, las lunitas*. Mexico: Era, 1994, 77–95.

———. "Monsiváis: cronista de un país a la deriva," *La Jornada Semanal* 305 7 Jan. 2000: 2–6.

———. "El movimiento estudiantil de 1968," *Vuelta* 1, no. 7 June 1977: 15–27.

———. *Nada, nadie: las voces del temblor*. Mexico: Era, 1988.

———. *La noche de Tlatelolco*. Mexico: Era, 1971.

Portilla, Jorge. *Fenomenología del relajo y otros ensayos*. Mexico: Fondo de Cultura Económica and CREA, 1984.

Pratt, Alan R., ed. *Black Humor: Critical Essays*. New York and London: Garland Publishing, 1993.

Praz, Mario. *The Romantic Agony*. Trans. Angus Davidson. 2nd ed. London: Oxford University Press, 1951.

Prieto, Francisco. "Constructivistas e iconoclastas en la generación del 68," in Kohut 107–17.

Prince, Gerald. "Narratology, Narrative, and Meaning," *Poetics Today* 12 (1991): 543–52.

———. "On Narrative Studies and Narrative Genres," *Poetics Today* 11 (1990): 271–81.

Pupo-Walker, Enrique. *La vocación literaria del pensamiento histórico en América: desarrollo de la prosa de ficción: siglos XVI, XVII, XVIII y XIX*. Madrid: Gredos, 1982.

Quintana, Claudia. "Carlos Monsiváis," trans. Jean Gottlob, *Caminos del aire* Jan. 1993: 14–15.

Rader, Ralph W. "Literary Form in Factual Narrative: The Example of Boswell's *Johnson*," in *Essays in Eighteenth-Century Biography*. Ed. Philip B. Daghlian. Bloomington and London: Indiana University Press, 1968, 3–42.

Radway, Janice. "Mail-Order Culture and Its Critics: The Book-of-the-Month Club, Commodification and Consumption, and the Problem of Cultural Authority," in Grossberg 512–30.

Rama, Angel. "El *boom* en perspectiva," in *La crítica de la cultura en América Latina*. Eds. Saúl Sosnowski and Tomás Eloy Martínez. Barcelona: Biblioteca Ayacucho, 1985, 266–306.

———. *Transculturación narrativa en América Latina*. Mexico: Siglo XXI, 1982.

Ramírez, Ramón. *El movimiento estudiantil de México*. 2 vols. Mexico: Era, 1969.

Ramiro Beltrán, Luis, and Elizabeth Fox de Cardona. *Comunicación dominada: Estados Unidos en los medios de América Latina*. Mexico: Nueva Imagen, 1980.

Ramos, Julio. *Desencuentros de la modernidad en América Latina: literatura y política en el siglo XIX*. Mexico: Fondo de Cultura Económica, 1989.

Revueltas, José. *El luto humano*. 10th reprint. Mexico: Era, 1990.

Retamar, Roberto Fernández. *Para una teoría de la literatura hispanoamericana*. 4th rev. ed. La Habana: Editorial Pueblo y Educación, 1984.

Reyes Matta, Fernando. "El concepto latinoamericano de las noticias," *Cuadernos de Comunicación* 54 (s.f.): 24–31.

Ricoeur, Paul. *The Reality of the Historical Past*. The Aquinas Lecture. Milwaukee: Marquette University Press, 1984.

———. *Time and Narrative*. Trans. Kathleen McLaughlin and David Pellauer. Chicago and London: University of Chicago Press, 1984, 1985, 1988. 3 vols.

Rieff, David. *Los Angeles: Capital of the Third World*. New York: Touchstone, 1991.

Rodríguez, Richard. "Mixed Blood. Columbus's Legacy: A World Made Mestizo," *Harper's* Nov. 1991: 47–56.

Rollin, Roger, ed. "Introduction," in *The Americanization of the Global Village: Essays in Comparative Popular Culture*. Bowling Green, Ohio: Bowling Green State University Popular Press, 1989, 1–10.

Ross, Andrew. "New Age Technoculture," in Grossberg 531–55.

Rotker, Susan. *La invención de la crónica*. Buenos Aires: Ediciones Letra Buena, 1992.

Rowe, William, and Vivian Schelling. *Memory and Modernity: Popular Culture in Latin America*. London and New York: Verso, 1991.

Ruffinelli, Jorge. "Los 80: ¿ingreso a la posmodernidad?" *Nuevo Texto Crítico* 3 (1990): 31–42.

Rulfo, Juan. *Pedro Páramo*. Ed. José Carlos González Boixo. 13th ed. Madrid: Cátedra, 1998.

Ruiz, Andrés. "De la vida de la *R*," *La Jornada* 29 Aug. 1993: 1, 10.

———. "Monsiváis: informarnos, método para combatir la impunidad. *Por mi madre bohemios*, humor de desquite," *La Jornada* 30 Aug. 1993: 10.

Ruiz, Ramón Eduardo. *Triumphs and Tragedy: A History of the Mexican People*. New York and London: Norton, 1992.

Russell, Bertrand. *A History of Western Philosophy*. New York: Book-of-the-Month Club, 1995.

Ryan, Marie-Laure. "The Modal Structure of Narrative Universes," *Poetics Today* 6 (1985): 717–55.

Sahagún, Fray Bernardino de. *Historia general de las cosas de Nueva España*. Eds. Alfredo López Austin and Josefina García Quintana. Madrid: Alianza, 1988. 2 vols.

Said, Edward. "Opponents, Audiences, Constituencies, and Community," in *The Anti-Aesthetic: Essays on Postmodern Culture*. Ed. Hal Foster. Port Townsend, Wash.: Bay Press, 1983, 135–59.

Sale, Kirkpatrick. *The Conquest of Paradise: Christopher Columbus and the Columbian Legacy*. New York: Plume, 1990.

Sánchez Susarrey, Jaime. *El debate político e intelectual en México*. Mexico: Grijalbo, 1993.

Sarduy, Severo. "El barroco y el neobarroco," in *América Latina en su literatura*. Ed. César Fernández Moreno. Mexico: Siglo XXI, 1972, 167–84.

Scherer García, Julio, and Carlos Monsiváis. *Parte de guerra: Tlatelolco 1968. Documentos del general Marcelino García Barragán. Los hechos y la historia*. Mexico: Nuevo Siglo Aguilar, 1999.

Schmidt, Siegfried J. "Towards a Pragmatic Interpretation of 'Fictionality,'" in *Pragmatics of Language and Literature*. Ed. Teun A. van Dijk. Amsterdam, Oxford, and New York: Horth-Holland Publishing Company, 1976, 161–78.

Scholes, Robert, and Carl H. Klaus. *Elements of the Essay*. New York: Oxford University Press, 1969.

Scholes, Robert, and Robert Kellogg. *The Nature of Narrative*. London and New York: Oxford University Press, 1966.

Schorske, Carl E. "History and the Study of Culture," *New Literary History* 21 (1990): 407–20.

Schwarz, Bill. "Where Is Cultural Studies?" *Cultural Studies* 8 (1994): 377–89.

Schwarz, Roberto. *Misplaced Ideas: Essays on Brazilian Culture*. Ed. John Gledson. London and New York: Verso, 1992.

Searle, John R. "The Logical Status of Fictional Discourse," *New Literary History* 6 (1975): 319–38.

Seidman, Steven, ed. "Introduction," in *The Postmodern Turn: New Perspectives on Social Theory.* New York and London: Cambridge University Press, 1994, 1–23.

Séjourné, Laurette. *Pensamiento y religión en el México antiguo.* Mexico and Buenos Aires: Fondo de Cultura Económica, 1957.

Shotwell, James. *An Introduction to the History of History.* New York: Columbia University Press, 1923.

Siebenschuh, William R. *Fictional Techniques and Factual Works.* Athens: University of Georgia Press, 1983.

Sims, Norman, ed. *The Literary Journalists.* New York: Ballantine, 1984.

Skirius, John, ed. *El ensayo hispanoamericano del siglo XX.* 3rd ed. Mexico: Fondo de Cultura Económica, 1994.

———. "Los intelectuales en México desde la Revolución," *Texto Crítico* 9 (1982): 3–37.

Sommer, Doris, and George Yúdice. "Latin American Literature from the 'Boom' On," in McCaffery 189–214.

Sontag, Susan. "Notes on 'Camp,'" in *A Susan Sontag Reader.* Intro. Elizabeth Hardwick. New York: Farrar, Straus and Giroux, 1982, 105–19.

Stabb, Martin S. *The Dissenting Voice: The New Essay of Spanish America, 1960–1985.* Austin: University of Texas Press, 1994.

———. "The Essay," in *Mexican Literature: A History.* Ed. David William Foster. Austin: University of Texas Press, 1994, 305–39.

———. "The New Essay of Mexico: Text and Context," *Hispania* 70 (1987): 47–61.

Staub, Michael E. "Black Panthers, New Journalism, and the Rewriting of the Sixties," *Representations* 57 (1997): 52–72.

Stavenhagen, Rodolfo. "Nation-Building in the Twentieth Century," in *Mexico Today.* Ed. Tommie Sue Montogomery. Philadelphia: Institute for the Study of Human Issues, 1982, 39–43.

Steele, Cynthia. *Politics, Gender, and the Mexican Novel, 1968–1988: Beyond the Pyramid.* Austin: University of Texas Press, 1992.

———. *Stories of Real Life.* Cincinnati: Story Press, 1996.

Swanson, Philip, ed. "Introduction: Background to the *Boom*," in *Landmarks in Modern Latin American Fiction.* London and New York: Routledge, 1990, 1–26.

Ticknor, George. *History of Spanish Literature.* Vol. 1 of 3. 6th rev. ed. New York: Gordian Press, 1965.

Todorov, Tzvetan. *Genres in Discourse.* Trans. Catherine Porter. Cambridge and London: Cambridge University Press, 1990.

Townsend, Richard F. *The Aztecs.* London: Thames and Hudson, 1992.

Traupman, John C., ed. *The New Collegiate Latin and English Dictionary.* New York: Bantam Books, 1966.

Trejo Fuentes, Ignacio. *Crónicas romanas.* Mexico: Diana, 1990.

———. *Faros y sirenas.* Mexico: Plaza y Janés, 1988.

Valverde, Jaime, and Juan Domingo Argüelles, eds. *El fin de la nostalgia. Nueva crónica de la ciudad de México.* Mexico: Nueva Imagen, 1992.

van Dijk, Teun A. *Some Aspects of Text Grammars: A Study in Theoretical Linguistics and Poetics.* The Hague and Paris: Mouton, 1972.

Varese, Stefano. "Los pueblos indígenas ante la globalización," *Revista de Crítica Literaria Latinoamericana* 23, no. 46 (1997): 19–35.

Vargas Llosa, Mario. "El nacimiento del Perú," in *Contra viento y marea, III (1964–1988).* Barcelona: Seix Barral, 1990, 365–78.

Veeser, H. Aram, ed. *The New Historicism.* New York and London: Routledge, 1989.

Vidal, Hernán. "The Concept of Colonial and Postcolonial Discourse: A Perspective from Literary Criticism," *Latin American Research Review* 28 (1993): 113–9.

Villanueva, Tino, prólogo. *Chicanos: antología histórica y literaria.* Mexico: Fondo de Cultura Económica, 1980, 7–67.

Villarreal, Rogelio. "El lado oscuro del buen *Monsi* . . .," *Sábado.* Supplement of *Unomásuno* 28 Aug. 1999: 4–5.

Waugh, Patricia. *Metafiction: The Theory and Practice of Self-Conscious Fiction.* London and New York: Methuen, 1984.

Weber, Ronald. *The Literature of Fact: Literary Nonfiction in American Writing.* Athens, Ohio: Ohio University Press, 1980.

———. "Some Sort of Artistic Excitement," in Weber, *Reporter* 13–26.

Weber, Ronald, ed. *The Reporter As Artist: A Look at the New Journalism Controversy.* New York: Hastings House, 1974.

White, Hayden. *The Content of the Form: Narrative Discourse and Historical Representation.* Baltimore, Md.: The Johns Hopkins University Press, 1987.

———. "The Fictions of Factual Representation," in *The Literature of Fact.* Ed. Angus Fletcher. New York: Columbia University Press, 1976, 21–44.

White, Hayden, and Frank E. Manuel. *Theories of History.* Los Angeles: University of California Press, 1978.

Wimsatt, James I. "The Mirror as Metaphor for Literature," in Hernadi, *What Is Literature?* 127–53.

Wolfe, Tom. *The Electric Kool-Aid Acid Text.* New York: Bantam Books, 1968.

———. *The Kandy-Kolored Tangerine-Flake Streamline Baby.* 18th reprint. New York: Farrar, Staus and Giroux, 1987.

———. "The New Journalism," in *The New Journalism.* Eds. Tom Wolfe and E. W. Johnson. London, Pan Books, 1975, 13–68.

———. *Radical Chic and Mau-Mauing the Flak Catchers.* New York: Farrar, Straus and Giroux, 1970.

Yáñez, Agustín. *Al filo del agua.* Mexico: Prologue Antonio Castro Leal. Mexico: Porrúa, 1988.

Yúdice, George. "Postmodernity and Transnational Capitalism in Latin America," in Yúdice, et al., *On Edge* 1–28.

Yúdice, George, Jean Franco, and Juan Flores, eds. *On Edge: The Crisis of Contemporary Latin American Culture.* Minneapolis and London: University of Minnesota Press, 1992.

Zavala, Lauro. *Humor, ironía y lectura: las fronteras de la escritura literaria.* Xochimilco, Mexico: Universidad Autónoma Metropolitana, 1993.

Zavarzadeh, Mas'ud. *The Mythopoetic Reality: The Postwar American Nonfiction Novel.* Urbana: University of Illinois Press, 1976.

Zermeño, Sergio. *México: una democracía utópica. El movimiento estudiantil del 68.* Prologue Carlos Monsiváis. Mexico: Siglo XXI, 1978.

Zimmerman, Bonnie. "Feminist Fiction and the Postmodern Challenge," in *Postmodern Fiction: A Bio-Bibliographical Guide.* Ed. Larry McCaffery. New York: Greenwood Press, 1987, 175–88.

Zolten, J. Jerome. "Joking in the Face of Tragedy: Why Would People Try to Turn Tragic Events into Humor?" Pratt 303–11.

index

about the author

Linda Egan is an associate professor of Spanish at the University of California, Davis, a Latin Americanist with a research emphasis in Mexican literature and culture. Among recent publications related to this book, "'Mechicanos' al borde del cambio en el valiente mundo nuevo de Carlos Monsiváis" (1996) examines his interest in the chicano as mediator between Mexican and U.S. anglo cultures. "Footnote to an Essay on Carlos Monsiváis (Reading *Mexican Postcards*)" (2000) analyzes his favored genre by way of a critical review of a groundbreaking selection of his chronicles in English translation. A forthcoming essay, "Peripeteia, anacronismo y otras herejías en *Nuevo catecismo para indios remisos*," analyzes literary aspects of the Mexican chronicler's sole work of fiction, a volume of satirical fables. Egan has also published frequently on the colonial poet Sor Juana Inés de la Cruz, most recently, a monograph exploring the nun's heterodox thought (*Diosas, demonios y debate: las armas metafísicas de Sor Juana*, 1997) and a study of Sor Juana's intertextual presence in novels of Carlos Fuentes ("Carlos Fuentes and Sor Juana between Times and Lines," 1999). A former journalist, her years as editorial page editor of a mid-size California daily helped shape the interest she subsequently developed in the literary nonfiction of U.S. New Journalists and contemporary Mexican *cronistas*. Egan's further investigative interests range from the historical chronicle of the conquest and colonial era in Spanish America to the emergent national literatures of the nineteenth century and include the chronicle, novel and short story of the twentieth and present centuries.

DATE DUE